An Only Child and *My Father's Son*

Born in 1903, Frank O'Connor begins his story with his
childhood and youth in Cork through to his release
from internment as a revolutionary at the age of twenty.

His autobiography continues with his experiences as
a public servant and librarian and takes us through
the turbulent early years of the Abbey Theatre in
Dublin until the death of Yeats in 1939, when O'Connor
resigned from the Abbey to become a full-time
writer.

Frank O'Connor died in 1966.

FRANK O'CONNOR

An Only Child and *My Father's Son*

an autobiography

Pan Books
in association with Macmillan

An Only Child was first published in 1961 by
Macmillan & Co. Ltd, and by Pan Books Ltd in 1970
© Frank O'Connor 1958, 1959, 1960, 1961
My Father's Son was first published in 1968 by
Macmillan & Co. Ltd, and by Pan Books Ltd in 1971
© Harriet O'Donovan 1968
This combined volume first published 1988 by
Pan Books Ltd, Cavaye Place, London SW10 9PG
in association with Macmillan London Ltd
9 8 7 6 5 4 3 2 1
© Frank O'Connor and Harriet O'Donovan 1988
ISBN 0330 30420 8

Photoset by Input Typesetting Ltd, London

Printed and bound in Great Britain by Richard Clay Ltd

CONTENTS

ILLUSTRATIONS

Lady Gregory

Frank O'Connor's mother and father
(*by courtesy of Harriet O'Donovan*)

The wharves, Cork
(*by courtesy of the Mansell Collection*)

'A.E' (George Russell)

J.M. Synge
(*by courtesy of Mander and Mitchenson*)

Lennox Robinson
(*by courtesy of the Radio Times Hulton Picture Library*)

W.B. Yeats
(*by courtesy of the Radio Times Hulton Picture Library*)

The Tailor and Ansty with Father Tim Traynor
(*by courtesy of Nancy Allitt*)

An Only Child

For William Maxwell

Four episodes from this autobiography have appeared in *The New Yorker*, and the author wishes to thank William Shawn and the other editors for their encouragement and assistance.

Throughout this book the author is referred to by his real name, Michael O'Donovan, not by the pen name that he later adopted.

Contents

ONE

Child, I know you're going to miss me

1

As a matter of historical fact I know that I was born in 1903 when we were living in Douglas Street, Cork, over a small sweet-and-tobacco shop kept by a middle-aged lady called Wall, but my memories have nothing to do with living in Douglas Street. My memories begin in Blarney Street, which we called Blarney Lane because it follows the track of an old lane from Cork to Blarney. It begins at the foot of Shandon Street, near the river-bank, in sordidness, and ascends the hill to something like squalor. No. 251, where we lived, is one of the cottages on the right near the top, though I realize now that it would be more properly described as a cabin, for it contained nothing but a tiny kitchen and a tiny bedroom with a loft above it. For this we paid two and sixpence – sixty cents – a week.

Up here we were just on the edge of the open country, and behind the house were high, windy fields that are now all built over. A hundred yards farther up the road the country proper began, and there a steep lane called Strawberry Hill descended past my first school into the classy quarter of Sunday's Well. The Women's Prison was at the foot of this lane, where it turned into Convent Avenue, and beside the Women's Prison was the Good Shepherd Convent. The convent had a penitentiary for 'fallen' women and an orphanage, and it was in the orphanage that Mother had been brought up. At the foot of Convent Avenue on the left was a house where Mother had been a maid for eight years with a family called Barry, and where she had been happier than at any other time in her life. To the right was a shop the owner of which had once wanted to marry her. All these places were full of significance to me – the convent because my mother and I often visited it to see

Mother Blessed Margaret and Mother of Perpetual Succour, who were her friends there, the Barrys' house because of the elegance of the life that Mother described in it, and the shop because of a slight feeling of resentment at the thought that if only Mother had been sensible and married a rich man I should have had a pretty elegant life myself.

That was the exalted end of Blarney Lane. At the other end it descended to the river and across the bridge to the North Main Street, where Mother took me shopping, and beyond the North Main Street, over another bridge to Douglas Street, where we had lived, and where my mother's brother, Tim O'Connor, had a cobbler's shop just across the street from Miss Wall. My memories of the cobbler's shop are hazy; I can remember my uncle only when he was dying in the South Infirmary of dysentery he had contracted in the Boer War; and yet I seem to have a very vivid recollection of him – tall, thin, and fair-haired, unlike Mother, who was small and had very dark hair – because he seemed to be always gay. One of the things I have inherited from my mother's side of the family is a passion for gaiety. I do not have it myself – I seem to take more after my father's family, which was brooding, melancholy, and violent – but I love gay people and books and music.

Not that Tim had much to be gay about; his wife, as I remember her, was common and jealous, and disliked Mother's politeness and gentleness, while Mother never ceased to resent the hysterical scenes Annie O'Connor had made over Tim's grave. Mother disliked and distrusted any form of demonstrativeness, and when Annie married again it was only what Mother had expected of her. How she thought Annie could bring up two children unaided I do not know, but she and Father shared an attitude which seemed to be commoner then than it is now, of regarding all second marriages as a form of betrayal.

On the other hand, Tim had objected to Mother's marrying my father, Michael O'Donovan. The two men, who were old friends, had been in the British Army together, and were stationed at Charles Fort, near Kinsale, where Tim's girl, Annie, and Mother visited him together. Mother came back to visit Father. Though they were friends and drinking companions, Tim told Father that he was not good enough for Mother, and Father, to give him his due, did not hold it against him. 'I'll get her in spite of you, Tim,' he said, and he did. Certainly neither Tim nor my mother had much to boast of in their marriages. Maybe there is about these men and women of

Mozartean temperament a certain unworldliness that makes them get the worst of any bargain.

Father played the big drum in the Blackpool Brass and Reed Band, and as I was the only child, I had often to accompany him, much against my will, on his Sunday trips to the band room or on band promenades at holiday resorts. The Cork bands were divided into supporters of William O'Brien and supporters of John Redmond, two rival Irish politicians with little to distinguish them except their personalities – flamboyant in O'Brien and frigid in Redmond. The Blackpool Band was an O'Brienite group, and our policy was 'Conciliation and Consent', whatever that meant. The Redmond supporters we called Molly Maguires, and I have forgotten what their policy was – if they had one. Our national anthem was 'God Save Ireland' and theirs 'A Nation Once Again'. I was often filled with pity for the poor degraded children of the Molly Maguires, who paraded the streets with tin cans, singing (to the tune of 'John Brown's Body'): 'We'll Hang William O'Brien on a Sour Apple Tree'. Sometimes passion overcame me till I got a tin can of my own and paraded up and down, singing: 'We'll Hang Johnny Redmond on a Sour Apple Tree'.

The bandsmen shared our attitude. There were frequent riots, and during election times Father came home with a drumstick up his sleeve – a useful weapon if he was attacked by Molly Maguires. There were even more serious incidents. Bandsmen raided a rival band room and smashed up the instruments, and one of Father's most gloomy songs listed some of the men who had done this:

> Creedy, Reidy, Dessy, and Snell,
> Not judging their souls, they're already in Hell.
> The night of the battle we'll show them some fun;
> We'll hang up the ruffian that stole our big drum.

Almost all the bandsmen were ex-bandsmen of the British Army, as Father was; and I think it may have been something of a tragedy to them that when once they returned to Cork, music became less important than the political faction for whom they made it. Father was devoted to the policy and personality of William O'Brien, who had married the daughter of one of the great Franco-Jewish bankers. It was Sophie Raffalovitch's mother who had started the romance by sending to O'Brien when he was in jail a verse of Racine with an eagle's feather enclosed, but I am glad that when Sophie O'Brien was old and poor in France during the German occupation, the

Irish Government protected her and paid her an allowance. Once, when there were threats of a Molly Maguire attack, Father, an enormously powerful man, acted as bodyguard for William O', and William O' thanked him personally and handed him a pound note. All the same, for several years Father had been big drummer of a Molly Maguire band. It was a superb band, and Father liked music so well that he preferred it to politics. For the sake of the music he even endured the indignity of playing for Johnny Redmond. Naturally, whenever he attended a demonstration at which William O' was criticized, he withdrew, like a good Catholic from a heretical service. What made him leave the Molly band and join the Blackpool Band I never knew. It was a period that for some reason he never liked to talk about, and I suspect that someone in the band must have impugned him by calling him a turncoat. That is the sort of thing that would have broken his spirit, for he was a proud man and a high-principled one, though what his principles were based on was more than I ever discovered. He was the one who insisted on the 'O'Donovan' form of the name, and it must have been his absence at the Boer War that explains my being described as 'Donovan' on my birth certificate. He would not permit a slighting reference to William O'Brien, and reading the *Echo*, the only evening paper in Cork and a Molly one, was as much a torment as a pleasure to him. 'There were about 130 people present, most of them women, with a sprinkling of children' was how the *Echo* would describe any meeting of O'Brien's, and Father would raise his eyes to Heaven, calling on God to witness that anything the *Echo* said was untrue. 'Oh, listen to George Crosbie, the dirty little caffler!' he would cry with mortification. In days when no one else that I knew seemed to worry about it, he was a passionate believer in buying Irish manufactures, and often sent me back to the shop with a box of English matches that had been passed off on me. He was a strong supporter of Jim Larkin, the Irish Labour leader; for months when he was out on strike we practically didn't eat but we always bought *The Irish Worker*, Larkin's paper, and I was permitted to read it aloud because my dramatic style of reading suited Larkin's dramatic style of journalism. According to Mother, there was a period in my infancy when Father didn't drink for two years. He had drunk himself penniless, as he frequently did, and some old friend had refused him a loan. The slight had cut him so deep that he stopped drinking at once. The friend was wrong if he assumed that Father would not have repaid that or any other loan, but, still, it was a great pity that he hadn't a few more friends of the sort.

It was no joke to go with Father on one of his Sunday outings with the band, and I often kicked up hell about it, but Mother liked me to go, because she had some strange notion that I could restrain him from drinking too much. Not that I didn't love music, nor that I wasn't proud of Father as, with the drum slung high about his neck, he glanced left and right of it, waiting to give the three taps that brought the bandsmen in. He was a drummer of the classical type: he hated to see a man carry his drum on his belly instead of his chest, and he had nothing but scorn for the showy drummers who swung or crossed their sticks. He was almost disappointingly unpretentious.

But when he was on the drink, I was so uncertain that I always had the feeling that one day he would lose me and forget I had been with him at all. Usually, the band would end its piece in front of a pub at the corner of Coburg Street. The pubs were always shut on Sunday until after last Mass, and when they opened, it was only for an hour or two. The last notes of 'Brian Boru's March' would hardly have been played before Father unslung the drum, thrust it on the young fellows whose job it was to carry it, and dashed across the road to the pub, accompanied by John P., his great buddy. John P. – I never knew what his surname was – was a long string of misery, with an air of unutterable gravity, emphasized by the way he sucked in his cheeks. He was one of the people vaguely known as 'followers of the band' – a group of lonely souls who gave some significance to their simple lives by attaching themselves to the band. They discussed its policies and personalities, looked after the instruments, and knew every pub in Cork that would risk receiving its members after hours. John P., with a look of intense concentration, would give a secret knock on the side door of the pub and utter what seemed to be whispered endearments through the keyhole, and more and more bandsmen would join the group peppering outside, while messengers rushed up to them shouting: 'Come on, can't ye, come on! The bloomin' train will be gone!'

That would be the first of the boring and humiliating waits outside public houses that went on all day and were broken only when I made a scene and Father gave me a penny to keep me quiet. Afterwards it would be the seaside at Aghada – which wasn't so bad because my maternal grandmother's people, the Kellys, still lived there and they would give me a cup of tea – or Crosshaven, or the grounds of Blarney Castle, and in the intervals of playing, the band would sit in various public houses with the doors barred, and if I was inside I couldn't get out and – what was worse for a shy small boy – if I was out I couldn't get in. It was all very boring and alarming, and I remember once at Blarney, in my discouragement, staking my last penny on a dice game called the Harp, Crown and Feather in the hope of retrieving a wasted day. Being a patriotic child, with something of Father's high principle, I put my money on the national emblem and lost. This was prophetic, because since then I have lost a great many pennies on the national emblem, but at least it cured me of the more obvious forms of gambling for the rest of my days.

On another occasion, after what had seemed an endless day in Crosshaven, I found myself late at night outside a locked public house in Cork opposite the North Cathedral, waiting for some drunk to emerge, so that I could stick my head in the door and wail: 'Daddy, won't you come home now?' At last, in despair, I decided to make my own way home through the dark streets, though I had never been out alone at night before this. In terror, I crept down the sinister length of Shandon Street, and crossed the street so that I might escape seeing what I might see by the old graveyard, and then, at the foot of Blarney Lane, I saw a tiny shop still open. There were steps up to the hall door, and railings round the area, and the window was small and high and barely lighted by one oil lamp inside, but I could plainly see a toy dog in it, looking out at me. Praying that it wouldn't be beyond my means, I climbed up the steps. Inside, a door on the right led from the hall to the shop, where the counter was higher than my head. A woman came out of the little back room and asked me what I wanted. I told her I wanted to know the price of the dog, and she said it was sixpence. I had earned a lot of pennies by standing outside public houses that day, and sixpence was exactly what I had, so I threw it all on the counter and staggered out, clutching my protector. The rest of the way up Blarney Lane I walked without fear, setting my woolly dog at every dark laneway to right and left of me with a fierce 'At 'em, boy!' Fortunately for myself, I was fast asleep when Father arrived home, distracted over losing me.

As for keeping him off the drink, I never did it but once, when I drank his pint, became very drunk, smashed my head against a wall, and had to be steered home by himself and John P., both of them mad with frustration and panic, and be put to bed.

Father had been brought up in the vicinity of Cork Barrack, a mile or two away at the other side of the town, and his family still lived there. For this neighbourhood he seemed to pine as an Irish immigrant in Brooklyn is supposed to pine for Galway Bay, though, unlike the Brooklyn immigrant, Father meant it. He used to take me to my grandparents' house in Harrington Square – an uneven unlighted piece of ground between the Old Youghal Road and the Ballyhooley Road that seemed to have been abandoned by God and was certainly abandoned by the Cork Corporation. One side was higher than the other, and a channel had been hollowed out before the houses on the lower side to give ingress, while, at the end of this, one lonesome pillar commemorated some early dream of railing the place off. In England such sites are politely known as 'non-adopted', a word that well suits their orphaned air. It was inhabited largely by washerwomen who worked mainly for the British officers in Cork Barrack, and there were three sets of iron poles in the middle of the square to support their lines. One set belonged to my grandmother, a stout, coarse peasant woman from Aghada, who flopped about the floor in bare feet because these were what she was used to and the boots still continued to give her trouble. She had a pronounced Mongolian appearance, and the protrusion of the brows and the high cheekbones gave her a constant look of peering at things. With it went a curious shrugging of the shoulders, which I never noticed again till I saw it in an eminent writer and traced it down to a common dislike of soap and water. After a huge meal of stockfish and boiled potatoes she would shrug and bless herself and then add her own peculiar grace: 'Well, thanks be to God, we're neither full nor fasting.' I remember little of my grandfather, a quiet, bearded old man. My aunt was a deaf-mute, and during the early part of my childhood I met her only once or twice, when she was home on holidays from Glasgow, where she lived with her husband – a tailor named Hanlon. She, too, seemed to pine for the old spot.

I had no nostalgia for it. The kitchen of my grandparents' house resembled that of a country cabin, and there was nothing in it but a table and a few chairs – no pictures, or anything else that could hold the attention of a child. It was criss-crossed with clothes lines, and in wet weather it smelled of damp linen and was warm with a big fire where the heaters for the box-iron were reddened. (I liked the heaters, and I wished Mother would get a box-iron instead of her own little flat-iron.)

Hospitality there was of the same order: strictly functional, and with none of the frills of cakes and jam that a child remembers. Sometimes my Uncle Laurence, my father's brother, came in, and Grandmother was sent out to the pub and returned with a great jug of porter under her old plaid shawl, and this was mulled with the big iron poker, and I was given half a mug of it with sugar. One night when I was about three or four and sitting on Father's knee, almost asleep, he suddenly put me down, lifted the poker, and slashed my uncle's face across with it. I remember the long red line on my uncle's face, which suddenly went white, and blood beginning to pour from it, and the quiet voice in which he said: 'Mick Donovan, if another man in the world did that to me, I'd have his life.'* Laurence was the only member of the family I liked, and the scene made a terrifying impression on me.

I can only have been five or six when a house fell vacant next door to my grandparents'. Mother did not want to take it; it would detach her from the convent, which was one of the nearest things she knew to a home, and from the neighbours in Blarney Lane, whom she liked and who liked her. It was probably characteristic of the orphan, but I never met anyone so firmly rooted in places and people. When she began visiting me in Dublin, she was at first very lonely; then she noticed a house that reminded her of one in Cork, and then she saw a woman with a child who reminded her of a neighbour in Cork, and she even observed a piece of furniture in a shop-window that reminded her of something we had once possessed, till at last she built up a world of remote analogies with comfortable and friendly memories that protected her from the unknown. She disliked my father's family even more than I did, and, besides, the rent – four and sixpence a week – was nearly twice what we paid for the little cottage in Blarney Lane. But Father was homesick for the delights of the Barrack Stream (as the old people called the locality), and he argued irritably that with a commodious house like that – four rooms instead of two – we could take in lodgers, and everyone knew the big money you could make out of lodgers. So one day we said goodbye sadly to the old neighbours, piled all our possessions on a little donkey cart, and set out after them down Blarney Lane toward the river. I carried the kitten in my arms.

* When I was growing up, 'O'Donovan' and 'Donovan' were almost interchangeable. English officials insisted on the latter form, and it was always used familiarly.

That night Mother sat in the dirty, dilapidated kitchen of the new house and wept, but Father's family were happily reunited in a neighbourhood where they were well known and – according to themselves – highly respected. At least, in Barrack Stream, Father was sure of a good funeral. Grandfather and Grandmother lived next door, my Uncle Laurence and his family lived up the Old Youghal Road, near Mayfield Chapel, and for a time my deaf-and-dumb aunt and her deaf-and-dumb husband lodged with the old people in the house next door. The homesickness of my father's family was really quite remarkable.

Barrack Stream, though richer than Blarney Lane, was rougher, like all places attached to military barracks. There were women who went with soldiers, and girls who went with officers, and sinister houses where people drank after hours. Of course, it had its advantages for me, particularly when we weren't plagued by lodgers. (Of these I remember two lots – a family so brutal and filthy that at last Father, who was out for most of the day and only pooh-poohed Mother's complaints, practically ejected them himself, and an old lady so scared of draughts that she nailed up the window and padded the door till the front room stank.) A lot of the time I had an attic to myself, where I could keep my treasures, and there was an outdoor toilet, with a door suitable for climbing. From the roof of this I could get on to the high back wall and command a view of the neighbours' back yards and of the hillside opposite as it sloped down into the valley of the city. I sometimes sat there for hours, till darkness crept up on me, and in order to enjoy the view a little longer I even climbed out of the attic window and up the roof to the ridge-pole. Besides, there was the Barrack, and the day was punctuated by bugle calls, and sometimes the soldiers went by on a route march, preceded by their band. When this happened in the evening and Father was at home, we both dashed for the front door. The regiments at the Barrack were always changing, and while the fast girls compared lovers – English, Scotch and Welsh – Father compared the height and smartness of the men, the quality of the band and, of course, the big drummers. If you went far enough afield, you could even see an occasional military funeral, with a gun-carriage draped in the Union Jack, and a band that played Chopin's Funeral March. With the O'Donovan morbidity, I loved military funerals, and when Father was in good humour I got him to hum dead marches for me. Though he was usually ready to oblige with Chopin, Handel or Beethoven, he maintained that the greatest of

dead marches was 'The Flowers of the Forest' as played by the pipe
band of the Scots Guards. Naturally, he performed all these as
though the principal instrument were the big drum, and I tested
them out, pacing the kitchen with reversed sweeping brush, lost in
ecstatic melancholy. Afterwards he would be bound to sing me 'The
Burial of Sir John Moore', one of his favourite songs and mine. So
far as music went, he and I got on excellently.

But the move to Barrackton brought to a head my sense of the
conflict between the two families whose heredity I shared. The more
I saw of my grandparents, the less I liked them. Children, who see
only one side of any question and because of their powerlessness
see this with hysterical clarity, are abominably cruel. And an only
child is worse. There was no way in which I could have avoided
seeing the contrast between my mother, on the one hand, and the
women of my father's family on the other, and it meant nothing to
me that one was old, another ill, another deaf-and-dumb.

Mother was dainty in everything she did. Women can observe
and describe that sort of fastidiousness better than men, and my
cousin's wife, whom Mother adored, gives a tart and amusing
description of her at the age of eighty-five, flouncing about the
kitchen of May's little house, demanding to be inspected and assured
that her hat was not crooked or her skirt too short. When she
returned from town, she would immediately take off her wet shoes,
stretch them with her hands, stuff them with newspapers (she had
never been able to afford shoe-trees), and set them to dry before
the fire. Only then would she produce the perfect pear or the perfect
peach that she had coveted in some fruit-shop window, not for
herself but May. This is the side of her I remember best, because
one of my earliest recollections of her is the way she would choose
a twopenny Christmas card, study it, price it, put it back, return
and study it again with a frown as though she were wondering if it
really was a Rembrandt etching, though all the time she was
thinking not of what it was but of its appropriateness to the person
she was buying it for.

Besides, she was an excellent cook and a first-rate housekeeper,
a woman to whom cleanliness and neatness came as natural as
untidiness does to me. Though, apart from our beds, the only
furniture we had was what went into the kitchen, she made even
that room look beautiful. Over the mantelpiece hung a long mirror,
and to the right of it the lamp. At either side of the window were
pictures of the Battle of Bethlehem, a Boer War relic which I

searched by the hour for a likeness of Father, and of Kathleen Mavourneen, with insets of the Lakes of Killarney. Facing the window was the little sideboard with one of our two clocks, and between that and the door was the bedroom wardrobe, which was too big to go up the stairs. Father used the top of it for his own treasures, his razors, clippers and pipes.

One of those peculiar romances of Mother's that I was always so curious about – not being very satisfied with the father she had supplied me with – had been with a French chef called Armady who had taught her to make superb coffee. I think he must also have taught her to hate fried food, that curse of Irish life, because the first thing she bought when I got a job and turned my wages over to her was a gas-stove on which she could grill. In the evenings, when I induced Father and herself to sing for me, his favourites were sentimental songs like 'Eileen Alannah' and 'Kathleen Mavourneen', and these he sang in the manner of a public-house singer, all sniffle and rallentando. When Mother was not singing Moore's melodies – her favourites were 'How Dear to Me the Hour When Daylight Dies', 'Farewell But Whenever You Welcome the Hour', and 'I Saw from the Beach' – she sang charming little drawing-room songs of the Victorian period like 'The Danube River', 'Alabama Moon', 'When the Old Man Died', and 'Three Students Went Merrily over the Rhine', and she sang them in good time, in her sweet, clear, girlish voice. It was, I suppose, typical of me that when I sang the same songs I tried to invest them with Father's trills, but I got ticked off for it. Even when I sang with her as a grown man I got a sharp 'No!' when I strayed from the correct time. Her harshest criticism was an impatient 'Ah, you have it out loud and all wrong.'

She was the sort of woman who is always called in when there is trouble in a house, and as she had to bring me with her in the years when I was still an infant, some of my earliest recollections of her are so extraordinary that to this day I cannot say if they weren't hallucinations. Once, when we were living in Blarney Lane, she carried me to a neighbour's house and put me sitting on a chair by the door. I could see into the little partitioned-off bedroom, and I watched her, in the candlelight, holding up the head of a young man who was coughing red stuff on to the bed. In a loud voice Mother said something that sounded like prayers, and he continued to cough till all the bedclothes were bright red, and then he seemed to fall asleep, and she laid him back on the pillow and knelt beside

him, praying into his ear. Another time she took me with her and
I saw a young man crouching under the bedroom window with his
hands raised, screaming: 'They'll never get me alive!' Mother went
up to him, smiling, her two hands out in a gesture that was most
characteristic of her, murmuring reproachfully: 'Ah, Johnny,
Johnny, don't you know who it is? It's only Mrs Donovan.' The
strange quality of these half-memories of her is best summed up in
one incident. I remember the mother of a very sick little girl coming
hysterically to the door and our running back with her to the
cottage, where Mother forced back the child's rectal passage, which
had become extruded. The incident is perfectly clear in my mind,
though I do not even know if what I think I saw is physically
possible.

She had always wanted to be a nurse and was an excellent one.
When Grandfather was dying, it was she who looked after him, and
I watched her scrubbing the floor, killing the lice that covered
the bedroom wall, and changing the bedclothes, while downstairs
Grandmother, huge, shiftless and dirty, drained her mug of porter
over the fire and moaned. 'I'm a bird alone, a bird alone!' she
whined, and Mother, sick with disgust, told her sharply that she
could at least wash her face before the priest came.

When my grandmother came to live with us after Grandfather's
death, I nearly lost my mind. Lodgers were awful, and the large
fortunes to be made from them were clearly illusory, but at least
they were not relations and I did not have to apologize for them to
any other kid I brought to the house and wanted to impress. I was
always trying to make an impression, particularly on one friend,
Bob O'Connell, whose father was a colour sergeant and who spoke
in a cultured English voice that I tried hard to imitate, but when I
glanced into the kitchen and saw Grandmother at one of her modest
repasts – a mess of hake and potatoes boiled in a big pot, with the
unpeeled potatoes afterwards tossed on the table to be dipped in a
mound of salt and eaten out of the fingers, and a jug of porter
beside these – I fled for very shame. And once, when Mother was
at work and Grandmother was supposed to give me my dinner, I
hid under the kitchen table, yelling bloody murder and refusing to
come out until Mother returned and fed me herself. Mother tried to
induce her to keep herself clean, but Grandmother, deeply offended,
shrugged herself in her dirty old clothes, blinked her eyes, and
retorted sullenly: 'Sure, what is it but clean dirt?'

I had already become a classic example of the Mother's Boy.

Later, when as a public official I had to be careful not to involve my employers in my literary activities and had to change my name, I took her name in place of my own. At that time all I could do was beg her to leave my father and come away to live with me, and though in those days I was little tempted to criticize her, I did frequently blame her in my own thought for timidity. I felt that she, on the one hand, and Father's family, on the other, were the two powers that were struggling for possession of my soul, and I hated every member of my father's family – even cousins I later grew fond of. It was not the people themselves I hated, of course, but drunkenness, dirt and violence. I made an exception of my Uncle Laurence, because he was gentler than the others and had a sense of humour that partly qualified the O'Donovan gloom. When he was leaving for the front during the First World War, Grandmother, with her alcoholic emotionalism, began a beautiful scene that would have reduced poor Father to helpless sobs, but Laurence punctured it wickedly by pretending to sob even louder, and left Grandmother with the outraged expression that Shaw once versified as

Respect a mother's grief
And give me time to finish my scene.

Much as I pitied my aunt, I didn't really like her either; her affliction was never anything but terrible; and her wordless rages and griefs were as horrifying as those of a chained animal. But, like Mother, I was very fond of her husband, Pat Hanlon, because he was a man of great expressiveness and gaiety, and made his affliction serve his purposes. He was a wraith of a man with small black eyes and a little black moustache, and he lurched about in a curiously disjointed way, his head rolling from side to side. I think he hated the O'Donovan atmosphere as much as Mother did. He never joined in the drinking and was very industrious. When things became too difficult, he got down off the table on which he sat cross-legged, and lurched into our house with a snort and a shrug. Then he threw himself into a chair with that loose-jointed air of his and began describing his day in the Jewish tailor's in Patrick Street, his fingers flying, his small dark eyes flashing – really flashing – and queer animal noises that were intended to be laughter bubbling in his throat. He was a man who observed everything. I had never met the Jewish tailor, but he was as real to me as Charlie Chaplin, and just as funny. Hanlon was a superb mimic, and of everybody at once – the tailor, the customers and the work-girls. Having no sound track to bother with, he acted at the speed of the earliest films, breaking off a scene or a part in an instant, impatiently grabbing and growling at Mother, who would be in hysterics, to tell her something new, though his thin face never lost its air of faint anxiety. At the end of a story he would give another shrug as a final commentary on the futility of human existence.

It was strange entertainment for a child, but I loved it – though, because I spoke slowly and only with my two hands, I often missed the point. Mother also used her two hands, but she spoke fast and clearly and could understand Hanlon when he grew so excited that he fell back on one hand, and between hysterical fits of laughter she carried on a sort of subdued commentary to herself that told the story to Father and me. Then Hanlon would return to that dirty, uncomfortable house, having enjoyed a couple of hours of intelligent conversation with people far better equipped by nature than himself, and knowing that he had given at least as good as he got. And how many of us, with all our faculties, can feel as much when we leave someone's house? It was a real triumph of art over nature, and something it would take me twenty years to learn.

2

Father was a really fine-looking man. He was a six-footer and built to match, and years of work as a navvy had not affected the soldierly erectness of bearing he had picked up as a young man in the Army. He had a long Scandinavian head, but because of the slightly Mongolian cast of feature he had inherited from Grandmother, the lines of his face were horizontal instead of vertical. At the same time the bulge of the brows and the height of the cheekbones, instead of making his eyes seem weak, made them look as though they were twinkling. He was extraordinarily like certain photographs of the young Maxim Gorky. He dressed carefully, in the manner of an old-fashioned tradesman, in a blue serge suit with the cuffs of the trousers turned down over the heels, a bowler hat cocked a little to one side, and a starched shirt-front. Dressing him for Mass on Sunday was a serious task for any woman, for his fingers were all thumbs. He could rarely fasten his own studs, and it sometimes ended with his stamping and cursing before the big mirror, and Mother's grabbing at a stool to stand on, so that she could reach up to him, and begging him for the Lord's sake to keep quiet and let her do it for him. Then he put an open white handkerchief, casually disposed, in his breast pocket, and went down the road, graciously bowing and raising his hat to any woman he met, a fine figure of a man, and as vain as a child in his first sailor suit. In the 'tall tales' he loved to tell of his soldiering days there was a great favourite of his about a review held by Queen Victoria during which she said: 'And tell me, General, who is that distinguished-looking man in the second rank?' to which the general replied: 'That, Your Majesty, is Michael O'Donovan, one of the best-looking men in your whole army.'

Nothing could ever persuade Father that he was anything but a naturally home-loving body – which, indeed, for a great part of the time, he was. Nobody but himself could lock up the house for the night, and he had a big bolt for the back door and two bolts for the front, and only he could properly check the catch on the window, wind the alarm on the clock, and see that the lamp was out before we retired. Often he would be up first in the morning, give Mother a cup of tea in bed, and have a tremendous wash-up under the tap in the yard, winter and summer. Indeed, if there was snow he rubbed himself all over with it because it prevented chilblains. It was a bitter disappointment to him that I was a sissy, and he made angry comments when I drew a basin of water and then poured hot water from the kettle into it. When he got in from work in the evening, he usually had a more leisurely, noisy wash, changed into old trousers and 'slippers' that were old boots cut down and hacked in all directions so that the leather did not press on his corns, and, with a cap on to protect his head from draughts, sat at the head of the table by the window to read the evening *Echo* aloud to Mother, with comments that went on longer than the news. He began with the Police Court news to put him into good humour, and reserved for the last the political meetings, which made him scowl and mutter 'Oh, that unspeakable scut, George Crosbie!' I liked that till I began to read myself, but even then it did not disturb me much, for I was always too involved in what I read even to notice when neighbours dropped in.

This was just as well, because any project of Father's, from cutting his corns to writing to Whitehall about his pension, involved preparation on a major scale and something like general mobilization, and in any detail of this he could become entirely lost. For instance, when he wrote to Whitehall – this usually meant no more than filling out some form to show he was still alive – he had first of all to get the penny bottle of ink, and a new nib for the pen, and a bit of blotting-paper, and lay them all out on the table before him; then he had to get his papers, which were in a locked tin trunk in the bedroom, and he could never take one of these out without re-reading the lot: and on going through his discharge papers and discovering again what a model soldier he had been, he would be moved like an old novelist re-reading a review of his first talented book, and would have to bring them down and read them all over again to Mother, who knew them by heart. Every question on a questionnaire he read over several times before replying to it, because he knew it had been drafted by an old and cunning hand with the deliberate intention of catching him out. When he spotted the trap – and there nearly always was a trap – his whole face lit up with approval and he explained the problem carefully to Mother while he considered how best to handle it. He liked a subtle enemy because it enabled him to show how subtle he could be himself. He was a born hob-lawyer, always laying down the law about regulations, and greatly looked up to by other old soldiers, like Bill Heffernan, who were too humble even to pretend that they knew what the War Office wanted of them. When the form was filled out and in its envelope on the mantelpiece, and Mother had been warned that she must post it with her own hand and not entrust it to me, he would become emotional again about the goodness of the British Government and its consideration for its old servants – unlike the gnats of employers he worked for in Cork, who would see an old workman dying in the streets and not lift a hand to help him. The pension meant much more to him than the trifle of money it represented. It gave him a personal interest in the British Government. A Liberal Government might be good for the Irish cause, but a Conservative one would be better for the pension. It gave him wild dreams, because no quarter passed without his toying with the idea of compounding it for a capital sum, the size of which staggered imagination. It gave him the prospect of a happy old age, for when Mother died he could hand it in in return for provision in one of the military hospitals like Chelsea or Kilmainham where every day for the rest of his life he would get his pint of beer for nothing.

When the time came to cut his corns, he got a chair and rooted about on top of the wardrobe, which was his hidey-hole, well out of my reach, or intended to be; and after contemplating his many treasures, he took down his current razor, wrapped in oiled cloth, and a couple of other, older razors that he had either abandoned or picked up from those who had no further use for them but that could be trusted to do the rough work of corn-cutting. Then he got the wash-basin, and a jug of cold water, and a kettle of boiling water, and a bottle of corn cure, and a paper of some sort to read while his feet soaked, and a hand mirror to see the parts of his feet that were normally hard to see, and anything else that could conceivably be of use to him, and then, with Mother or myself lined up to hold the mirror, he was set for the evening. Not that I ever remember his doing it without cutting himself.

Or else it was an evening with his pipes. He was an inveterate magpie, and everything that anyone else threw away Father would pick up, in the full conviction that if you kept it for seven years it would be bound to come in useful, while the person who had discarded it would probably pay for his improvidence by dying in the workhouse. Old broken pipes were a tremendous temptation to him, and he had a large collection of bowls and stems, all of which needed only careful handling to turn them into brand-new pipes of the most expensive kind. This task would have been considerably easier if he had ever had anything like a gimlet handy, but as he rarely did, he had to make a tool. Usually, the treasure chest yielded some sort of blade, and some sort of handle, and the blade had to be heated and set in the handle, and then the handle usually burst and had to be bound with a bit of string or wax-end. Then the improvised tool had to be heated again, and the bowl or the stem burned till the two pieces could be joined. I can still remember the rancid smell of burned amber. The result was usually most peculiar – a delicate bowl joined to a colossal stem or a delicate stem to a rural bowl – but Father puffed it with great satisfaction, in the belief that he had cheated some ruffian of a tobacco merchant out of the price of a brand-new pipe.

Father was, I think, a naturally melancholy man; though he was always pleased when people called, he rarely called on anybody himself; and, like all melancholy men, he made his home his cave, and devoted a great deal of thought to its beauty and utility. Unfortunately, he was one of the most awkward men who ever handled a tool, and it is a subject I can speak on with some authority, for I have inherited his awkwardness. Along with the razors, the pipe bowls and stems and the rest, he had a peculiar hoard of tools and equipment, mostly stored on top of the wardrobe. They had been lovingly accumulated over the years in the conviction that eventually they would be bound to come in useful. Prior to tackling any major job, all this had to be unloaded on to the kitchen table, and Father put on his glasses and studied it affectionately in the way in which he studied the documents in the tin trunk, forgetting whatever he was supposed to be looking for as he recited the history of hinges, bolts, screws, wooden handles, blades, clock springs, and mysterious-looking bits of machinery that had probably fallen out of a railway engine in process of dissolution, and wondered what some of them could be used for.

Finally, having selected his equipment – the nice bit of timber that would nearly do for a shelf, and the brackets that didn't quite match, and the screws or nails that were either a bit long or a bit too short, and the old chisel that would do for a screwdriver, and the hammer with the loose head – Father set to work. He had lined up my mother and myself as builder's mates, to hold the plank and the hammer, the saw that needed setting, and the nails and screws. Before he had been at work for five minutes, the top of the hammer would have flown off and hit him in the face, or the saw would have cut the chair instead of the plank, or the nail that was to have provided the setting for the screw would have carried away inches of the plank with the unmerciful wallops he gave it. Father had the secret of making inanimate objects appear to possess a secret, malevolent life of their own, and sometimes it was hard to believe that his tools and materials were not really in a conspiracy against him.

His first reaction to this behaviour was chagrin that, for all his love and care, they were turning on him again, but this soon changed to blind rage and an autocratic determination to put them in their places. Hacking away great chunks of the plaster, he nailed in the brackets any old way, while Mother and I, our hearts in our mouths, stood by with anything we thought might come in handy. He swore bloody murder, exactly as he did when the studs in his shirt-front turned against him before Mass on Sunday and it became a toss-up whether, to spite them, he might not go to Mass at all; and in the same gentle voice Mother besought him to let it alone and not to be upsetting himself like that. And when it was all over, and the kitchen a wreck, he would sit down with gloomy pride to read a paper he could not concentrate on, obsessed by the image of himself as a good man and kind father on whom everybody and everything turned.

That was why, in spite of the fact that he had a cobbler's last among his treasures, and that I was forever hacking the good boots that were bought for me with his money, he didn't try his hand at cobbling. A man who could hardly hit a three-inch nail with a large hammer could not be expected to do much with a shoemaker's tack. Most often it was Mother who did the cobbling, buying a patch or a pair of half-soles in town and tacking them on herself. But I seem to remember that his hoarding instinct betrayed him once when he discovered a large strip of fan-belting from a factory, made of some extraordinary material which he maintained was stronger than leather and would save us a fortune, and he did cut strips of this and nail them to his working boots, on which they looked like pieces of board. On the other hand, he liked rough tailoring, and was perfectly happy sewing a patch on to his working trousers.

But I never minded Father as a handyman the way I minded him as a barber. He always had one pair of clippers, and sometimes two, wrapped in oily rags among the other treasures, and, according to him, these clippers had saved him untold expense. Given a pencil and paper, he could even work it out, as he worked out the amount he saved by being a teetotaller. He was a great man for saving. 'My couple of ha'pence,' he used to call it. Mother, I suspect, never knew how much he really earned, and when he was sober he usually had a substantial sum in the locked trunk in the bedroom. When he was feeling depressed, he went upstairs by way of consulting his documents and counted it softly, but not so softly that we couldn't hear the chink of the coins as he caressed them. He was a bit of a skinflint and disliked the improvident way Mother bought me sweets, biscuits or boys' weeklies, not to mention toys at Christmas – a season that seemed to have been specially invented for his mortification. Father, of course, was only providing for the rainy day.

So, on a sunny afternoon, he would take down the clippers, pull off the oily rags, adjust the blades, set a chair in the back yard and, with a towel round his neck, let Mother cut his hair. There was no great difficulty about this, since all Father wanted was the equivalent of a close shave. According to him, this was excellent for the growth of the hair, and one of his ambitions was to double his savings by protecting my hair as well. I didn't want my hair protected, though he assured me angrily that I would be bald before I was grown up at all; neither did Mother want it, and so, the moment it grew a bit too long and she saw Father casting brooding glances at it, she gave me tuppence to go to the barber. This made Father furious, for not only had she again demonstrated her fundamental improvidence, but Curtin, the barber, would have left me with what Father called 'a most unsightly mop'. It was like the business of wanting me to wash under the tap. But no matter how carefully she watched over me, he sometimes caught me with the clippers in his hand, and I had to sit on a chair in the back yard, sobbing and sniffling, while he got to work on me and turned me into a laughing-stock for the neighbourhood. He went about it in exactly the same way that he went about cutting his corns or putting up a shelf. 'Wisha, is it the way you want to make the child look like a convict?' Mother would cry indignantly, and Father would stamp and curse and pull at a whole chunk of hair till I screamed, and then curse again and shout: 'It's your own fault, you little puppy, you! Why can't you stop quiet?'

Then one evening Father would be late, and Mother and I would sit over the fire, half crazy with panic, and I would say prayers to the Sacred Heart and the Blessed Virgin to look after him. I can never remember that my prayers had any effect. Finally, he would come in, full of fallacious good humour, and stand at the door, rubbing his palms and puckering up his lips in a sly grin. He expressed great – indeed, undue – surprise at the lateness of the hour. He had been detained talking to a man he hadn't met for fifteen years – not since the funeral of poor Jack Murphy of the Connaught Rangers in September '98, which he remembered distinctly because Tim O'Connor, God rest him, had been there as well, and the three of them had left the funeral together and spent the evening in a pub called Keohane's that used to be at the corner of Windmill Road but had since been torn down. He would ramble on like that for half an hour, in loosely related clauses that gave the impression of coherence but were difficult to follow, and towards ten o'clock would decide to take a little stroll. That was the end of Father in his role as a home-loving body. Next evening he would slink upstairs to the locked trunk where he kept his savings, and then go out again. The rainy day had at last arrived. He would return in a state of noisy amiability that turned to sullenness when it failed to rouse a response. I was most often to blame for this because, in spite of Mother's appeals to me not to answer him back, I could not bear his maudlin attentions, which made him so like my grandmother, and, like her, he was offended, and snarled that I was 'better fed than taught'. The day after, he would not go work and at twelve or one would be at the trunk again and off for a longer carouse.

The savings usually lasted him for a week or ten days. When they were exhausted, Mother had to go to the pawnshop with his best blue suit. So that the neighbours would not see what she was doing, she would put on her long black shawl. I hated the very sight of that shawl, even though I knew that it suited her long, thin, virginal face; it meant an immediate descent in the social scale from the 'hatties' to the 'shawlies' – the poorest of the poor. I also hated the pawning of the blue suit, because it meant that Father stopped going for walks or to Mass – especially to Mass, for he would not have dreamed of worshipping God in anything less dignified than blue serge – and it meant that we had him all day about the house, his head swollen, his eyes bloodshot, sitting by the fire and shivering in the fever of alcoholism or getting up and walking to and fro, unable to read, unable to work, unable to think of anything except drink. Home was no longer a refuge for him. It had become a prison and a cage, and the only hope of escaping from it was more money. When Mother returned from the town and put the five or six shillings on the table with the pawn tickets, he sometimes turned on her with an angry 'Lord God, was that all you got on it?' It was not so much that he expected more as that staging a quarrel at this point meant that she would not dare to ask him for money for food or the rent or the insurance or Levin the peddler, who had sold her a suit for me.

Two days later she would be off again with one of the two clocks – her own clock from the bedroom, which did not have an alarm. After that came the clock with the alarm, which was no longer necessary as he did not go to work, and then his silver watch. 'In God's name, Mick Donovan, do you want to put us on the street?' she would cry, and he would stamp and shout like a madman. He didn't know what being put on the street meant as she, the orphan, did. Then her blue costume went, and his military medals and, lastly, his 'ring paper' – so called because it was printed in a series of small circles intended for the post-office date stamp – his authority for drawing his Army pension. Though the transaction was illegal, the security was excellent. Even then he would be greedily eyeing the wedding ring on her finger and whining at her to pawn this as well, 'just for a couple of days till I steady up,' but it was only when she was really desperate that she let this go, and it took precedence of everything else when the time came to reclaim the little bits of married life. By this time all the money coming into the house would be the ninepence or shilling she earned as a charwoman, and he would be striding like a caged tiger up and down the kitchen in the dusk, waiting for her to come in from work so that he could get this from her.

'Come on!' he would say with forced joviality. 'Tuppence is all I want. Me entrance fee!'

'And where am I to get the child's dinner?' she would cry in despair. 'Or is it the way you want us to starve?'

'Look, it's all over now. No one is going to starve. Can't you see I'm steadying up? Come on, woman, give us the money!'

'Stay here, then, and I'll go and get it for you!'

'I don't want you to get it for me,' he would say, turning nasty. 'Getting it for him' was a later stage, which occurred only when he had completely exhausted his credit and old friends cleared out when he came red-eyed and fighting mad into the pub. With his 'entrance fee', as he called it, he had not only the price of a drink but the chance of cadging more, either from the barmaid, if the publican was out, or from one of his old cronies.

If he did not get the money immediately, his tone would change again and he would become whining and maudlin. As night came on and his chances of a real debauch diminished, he would grow vicious. 'Jesus Christ, I'll put an end to this!' he would mutter, and take down his razor. His threats were never empty, as I well knew since the night when I was an infant and he flung the two of us out into Blarney Lane in our night clothes, and we shivered there in the roadway till some neighbours took us in and let us lie in blankets before the fire. Whenever he brandished the razor at Mother, I went into hysterics, and a couple of times I threw myself on him, beating him with my fists. That drove her into hysterics, too, because she knew that at times like that he would as soon have slashed me as her. Later, in adolescence, I developed pseudo-epileptic fits that were merely an externalization of this recurring nightmare, and though I knew they were not real, and was ashamed of myself for indulging in them at all, I could not resist them when once I had yielded to the first nervous spasm.

In those days, the house would be a horror. Only when he had money for drink would we have peace for an hour, and sometimes Mother borrowed it just to get him out of the house. When I was old enough to go to school, I would come back at three o'clock and scout round to make sure that he was not at home. If he wasn't, I would sneak in and hastily make myself a cup of tea. If he was, I did without the tea and wandered round the rest of the afternoon, waiting till it was time to intercept Mother on her way home from work. I never went near my grandmother. From the moment Father began his drinking bout, you could feel her disapproval of Mother and me – the two heartless creatures who did not sympathize with her darling son. This, she seemed to say, all came of Father's mistake in marrying a woman who did not know her place, a would-be lady. When I talked of him to Mother, I always called him 'he' or 'him', carefully eschewing the name of 'Father' which would have seemed like profanation to me. 'You must not speak like that of your father, child,' Mother would say severely. 'Whatever he does, he's still your father.' I resented her loyalty to him. I wanted her to talk to me about him the way I knew the neighbours talked. They could not understand why she did not leave him. I realize now that to do so she would have had to take a job as housekeeper and put me into an orphanage – the one thing in the world that the orphan child could not do.

It always ended in the same way – only when we were completely destitute; when the shopkeepers refused Mother even a loaf of bread, and the landlord threatened us with eviction, and Father could no longer raise the price of a single pint. At that point only did he give in – 'cave in' better describes what really happened to him. Sour and savage and silent, he began to look for another job. He rarely went back to the job he had left, and in those days I believed it was because he had lost it. Now I am certain that he was far too good a workman to be put off because of a drinking bout, however prolonged, and that he was too humiliated to go back. To have done that would have been to admit his weakness and guilt. He was, as I have said, a proud man, and he would never have admitted to the other poor labourers, whom he despised, that he had sunk so low. And because something had to be done about the mass of debt that had accumulated in the meantime, he and Mother would have to go to the loan office in Paul Street, accompanied by some friend to act as guarantor. Mother had to go with him, because even at this stage he would still have taken the money and drunk it along with the rest. I was very impressed by the big interest we had to pay, and it struck me that if only I could accumulate a little capital and lend them the money myself, it would be an excellent way both of getting rich and of saving Mother anxiety – the money would, at least, be in the family. But my own savings usually evaporated in the first few days of strain, and I realized that I would need a more settled background before I could set up in business as a moneylender.

With the aid of the loan, Father would take out his 'ring paper' and draw his pension, and out of that he would release his best suit, so that he could again worship God on Sundays in the Dominican Church on the Sand Quay. Then would come the clocks and the watch and chain and the military medals, and finally Mother's blue costume. It was characteristic of him that when he started to put money aside again, it was to pay the publicans. He preferred to let Mother work for a shilling a day rather than defer the payment of his drinking debts. It would seem to be obvious that he was only preparing the way for another debauch – because this, in fact, was the ultimate effect of it – and yet I should still say that this was untrue. I am sure it was pride that moved him. I don't think Mother had much pride. Gay people have no need of pride because gaiety is merely the outward sign of inward integrity; as with all mentally sick people, the two sides of his nature hardly communicated and were held together by pins and Hail Marys, and pride was one of the ways in which he protected the false conception of his own character that was one side.

And once again the little house was reconstituted about that incomplete conception of Father as a home-loving body, and a new cycle began. Brisk and cheerful, he rose in the early morning to wash under the tap and bring Mother a cup of tea in bed, and in the evening he read the *Echo* to her while I sat in some corner, absorbed in my own boys' weeklies, and a wind blew up the river and seemed to isolate us as on a ship at sea. On such evenings, no one could doubt his love for her or hers for him, but I, who had no other security, knew better than she did what he was really like, and watched him suspiciously, in the way that only a child can watch, and felt that all authority was only a pretence and that God Himself was probably not much better, and directed my prayers not to Him, but to His mother, who had said nothing but merely suffered.

Because I was jealous of him, I knew that there was real devotion between that strangely assorted pair, and yet I often wonder what really went on in Mother's mind during those terrible years. I think when she wasn't entirely desperate, pity was what was uppermost in her mind, pity for this giant of a man who had no more self-knowledge or self-control than a baby. The least pain could bewilder and madden him and even a toothache could drive him to drink. He died as he had lived, wandering about Cork, looking for drink when he was in the last stages of pneumonia, and I, who might have controlled him, was not informed because it would upset me too much, and besides Mother felt I wouldn't understand. Even God wouldn't understand. Whenever his anniversary came round, she withdrew herself for weeks and, without a word to anyone, the offering for Masses was sent to the Cistercians at Mount Melleray, because God might fail to realize that poor Father really was at heart a home-loving body and a good husband and father, and might keep him too long in Purgatory, a place he would not be happy in at all because he could not stand pain, and even a toothache would drive him mad.

Once only did she say anything significant, and that was while she was raving. I was a grown man and living in Dublin, and I came back to Cork on holiday to find her desperately ill, and poor Father – the world's most hopeless man with his hands – devotedly nursing her with nothing but neat whiskey. I blasted him for not wiring for me, and he snarled back: 'How could I, when she wouldn't let me?' And then he sat over the fire, flapping his hands and snivelling: 'What would I do without her?' When I had made her comfortable for the night, I sat with her, holding her hand, and heard her muttering about him as though I were not there.

'God! God!' she whispered. 'He raised me from the gutter where the world threw me. He raised me from the gutter where the world threw me!'

3

Whenever I read about juvenile delinquents, I find myself thinking of Mother, because she was whatever the opposite of a juvenile delinquent is, and this was not due to her upbringing in a Catholic orphanage, since whatever it was in her that was the opposite of a juvenile delinquent was too strong to have been due to the effect of any environment and, indeed, resisted a number of environments to which no reasonable person would subject a child; the gutter where life had thrown her was deep and dirty. One way of describing this quality is to call it gaiety; another is to say that she was a woman who passionately believed in the world of appearances. If something appeared to be so, or if she had been told it was so, then she believed it to be so. This, as every psychologist knows, leads to disillusionments, and when a juvenile delinquent is disillusioned we describe it as a traumatic experience. So far as I could see, up to her death practically all Mother's experiences were traumatic, including, I am afraid, her experience with me. And some small portion of her simple-mindedness she did pass on to me.

She was small and dainty, with long dark hair that she was very proud of. She had only two faults that I ever knew of – she was vain and she was obstinate – and the fact that these qualities were masked by humility and gentleness prevented my recognizing them till I was a grown man. Father, who was as grey as a badger at thirty-five, and in danger of growing bald, in spite of his clippers, was very jealous of her beautiful dark hair, and whenever he wanted to make her mad he would affect to discover white strands in it. Being an orphan, she had no notion of her own age, and had never known a birthday, but Father had discussed it with my Uncle Tim and satisfied himself that she was several years older than himself. When he believed she was seventy, he got really angry because he was sure she was going to let her vanity deprive her of a perfectly good pension. Mother shrugged this off as another example of his jealousy. To tell the truth, that was what I thought myself. She looked, at the time, like a well-preserved fifty-five. However, to put his mind at rest, I had the date of her birth looked up in the Customs House in Dublin, and discovered that she was only a few months short of seventy. Father was triumphant, but I felt guilty because I feared that the knowledge of her real age would make her become old. I needn't have worried. I think she probably decided finally that though the Registrar of Births and Deaths was a well-intentioned man, he was not particularly bright.

She had a lordly way with any sort of record she could get her hands on that conflicted with her own view of herself – she merely tore it up. Once, the poet George Russell did a charming pencil drawing of her, which I had framed. The next time I came home on holiday, I found the frame filled with snapshots of me, and my heart sank, because I knew what must have happened. 'What did you do with that drawing?' I asked, hoping she might at least have preserved it, and she replied firmly: 'Now, I'm just as fond of A.E.

as you are, but I could not have that picture round the house. He made me look like a poisoner.' When she was eighty-five, and we were leaving to live in England, I discovered that she had done the same thing with the photograph in her passport. She was entirely unaffected by my anger. 'The sergeant of the police at St Luke's said it,' she proclaimed firmly. 'The man who took that picture should be tried for his life.' I think she was glad to have official authority for her personal view that I had been very remiss in not bringing proceedings against the photographer. When my wife and I separated, the only indication I had of Mother's feelings was when I looked at my photograph album one day and saw that every single photograph of my wife had been destroyed. Where she had been photographed with me or the children her picture had been cut away. It was not all malice, any more than the destruction of her own pictures was all vanity. I am certain it went back to some childish technique of endurance by obliterating impressions she had found too terrible to entertain, as though, believing as she did in the world of appearances, she found it necessary to alter the world of appearances to make it seem right, but in time it came to affect almost everything she did. It even worked in reverse, for one Christmas an old friend, Stan Stewart, sent her a book, but because it came straight from his bookseller, it did not contain an inscription, as books that were sent to me did. After her death, I found the book with a charming inscription from Stan, written in by herself. Her affection for him made her give herself away, for she wrote 'From dear Stan'.

She was beautiful, and – in later life at least – she knew it. Once a well-known woman writer came to the house, and when she was introduced to Mother, she threw her arms about her neck and hugged her. 'But she's so beautiful!' she said to me later in apology, and Mother accepted the tribute modestly as indicating that our visitor showed nice feelings. She had a long, pale, eager face that lit up as though there had been an electric torch behind it, and whenever people told her anything interesting, she studied their faces with a delighted or grieved expression. It was part of her belief in the reality of the objective world. She knew that when people were happy they laughed, and she laughed with them – not so much at what they said, because sometimes she didn't understand what they were saying, as in sympathy with their happiness. In the same way, when they were sad she looked grieved. It never occurred to her that people could be happy and wear a mournful face. From her point of view, this would have been a mere waste of good happiness. For the same reason, she never teased and could never understand teasing, which was the amusement of people like Father, who do not believe in the world of appearances, and though she was clever and sometimes profound, she went through life burdened with the most extraordinary misapprehension, which she clung to with gentle persistence.

When I was a child, our walks often took us to the Good Shepherd Convent, in the orphanage of which she had grown up. I liked it because it had trees and steep lawns and pleasant avenues. On fine days we sat with one of her old friends on the lawn that overlooked the valley of the river or, on showery ones, in the grotto of the nuns' cemetery, and Mother of Perpetual Succour, who was in charge of the garden, took me round and picked me fruit, and I suspect that sometimes, when things were not going well at home, Mother Blessed Margaret gave Mother small gifts of money and clothes. In the convent cemetery, among the tiny crosses of the nuns, was a big monument to one of the orphans, an infant known as Little Nellie of Holy God, who had suffered and died in a particularly edifying way and about whom, at the time, a certain cult was growing up. I had a deep personal interest in her, because not only was I rather in that line myself, but Father had assisted at her exhumation when her body was removed from a city cemetery, and verified the story that it was perfectly preserved. Having attended several funerals, seen the broken coffins and the bones that were heaped on the side, and heard my relatives say knowingly: 'That was Eugene now. The one below him was Mary,' I was strongly in favour of the saintly life. When they dug me up, I wanted to be intact.

But much as I enjoyed the elegance of the convent gardens and avenues, it was here that I picked up the fragments of Mother's past life that have never ceased to haunt me. At that time, of course, they were merely a few hints, but they were sufficient to sustain my interest through the years, and later I wrote down and got her to write down as many of the facts as she remembered – or cared to remember. I stopped doing this one day when she put down her pen with a look of horror and said: 'I can't write any more – it's too terrible!'

It was. She had been the oldest of four children whose parents lived in a tiny cabin at the top of Blarney Lane beyond the point where I grew up. After her had come Margaret, then Tim and then Nora, the baby. My grandmother was a country girl from Donoughmore, and had been married in the hood cloak, the traditional dress of country women of her day. My grandfather was a labourer in Arnott's Brewery, which was near St Mary's of the Isle Convent, at the other side of the city. Mother was his pet, and sometimes when he went to work he carried her with him in his arms, left her in the playground of the convent to amuse herself, and then came back later to carry her home again. He was a powerful man, a bowls player and athlete, and one day, for a bet, he began lifting heavy casks and injured his back. While he was in Mercy Hospital Mother was not allowed to visit him – I fancy because my grandmother had to work and Mother looked after the children – and, being his pet, she resented it. One day she left the children behind and ran all the way down Sunday's Well and Wyse's Hill and across the old wooden bridge where St Vincent's Bridge now stands to the hospital. She found him, fully dressed, sitting on his bed in the men's ward upstairs, with a group of men about him who played with her and gave her sweets. When she was leaving he came down the stairs with her, and at the front door, asked if she knew her way home. She said that she did, but he realized that she was confused, caught her up in his arms and made off with her for home. Mother told that part of the story in a rather tentative way, and I suspect that, with a child's belief in magic, she had always felt that her visit had cured him, and could not face the possibility that it might have been the cause of his death. Anyhow, I doubt if it was. I think he knew he was dying, and wanted to die at home. He lingered only a short while, and Mother remembered how he reported the stages of dying to my grandmother. 'The end is coming, Julia,' he said once. 'The hearing is going on me now.'

After his death, neighbours and friends took the children in. My grandmother's people in Donoughmore, who were comfortably off, refused to do anything for her. Nora, taken by one couple, was never heard of again in this world, though in later years Mother tried hard to track her down. Someone else took Tim. Margaret, I fancy, remained on with Grandmother. Mother fell to the lot of a foreman in the Brewery named O'Regan, who lived with his childless wife in a place called Brandy Lane on the south side of the city. They were a good-natured couple, but with no comprehension of a child's needs. After the intimacy of the little cabin, Mother was terrified of her own tall solitary bedroom and the streetlamp outside that threw its light up on to the ceiling, and in the daytime Mrs

O'Regan went out and left her alone in the house. One day she dragged a chair into the hall and managed to lift the latch. Then she ran wild through the city streets till a policeman picked her up and brought her home by the hand.

It was only a brief respite, because a couple of days later they were evicted for not paying the rent, and Mother and Margaret sat for hours on the roadside with the remains of their little home: the tester bed, the picture of Sir John Arnott, the brewer, and the picture of the Guardian Angel – the two protectors who had done so little for them. After that, Grandmother took Mother and Margaret to the Good Shepherd Orphanage, and when Mother realized that they were being left behind, she rushed after my grandmother, clinging to her skirts and screaming to be taken home. My grandmother's whispered reply is one of the phrases that haunted my childhood – indeed, it haunts me still. 'But, my store, I have no home now.' For me, there has always been in imagination a stage beyond death – a stage where one says 'I have no home now.'

My grandmother went mad under the strain and was for a time in the Lunatic Asylum. When she came out, she worked for a few months as a maid. She used to visit Mother and Aunt Margaret at the orphanage, and once she brought Tim, then two, who was on his way to an infants' orphanage in Waterford. To begin with, the two little girls were comfortable enough. They were too young to dress themselves, so they were dispensed from the necessity for going to Mass, and for the same reason they didn't attend classes and were left in the kitchen with the older girls who did the cooking. Their cots were side by side in the dormitory, and sometimes Mother got into Margaret's bed and was caught there at 6.30 when Mother Cecilia came into the dormitory, clapping her hands and reciting the morning offering.

By the time Mother was attending classes, fever broke out in the school and a temporary hospital had to be erected in the grounds. Margaret disappeared with many of the others, but by this time Mother was growing used to disappearances. One day two girls entered the classroom, carrying a third whose legs dragged dead behind her.

'Minnie,' they said. 'Here's your sister.'

Mother ran away, and then the tall, thin girl they were carrying began to cry. Margaret was now a cripple for life and lived in the infirmary. It was Mother who carried her to and from the classrooms, where she could move about fairly well by swinging on the desks. She had developed into something of a pet and a tyrant. She was precocious, and read everything that came her way. Whatever poetry she read, she immediately memorized. She developed a hatred of injustice, and attacked even the nuns when she thought they were doing wrong. She despised Mother's timidity, and when Mother peered in the infirmary door to see if any nuns were around, Margaret called out to her not to be such a coward. The owner of the Queen's Old Castle, one of the big city stores, who sometimes visited the convent, had a wheelchair made for her so that she could be pushed around.

When Grandmother was dying in the workhouse, only Mother could make the journey to say goodbye to her. Grandmother wept, and Mother took out her own handkerchief to dry her tears. As she left the workhouse, she remembered the handkerchief. It was school property, and she might be punished for the loss of it, so she rushed back to the ward. Grandmother was still weeping, but Mother could not keep the lay sister waiting in the convent cab.

Grandmother's gentleness and humility had endeared her to some of the nuns, and when she died, Reverend Mother decided to save her from what was considered the shame of the pauper's hole, where the unclaimed bodies of the dead were thrown. Mother Mary Magdalen was a lady, and did not allow the other nuns to forget it. Her family had been of Isaac Butt's party, as opposed to the popular party of Parnell. 'My brothers were in Parliament when there were none but gentlemen there,' she told the children. She also told them that she had found her vocation at the age of twenty-eight, while attending a performance of *The Colleen Bawn* at the Opera House in Cork. I wonder whether the subject of the play, which deals with the seduction of an innocent Irish girl, and her peculiar choice of a name in religion do not imply that she considered herself to have been flighty. She sent for Mother to find out where Grandfather was buried, but Mother did not know. So Grandmother was buried in a city graveyard, and Reverend Mother ordered a hearse and two covered cars – the old-fashioned two-wheeled vehicles known only in Cork. In one rode Mother with a lay sister, and in the other a couple of orphans.

There was little of the agony of the orphan child that Mother did not know, either through her own experience or the experiences of the other children, which she observed in her sympathetic way. It was the height of the Land War, and all over Ireland poor cottagers were being thrown on to the roadside by police and British troops. One frightened little girl went about for days asking: 'Will the men with the wed wousers (red trousers) come here too?' Once, a baby girl called Lynch, from Kerry, whose family had been drowned, was missing for hours, and was finally discovered in the empty chapel, patiently knocking on the altar and calling: 'Holy God! Holy God! Are 'oo there? Will 'oo send up my Daddy?' Some of the children did not realize for days the immensity of the change that had come over their lives. For a whole week one little girl called Anne Dorgan patiently watched the clock till it came to half past three and then stood up and raised her hand, asking meekly: 'Please ma'am, can I go home now?' 'Sit down, Anne Dorgan,' the nun would say gently, but Anne would stick to her point. 'But, ma'am, 'tis half past three. 'Tis time to go home, ma'am.'

In time she too realized as Mother had done that she had no home now, and tried to divert her feeling for home to the convent, and for her parents to some nun. In some girls that switch was never affected at all and they remained to the end of their lives aloof and cold and conscious of some lack of warmth in themselves, like Kate Gaynor, a friend of Mother's whom I knew in later years and who said bitterly that every orphanage in the world should be torn down because they robbed a child of natural affection, but others were luckier or maybe less exacting. Mother used to quote a snatch of conversation that she had overheard between two infants sitting on the ground under a window, the one eager and serious, the other bored and pompous.

'Do you love God?'
'I won't tell you.'
'Do you love Mother Saint Paul?'
'I won't tell you.'
'Do you rather God or Mother Saint Paul?'
'I won't tell you.'
'I think I rather God, and then Mother Saint Paul.'

Then there was silence. Perhaps the child who would not tell was one whose natural affection was being killed.

Mother herself did not see my Uncle Tim for five years, and in the meantime he had been transferred to the Boys' Orphanage at Greenmount on the south side of the river. On her feast day, Reverend Mother decided that girls who had brothers there should be allowed to entertain them in Sunday's Well. Mother was now quite an important person, and she allowed one of her friends to join her in collecting candies and biscuits for the expected visit. My Aunt Margaret in the infirmary had a hoard. When the orphan boys marched up the convent avenue behind their band, Mother and her friend ran screaming through the ranks calling 'O'Connor! Tim O'Connor!' A small boy said modestly 'That's me,' and the two little girls stuffed his pockets with sweets and marched him off in triumph to the infirmary. But another little girl, called Eileen O'Connor, rushed after them weeping and crying that they had stolen her brother. When they realized their mistake, Mother and her friend beat the pretender and took back the sweets before returning to look for the real Tim O'Connor. After that, the experiment of allowing brothers and sisters to meet for one afternoon in the year was not repeated.

Meanwhile, Mother had her living to earn. She had been trained as a bookbinder, and was neat and skilful at this, as she was at almost anything she tackled, but she was always getting into trouble for reading the books she should have been binding. Maria Condon, who was in charge of the bookbinding class and was a gentle, grave, responsible girl, used to smile sadly and shake her head over Mother's tendency to be distracted by printed pages. She was the daughter of one of the 'fallen' women in the penitentiary and was allowed to see her mother once a week in a convent parlour. One of Mother Mary Magdalen's reforms had been to make a clean sweep of illegitimate girls from the school on the plea that it was unfair to the orphans to have an additional presumption of illegitimacy against them, but an exception had been made of Maria because her mother, who had been seduced by a well-known doctor, had taken vows and become what was known as a 'dedicated penitent', serving a life term by choice in atonement for her fall. There was a moving sequel to the story of Maria and her mother which disturbed me greatly when I was an adolescent and caused endless argument between Mother and myself.

When Maria was sixteen or seventeen she had to be sent out to work as a maid, but the nuns decided that it was unsafe for her to work in Ireland, where people would get to know of her illegitimacy. Maria, who had been told nothing about this, wanted to remain in Cork, where she could be close to her mother, but instead the nuns sent her to New York as maid in a rough Irish boarding house. An older girl who was also a maid in New York was told to look after her. Maria was homesick; she wanted to save her wages to earn her fare back to Ireland, and finally the older girl told her why she could not go back. Maria returned to the horrible boarding house, packed her few possessions, and was not heard of again for a long time. She had been so horrified at her mother's 'sin' and her own illegitimacy that she had decided to break off all connexion with her mother and the convent.

After the revelation, she had gone out and taken the first job she was offered. Fortunately for her, this was with an old American family who soon realized that she was a superior and intelligent girl. But they could not understand why she never received or wrote letters. Finally, the mistress of the house questioned her, and Maria, believing that since she was illegitimate she would be dismissed, broke down and told her everything. Her employers were shocked, and they insisted on her writing at once to her mother. Correspondence with her was resumed, but the nuns were hostile – Maria had left the good Catholic home they had found for her. Her employers encouraged Maria to get a better job and save for a little home of her own to which she could bring her mother. When she had saved enough she returned to Cork, but she found the nuns openly hostile to her plans, and her mother refused to go back to her. She had taken her vows and would end her days as an unpaid trusty in a penitentiary.

As was only natural, when I learned the truth about Maria, I had no sympathy for anyone but her, but Mother refused to let me criticize the nuns. 'They did what they thought was right,' she said obstinately and that settled it for her. But it didn't settle it for me, and I have never ceased to be haunted by the images of Maria and her mother, whose innocent lives had been blasted by an introverted religion.

Mother must have been a dreamy, sensitive child, because she had spells of somnambulism, and once she was found walking up and down a convent corridor in her nightdress, reciting Wolsey's speech from *Henry VIII* – 'Farewell, a long farewell, to all my greatness!'

She was not sent to a bookbinder's to work. One winter evening, when she was fourteen or fifteen, the Mistress of Studies came to her in the orphanage workroom where she was sewing and told her she had found a nice home for her with two ladies who had called to inquire for a maid. The Mistress of Studies then went out and returned with a regular convent outfit for girls who were leaving school – a black straw sailor hat and black coat, a pair of gloves and a parcel of clean aprons. Mother gathered up her own possessions

– a statue of the Blessed Virgin and a couple of holy pictures – said goodbye to her friends, and went off in the darkness down Sunday's Well in a covered car with the two ladies, a Mrs Bowen, who was a widow, and her daughter-in-law. The car stopped outside a terrace of new two-storey houses on Gardiner's Hill.

Mother thought the Mistress of Studies had probably been mistaken, because it didn't seem a very good home. The younger of the two women lit a candle and showed her her room, which was a little cubbyhole with a fireplace, a bed and two or three framed Bible texts. Mother unpacked her belongings and ranged the statue of the Blessed Virgin and the holy pictures on the mantelpiece to keep her company. After her tea she sat in the kitchen till Mrs Bowen told her it was time for her to go to bed. Then she lit her candle and went up to her room. That night all her old fears came back. Since she had been taken by the O'Regans she had never slept alone in a room. She had become used to the big classrooms and dormitories, the voices and the loud footsteps along the corridors, and she was terrified. When she left her room, she stooped for fear of knocking her head on the lintel, which was so much lower than in the big doorway she was used to, and dreaded to move lest she knock something over.

The Bowens were poor, and Mother got no wages, but the younger woman was a dressmaker, and made Mother some clothes of her own, which she liked just as well. Anyhow, she was not accustomed to money. (One of the orphans had once stolen a pound and gone straight to a sweet store, where she ordered 'a pound's worth of sweets' – as though a child of our own time should ask for ten pounds' worth of sweets.) The Bowens kept two lodgers, and the younger woman waited on them. She was an eager, earnest housekeeper, forever on the rush, and so careful of the scraps that she sometimes kept bread till it turned green. Once, Mother was throwing it out, but Mrs Bowen gave her a lecture on waste and explained that bread was healthier that way. Being a great believer in the world of appearances, Mother tried to like it, but couldn't. She decided that, like the view that the Mistress of Studies held of the Bowens' house, this was just a mistake.

Mr Bowen had a job in a wine store on Merchant's Quay, but his health was poor, and Mother was frequently sent into town to explain his absences. She was very sorry about his bad health, but she enjoyed the trips into town. At nights she was allowed to read in the parlour while the Bowens sang sentimental or comic songs or, on Sunday, hymns – Protestant hymns of course. Mother's own favourites were always the old Latin hymns like *Ave Maris Stella* and *Stabat Mater*, but she thoroughly enjoyed the Protestant ones, having, like her son, an open mind on the subject of anything with a tune. The books at her disposal were limited in appeal, boys' school stories with a strongly sectarian bias and standard editions of the poets, but at least she was able to read Shakespeare right through.

When she was hanging out the washing, she became friendly with the sour-faced maid next door, one Betty, who kept house for two old maids called Bennett. Mother talked to her at great length about the convent and about Mother Blessed Margaret, her favourite among the nuns, but Betty hinted darkly that there was nothing she did not know about nuns and chaplains and the dark goings on in convents, and Mother realized, to her great astonishment, that Betty was a Protestant as well. Nobody had ever explained to Mother that Protestants could also be poor. I have a strong impression that from this moment Mother was bent on converting Betty. Betty told Mother that Mr Bowen was a drunkard, but Mother denied this indignantly, and explained that it was just bad health.

Mother, with her belief in the world of appearances, was always being impressed by the curious mistakes that people made. The Mistress of Studies had been mistaken about the Bowens' house, Betty thought that Mr Bowen was a drunkard, and Mr Bowen himself made mistakes that were nearly as bad. One evening his wife, who usually opened the front door when he knocked, was upstairs; Mother opened it instead, and Mr Bowen beamed on her, put his arm about her waist and kissed her. She was taken by such a fit of giggling that she was ashamed. 'Oh, sir, I'm only Minnie,' she explained, and then went off to the kitchen to laugh in peace at the notion that anybody could take *her* for Mrs Bowen. She was longing to tell the joke to the mistress, but finally decided that it might seem forward.

But his mistake was nothing to that of Mr Daly, one of the lodgers, who was a reporter on the Cork *Examiner*. He had a blue overcoat with a velvet collar that Mother thought the height of elegance and which she stroked every time she passed it hanging in the hall. One night she woke and felt a hand on her throat. Her first impulse was to reach for the statue of the Blessed Virgin, which was on the mantelpiece over her bed, but what she grabbed instead was the velvet collar she knew so well.

'Oh, Mr Daly, is that you?' she cried in relief.

'Don't shout, Minnie!' he whispered crossly. 'I'm only looking for the candle.'

'But what are you doing in here?' she asked. 'Your room is the other way.'

'I lost my way in the darkness, that's all,' he said with a sigh, and after a couple of minutes went out quietly.

It was only then that Mother, having got over the shock, could laugh in comfort. Here was an educated man with a big job on the Cork *Examiner* who could not even find his own way upstairs in the dark! And she knew from the way he had sighed that this was something that must often happen to him and cause him a great deal of concern.

Next morning, she simply could not resist reporting his mistake to the younger Mrs Bowen, and then she wished she hadn't, because Mrs Bowen did not laugh at all. Instead, she rushed upstairs to her husband, who was still in bed, and repeated the story to him. He jumped out of bed in his nightshirt and went and threw open the door of Daly's room. Mrs Bowen was still angry when she came downstairs.

'His bed hasn't even been slept in,' she said bitterly. 'I don't think you need worry, Minnie. I fancy he won't trouble us again.'

She was right about that, because in the afternoon a messenger came from the *Examiner* for Daly's clothes, and Mrs Bowen was still so furious that she hurled them at him from the head of the stairs. She even refused to let Mother parcel them for him. Mother was full of pity for the poor little messenger. who sat at the front gate trying to fold the shirts and suits, but, indeed, I think she was sorrier for poor Mr Daly, who had been so ashamed of his own mistake that he had walked blindly out of the house and probably got no sleep at all that night. She thought it was very unforeseen of him not to explain to her how seriously Protestants regarded mistakes.

Then the Bowens had a baby, and Mother had one of her many traumatic experiences about him. She made the midwife promise that when she brought the baby, before giving it over to the mother, she would let her see it first, and when Mr Bowen invited her up to the bedroom to see the new arrival, Mother, after a stunned silence, turned to the midwife and called her a false and wicked woman. Mother hardly ever lost her temper, and never except under what she regarded as intolerable provocation, but when she did, she was magnificent. She reduced everybody to silence. The midwife apologized and excused herself on the ground of the baby's having no clothes, but Mother regarded this as a very lame excuse.

Mother, of course, was enchanted with the baby, and insisted on showing him off to Betty next door. She had no idea of the emotions she was rousing both in Betty and the two old maids she worked for. One Sunday morning the Bowens stormed back from church and denounced Mother for having said of herself and the baby that she was 'bringing up a heretic for Hell'. Mother found it difficult to deny this accusation, because she didn't know what a heretic was, even when the Bowens explained that it was something Catholics called Protestants. Mother, weeping, explained that she had never heard Protestants called that by anyone she knew, and finally the Bowens apologized, realizing that they had been victims of a plot of the Bennetts and Betty, but Mother did not lightly recover from the scene. It was quite plain now that Betty would never be a Catholic.

Mother went a few times to the convent to visit my Aunt Margaret, who was seriously ill, her two arms swathed in cotton wool. One day she was sent for, and when she arrived my aunt was dead. The nun who brought her in to see the body told her she should not cry. Margaret was better off. The nun may have been right. It was bad enough to be an orphan, but to be a cripple as well! Margaret's confession had to be heard after that of all the other children because the chaplain had to leave the confession box and sit beside her in her wheelchair. A little while before she died, one of the girls had pushed her wheelchair into the chapel in the evening, and then forgot all about her. The chaplain, too, forgot, and it was only at bedtime that they discovered her missing and found her at last, having sobbed herself to sleep in the deserted chapel.

But the Mistress of Studies, who always seemed to have Mother's best interests at heart, did not forget *her* and, deciding that it was bad for her to be in a Protestant home, found her a place in a respectable Catholic lodging house on Richmond Hill. It was kept by a Mrs Joyce, who had five daughters. The eldest, Kathleen, was Mother's age, and a good-natured girl, but foolish and affected. She spent her life reading sentimental novelettes. As in the Bowens' there were two lodgers. Mannix and Healy – both medical students of a violently patriotic temperament who sometimes came in covered in blood after some political riot – and when Kathleen waited on them they ridiculed her affected airs, but both were fond of Mother and brought her presents of sweets and fruit. Neither of them realized the damage they were doing her in the eyes of her mistress, a coarse and ignorant woman with a violent temper. Every little gift they brought Mother became a further slight on Mrs Joyce's fine, educated daughter, and she harried Mother relentlessly, shouting 'Gerril, do this!' and 'Gerril, do that!' One evening she came into the sitting-room and saw Mannix pull Mother's pigtail. This was sufficient to put her in one of her usual furies.

'Aha, Gerril!' she said. 'The same thing will happen you as happened Madge Murphy.'

'What happened her?' Mother asked with genuine interest.

'She had a baby!'

'Well, that isn't true, anyway.' Mother said heatedly. (She never liked people to flout her intelligence.) 'How could she have a baby when she isn't even married?'

Joyce, who was eating his supper, looked up at his wife as she was about to reply, and said shortly: 'Let the child alone! She's better off as she is.'

However, that could not keep Mother off the subject of sex, on which her experience with the Bowens had made her an expert. Mrs Joyce was having her sixth and Mother, who was nothing if not conscientious, decided to enlighten Patricia, the youngest but one of the children, about the facts of life and the untrustworthiness of midwives. She explained to Patricia that she had personally known a midwife who had promised to show her the baby as soon as she bought it and, instead of that, had taken it straight up to the mother, concealed. Patricia, who wasn't much more than a baby herself, listened with growing stupefaction and then said: 'But you don't buy babies.'

'Don't you, indeed?' Mother asked good-naturedly. 'And how do you get them?'

'You make them, of course,' cried Patricia indignantly, and Mother laughed heartily at this example of childish innocence. Her laughter made the little girl furious, and when they reached home she rushed in to her eldest sister, and, pointing an accusing finger at Mother, yelled: 'She says you buy babies!'

'Ah, she only says that because you're so young,' Kathleen replied good-humouredly.

'She doesn't!' screamed the infant. 'She believes it!'

I never had the heart to ask Mother if she had taken example by the child and really learned the facts of life. The one dirty story she knew suggested that she had, but I was never quite certain that she knew what it meant. My impression is that she accepted the evidence in the spirit in which she accepted the evidence of her birth certificate and marked the case 'Not Proven'. Once in Geneva I overheard an extraordinary conversation between her and a Swiss manufacturer's wife whose son was leaving for Paris and who was very concerned about the sort of women he might meet there.

'It is such a dangerous place for a young man,' said the Swiss woman.

'Oh, the traffic!' exclaimed Mother, delighted to have found a kindred spirit. 'It took the sight from my eyes.'

'And it isn't only the traffic, is it?' the Swiss woman asked gently. 'We send them away healthy and we wish them to come back healthy.'

'I said it!' Mother cried passionately. 'My boy's digestion is never the same.'

A certain simplicity of mind that is characteristic of all noble natures, says some old Greek author whose name I cannot remember.

The real nightmare began only after the Joyces moved to a house in Mulgrave Road, near the North Cathedral. Mother no longer had a bedroom, and slept on a trestle bed in the corridor. The painters were still at work in the house, and one of them, after trying in vain to get Mother to walk out with him, proposed to her. He told her he thought she'd make 'a damn nice little wife'. Mother didn't mind the proposal so much, but she thought his language was terrible.

'What was that fellow saying to you?/ Mrs Joyce asked suspiciously when the painter left the room.

'Ah, nothing, only asking me to marry him,' Mother replied lightly, not realizing what she was doing to a woman with five daughters and a probable sixth on the way.

'A queer one he'd be marrying!' growled Mrs Joyce.

A few days later some nuns of the city order called and addressed Mother under the impression that she was the eldest of the family, which seemed such a good joke to Patricia that she told her mother. It drove Mrs Joyce into a tempest of fury.

'A nice daughter, indeed!' snarled Mrs Joyce. 'A creature that doesn't know who she is or where she came from. She doesn't even know who her own mother was.'

This was too much for Mother. Insults directed against herself she could stand, but not insults to her mother's memory.

'My mother was a lady, anyhow,' she said. 'You're not a lady.'

After that, Mrs Joyce made her life a hell. The clothes her previous employer had made fell into rags, and Mrs Joyce refused to replace them. Instead, she gave Mother a ragged coatee, which she had bought from a dealing woman for a few pence, and an old skirt of her sister's who had just died in the Incurable Hospital. After each meal served to the lodgers, Mrs Joyce rushed in to gather up the scraps, so that there was nothing left to eat. Hunger was no new thing to any of the orphanage children, but starvation was a new thing to Mother. Instead of candies and biscuits, the medical students now gave her an occasional sixpence, and she bought a loaf of bread which she concealed, and from which she cut a slice when Mrs Joyce went out. At night she was so tired that sometimes she never reached her trestle bed in the corridor. Once, walking across the yard with the lamp, she fell asleep and was wakened only by the crash of the falling lamp. Another time, she fell asleep crossing the Joyces' bedroom with a lighted candle, and when she woke up the curtains were in flames about her.

Then her long beautiful hair grew lousy, and Mrs Joyce ordered her to cut it off. Mother did not perceive that this was the chance the woman had been waiting for all the time. Slight her beautiful, educated daughter indeed! She would show the medical students what a girl looked like when she was ragged and starved and without hair.

That evening, when Mother served the dinner, Mannix looked at her in astonishment. 'What the hell did you do that to yourself for?' he shouted, and when she had told him he went on: 'For God's sake, girl, will you get out of this house before that woman does something worse to you? Can't you see yourself that she hates you?'

'But why would she hate me?' asked Mother.

'Because she's jealous of you. That's why.'

But Mother could not see why anyone should be jealous of somebody as poor and friendless as herself. I doubt if it occurred to her to the day of her death that the Mistress of Studies was also jealous of her. With that simplicity of mind the old author praised, she never really understood the hatred that common natures entertain for refined ones.

She was now ashamed to leave the house, even to buy food. And then something happened that showed how far she had really sunk.

55

The Good Shepherd nuns had at last learned that the lodgers in the house were medical students, and medical students were notorious for their depravity, though this instantly ceased the moment they got a degree. It is a superstition from the early days of scientific medicine, and it has not yet died out. One day two nuns came to the house in a covered car, and ordered Mother to return to the orphanage with them. She refused, and they reminded her of the penalty she was incurring. Any girl who left one of the pleasant homes provided by the nuns without permission was not allowed to return to the orphanage, which was the only home most of the girls had. In the same way, one who refused to leave immediately when ordered was not allowed to return. Mother still refused to go back with them, and when they left in anger, she knew she had now no place in the world to go. When I tried to get her to explain this extraordinary conduct, she said, almost impatiently, that she could not go back in that state among clean, well-dressed girls. Possibly behind her refusal to return there was an element of almost hysterical vanity, but that cannot be the real explanation. My own guess is that it was despair, rather than vanity. Children, and adolescents who have retained their childish innocence, have little hold on life. They have no method of defending themselves against the things that are not in their own nature. I think that, without knowing it, Mother hated the nuns for what they had made of her innocent life, and had already decided to commit suicide. Her parents were dead, Margaret had died while she was at Bowens', Tim she had seen only once for a few hours in all the years, and she had nothing left to live for.

For eight or nine months longer, it dragged on like that. The eldest girl took pity on her, helped with the housework when her mother wasn't looking, and even checked her mother when the scurrility went too far. The youngest also helped in her own enlightened way, hiding Mother's brushes and mops and dusters in order to be able to ask: 'Minnie, what are you looking for? I get it for you.' Even in her own misery, Mother laughed at the baby's goodwill. But one winter day Joyce came in at one o'clock for his dinner and it wasn't ready. His wife ordered Mother out of the house. She put off the apron she had been wearing, put on her black straw hat, threw the ragged old coatee over her shoulders – the hat, jacket and skirt were all the possessions she had left in the world – and went out into Mulgrave Road. She saw people stop and stare at her, and realized the extraordinary figure she cut. She ran up a laneway by the North Infirmary and threw the ragged jacket there, but people still continued to look. She ran for shelter to the Dominican Church on the Sand Quay, and prayed.

She knew now that only one hope remained to her, and that a miracle. None of the nuns – not even her favourite, Mother Blessed Margaret – could overrule the Mistress of Studies, and if she went to the orphanage she would be turned away. She knew too many to whom it had happened. The only one who could overrule the Mistress of Studies was Reverend Mother. It was she who had arranged for my grandmother's funeral. But lay sisters, not Reverend Mothers, answer convent door bells, and from one o'clock until darkness fell Mother waited in the church, most of the time on her knees, praying for a miracle to happen. She had decided that if it didn't she would return to the river and drown herself. It was only when she was telling me about this period of her life that I ever heard her use such an expression in any matter that concerned herself, for not only did she believe suicide was wrong, she thought it demonstrative, and she was almost fiercely undemonstrative in grief or pain. Nor, when she talked of that afternoon, as an old woman, did she exaggerate it. Father and I, with our deep streak of melancholia, would have added something to it that, by making it more dramatic, would also have made it less terrible. It is an awful moment when gaiety dies in those who have no other hold on life.

On the dark, stepped pathway up to the convent, she met two ladies who were coming away from it, chattering, and paid no heed to them. She went up the steps to the front door and rang, and immediately the door opened and Reverend Mother stood inside. In sheer relief, Mother broke down and began to sob out her story. Reverend Mother did not recognize her at first; then something seemed to strike her. 'Aren't you the girl we told to come back from that terrible house?' she asked.

'Yes,' said Mother.

'And why *didn't* you come?'

'I had no clothes. I was ashamed.'

'It's strange I should have answered the door,' said Reverend Mother. 'I was just seeing off some friends, and something kept me here thinking. I was just walking up and down the corridor.' Clearly, she was aware of the coincidence, but Mother knew it was something more.

She brought Mother into her own parlour, sat her before the fire to warm herself, and rang the bell for the Mistress of Studies.

'Minnie O'Connor has come back from that terrible house to stay,' she said quietly, and then as the Mistress of Studies burst into a stream of abuse she added: 'Don't scold, Mother!'

Turning to Mother, the Mistress of Studies cried: 'If you're in that state, you can go to the workhouse. You will not stay here!'

'She is not in that state, and she will stay here,' Reverend Mother said firmly, and that night, for the first time in years, Mother had enough to eat, and bathed, and slept in a clean bed.

She never made much of her own misery. Other girls, as she said, had had a worse time. But she never ceased to speak of what happened as a miracle and, in the way of those to whom miracles occur, never by so much as a harsh word attempted to blame the Mistress of Studies. Not that she did not realize that for the future she must be on her guard. I feel sure it was significant that when, a week later, the Mistress of Studies found her another nice home, in a public house off Blarney Lane that was a lodging house for cattle dealers, Mother, without even unpacking her bag, returned to the convent and told the Mistress of Studies that it was not a suitable place for a young woman. It was also significant that, a few days later, the Mistress of Studies was replaced by Mother's great friend, Mother Blessed Margaret, whom I knew and loved when she was an old lady. Old or young, she, like Reverend Mother, was a lady.

4

Mother Blessed Margaret's way with the girls was to say: 'There is a situation free in the Xs'. I think you might try it and see what you think of it.' So Mother took a situation with the Stewarts, and after sticking it for six months did not think much of it. Mr Stewart came from the North of Ireland, and was a tight-fisted, small, dark, dingy man. Every morning he ground and prepared his own coffee on the landing. His wife was very tall, thin, ailing, devout and fussy. There were two daughters. Kathleen, the eldest, took after her father; Nan was small, with frizzy hair and a good-natured friendly manner, and was forever singing Methodist hymns. Mrs

Stewart, as Mother described her, had a lot in common with Trollope's Mrs Proudie. Once when a girl called Ethel Richards was staying with them, Kathleen and Nan chaffed her about her young man.

'Do tell us what his name is!' one of the girls cried.

'Oh!' Ethel said ecstatically. 'That name above all other names!'

At this, Mrs Stewart sat up in her chair, red with horror and indignation.

'Ethel!' she cried. 'Unsay those words!'

Mrs Proudie could scarcely have phrased it better. But for Mother it was too like the dingy atmosphere of the Bowens' house. Then Mother Blessed Margaret got her the job that for eight years was to provide her with a real home, and for the rest of her days with memories that I can only describe as enchanted. It was in a house whose gardens reached to the convent wall, so that Mother could talk to the nuns across it, and it was occupied by a butter-and-egg merchant named Barry and his unmarried sister, Alice. I do not think life can ever have been as good anywhere as it seemed to Mother there, but for the orphan girl who had never asked anything but that people should value her, it was happiness enough. Ned Barry was a man of forty, tall and fat, with a hook nose and high colour. His main weakness was vanity, but he was the kindest of men and the gayest, and she loved gaiety even more than she loved kindness. When she told me about him, later in life, I did not guess what now seems so obvious – that she was very much in love with him – nor did I wonder, as I now find myself doing, whether he was not just a little attracted by her. She admitted that he had been 'flighty' with her, and she was not the sort of woman who admitted, or permitted 'flightiness'.

He gave great stag parties, and after them the men had to be carried up to bed, and Mother brought them their breakfast of whiskey and soda in the morning, while their wives sat in the hall waiting for them to get up. There was a piano in Barry's bedroom, and sometimes the party was resumed there by men in their nightshirts who played the piano and danced hornpipes by the hour. To judge by Mother's accounts, all the men were unbelievably good, brave and generous, and often there would be as much as twenty-five shillings in tips on the hall table in the morning. Twenty-five shillings was big money for a poor girl who up to the age of eighteen had had no wages at all, and she saved it, though I suspect my

Uncle Tim, who was now an apprentice in a cobbler's shop in Barrack Street, lightened it considerably.

One day he called to the house to ask for money and to say goodbye. That night he stowed away on a cattle boat, was discovered and brought before the captain, and then put ashore in an English port. He tramped across England to Colchester, where he enlisted, and Mother did not see him again for some years till Alice came to her in great distress and said: 'Minnie, there are two soldiers here, asking for you, and I'm afraid they'll run away with Towser.' But when Alice discovered that one of them was Mother's brother, she set to making supper with her and produced a bottle of her brother's whiskey.

She was like that, a magnificent woman with a great head of golden hair, and she had all her brother's good nature. From the beginning the two girls were never mistress and maid. Alice had had a succession of servants who were drunkards or thieves, and was glad of Mother, and Mother had had a succession of heartless mistresses, and was grateful for one who treated her as a friend. Alice confided her love affairs to Mother, and I have no doubt that if Mother had love affairs, she confided them to Alice. Alice had few friends, and she and Mother spent the summer afternoons taking long walks or sitting under a hedge by the river while Alice painted a water colour and Mother read a book. When the two went to town together, people stopped in the street to stare at Alice's beauty, and Mother was as proud as though it were at her own. But Alice had periods of depression that sometimes lasted for a whole week, and all that time she did not speak, and after the first few months Mother, believing that Alice was going insane, gave notice. Alice apologized, and Mother became even more devoted to her than she already was to her brother. I can answer for their mutual affection, because by a curious coincidence I was able to bring them together again when they were elderly women, and they rattled on delightedly like two schoolgirls who had not met for a whole vacation.

Each of them had had one son: Alice's had died tragically under a cloud, the sort of cloud that Irish respectability creates over a mere indiscretion: I was just beginning to make a small reputation for myself; and even the touch of envy on Alice's part, of complacency on Mother's, could not conceal the deep affection between two women who had shared real happiness together.

It was the great age of the butter-and-egg trade. The Barrys were wealthy and lived in a beautiful house, with gardens before and behind producing strawberries, raspberries, pears, apples and peaches. Like the Jewish merchants of the time, the Catholic merchants did things in style, far beyond the level of their Protestant neighbours. Like the Jews, they were emerging from an age of persecution and, full of self-confidence, were the principal supporters of Charles Stewart Parnell. His fall was the first real shock to their self-confidence. On the day he died, Alice came down to the kitchen to tell Mother, and the two of them sat there all evening, weeping.

Meanwhile, the great stag parties went on, catered for by a restaurant in town, and the big house was always full of life, for Barry was so good-natured that he could not pass a policeman on his beat without bringing him home for a drink, or a poor prostitute without bringing her home for a meal, and often when Mother came down to the kitchen in the morning the pantry was bare and the decanter empty. Half the girls in town seemed to want to marry him, but his sister took their letters from the hall stand and, having read them out scornfully to Mother, destroyed them. Of course, he never noticed. He was a rattlepate and never in time for anything. He would arrange to take Alice to the theatre, and she would dress and wait for him, but he never showed up on time. After the performance had already begun, he would rush in in a frenzy of efficiency and dash upstairs to dress, with Mother at his heels to fix the studs in his dress shirt. But Alice was endlessly patient with him.

Then a child, a niece who had been left an orphan, came to live with them, and soon after that Alice married. She married because she felt she ought to be married rather than because she really wanted to marry. I suspect she was one of those dreamy, romantic women whose marriage, to be successful, must first make smithereens of their personality, but, in the way of women like that, she drew back from the danger. She had been very much in love with a doctor, but refused to marry him because he drank. He took up with another girl, and one day when the three of them met at the races, he threw his arms about Alice and said: 'I have you now, and I'll never let you go.' 'Oh, yes, you will,' the other girl said not in the least discomposed, and detached him from Alice. Alice came home in a state of collapse. The kind, bookish man she finally married was not the sort to make smithereens of anyone, and she returned from the honeymoon in despair. 'I should never have left

Ned,' she told Mother. When it was all over and Alice was settled with her husband in a little village in East Cork, Mother was sick with loneliness. While the child stayed with them, Barry pulled himself together and took Mother and her to the Opera House every week, but when she went off to school, he did his entertaining in a hotel in the city, and Mother lay awake half the night listening for the sound of his step. The old house was full of noises and had the reputation of being haunted.

Reverend Mother insisted that she must not stay on in the house unchaperoned, and pressed her to leave, but Mother hated to do that. Her reputation never worried her much at any time. There were good people and bad people, and she had her own standards of both, and the reputation she might retain by not associating with people she thought good did not interest her. She had been happier there than she had ever been in her life before, and she clung to her position like an old dog to a deserted house, waiting for Alice's brief visits and the child's return from school. When she had been living there for a year without a chaperon, Reverend Mother issued an ultimatum: Mother must choose between Barry and her, between the house and convent. Mother wrote distractedly to Alice, who replied shrewdly that Mother should take in another of the orphans as maid. Reverend Mother refused to accept the suggestion, saying that Barry's reputation was too bad. This is the point in the story at which I begin to wonder whether Reverend Mother's ultimatum was not directed at him rather than at her – she may well have been trying to prevent Mother's staying on as housekeeper so that she could come back as mistress of the house. I am quite sure that Mother never considered that aspect of it at all. She was blinded to everything in the world by the fact that she regarded the house as her home.

Terrified of a breach with Reverend Mother, Mother at last gave notice and told Barry that the nuns refused to let her remain. He was bitterly offended.

'The nuns are no friends of yours, Minnie,' he said – a phrase that, again, could mean something different from what she saw in it. I have a suspicion, which may be mere daydreaming, that he had considered marrying her, and that only his vanity had kept him back. The man who married his housekeeper was too obvious a subject for ridicule. And now that she had given notice, Mother was almost insane with worry and fear and loneliness. Finally, unable to bear it any longer, she told her friends in the convent that she intended to remain on, and withdrew her notice. But now it was his turn to be stiff. He told her that he had already engaged another housekeeper, and, seeing her gesture of love slighted, she grew really angry. She told him curtly that it was just as well that way. It wasn't, as she soon discovered. When she tried to show the new housekeeper, a crude country girl, the workings of the house, she showed no interest, and spent her time in Mother's bedroom, trying on her hats.

The night the covered car came to take Mother and her trunk away, she was broken-hearted. All she had ever asked was a home, and for eight years she had had a perfect one, with a man and woman she loved and who valued her love, and she knew that no other house in the world would mean as much to her. It was, as she said, the tragedy of the orphan, who clings to any place where she is happy. She still went back in the mornings, to try to train the new housekeeper, and afterwards, during the school holidays, to act as companion to Barry's niece and buy whatever she needed. The new housekeeper, who by this time had managed to introduce her mother into the house to help her, and later brought her sisters as well, was very cordial and insisted on showing all the presents she received from Barry. One day as Mother and she were passing through his bedroom, she pointed slyly to a pair of women's slippers under his bed. 'He gave me them too,' she said.

Mother did not see Barry again until six years later, when she was married and I a baby in her arms. During the first three of these she was employed in four houses, sufficient indication of the fever of restlessness in which she found herself. After Barry's she found it impossible to settle anywhere, and that, too, I think, is part of the orphan pattern. For me, it was best illustrated in one of the most moving stories she told about the orphanage. Reverend Mother, whose brother, a priest, had died young, was convinced that the reason for his death was that he, like other priests, was confined to the dragons who in Ireland become priests' housekeepers. She decided to train as housekeepers a few of the orphans who had real intelligence, and one of these, May Corcoran, first underwent training in a really good town house and was then sent as housekeeper to a young priest in the country. After six months she returned to the orphanage, nobody knew why. She went out again as housekeeper to a priest of more settled age and again in a short time she returned. This time the secret was out. She had 'made herself cheap' – that is, she had fallen in love with each priest in turn, until her innocent adoration of him and concern for his comfort had made him a laughing-stock among his fellow priests and his parishioners. The experiment of training priests' housekeepers was at an end, and May was found a job as nursery governess with a wealthy family who were delighted with her gentleness and gracious manners. She, on the other hand, filled with restlessness and resentment, had no affection to spare for them. She fell ill and an operation became necessary, but she refused to undergo it in Cork. She arranged for her admission to a Dublin hospital and on the evening before the operation was to take place, destroyed every particle of writing by which she could be identified, and then went into the hospital and died after the operation. Only a letter from Reverend Mother that had slipped down inside the lining of her coat showed who she was.

Mother's restlessness led her to take a job in England, but she stood this only six months, and preferred to repay the advance that she had received for her passage money. By August of '98 she was in a position in East Cork with a well-to-do family of millers who behaved in the way of lords of the manor in England, had their old pensioners to the house every Saturday to draw their pensions, and gave expensive entertainments to the children of their mill-hands at Christmas. The lady of the house was the daughter of a general much in favour with the Queen, who was godmother to the second son – called, of course, Victor – and presented him with a silver baby service. The second maid was a girl from Limerick called Molly, who arrived while Victor was being born, with references that were not checked until later and that turned out to have been forged. Molly was the mistress of a son in another big house closer to Cork, and had taken the situation to be nearer him. When he wished to take her off on holiday, Molly sent herself a wire announcing that her father was dying, and went off, wearing Mrs Armitage's jewellery and clothes. Molly returned from the holiday and presented herself before Mrs Armitage wearing a gold locket that had been one of Mrs Armitage's wedding presents. When she looked at it and took it, Molly tried to grab it back. Discharged next morning, she wrote from Cork to say that she was employing a solicitor, but, she added, 'what better could you expect from a woman who did not go to Confession and Communion?' Like many of her race, Molly believed firmly in the superiority of faith over morals.

Here at least Mother was able to visit Alice Barry and her

husband. By this time Tim had become engaged, and Alice insisted on Mother's bringing him and his girl as well. There was a brief interlude when one of the orphans induced her to take a job outside Limerick where the boss and the Swiss butler, Armady, fought a running battle in the manner of *Figaro* as to which was to pay attention to the maids. In 1901 she took a job with the family of a naval paymaster in Queenstown. In the meantime Tim had married; his daughter, Julia, was born on a Saturday and on the following Monday he set sail from Queenstown for the South African War. He had to be carried, blind drunk, on to the troopship while Mother held his hand, and my conscientious father, afraid he would die of thirst on the long voyage, hurled a bottle of whiskey on board, to be caught by his comrades. As the troopship moved away, my uncle distinguished himself further by trying to throw himself overboard, but his companions caught and held him. Along with a holy medal, Mother had given him her gunmetal watch, which contained a photograph of Mother Blessed Margaret. On the second day out, he staked it at cards and lost it. That was typical of Tim. But it was also typical of him to order from London an expensive gold watch to replace it, and in his letters he continued to warn her against my father. 'Have nothing to do with Mick Donovan,' he wrote. 'He's a good friend, but he'll make a poor husband.' Poor man, I'm afraid he did.

The marriage may have been precipitated by a mean trick of the paymaster's wife. She brought Mother on a long holiday to her own mother's house in Sheerness as nurse to her daughter, aged five, but in England she decided that what she really wanted was an English nurse, and she proposed to bring her back to Ireland on the return half of Mother's ticket. Without consulting Mother, she arranged employment for her as parlourmaid in a house in the dockyards. 'I told you I would not live in this country,' Mother said angrily. 'I came with you and I intend to go back with you.' On her return she married Father, and they went to live with his parents, who then had a house in Maryville Cottages in Barrackton that they could not afford to keep on their own. There was some ugly story about this incident, but I have forgotten the details. I know that Mother was disgusted and horrified by the dirt and drunkenness and complained that it had not been part of their bargain. I think it was probably Father who said: 'It's done now, and it can't be undone,' because the words rankled in her mind for forty years. When he went off to the South African War, she took rooms with Miss Wall in Douglas Street, and I was born when he was still away. When he returned they set up house in Blarney Lane, and Mother opened a little shop. This was the one period of her life that she always refused to speak about, and it was clearly a horror to her. The whole idea of her keeping a shop was absurd, because she could never refuse anybody anything, and when at last she had to abandon it she was owed money all over the place. But I don't think Father gave her any chance of continuing. For Tim had proved to be a prophet. Father drank his way through the shop, and with it all her other treasures, including Tim's gold watch, which she sold for five pounds.

One morning at Mass in Sunday's Well Church, I cried and had to be taken out on to the porch. The church door opened and Ned Barry came out. Mother was horrified at his appearance. He was pale and hollow-cheeked, and she felt sure he was dying. In the old, good-natured way he stopped to speak to me and pat me on the head, as he would have done with any baby, but without once looking at her or recognizing her, and she was too taken aback to remind him of who she was. He had reached the chapel gate before she made a move. But he was a brisk walker, and she was burdened with me and, hard as she ran, she could only keep him in view down the length of Sunday's Well, till he turned in the gateway of his house. As the door closed behind him, she ran up the avenue. She rang the bell, and the housekeeper put her head out of a bedroom window.

'The Boss isn't in,' she said shortly.

'I saw him go in just a moment ago,' said Mother.

'Well, he's not in now, anyway,' the other woman said, and banged the window shut.

When Mother saw Barry again a few months later, he was dead. Alice had looked through the house, which was filthy, and found a compromising letter from the housekeeper to a man, inviting him to the house while her mother was at the church. The lawyers, too, had stepped in and cancelled the order for a piano which the housekeeper had issued for her own entertainment. Alice and she sat with the body in the bedroom of the house where all three of them had been so happy together. I was put to sleep on the sofa beside him, and the two women talked till night fell of his kindness and his charm, while the housekeeper and her many relations sat below in the kitchen and did not once approach them.

5

I suspect that it was that house, rather than the convent, that really left its mark upon my mother's character and established, if it did not give her, standards of behaviour that would have been exacting in any social group and were impossible in the gutter where the world had thrown her. She rarely permitted herself to comment on any tiny treachery she had observed in one of my friends, and I used to persuade myself that she had not noticed, but if worse happened, and she felt free to speak, it became clear that she had seen every detail and felt it more than I. Sometimes she observed things that nobody else had observed. Once I laughed outright at her when she said of a brilliant young artist who came to the flat: 'I'd have nothing to do with that boy. There's a streak of imbecility in him,' but time proved her right.

She rarely asked anything for herself, never made scenes, and often went for months without the commonest necessities rather than complain. On her seventieth birthday she had a very bad fall, and the doctor who examined her told me that all her life she had suffered from chronic appendicitis. When she really did want something – usually something that involved the pleasure of a third party, like the cousins of mine to whom in her last years she was devoted – she dripped hints like a leaky old tap. On the other hand, 'hints' is a crude word for the photograph casually dropped where I would be bound to see it, or for the gossamer off-key phrases that seemed to be intended as a sort of psychological conditioning that might ultimately influence my conduct subconsciously; and I noticed that when the hints went on too long and I shouted at her, she seemed to be less hurt by the shout than by my discovery of her innocent little plot. At such moments, I fancy, she probably blamed herself severely for a lack of delicacy.

That curious negative energy gave her an almost uncanny power of inducing people to confide in her. She woke very early, with a passion for tea, and when we were staying in a London hotel I made a deal with the chambermaid to bring it to her when she herself came on duty. When I called for her at nine o'clock Mother had acquired the material for a full-length novel of life in Devon from the maid. On the same morning I had an interview with my agent, and left her sitting in Trafalgar Square. When I returned forty-five minutes later, a good-looking woman was sitting beside her. Mother had got the material for another novel. By that time she knew as much about the life of ordinary people in England as I would learn in years. She was uncomfortable abroad even more than I was but for the same reason – all that lovely material going to waste – but in Switzerland she met the Swiss woman who spoke English and got her life story as well.

Naturally, with that sort of mind she loved novels, particularly Victorian novels, but she had a similar passion for classical music. She made a point of never intruding on me, because I might be 'thinking', but she reserved her rights in respect of thinking to music, and I had only to put the needle on a gramophone record to see her shuffle in, smiling, her shawl round her shoulders, and settle on the chair nearest the door. The smile, as well as the choice of chair, clearly indicated that she was not disturbing me because she wasn't really there. Sometimes if I had visitors she didn't want to interrupt, she would give the handle of my door a gentle twist, leave the door ajar, and then sit on a chair outside. She had a passion for Schubert and Mozart, and loved soprano voices and violins – the high, pure, piercing tone. It took me longer to discover her taste in fiction, because her comments on anything were so direct and simple that they could appear irrelevant. She talked as a child talks, completely without self-consciousness. Once she practically burst into tears when I brought her a novel of Walter Scott's and cried: 'But you know I can't read Scotch!' It took me years to discover that she didn't really like dialect. Another time I brought her a novel by Peadar O'Donnell, whom she loved, but she had read only a few pages when I saw her getting fretful.

'What is it now?' I growled.

'Ah, didn't you notice?' she asked reproachfully, looking at me over her glasses. 'Nearly every sentence begins with "I".'

From remarks like these one had to deduce what she meant, but often no deductions were necessary. Once I took her on a funicular to the top of some Alp, and as we sat on the terrace of a restaurant far above the glittering lake, I enthused about the view. 'There should be great drying up here,' she said thoughtfully, her mind reverting to the problem of laundry.

In spite of her gentleness, there was a streak of terribleness in her – something that was like a Last Judgement, and (as I suspect the Last Judgement will be) rather less than just. I think it was linked in a curious way with her weakness for tearing up pictures of herself that she didn't like and removing pictures of the woman she disapproved of from photograph albums, and echoed some childish magic, some reconstruction of reality to make it less intolerable. During court proceedings about my right to visit my children, after my wife and I were separated, Mother learned that they were in court and, against my wishes, insisted on seeing them. I went with her to the witnesses' room, and when the children saw her they slunk away with their heads down. She went up to them slowly, her two hands out, as she had gone up to the mad boy in Blarney Lane, saying in a whisper: 'Darlings, won't you speak to me? It's only Dunnie.' (Dunnie was their pet name for her.) I could bear it no longer and, putting my arm round her, made her leave the room. She stood against the wall outside with her face suddenly gone white and stony, and said: 'I'm eighty-five, but I've learned a new thing today. I've learned that you can turn children into devils.' Then and later I argued angrily with her, pleading that you cannot hold children responsible for what they do when they are frightened, but she never spoke their names again. I insisted on speaking to her about them, and she listened politely because she knew I was doing what I thought 'right,' which was the only test of conduct she admitted, but she offered no opinion, and it was clear that their photographs had been taken out of whatever album she carried in her mind. The woman who all her life had sought love could not entertain the idea of a child who, she thought, rejected it.

A couple of weeks before that, our next-door neighbour in the little 'development' where we lived had died. His younger daughter had put in a good deal of unpaid work as secretary of the Tenants' Association. But the family was Protestant, and by this time Irish Catholics no longer attended Protestant funerals – a refinement of conscience that had completely escaped Mother's attention. She only realized it when the funeral was ready to start and none of the hundred families in the estate development had shown up. I was waiting at the front door, with my coat and hat on, and as she rushed out I tried to detain her. 'How dare you!' she cried frantically. 'Let me go! Do you think I could let that poor woman go with her husband's body to the grave thinking that those miserable cowards are Catholics?' She ran out in front of the house, her grey hair blowing in the wind, and held out her hands to the widow. 'I'm old and feeble, or I'd be along with you today,' she said, glaring round at the estate houses, where people watched from behind drawn blinds. 'What those creatures are doing to you – that's not Catholic; that's not Irish.'

When she was dead, and I had done all the futile things she would have wished, like bringing her home across the sea to rest with Father, and when the little girl who had refused to speak to her in court had knelt beside the coffin in the luggage van at Kingsbridge, and the little boy had joined the train at Limerick Junction, I returned to the house she had left. When she fell ill, I had been teaching the child who was left me a Negro spiritual, and now when we came home together and I opened the front door, he felt that everything was going to be the same again and that we could go back to our singing. He began, in a clear treble: 'Child, I know you're going to miss me when I'm gone.' Then only did I realize the horror that had haunted me from the time I was his age and accompanied Mother to the orphanage, and learned for the first time the meaning of parting and death, had happened at last to me, and that it made no difference to me that I was fifty and a father myself.

And I await the resurrection from the dead and eternal life to come.

TWO

I know where I'm going

6

There was only one thing to be said in favour of Father's home ground – it was colourful. There were fifteen houses in the little square, and the occupants were as sharply distinguished as though they had all been of different races and religions. They had little appeal to me, because I dreamed of families that lived in the Bally-hooley Road, who kept their front doors shut, played the piano in the evenings, and did not go to the neighbours' houses to borrow a spoon of tea or a cupful of sugar, but they are all very distinct in my memory.

In one house lodged a married couple who provided a strange counterpoint to my own parents. Mrs MacCarthy was a big, bosomy woman with a round, rosy face who was the living image of Kathleen Mavourneen in the picture in our kitchen, and must have been a girl of great beauty. Her personality was like her looks, warm and sunny, and she had a deep, husky voice. Her husband was a small, taciturn man who worked in the Harbour Commissioners. At regular intervals, Mrs MacCarthy went on batters that were as bad as those of my father in their utter destructiveness. Mother would rescue her from the road where she had fallen, and bring her home, caked with blood and dirt, and wash her face and comb her hair, while she scolded her gently. 'Ah, Mrs MacCarthy,' she would say, 'indeed and indeed you should be ashamed of yourself, making an exhibition of yourself like that, and what will your poor husband say?' But by this time Mrs MacCarthy would be threatening what she would do to that miserable little gnat of a man when he came home.

The woman who lived in the house on our left was a Cockney called Gertie Twomey. At first, I think, she lodged with my grand-mother, and then took over the house when Grandmother came to live with us. She had married a nice gentle Cork sailor called Steve

Twomey who had picked her up on one of his trips and brought her home in the spirit in which he would have brought home some flaming, chattering parakeet from the Congo to hang with his dispirited goldfinches and canaries. She was a tiny little woman with a face shaped like a box and coloured a brilliant red as though she never drank anything but gin, though I have no recollection of her drinking at all. In the middle of the box was a gleaming snub nose like a holy medal, and above it two small, crafty, merry eyes that seemed as though they had been sunk into the head with a metal-worker's tool. She haunted our house, perhaps because Father, as a travelled man, could talk to her about London, or perhaps because Mother, as a superior woman and a good housekeeper, might be expected to understand her scorn of the 'natives'. She usually came accompanied by her two pretty daughters, one attached to either hand and trailing behind in the wind of her approach like after-thoughts – 'pore little eyengils', as she called them with a sudden brilliant glare that was probably supposed to suggest mother love – and the beady little eyes started to flicker inquisitively about the kitchen in quest of anything new or useful. She missed nothing, had no shyness about asking for anything she wanted, and distressed Mother, who preferred the shyer manner of the 'natives'. 'A great maker-out,' Mother sometimes called her with real disapproval.

Gertie thought Irish Catholics impractical, and small wonder, for behind the English sentimentality and gab was a mind like a razor. I suppose she had had to become a Catholic to marry Steve, but the Catholicism had not taken. As a girl in London, Gertie had heard all about the bloke in the Holy Land who started religion, and knew that his idea was to give things away to people who wanted them, a view that was the very opposite of that held by the Catholic priests in Ireland. They acted as though the bloke in the Holy Land had intended them to get the dibs, but they couldn't take Gertie in with that sort of nonsense. I doubt if any priest looking for dues ever got a penny out of her. He didn't have two kids to keep, as she did, and if money ever changed hands – which I doubt – it must have been in the other direction. 'Why,' she said one day, grabbing a gold chain on the priest's fat belly, 'that beautiful gold chain you're wearing would keep me and my two poor helpless little angels for months . . . And wasn't I right?' she added sharply, reporting the incident to Father and Mother, who didn't know where to look. Mother out of a sense of duty would have given the priest her last half-crown, as I suspect she often did, and Father, whose views of religion were always a mystery to me, would have been afraid to refuse him. Though always very respectful to priests, he didn't like them and thought them unlucky, like magpies, and though he went to Mass regularly, he never attended the Sacraments. He probably thought them unlucky too. At the same time, with English practicality Gertie also had English tolerance and grit. Not only did she not hold it against the priest that he hadn't given her his gold watch and chain; she rather enjoyed the tussle for it.

However, her great entries were reserved for stormy nights when Father was sitting under the lamp, reading the *Echo*. Steve worked on a tub called the *Hannibal* that must have been about the one age with Carthage, and when a big wind began blowing up the river, Gertie, with her vivid imagination, immediately began to picture it at the bottom of the Irish Sea, herself a widow, and her two little angels orphans. On nights like these she could not remain at home. She had to know what Father, the universal expert, made out of the shipping news. We would hear her bang the front of her house, chattering like a monkey to herself or the children, and then came the hasty shuffle of her feet down the channel in front of our house as she dragged the children behind her to our squeaking gate. 'It's that woman again!' Mother would say in disgust, and the string of the latch would be pulled, and Gertie would be framed in the kitchen doorway, her hair wild, her shiny face, which seemed to be haunted, reflecting the lamplight. Her right hand would be raised in a dramatic gesture.

''Ark to that!' she would mutter as the wind howled in the yard outside. 'The sea must be mountains high. Nothing could ever live through that.'

'Oh, now, now, Mrs Twomey! I wouldn't let myself be upset by a bit of wind like that,' Father would say gravely, in the ingenuous belief that he was really comforting her instead of driving her mad. Father was an intensely conventional man, and he knew that this was how a woman whose husband was at sea on a stormy night should feel, and that this was the sort of thing you should say to her.

'A bit of wind?' she would mutter wonderingly. 'How can you, Mr O'Donovan! You know that ship should have been scrapped years ago. I warned him! Now he has only himself to blame.'

'Ah, well,' Father would say, doing the hob-lawyer, which seemed to be what was expected of him, 'a lot would depend on what it was like at sea, or what way the ship was going.'

'It's in the hands of God,' Mother would say. 'You should be praying for him.'

Now, this was the sort of talk that Gertie didn't like at all. Praying was what the natives did when there was nothing to eat in the house, instead of going after the sky pilots with horse, foot and artillery.

'God helps those who help themselves,' she snapped. 'I told him years ago to get off that boat. I have my children to think of, don't I? This time tomorrow they may be orphans.' Her eyes settled unseeingly on the children, and she asked menacingly: 'What'll you do when you have no father?' At this they would burst into loud harmonious wails that for some reason seemed to give her deep satisfaction, because she beamed and patted them and assured them fondly that Mummy would look after them.

I never saw a woman who got so much value out of her troubles, but they were too intense to last. Having exhausted all the phases of her tragedy – the terrors of the deep, the temptations of widowhood, and the sad fate of orphaned children – in ten or fifteen minutes, she hadn't much more left to grieve for and began to see the bright side of things. Or rather, she became practical, and you saw what was really behind all that English guff. She sat bolt upright in her chair, her little eyes half shut as they darted shrewdly from Father to Mother, to see how they were taking it. Mother was not taking it too well. Having been an orphan herself, she did not like to see it turned into a subject for play-acting. Father was completely mystified. He had a conventional mind, and a slow one, and he never really saw where Gertie was getting.

Compensation was now her theme – purely for the children's sake, of course. She knew several sailors' widows who had been impractical in the usual Irish way. They should have got more compensation, and they should have handled more wisely whatever they had got. The English were better at handling lump sums than the Irish. And, of course, though wages were bad and jobs uncertain, they did bring in the regular dibs while no one could be sure of a lump sum unless it was wisely invested. She would have a solicitor on the job to see that she got her rights, and then she would have enough to buy or rent a big house in London which she would run as a superior boarding house, furnished in style and confined to lodgers of the best class. There her children would get a real education, not the sort of thing that passed for education among the natives. The first thing she would buy would be a piano, and they would have lessons and grow up as real little ladies. There was something about being able to play the piano that raised a girl in a man's estimation, wasn't there?

And subtly, almost imperceptibly, as she talked her tone changed, and she was no longer practical but giddy and gay. That was where Father's reminiscences of London came in handy, because they reassured her that everything was as she remembered it, with parks and bands and music-halls and toffs, and all at once, her red face beaming, she began to run her fingers over the keys of an imaginary piano and sang in a cracked voice:

O, won't we have a merry time,
Drinking whisky, beer and wine,
On Coronation Day?

By this time she would be in the highest of spirits, cracking jokes and making the children laugh. But, as though she found it difficult to sustain any mood for long, that, too, would pass and she would remember her bad neighbours and her many wrongs and snap at the children to tell them keep quiet and not break their mummy's heart. In those days I did not understand it, and I doubt if my parents understood it either, but nowadays I fancy she was thinking that even if the wind was still howling about the house, the old ship had weathered worse, and she would never return to dear old London Town but end her days among ignorant Irish Catholics, who didn't even know what the bloke in the Holy Land had said about giving people things. Then she would accuse the children of having no heart, and when they cried she would spank them till Mother protested, and finally she would shuffle off as she had come, into the storm, dragging the yelling kids behind her and muttering rapidly to herself. No wonder Mother told Minnie Connolly that she was 'never right'.

7

But, if she wasn't 'right', what could one say of Ellen Farrell, who lived in the house at the other side of us? She was one of the handsomest old women I have ever seen. In the summer and autumn evenings you could see her standing for hours at the gate of her little house, resting her right arm on the broken-down gate post, and occasionally pushing back the thin white hair from her long, bloodless, toothless face with its jutting chin and bitter mouth. Sometimes a passer-by would stop to greet her, and then the right hand on its pedestal would be used as an ear trumpet, and Ellen would shout back some savage jest. When she went out to the pub to fetch a jug of porter, she moved almost without raising her feet and this gave her what seemed a firm and stately demeanour. As she grew older, and walking became harder, she would grasp a garden railing and hang on to it for as long as it took her to recover breath, but she always held her head high, and looked angrily up the road as though she had paused only to study the view. She came from Carlow, and despised and hated Cork.

A few doors down from her lived her old husband and daughter, who were almost as odd as herself. Farrell was an old pedlar; he wore a beard and had a hump and possessed a bit of the miraculous Knock stone that was supposed to cure all aches and pains. I was brought to him once by Mother for the cure of a recurring headache, and sure enough it went away for a day but came back again. (I was losing my sight, but nobody had noticed it.) His daughter, Annie, who was a laundress like her mother, limped because of some disease of the hip. She never went to bed at all because in her early years she had seen someone die in bed, and never cared for beds after. When she died herself, she was sitting bolt upright in the chair where she had slept for twenty years. For a period longer than that her mother had never spoken a word either to her or her father except when she shuffled by their gate in a wicked mood and snarled a curse at them. Ellen was an old woman with a long, long memory for injuries.

Yet there was a queer romance about the Farrells. They had been great supporters of Charles Stewart Parnell, and when he married a divorced woman and the priests went from door to door, threatening hell fire on anyone who voted for him, they refused to be intimidated, and Ellen even hung his portrait over the front door for the whole world to see. When the priest came to remove it, she chased him with a stick, and took an oath never again to enter a Catholic church as long as she lived. She never did, nor did her old husband, though by this time he and she had separated. Disunion in the home there might be, but not disunion about Parnell. At the same time, she continued to regard herself as a good Catholic and to pay her dues at Christmas and Easter. Once, when she had to have an official document witnessed by a clergyman, she went to Father O'Mahoney, a big, loud-voiced man whom most of the poor people were scared of. 'Never saw you in my life before, my good woman,' he said pompously. 'Oh, yes, you did, Father,' she replied with her bitter humour. 'Twice a year regularly – at Christmas and Easter. However, I dare say the Protestant minister will remember me.' 'Give me that at once!' he shouted, but she strode scornfully away up the chapel yard and he had to run after her, snatch the document from her hand, and sign it against the church wall. 'You're a very impudent old woman!' he shouted as he returned it to her. 'There's a pair of us there, Father,' she retorted. She was never at a loss for a dirty crack.

For six months or so after we came to Harrington's Square Mother looked after old Ellen, brought her breakfast in the morning or tea in the evening, collected her old-age pension from the post office at St Luke's, and did whatever shopping the old woman wanted done. It wasn't much, God knows, for her house was even dirtier and barer than Grandmother's, but Mother was full of pity for her, as she was for anyone who was old or helpless or sick. Her friend, Minnie Connolly, from the other side of the square pursed her lips and shook her head over it. 'I only hope she doesn't repay you the way she repaid others, Mrs Donovan,' she said. By 'others,' of course, she meant herself.

And, sure enough, one day when I followed my ball into Ellen's front garden, she was waiting for me behind the front door with a stick, and chased me, screaming and cursing. The honeymoon with humanity was over. Ellen had tolerated Mother rather longer than she had tolerated other specimens of the human race, but her patience could not be expected to last for ever. She even accused Mother of stealing her old-age pension! 'What did I tell you, Mrs Donovan?' asked Minnie. 'The woman is bad.'

She was bad, but that wasn't the worst feature of her character. She had a little house to herself, and usually there was a printed notice in the front window saying 'Rooms to Let'. The people she rented the rooms to were not old women of her own age but young married couples. This was in the days before council houses, and the real bait was not so much the accommodation as the prospect of permanence. The young couples, coming up the road hand in hand, knew that the old woman, leaning on her gate post, could only have a short while to live and that whoever was there when she died could not be dispossessed. And potentially it was such a nice home, with a tiny garden in front where you could grow flowers, a sitting room from which you could see everyone going by, and a back yard and toilet to yourself. Lust and hunger have no greater grip on human beings than the need for a home.

Now, there was something in the old woman that made her want young people in her house, but there was also a fiendish possessiveness and jealousy that made her realize clearly what they wanted, and no sooner had they settled in than she set herself frantically to getting rid of them. She had no scruples about what a poor, friendless old lady in her position might or might not do. First, she would lock them out at night; then she would throw away the bit of food they might have left in the kitchen; then she would scare the child from going to the back yard. If that didn't shift them, she took them to court and accused them of keeping a 'bad' house or of stealing her money. Like all power maniacs, she was mad about the law, and had considerable skill in taking in magistrates. All she had to do was to put her hand to her ear when they asked her a question and give them a witty reply. Her tenants could rarely afford a lawyer, and they probably knew that even if they won, she would continue to harass them in ways no law could control, so after dark one night you would see a donkey cart outside her gate, a small boy driving, and no light but the butt of a candle; and, taking their handful of possessions, the young people would slink back to whatever slum they had emerged from. By the time the last couple came we knew the pattern well.

8

But the most extraordinary of the neighbours was Minnie Connolly, who lived with her brother and mother, and later with her brother and his wife in the house across the square. She was a laundress, too, like her mother, and had once been maid to an old Quaker family, and while the older generation of the family lived, they were, as Minnie described it, 'good to her', meaning that they sent her an occasional postal order, which, with whatever else she earned, just kept her this side of starvation. As I knew myself, the line was often indeterminate. When Mother was at work, Minnie was the only person I would stay with, and I often sat for hours in the steaming little attic where she did her laundry, and turned over the pages of the religious books of which she had a small library. I remember with particular vividness a manuscript prayer book of which the binding had been removed. It was written in an exquisite hand – some Catholic of a hundred or so years before who had not been able to afford a printed book, or despised those he knew, had written it for his own pleasure. I confided all my ambitions to Minnie, who listened with her almost toothless mouth primmed up in amusement and replied ironically in phrases like: 'Well, you don't tell me so!'

Minnie was a regular visitor to our house, and her favourite topic was priests. 'Mrs Donovan,' she would say, pulling her old shawl round her as she sat on a kitchen chair in the middle of the floor, 'if you were at eleven o'clock Mass yesterday, you'd never do another day's good.' 'Who was it?' Mother would ask, knowing that there was a good story coming. 'Was it Father Tierney?' 'Wisha, who else, woman?' Minnie would cry. 'Himself and his ghosts!' Tierney, a white-haired, unctuous old man who saw ghosts everywhere, was more a source of interest than of edification to Minnie – not that she didn't believe in ghosts or had not had strange experiences herself, but she pooh-poohed Tierney's, and when he died, having failed to leave his money back to the Church, and no Month's Mind was said for him, it was as juicy a bit of gossip to her as if he had been found dead in the arms of one of the Holy Women. Some young English Protestant who wanted to marry a local girl had gone to Tierney for instruction, but Tierney had refused to listen to his explanations and ordered him to kneel down. The young man had told Minnie, and she did an excellent imitation of the old priest climbing a ladder to take down a large book and muttering incantations over the unfortunate boy before sending him away as wise as he had come. Later, when an attempt was made locally to get Tierney beatified, and bits of his underpants were being distributed as miraculous relics, she was savagely sarcastic about it all.

She also did excellent imitations of Sexton, the Dean in St Patrick's Church, who gave extraordinary sermons in a thick Cork accent. Sexton, a big, rough man, did not like talking about matters of doctrine; he preferred to take his text from a new movie or a newspaper, and he leaned over the edge of the pulpit, bawling away in the voice of a market woman. 'Dearly beloved brethren,' he cried, 'ye all saw it in the paper; the advertisement for the new film at the Coliseum. Ye all saw that it was supposed to be "hot stuff", and there was nothing in it at all. That is what I call deceiving the public.' I have a vivid recollection of one of his sermons when an episcopal ordinance compelled him to preach on the Commandments, Sunday by Sunday. He was discussing the Second Commandment, and obviously in agony, because he felt that the Commandments were all out of date and should be scrapped. 'Dearly beloved brethren,' he began, 'of course we're not supposed to take that seriously. Sure, we all take the Lord's name in vain. I do it myself. If I lose my temper I say "Ah, God damn it!" There's no harm in that at all. What the Commandment means, dearly beloved brethren, is that we shouldn't be using the Holy Name in public, the way a lot of people do. You can't go along King Street on Saturday night without hearing someone using the Holy Name. That's very bad. At the same time, there isn't any harm in that either. Sure, half the time people don't be thinking of what they're saying. But, dearly beloved brethren, if you do use it, don't use it in front of children. A child's mind is a delicate thing. A child's mind is like that marble pillar there (slapping the column beside him). It's smooth, and it doesn't hold dust nor dirt. One rub of a duster is all you need to clean that marble. A child's mind is like marble. Don't roughen it.' I thought it the best sermon I had ever heard, and I liked Sexton and his rough-neck oratory, but neither Mother nor Minnie could tolerate it. Minnie did a first-class imitation of him, preaching on the text that 'Not a bird shall fall' and announcing in scandalized tones that it was 'all nonsense – my goodness, they're falling by thousands all over the world every minute'. She had her crow over Sexton as well, when an impostor who called himself the 'Crown Prince of Abyssinia' served his Mass and reviewed the troops before the police caught up on him.

After religion – a long way after religion – she loved novelettes, and these she brought to Mother and discussed them as though they were police reports. I don't think it ever once crossed her mind – which in some ways was so profound – that they might not be literally true. 'Ah, woman,' she would cry impatiently with a hasty flick of her skinny arm, 'sure he was a fool to have anything to do with a girl like that. Do you mean to tell me that he couldn't see for himself the sort of girl she was?' I fancy that she had a great interest in the passions because she had quite an attachment to the Bad Girl of the neighbourhood and though she would anyway have tried to have an influence for good on the girl and protect her from the Holy Women, she seemed to love hearing about married men and jealous wives and officers from the barrack. She would stride hastily into our kitchen, clutching the shawl or old coat about her as though she were cold, her head bowed, but with a little smile on her thick negroid lips. 'Wisha, wait till you hear what's after happening, ma'am,' she would cry modestly. 'You'll never be the better of it.' (For some reason, that and 'You'll never do a day's good' were her blurbs for the dust jacket of some new romance.) Then, for an hour or more you got the whole story as if it were a novelette. 'But if he did not feel that way towards her, Mrs Donovan,' she would cry dramatically, letting her hand fall on Mother's knee while she looked up from under her thick brows with a penetrating glance, 'why did he use those particular words?'

Minnie had an extraordinarily striking face, with a high forehead, high cheekbones and sunken, dreaming eyes, thick poet's lips and a toothless mouth. She shuffled hastily about the locality in some foot-gear that never seemed to fit, clutching her ragged old coat across her breast and with her head well down till she recognized someone she liked, and then it would be suddenly raised to reveal the most enchanting smile in the world. I do not think I am exaggerating. Sometimes it comes before me in the early hours of the morning, and it seems as though all the suffering and delight of humanity were in that one strange smile. Minnie had spent some time in the Big House, as she euphemistically called the Lunatic Asylum, and someone once told me that while she was there she wept almost without ceasing. The doctors called it acute melancholia, but what does melancholia mean, and what do the majority of doctors know about people of Minnie's quality? Whatever it was, it had left no trace on her character, except when she saw suffering inflicted on an animal, and then she seemed to go off her head; screamed in the middle of the street and stamped off to complain to the police or the Society for the Prevention of Cruelty to Animals. They, of course, knew that she was only an old maid and had spent some time in the Lunatic Asylum and so they paid little heed to her.

Yet that woman who had been in the asylum was one of the sanest women I have ever met, and probably the finest. Sometimes when I think of her I seem to see her holding a starving dog or a poisoned cat, talking to it gently, her whole face lit up, and I realize how vulgar are all the pictures we see of the Good Shepherd.

Wherever there was sickness or death, there would come the knock, and Minnie would be outside the door in her ragged old coat, asking in her expressionless voice: 'Is there anything I can do for you, ma'am?', ready to scrub or cook or nurse or pray; to hold the hand of some dying man in hers or to wash his poor dirty body when the life had gone from him. If someone offered her sixpence or a shilling, she was too humble to refuse it, unless it was someone as poor as herself, and then she pushed it away with a smile and said dryly: 'You'll be wanting that yourself, ma'am,' though what she was rejecting might be her own dinner for the day. When I grew up and realized that the woman I had known was a saint I understood something of her demonic pride and her terrible abnegation. At the best of times she must have been a cruelly difficult woman to get on with, for though she and Mother adored one another, and up to the day of Minnie's death Mother shared whatever few shillings she had with her, there were long spells of not speaking, and Minnie would not glance at the side of the road Mother was on, and Mother was as hurt as a schoolgirl.

As I say, she had a passion for novelettes which she fed to poor Mother, who, though she could never resist a love story, no matter how bad, or deny a tear to suffering virtue, had a natural distinction of taste. I suspect that Minnie had no taste, but she had a fierce, combative masculine intellect, which, if it had been trained, might have made her a formidable logician or philosopher, and she would have no hesitation about telling the Pope himself where he went wrong. What she really enjoyed about a sermon was when a priest made a fool of himself about some matter of doctrine. 'Heresy, ma'am, plain heresy!' she would say flatly. 'St Ignatius Loyola distinctly lays it down.' I am sure it was she who told Mother that the Church was going to hell with all the vulgarians who were being raised to the altars, and I seem to remember one angry speech of hers on the subject in which she contrasted Teresa of Avila with some modern saint – probably Thérèse of Lisieux, who from Minnie's point of view would be only a stage-struck child. The great Teresa would have had no difficulty at all in placing Minnie Connolly.

9

Gertie, Ellen and Minnie had very different fates. So far as Gertie was concerned, it all happened as in a storybook. One winter night, the *Hannibal* went down with all hands. Gertie got the lump sum, and as she had always known she would, she left Cork for London to open a superior lodging house. I remember her bouncing with glee and confidence when she came in to say goodbye, and I remember that to my astonishment both my parents seemed sorry to lose her. They too had become used to that flaming parakeet of a woman, and I think they suddenly realized that without her their lives would be poorer and less interesting.

Ellen Farrell's was different but equally characteristic. One day there arrived at her house a newly married couple, of which the young husband would strike pity into anyone's heart, he was so guileless and gentle. He was so unsure of himself in the part of husband and father that he talked to kids like myself as equals and called all the other married men 'Sir', an example of modesty that made Father his slave for life. He loved coming to his door in shirt sleeves and carrying on conversations with Father and the man in the house at the other side, and in the evenings he dug the little front garden.

Within a few weeks Ellen was on the war-path again. She locked the front door on him, and he got in through the bedroom window. She did it again and he started to break down the front door. By this time Father was beginning to see that his politeness was not obsequiousness and to say approvingly that he was 'no balk'. When the plants began to root in the front garden, Ellen poured buckets of red-hot cinders on them. He didn't seem in the least put out. He affected to believe that the plants only needed water and dragged buckets of it from the back yard, spilling each one in the kitchen as though by accident till he flooded the old woman out. She took him to court, but he defended himself, and the magistrate, beginning at last to get suspicious of the bonneted old lady with the amusing tongue, decided in his favour. There was great rejoicing in the neighbourhood. Ellen shouted defiantly as she left the court; 'The Corkies has me bet at last.' To the end she remained a loyal Carlow woman.

But it was not in her to admit that she really was defeated. She would remain for weeks in sullen silence, and then remember that when she was dead, the lodgers would be growing flowers in her front garden, and children would be playing about her fireplace, and then she would start to curse them, sullenly and bitterly, leaning on her gate post with her hand to her ear, her grey hair blowing in the wind. The young husband with his sly humour would intercept the occasional letters that reached her and re-address them to 'The Beautiful Mrs Ellen Farrell,' or 'Ellen, the Tinker from Carlow, Cork'.

My memory of her end is uncertain, but I have a strong impression that it was Minnie Connolly who came to look after her when she was dying. It was certainly Minnie who wrote to the woman's second daughter, who was married to a baker in the French provinces. The hunchback husband and crippled daughter came and sat for hours in the bare kitchen downstairs, waiting for her to speak the word of reconciliation, but she only spat when their presence was mentioned. She was so deaf that her confession could be heard all over the terrace. She still retained her savage humour, and agreed to forgive all her enemies, but made an exception of Parnell's successor, John Redmond, because, she maintained, she had it on the best authority that he had betrayed Ireland. The Catholic Church is wonderfully tolerant of political vagaries like that, and the exception was allowed to pass. Maybe the priest did not think much of John Redmond himself.

Minnie Connolly is probably astonished if she knows that the solemn little boy who read prayer books in her attic bedroom while she ironed remembers her as a myth, a point in history at which the whole significance of human life seems to be concentrated, rather as Ellen Farrell thought of Parnell. She would be still more astonished at the company she keeps, but what she had in common with Gertie Twomey and Ellen Farrell was that each of them knew exactly where she was going. Ellen was going to hell, or wherever it is people go who think only of themselves. Minnie was going to Heaven, if that is the right name for the place where people go who think only of poisoned cats and starving dogs and dying people. Gertie, of course, was merely going to London.

THREE

Go where glory waits thee

10

For kids like myself social life was represented by the shop-front and the gas-lamp. This was mainly because we could rarely bring other kids home in the evenings; the houses were too small, and after the fathers came home from work, children became a nuisance. Besides, most families had something to hide; if it wasn't an old grandmother like mine or a father who drank, it was how little they had to eat. This was always a matter of extreme delicacy, and the ultimate of snobbery was expressed for us by the loud woman up the road who was supposed to call her son in from play with: 'Tommy, come in to your tea, toast and two eggs!'

But as well as that, there was a sort of fever in the blood that mounted towards evening. After tea, you would hear the children whistling and calling from every direction, on a falling note: 'SUsie! JOHNnie!' at least those of them whose parents did not set them at once to their homework; and then by some immemorial instinct they would begin to converge like wild animals or savages from the jungle of the streets on the campfires of the shop-windows that glowed warmly in the cold evenings. The shopkeepers didn't like these gatherings at all because they gave their shops a bad name, and now and then one would come out and clap her hands and cry: 'Let ye be going home now, children! This is no place for ye at this hour of night.' But the children would rarely go further than the nearest lamp-post and after a while they would drift back to the shop-front until their mothers' voices began to fill the night with names uttered on a rising note: 'SuSIE!' or 'JohnNIE!'

The shop-fronts and gas-lamps were quite as exclusive as city clubs. The boys from our neighbourhood usually gathered outside Miss Murphy's shop at the foot of the Square, while the respectable boys of the Ballyhooley Road – the children of policemen, minor officials and small shopkeepers – gathered outside Miss Long's by the Quarry. I lived in a sort of social vacuum between the two, for though custom summoned me to Miss Murphy's with boys of my own class who sometimes went without boots and had no ambition to be educated, my instinct summoned me to Miss Long's and the boys who wore boots and got educated whether they liked it or not.

As nothing would persuade Father but that he was a home-loving body, nothing would persuade me but that I belonged to a class to which boots and education came natural. I was always very sympathetic with children in the story-books I read who had been kidnapped by tramps and gipsies, and for a lot of the time I was inclined to think that something like that must have happened to myself. Apart from any natural liking I may have had for education, I knew it was the only way of escaping from the situation in which I found myself. Everyone admitted that. They said you could get nowhere without education. They blamed their own failure in life on the lack of it. They talked of it as Father talked of the valuable bits of machinery he had stored on top of the wardrobe, as something that would be bound to come in handy in seven years' time.

The difficulty was to get started. It seemed to be extremely hard to get an education, or even – at the level on which we lived – to discover what it was. There was a little woman up the road called Mrs Busteed whose elder son was supposed to be the most brilliant boy in Ireland, and I watched him enviously on his way to and from the North Monastery, but his mother had been a stewardess on the boats and it was always said that 'they made great money on the boats'. Of course, education implied nice manners instead of coarse ones – I could see that for myself when I contrasted Mother's manners with those of my father's family – and I was a polite and considerate boy most of the time, except when the business of getting an education proved too much for me, and I had to go to Confession and admit that I had again been disobedient and disrespectful to my parents – about the only sin I ever got the chance of committing till I was fifteen.

So I was drawn to the policemen's sons and the others on the Ballyhooley road who produced all those signs of a proper education that I had learned to recognize from the boys' weeklies I read. One boy might have a bicycle, another a stamp album; they had a real football instead of the raggy ball that I kicked around or a real cricket bat with wickets; and occasionally I saw one with a copy of the *Boy's Own Paper*, which cost sixpence and had half-tone illustrations instead of the papers that I read, which cost a penny and had only line drawings.

Between those two groups I felt very lonely and unwelcome. Those who frequented them must have thought me a freak – the poorer kids because I spoke in what probably sounded like an affected accent, and used strange words and phrases that I had picked up from my reading; the others because I was only an intruder from the shop-front where I belonged, trying to force his company on them. The only one of them I became really acquainted with was Willie Curtin, whose family kept a florist's shop in which he did messages. He was a lame lad with a long, pale, handsome, desperate face and a loud, boisterous voice, who smoked cigarette butts by the score and broke in defiantly on any group, pushing people aside with his arms like a swimmer. Like myself, he read endlessly, and he ate whatever he was reading right down to the type – a habit I detested because I treasured everything I read. We carried on complicated swaps, which with Willie were always complicated further by considerations like a foreign coin or a magic-lantern slide. I envied him his warm welcome for himself, and it wasn't until long after that I guessed he was really a lame, lonely, neglected boy who also did not belong anywhere.

That was probably why we both read so much, but whereas Willie read indiscriminately, I had a strong preference for school stories and above all for the penny weeklies, the *Gem* and the *Magnet*. Their appeal for me was that the characters in them were getting a really good education, and that some of it was bound to brush off on me. All the same, a really good education like that demanded a great many things I did not have, like an old fellow who didn't drink and an old one who didn't work, an uncle with a racing car who would give me a tip of five pounds to blow on a feed in the dormitory after lights out, long trousers, a short jacket and a top hat, bicycles, footballs and cricket bats. For this I should need a rich relative in the States, and we were short of relatives in the States. The only one I could get certain tidings of was a patrolman in the Chicago Police known as 'Big Tim' Fahy. He was a cousin of Mother, and such a giant that even Father, who was a six-footer, said he felt like a small boy beside him. Tim's only ambition was to join the Royal Irish Constabulary, where height was as well regarded as it had been in the court of Frederick the Great, but one day in the Western Star pub, six English soldiers had jeered him about his height, and he had thrown the whole six into the street. The police had been sent for, and he had thrown them after the soldiers. And that was the end of Tim's ambition, for no one with a conviction against him would be accepted in the RIC. Murphy's Brewery had offered him a handsome job as sandwichman to illustrate what Murphy's stout did for you, but he was too proud for a job like that, so he emigrated. He was famous enough in Chicago, to judge by the newspaper clippings the Fahys showed us when we visited them, and we had a photograph of him on the sideboard, wearing a sword, but I didn't know if even he could afford to send me to a school like those I read about.

So I adored education from afar, and strove to be worthy of it, as later I adored beautiful girls and strove to be worthy of them, and with similar results. I played cricket with a raggy ball and an old board hacked into shape for a bat before a wicket chalked on some dead wall. I kept in training by shadow boxing before the mirror in the kitchen, and practised the deadly straight left with which the hero knocked out the bully of the school. I even adopted the public-school code for my own, and did not tell lies, or inform on other boys, or yell when I was beaten. It wasn't easy, because the other fellows did tell lies, and told on one another in the most shameless way, and, when they were beaten, yelled that their wrists were broken and even boasted later of their own cleverness, and when I behaved in the simple, manly way recommended in the school stories, they said I was mad or that I was 'shaping' (the Cork word for swanking), and even the teachers seemed to regard it as an impertinence.

I was always very fond of heights, and afterwards it struck me that reading was only another form of height, and a more perilous one. It was a way of looking beyond your own back yard into the neighbours'. Our back yard had a high wall, and by early afternoon it made the whole kitchen dark, and when the evening was fine, I climbed the door of the outhouse and up the roof to the top of the wall. It was on a level with the respectable terrace behind ours, which had front gardens and a fine view, and I often sat there for hours on terms of relative equality with the policeman in the first house who dug close beside me and gave me ugly looks but could not think up a law to keep me from sitting on my own back wall. From this I could see Gardiner's Hill falling headlong to the valley of the city, with its terraces of tall houses and its crest of dark trees. It was all lit up when our little house was already in darkness. In the mornings, the first thing I did when I got up was to mount a chair under the attic window and push up the windowframe to see the same hillside when it was still in shadow and its colours had the stiffness of early-morning light. I have a distinct recollection of climbing out the attic window and, after negotiating the peril of the raised windowframe, crawling up the roof to the ridge to enlarge my field of view, but Mother must have caught me at this, because I do not remember having done it often.

Then there was the quarry that fell sheer from the neighbourhood of the barrack to the Ballyhooley Road. It was a noisome place where people dumped their rubbish and gangs of wild kids had stoning matches after school and poor people from the lanes poked among the rubbish for spoil, but I ignored them and picked my way through the discarded bully-beef tins and climbed to some ledge of rock or hollow in the quarry face, and sat there happily, surveying the whole neighbourhood from Mayfield Chapel, which crowned the hillside on the edge of the open country, to the spire of Saint Luke's church below me, and below that again in the distance was the River Lee with its funnels and masts, and the blue hills over it. Immediately beneath me was the Ballyhooley Road, winding up the hill from St Luke's Cross, with its little houses and their tiny front gardens, and (on the side nearest me) the back yards where the women came to peg up their washing; and all the time the shadow moved with a chill you could feel, and the isolated spots of sunlight contracted and their colour deepened. I felt like some sort of wild bird, secure from everything and observing everything – the horse and cart coming up the road, the little girl with her skipping rope on the pavement, or the old man staggering by on his stick – all of them unconscious of the eagle eye that watched them.

But whatever the height, whether that of storybook or quarry, the eagle had to descend. Up there I was cold and hungry, and the loneliness and the longing for society made me feel even worse. Mother would soon be finished work. At some houses she did half a day, which ended about three o'clock and for which she was paid ninepence, and at others a whole day that did not end until six or later and for which she was paid one and sixpence. Depending on the humour of the mistress or maid she worked for, I might be allowed to call for her a little before she finished work, and in one house in Tivoli, beside the river, where the maid – Ellie Mahoney – was also an orphan from the Good Shepherd Orphanage, I was not only admitted to the big, warm area kitchen after school and given my tea, but, if the family was out, I was allowed to accompany Mother upstairs while she did the bedrooms, or go to the lumber room in the attic which was chock full of treasures – old pamphlets, guide books, phrase books in French and German, school books, including a French primer, old dance programmes from Vienna and Munich that contained musical illustrations of Schubert's songs and – greatest prize of all – an illustrated book of the Oberammergau Passion Play with the text in German and English. It was junk that would have meant nothing to anyone else, but for me it was 'the right twigs for an eagle's nest', and, seeing my passion for it, Ellie Mahoney soon cleared it out and let me have my pick. It filled my mind with images of how educated people lived; the places they saw, the things they did, and the lordly way they spoke to hotel managers and railway porters, disputing the bill, checking the two trunks and five bags that were to go on the express to Cologne, and tipping right, left and centre.

It was only another aspect of the vision I caught in the master bedrooms that overlooked the railway line and the river. There were triptych mirrors, silver-handled brushes with engraved designs, and curiously shaped bottles that contained oils and scents and with which I experimented recklessly when Mother's back was turned. Sometimes, since then, whenever I stay in such a house, I wonder what really goes on when I am not looking; what small black face has studied itself in the mirror of the dressing table, or what grubby little paw has plied the silver-handled brushes and poured on the bay rum, and I turn round expecting to see a tiny figure dash recklessly down the stairs to the safety of the kitchen. For these were dangerous heights, and sometimes I became so fascinated by a passing boat or a lighted train on its way down to Queenstown between the roadway and the house that I failed to notice someone crossing the railway bridge from the river road till I heard the bell jangle below in the kitchen, and took the stairs three or four at a time, almost knocking down Ellie as she trotted up, nervously arranging her starched cap.

Ellie was typical of the orphan children – a thin, desiccated, anxious old maid with tiny, red-rimmed eyes, a little scrap of grey hair screwed up under her old-fashioned cap, and a tinny, tormented voice. But her heart was full of girlish passion, and she loved to discuss with Mother whether or not she should accept the proposal of the milkman, who was now becoming pressing. Ellie's wages, as

I remember distinctly over all the years, were five shillings a week, but I fancy that in her forty-odd years of service she had managed to put by a few pounds, and with her little dowry and her blameless character, considered herself an eligible partner for a settled man like the milkman. At least, as she said, she would have someone to look after her in her old age. I think this must have been something of a dream to the orphan girls, because Mother caused me fierce pangs of jealousy when she told me that she had prayed for a girl – someone who would look after her in her old age. But, instead of marrying the milkman, Ellie contracted lupus, and while her poor little face was being eaten away, Mother (and, of course, I) visited her regularly in the Incurable Hospital on the Wellington Road, and until the end she continued to congratulate herself on having had employers who did not throw her into the workhouse to die. I was sorry when she did die and I saw her laid out for burial with a white linen cloth covering her demolished face, because I had planned everything differently, and had arranged with Mother (and I suspect with Ellie herself) that when I made a fortune she would come as maid to us, and be paid a really substantial wage – I think I had fixed it at seven shillings a week.

So I scampered down the quarry face to the snug, suburban road with its gas-lamps and smooth pavements, and waited by the tram stop at Saint Luke's Cross where I could be sure Mother would not escape me. I would feel guilty because I knew I should have stayed at home and lit the fire so that she would not have to re-light it after a hard day's work, but I hated to be in the house alone. I sat in the dusk on the high wall overlooking the church, afraid to look back for fear I might grow dizzy and fall, and when a tram came wheezing up the hill from town I followed the men who got off it in quest of cigarette pictures. Sometimes she would have only her wages, but occasionally a maid would give her a bit of cold meat or a slice of apple pie for my supper. Sometimes, too, we would have the house to ourselves, and we would light the fire and sit beside it in the darkness, and she would tell me stories or sing songs with me. These were almost always Moore's Melodies. A whole generation has grown up that has what seems to me an idiotic attitude to 'Tommy' Moore, as it calls him in its supercilious way – mainly, because it has never learned to sing him. His songs were the only real education that the vast majority of Irish people got during the nineteenth century and after, even if it was an education of the heart, of which we all had too much, rather than an education of the intelligence, of which we had too little. My own favourites were 'Farewell, but Whenever You Welcome the Hour' and 'How Dear to Me the Hour When Daylight Dies'. I took the songs I sang with a deadly literalness that sometimes reduced me to sobs, and with the paternal melancholia I loved songs of twilight like 'Those Evening Bells' (a choice which, I subsequently learned, I shared with the great actor Edmund Kean). But Mother was very fond of 'I Saw from the Beach', and I can still remember the feeling of slight jealousy and mortification that possessed me when she sang:

> Ne'er tell me of glories, serenely adorning
> The close of our day, the calm eve of our night;–
> Give me back, give me back the wild freshness of Morning.
> Her clouds and her tears are worth Evening's best light.

As I say, I took things literally, and it seemed to me as if she were appealing to some happiness she had known in youth of which I was not a part, but she made it up to me by singing her own favourite, 'Go Where Glory Waits Thee', and I put up with the dull tune for the sake of the words that seemed to be addressed to myself.

> Go where glory waits thee,
> But, while fame elates thee,
> Oh! Still remember me.
> When the praise thou meetest
> To thine ear is sweetest,
> Oh! then remember me.

But often it was misery to return from the heights, and I shuddered at the difference between the two worlds, the world in my head and the world that really existed. The fever in my blood would drive me out of the kitchen, where I had been reading or singing Moore's Melodies to the club-like atmosphere of the pool of light outside the shop-window, and everything would go well for a few minutes till I said something wrong or used a word that no one understood, and then the whole group jeered me, and called me 'Molly' (our word for 'sissy') and later 'Foureyes', and I realized that once again I had been talking the language of the heights, which the others did not speak, and that they thought me mad. Sometimes I didn't know but that I was mad.

The trouble was that I was always a little bit of what I had picked up from book or song or picture or glimpse of some different sort of life, always half in and half out of the world of reality, like Moses descending the mountain or a dreamer waking. Once I had read about Robin Hood, I had to make myself a bow out of a bamboo curtain rod and practise archery in the Square. Going along the street, remembering Chopin's Funeral March, I was never just a small boy remembering a piece of music; I was, like any other imaginative boy, everything from the corpse to the brass band and the firing party. When I induced a couple of younger boys to assist me at cricket and stood with a homemade bat before a wicket chalked on a wall, I was always the Dark Horse of the school, emerging to save its honour when all seemed lost, and I even stood my ground when a policeman came stalking towards us, and the 'school' took to its heels round the nearest corner.

'What do you mean playing ball on the public street?' the policeman asked angrily.

'Excuse me, this is not a public street,' I replied firmly. 'This square is private property.'

That day the bobby was so stunned at being cheeked by a small spectacled boy with an imitation bat that I got away with it, but most of the time I didn't get away with it. I got in trouble for being cheeky when I was only acting out a part and was called a liar when I was still half in, half out of the dream and only telling the truth as best I could.

It was still worse when I interfered to prevent what I thought an injustice. This was more than mere imitation of the head boy of the school, more even than the gentle nostalgic sentiment of Moore applied to a half-barbarous society – it was the natural reaction of a mother's boy who knew what suffering and injustice really were, but it was more dangerous, because the one thing a Sir Galahad needs is a more than theoretical knowledge of the Noble Art of Self-Defence. Sometimes surprise was enough, as it was sometimes enough for Minnie Connolly when she bawled at a brutal carter, but often it was not, and before ever I got in the deadly straight left I had developed from shadow boxing before the mirror, I got a knee in the groin or a kick in the shin or had my glasses knocked off, and went home, weeping and determined that for the future I would carry a Chinese dagger, preferably poisoned.

And yet I could not help brooding on injustice, and making a fool of myself about it. I must have been several years older when I heard that a young fellow I knew – a wild, handsome boy whose father beat him savagely – had run away from home and was being searched for by the police. The story was told in whispers. He would be picked up and sent to a reformatory. That evening I found him myself, lurking in an alleyway, his long face dirty with tears, and tried to make him come home with me. He wouldn't, and I could not leave him there like that, lonely and lost and crying. I made it clear that I would stay with him, and at last he agreed to return home if I went with him and pleaded for him. When I knocked at the door he stood against the wall, his hands in his pockets and his head bent. His elder sister opened the door, and I made my little speech, and she promised to see that he wasn't punished. Then I went home in a glow of self-righteousness. feeling that I had saved him from the fate I had always dreaded myself. I felt sure he would be grateful, and that from this out we would be good friends, but it didn't happen like that at all. When we met again he would not look at me; instead, he turned away with a sneer, and I knew his father had beaten him again, and that it was all my fault. As a protector of the weak, I was never worth a damn.

11

Christmas was always the worst time of the year for me, though it began well, weeks before Christmas itself, with the Christmas numbers. Normally I read only boys' weeklies, but at this time of year all papers, juvenile and adult, seemed equally desirable, as though the general magic of the season transcended the particular magic of any one paper. School stories, detective stories and adventure stories all emerged into one great Christmas story.

Christmas numbers were, of course, double numbers; their pale-green and red covers suddenly bloomed into glossy colours, with borders of red-berried holly. Even their titles dripped with snow. As for the pictures within, they showed roads under snow, and old houses under snow, with diamond-paned windows that were brilliant in the darkness. I never knew what magic there was in snow for me because in Ireland we rarely saw it for more than two or three days in the year, and that was usually in the late spring. In real life it meant little to me except that Father – who was always trying to make a manly boy of me as he believed himself to have been at my age – made me wash my face and hands in it to avert chilblains. I think its magic in the Christmas numbers depended on the contrast between it and the Christmas candles, the holly branches with the red berries, the log fires, and the gleaming windows. It was the contrast between light and dark, life and death; the cold and darkness that reigned when Life came into the world. Going about her work, Mother would suddenly break into song:

Natum videte
Regem angelorum . . .

and I would join in. It was the season of imagination. My trouble was that I already had more than my share of imagination.

Then there were no more Christmas numbers, but I managed to preserve the spirit of them, sitting at my table with pencil and paper, trying to draw Christmas scenes of my own – dark skies and walls, bright snow and windows. When I was older and could trace figures, these turned into the figures of the manger scene, cut out and mounted on cardboard to make a proper crib.

Christmas Eve was the culmination of this season, the day when the promise of the Christmas numbers should be fulfilled. The shops already had their green and red streamers, and in the morning Mother decorated the house with holly and ivy. Much as I longed for it, we never had red-berried holly, which cost more. The Christmas candle, two feet high and a couple of inches thick, was set in a jam crock, wrapped in coloured paper, and twined about with holly. Everything was ready for the feast. For a lot of the day I leaned against the front door or wandered slowly down the road to the corner, trying to appear careless and indifferent so that no one should know I was really waiting for the postman. Most of the Christmas mail we got came on Christmas Eve, and though I don't think I ever got a present through the post, that did not in the least diminish my expectations of one. Whatever experience might have taught me, the Christmas numbers taught differently.

Father had a half-day on Christmas Eve, and came home at noon with his week's pay in his pocket – that is, when he got home at all. Mother and I knew well how easily he was led astray by out-of-works who waited at the street corners for men in regular jobs, knowing that on Christmas Eve no one could refuse them a pint. But I never gave that aspect of it much thought. It wasn't for anything so commonplace as Father's weekly pay that I was waiting. I even ignored the fact that when he did come in, there was usually an argument and sometimes a quarrel. At ordinary times when he did not give Mother enough to pay the bills, she took it with resignation, and if there was a row it was he who provoked it by asking: 'Well, isn't that enough for you?' But at Christmas she would fight and fight desperately. One Christmas Eve he came home and handed her the housekeeping money with a complacent air, and she looked at the coins in her hand and went white. 'Lord God, what am I to do with that?' I heard her whisper despairingly, and I listened in terror because she never invoked the name of God. Father suddenly blew up into the fury he had been cooking up all the way home – a poor, hard-working man deprived of his little bit of pleasure at Christmas-time because of an extravagant wife and child. 'Well, what do you want it for?' he snarled. 'What do I want it for?' she asked distractedly, and went through her shopping list, which, God knows, must have been modest enough. And then he said something that I did not understand, and I heard her whispering in reply and there was a frenzy in her voice that I would not have believed possible; 'Do you think I'll leave him without it on the one day of the year?'

Years later I suddenly remembered the phrase because of its beauty, and realized that it was I who was to be left without a toy, and on this one day of the year that seemed to her intolerable. And yet I did not allow it to disturb me; I had other expectations, and I was very happy when the pair of us went shopping together, down Blarney Lane, past the shop in the big old house islanded in Goulnaspurra, where they sold the coloured cardboard cribs I coveted, with shepherds and snow, manger and star, and across the bridge to Myles's Toy Shop on the North Main Street. There in the rainy dusk, jostled by prams and drunken women in shawls, and thrust on one side by barefooted children from the lanes, I stood in wonder, thinking which treasure Santa Claus would bring me from the ends of the earth to show his appreciation of the way I had behaved in the past twelve months. As he was a most superior man, and I a most superior child, I saw no limit to the possibilities of the period, and no reason why Mother should not join in my speculations.

It was usually dark when we tramped home together, up Wyse's Hill, from which we saw the whole city lit up beneath us and the trams reflected in the water under Patrick's Bridge; or later – when we lived in Barrackton, up Summerhill, Mother carrying the few scraps of meat and the plum pudding from Thompson's and me something from the Penny Bazaar. We had been out a long time, and I was full of expectations of what the postman might have brought in the meantime. Even when he hadn't brought anything, I didn't allow myself to be upset, for I knew that the poor postmen were dreadfully overworked at this time of year. And even if he didn't come later, there was always the final Christmas-morning delivery. I was an optimistic child, and the holly over the mirror in the kitchen and the red paper in the lighted window of the huxter shop across the street assured me that the Christmas numbers were right and anything might happen.

There were lesser pleasures to look forward to, like the lighting of the Christmas candle and the cutting of the Christmas cake. As the youngest of the household I had the job of lighting the candle and saying solemnly: 'The light of Heaven to our souls on the last day', and Mother's principal worry was that before the time came Father might slip out to the pub and spoil the ritual, for it was supposed to be carried out by the oldest and the youngest, and Father, by convention, was the oldest, though in fact, as I later discovered, he was younger than Mother.

In those days the cake and candle were supposed to be presented by the small shopkeeper from whom we bought the tea, sugar, paraffin oil and so on. We could not afford to shop in big stores where everything was cheaper, because they did not give credit to poor people, and most of the time we lived on credit. But each year our 'presents' seemed to grow smaller, and Mother would comment impatiently on the meanness of Miss O' or Miss Mac in giving us a tiny candle or a stale cake. (When the 1914 War began they stopped giving us the cake.) Mother could never believe that people could be so mean, but, where we were concerned, they seemed to be capable of anything. The lighted candle still left me with two expectations. However late it grew I never ceased to expect the postman's knock, and even when that failed, there was the certainty that Christmas Morning would set everything right.

But when I woke on Christmas Morning, I felt the season of imagination slipping away from me and the world of reality breaking in. If all Santa Claus could bring me from the North Pole was something I could have bought in Myles's Toy Shop for a couple of pence, he seemed to me to be wasting his time. Then the postman came, on his final round before a holiday that already had begun to seem eternal, and either he brought nothing for us, or else he brought the dregs of the Christmas mail, like a Christmas card from somebody who had just got Mother's card and remembered her existence at the last moment. Often, even this would be in an unsealed envelope and it would upset her for hours. It was strange in a woman to whom a penny was money that an unsealed envelope seemed to her the worst of ill-breeding, equivalent to the small candle or the stale cake – not a simple measure of economy, but plain, unadulterated bad taste.

Comparing Christmas gifts with other kids didn't take long or give much satisfaction, and even then the day was overshadowed by the harsh rule that I was not supposed to call at other children's houses or they at mine. This, Mother said, was the family season, which was all very well for those who had families but death to an only child. It was the end of the season of imagination, and there was no reason to think it would ever come again. Nothing had happened as it happened in the Christmas numbers. There was no snow; no relative had returned from the States with presents for everyone; there was nothing but Christmas Mass and the choir thundering out *Natum videte regem angelorum* as though they believed it, when any fool could see that things were just going on the same old way. Mother would sigh and say: 'I never believe it's really Christmas until I hear the *Adeste*,' but if that was all that Christmas meant to her she was welcome to it. Most Christmas days I could have screamed with misery. I argued with Mother that other kids were just as depressed as I was, and dying to see me, but I never remember that she allowed me to stray far from the front door.

But, bad as Christmas Day was, St Stephen's Day was terrible. It needed no imagination, only as much as was required to believe that you really had a dead wren on the holly bush you carried from door to door, singing:

> I up with me stick and I gave me a fall,
> And I brought him here to visit ye all.

Father was very contemptuous, watching this, and took it as another sign of the disappearance of youthful manliness, for in his young days not only did they wash their faces in snow, but on Christmas Day they raised the countryside with big sticks, killing wrens – or droleens, as we called them. Everyone knew that it was the droleen's chirping that had alerted the Roman soldiers in the Garden of Gethsemane and pointed out to them where Christ was concealed, and in Father's young days they had carried it around with great pomp, all the mummers disguised. It seemed to him positively indecent to ask for money on the strength of a dead wren that you didn't have. It wasn't the absence of the wren that worried Mother, even if he was an informer, for she adored birds and supported a whole regiment of them through the winter, but the fear that I would be a nuisance to other women as poor as herself who didn't have a penny to give the wren boys.

In the afternoon she and I went to see the cribs in the chapels. (There were none in the parish churches.) She was never strong enough to visit the seven cribs you had to visit to get the special blessing, but we always went to the chapel of the Good Shepherd Convent in Sunday's Well where she had gone to school. She was very loyal to those she called 'the old nuns', the nuns who had been kind to her when she was a child.

One Christmas Santa Claus brought me a toy engine. As it was the only present I had received, I took it with me to the convent, and played with it on the floor while Mother and 'the old nuns' discussed old times and how much nicer girls used to be then. But it was a young nun who brought us in to see the crib. When I saw the Holy Child in the manger I was very distressed, because little as I had, he had nothing at all. For me it was fresh proof of the incompetence of Santa Claus — an elderly man who hadn't even remembered to give the Infant Jesus a toy and who should have been retired long ago. I asked the young nun politely if the Holy Child didn't like toys, and she replied composedly enough: 'Oh, he does, but his mother is too poor to afford them.' That settled it. My mother was poor too, but at Christmas she at least managed to buy me something, even if it was only a box of crayons. I distinctly remember getting into the crib and putting the engine between his outstretched arms. I probably showed him how to wind it as well, because a small baby like that would not be clever enough to know. I remember too the tearful feeling of reckless generosity with which I left him there in the nightly darkness of the chapel, clutching my toy engine to his chest.

Because somehow I knew even then exactly how that child felt — the utter despondency of realizing that he had been forgotten and that nobody had brought him anything; the longing for the dreary, dreadful holidays to pass till his father got to hell out of the house, and the postman returned again with the promise of better things.

12

The principal difficulty about the world in my head was that there seemed to be no connexion at all between the idea of education I formed from the boys' weeklies and education as it was practised in the schools I knew. There was the boys' school at St Luke's, for example, where the headmaster was called Downey, a fierce, red, sweaty bull of a man with a white moustache, a bald head he was for ever wiping with a huge white handkerchief, and a long cane that he flourished joyously. The boys had a song about him that was probably first sung about an Elizabethan schoolmaster, but it fitted him perfectly:

> Tommy is a holy man,
> He goes to Mass on Sunday,
> He prays to God to give him strength
> To slap the boys on Monday.

This was probably true, because he combined the sanctimoniousness of a reformed pirate with the brutality of a half-witted drill sergeant. With him the cane was never a mere weapon; it was a real extension of his personality, like a musician's instrument or a ventriloquist's dummy – something you could imagine his bringing home with him and reaching out for in the middle of the night as a man reaches out for his wife or his bottle. He was a real artist with it, and with his fat, soft, sexual fingers he caressed your hand into the exact position at which a cut would cause the most excruciating pain. He sent the boys out for canes on approval, and tested them carefully, swishing them and peering at them with his small piggy eyes for flaws that would be invisible to anyone else, and when one of them broke in his hand, as happened occasionally when he was flogging some slow child about the bare legs, one glance was enough for him to size up the possibilities of the two pieces so that he could carry on the job with the more formidable one. When, in those odd moments of recollection that afflict the most conscientious of men, he stood at the front door and looked out at the spring sunshine with a puzzled frown, as though wondering how it had got out and what it was doing there without his permission, he still kept the cane pressed close to his spine, where it continued to wave gently from side to side, as though, like a dog's tail, it had a life of its own. Sunshine, it seemed to say, wouldn't last long if only Tommy could get at it.

Frequently, I carried a boys' paper in my satchel as a sort of promise of better things, and Downey watched me closely because he knew my weakness for glancing at it under my desk, as a man in mortal agony will glance at a crucifix. Once, he caught me with a paper called *The Scout* and held it up before the class with a roar of glee. 'Ho! ho! ho!' he chortled. 'Look who we have here! Look at our young scout! We'll soon knock the scouting out of him . . . Hold out your hand, you little puppy!' I think he took more delight in catching us out than in beating us, because his stupidity was even greater than his brutality, if that was possible, and he seemed to regard all small boys as criminals with minds of extraordinary complexity and cunning, and greeted each new discovery of a plot with a sort of *Te Deum* of 'Ho! ho! ho's', like a dictator who has just cracked a fresh liberal conspiracy.

The religious instruction never fell below the high standard of secular instruction set by Downey. We were prepared for our First Communion by a well-to-do old lady on Summerhill, who wore a black bonnet and cloak such as my grandmother wore on state occasions, and who was welcomed by Downey with the sugary amiability he otherwise reserved for his boss, the parish priest. She came to the school with a candle and a box of matches, stuck the candle on the desk before her and lit it. Then she put a half-crown beside the candle, and, when we had watched these fascinating preparations long enough, offered to give the half-crown to any small boy who would hold one finger – mind, only *one* finger! – in the candle flame for five minutes. Then, having studied us carefully, apparently waiting for offers, she cocked her head and said sharply: 'And yet you'll risk an eternity of hell when you won't even put your finger in the candle flame for five minutes to earn half a crown!'

I think at any time I would cheerfully have risked an eternity of hell sooner than spend a day in that school, and one of the few painful recollections I have of Mother is the morning she tried to pull me out from under the table to make me go to school, and I pulled the table along with me. On the other hand, when the impersonal brutality of doctor and dentist (there were no painless extractions for me) left me free, it was heaven to stand at the foot of Gardiner's Hill, sucking a sweet, and listen to the chant of the other victims roaring the multiplication table on the first three notes of the scale, as though at any moment they might burst into 'Yankee

Doodle', and catch a glimpse of Downey shooting past the front door, brandishing his cane. It enabled even a born Sir Galahad like myself to understand how, through all eternity, the blessed can contemplate the sufferings of the damned with no diminution of their own ecstasy. Anyone who was lucky enough to get out of that inferno, even for a day, had no time to spare for the sufferings of others.

Beside Downey, the assistants were all shadowy figures, like the kindly teacher we unkindly called 'Tom Louse' who taught us Moore's lovely song *To Music*, with its promise that when we grew up and life became harder, we would welcome such strains as these. In that atmosphere it made the future sound very unpromising. But one day an assistant came who made an immediate impression on my imagination. He was a small man with a lame leg who trailed slowly and painfully about the classrooms, though whenever he wanted to, he seemed to glide round on skates and had a violent temper that sent the blood rushing to his head. In spite of his affliction, he was like that, light and spare and clean. He had a small, round head and a round face with a baby complexion on which a small, dark moustache and the shadow of a beard looked as inappropriate as they would have done on a small boy. His eyes were strange, because one eyebrow descended till it almost closed the eye, and the other mounted till it made the eye seem to expand. Afterwards, when I saw him do it with landscapes, I decided it was probably only a painter's trick of focusing a picture. His voice was the queerest part of him, because it had practically no modulation: each syllable emerged, harshly articulated and defined, with no perceptible variation of pitch, as though it were being cut off with a bacon slicer; and when he raised his voice, he raised his head as well, and pulled in his lower lip till the chin seemed to sag. That too someone explained to me later as a device for curing himself of a bad stammer, and it sounds probable enough, for though I did not realize it until later, the most striking thing about the Daniel Corkery of those years was his self-control.

One afternoon, at three o'clock, when we should have been going home, he kept us in, wrote a few words in a mysterious script on the top of the blackboard, and went on to give us our first lesson in what he called in his monosyllabic articulation 'Eye Rish', a subject I had never heard of, but which seemed to consist of giving unfamiliar names to familiar objects. With my life-long weakness for interesting myself in matters that are no concern of mine, I noticed that he never referred once to the words on top of the blackboard. I waited politely until he was leaving, and then went up to him to ask what they meant. He smiled and said: 'Waken your courage, Ireland!' – a most peculiar thing, as it seemed to me, for anyone to write on top of a blackboard, particularly when it didn't seem to be part of the lesson. He might, of course, have had a reason for not explaining it to the class, because the English were still in control, and neither they nor his other employers, the Roman Catholic Church, would have stood for much of that nonsense.

In singing class, instead of the Moore songs I loved, he taught us a song by someone called Walter Scott, which struck me as very dull indeed, and must have had a tune as uninteresting as the words, since a melomaniac like myself has forgotten it:

> Breathes there a man with soul so dead
> Who never to himself has said
> 'This is my own, my native land?'

But I remember the angry passion with which he chopped off the syllables of the third line, flushing and tossing his small, dark head. I was too young to realize what he was doing – using the standard English texts to promote disaffection in the young, right under the nose of the old policeman-schoolmaster, Downey, and there must have even been moments when Downey suspected it, for though he was perceptibly more deferential to Corkery than to the other assistants, he sometimes stood and looked after him with a stunned air.

Still, wonders continued to occur. In the smaller classroom Corkery removed some charts of an informative kind and replaced them by two brightly coloured pictures that immediately engaged my roving attention. I had a passion for tracing and copying illustrations from magazines and books I had borrowed, which was the next best thing to owning the books myself, and it made me regard myself as something of an authority on art. I asked Corkery who had painted the pictures, and he smiled and said: 'I did', as though he did not expect me to believe him. Really, they merely confirmed my favourable view of his abilities. They weren't *very* good pictures, not the sort that would get into the *Boy's Own Paper*, but they showed promise. One was of a laneway in the Marsh with washing strung from window to window across the dark lane, and in the background a misty white tower that he said was Shandon. It didn't look like Shandon, and I told him so, but he said that this was the effect of the light. The other picture was much stranger, for it showed an old man facing the wall of a country cottage, playing his fiddle, and a small crowd standing behind him. When I asked why the fiddler was looking at the wall, Corkery explained that it was because he was blind. If my memory of the picture is correct, he had written beneath it twelve lines of verse in the peculiar script he used for Irish. I know that I learned them, as I learned everything, by heart, and though they bore out his explanation of why the fiddler did not face the crowd, it still struck me as a tall story:

> Look at me now!
> My face to the wall,
> Playing music
> To empty pockets.

I took the poem home for my grandmother to interpret. I had at last discovered some use for that extraordinary and irritating old woman, because it turned out that Irish, not English, was her native language, as it was of several old people in the neighbourhood.

My grandmother didn't think much of the poem; she said she knew better ones herself and wanted to say them for me, but they were too hard, and she contented herself with teaching me my first sentence in Irish – A *chailín óg, tabhair dhom póg, agus pósfaidh mé thu* (Young girl, give me a kiss and I'll marry you). No more than Downey's type of education did this resemble anything I had read or heard of, but I found it considerably more interesting.

Besides, as will become clear, I am a natural collaborationist; like Dolan's ass I go a bit of the road with everybody, and I enjoyed having a hero among the hereditary enemy – schoolmasters. I hung on to Corkery's coat-tails at lunch when he leaned against the jamb of the front door, eating his sandwich; I borrowed Irish books from him that I could not understand, though this never hindered me from having a crack at something, and sometimes I waited for him after school to accompany him home as he butted his way manfully up the cruel hill, sighing, his hat always a little askew, one shoulder thrust forward like a swimmer, and the crippled foot trailing behind him. I imitated the old-fashioned grace with which he lifted his hat and bowed slightly to any woman he recognized; I imitated his extraordinary articulation so carefully that to this day I can render it with what seems to me complete fidelity, and for a time I even imitated his limp. I never loved anyone without imitating him, and having a quite satisfactory mother, I was not particularly attracted to women or girls, but in the absence of a father who answered my needs, I developed fierce passions for middle-aged men, and Corkery was my first and greatest love. 'Love' is a word that educationists dislike because it has so many unpleasant associations, but it is a fact that in many children the intellectual and emotional faculties are indissolubly knit, and the one cannot develop without the other. Any intellectual faculty I possessed was now developing like mad.

It developed so much that at Christmas Corkery – out of his own pocket, I fancy – gave me a prize book called *Kings and Vikings* by someone called Lorcan O'Byrne, and this, being the only prize I ever received in any walk of life, has impressed itself on my memory. Of course, from Corkery's point of view, it was probably further subversive action, though I didn't realize this.

The headaches that had plagued me for a year were explained when a doctor sent me to have my eyes tested, and I had to wear black glasses and stop going to school for months. When I resumed, it was not at St Patrick's but the North Monastery, run by the Christian Brothers – I cannot think why unless it meant that I should be out of Corkery's class and back in Downey's. Mother, I suspect, may have been influenced by her friendship with Mrs Busteed, whom she met regularly at Mass, for her brilliant son, who had gone to the North Monastery, had had his picture in the paper and was now at the University, and it would never have occurred to Mother that what had worked for him would not work for me.

It was very inconvenient, because it was miles from home, and on rainy days I reached school drenched and cold. The road led past the military barrack on the brow of the hill and then down a dirt track called Fever Hospital Hill to the Brewery, before climbing again through slums to the top of another hill. But the view from Fever Hospital Hill was astonishing, and often delayed me when I was already late. The cathedral tower and Shandon steeple, all limestone and blue sandstone, soared off the edge of the opposite hill, and the hillside, terraced to the top with slums, stood so steep that I could see every lane in it, and when the light moved across it on a spring day the whole hillside seemed to sway like a field of corn, and sometimes when there was no wind to stir the clouds, I could hear it murmuring to itself like a hive of bees.

I was happy enough for the first few months in a classroom where there was a statue of the Blessed Virgin (religious images were not allowed in the national schools), and when the best of the English compositions were shown along the partition in the classroom mine were often among them. But the monks had already made up their minds that I would never be a passer of examinations and never have my picture in the Cork *Examiner*, as John Busteed had. I was hurt when I was rejected from the singing class because of my defective ear because I knew perfectly well that my ear was not defective. Over-enthusiastic, perhaps – it still is, since my temperament makes me rush at things I like without paying too much attention to intervals and time – but not defective. And yet I had to sit there, listening to songs I loved without being allowed to join in them. It was very hard.

However, I was busy in other fields. The First World War had broken out; Father was called up, leaving comparative peace in the home, though to make up for that my grandfather had died and my grandmother had come to live with us. Inflamed with emotion by the supposed atrocities of the Germans against the Belgians, I had engaged in beating them myself in my own small way. On the kitchen wall I had pinned a map of the Western Front into which I stuck flags to show the position of the two armies, and I conducted brilliant campaigns of my own that beat the Germans to their knees in twenty-four hours. Father was also conducting a campaign, the details of which eluded me till later, but it was much more practical than mine. He loved pensions, and as there was no chance of a service pension out of the War, he was quietly building up a case history of rheumatic pains that would get him a disability pension when the War came to an end. Not a very large pension; you can't do much with occasional rheumatism, and anything more might have caused him to be sent home, but every little helps.

Father, I am certain, really enjoyed the War in the way that a middle-aged man enjoys a second marriage – as a renewal of youth. Though he liked his brief and dangerous reunions with his family, he was an old soldier among a whole army of young ones; he could make himself comfortable where they died of misery, and he enjoyed his opportunities for wrangling, and never came home without his pockets and kit-bag filled with bits of equipment that would all come in useful if he kept them for seven years. But Mother and I had never been happier. For the first time since I knew her, she had a regular allowance, and I had regular pocket money which I divided up between boys' weeklies and illustrated papers that dealt with the story of the War. I was interested in the War, not only because Father was engaged in it, but because there were several

Belgian kids in my class at school who had been driven from their homes by the Germans. They lived in the big Montenotte house of the Countess Murphy. The Countess had been one of my big disappointments. Her companion was another of the orphans, called Kate Gaynor, but Kate's family had apparently been well-to-do, and she and her sister had gone to the Orphanage as paying pupils. They were brought up a little apart from the other orphans and allowed to continue their piano lessons. Kate was a stiff, pompous woman with a cutting tongue, and she and Mother disagreed – in so far as Mother disagreed with anybody – about the Orphanage. Nothing would ever have induced Mother to say a word against it, but Kate said bitterly that if she had her way all the orphanages in the world would be torn to the ground because they 'robbed a child of natural affections'. What she meant by that, I realized later, was that in middle age it left her nobody to love but an ageing, cranky woman.

The Countess (the title was a Papal one, for the Count, who, I think, was a brewer, had written a defence of Catholicism that was always on view on the drawing-room table) had been very impressed by my good manners and piety, and promised to provide for my education as a priest. For a little while this made Mother and myself almost insane with happiness. But one Christmas either the Countess or Kate gave me a painting book and a box of paints, and, never having had paints to play with before, I had a beautiful time with them. When next Kate visited us and inspected the painting book, she asked in a cold, disgusted voice where I had seen green cows. Mother and I were equally mortified at my lack of observation, and when the Countess died, having failed to provide for my education as a priest, I was left with the guilty feeling that I had forever forfeited my hope of advancement by failing to notice that cows were not green.

And now the Countess was dead, and the beautiful house on Montenotte was a hostel for Belgian refugees, and whenever we knocked on her door Kate called out wearily 'Entrez'. She found the refugees disgusting, but I was devoted to them, first because they had been driven from their homes by the beastly Germans like the Holy Family by Herod, and second, because they spoke a different language. In the North Monastery we said our prayers in Irish, a language I had begun to lose interest in because it was obviously useless in the modern world. The Belgians said theirs in Flemish, and I was not happy till I could do the same. For some time after that I never used any other language for my night and morning prayers. The monks were wrong in thinking me a complete fool: I was really a serious student, but it was always of something that could be of no earthly use to me; which is probably why they summoned Mother to the school and explained to her that I would never be able to pass the regular Intermediate examinations, and put me into the Trades School, where I could pick up something more suitable to my station in life than Flemish. It was a blow to both of us, because, though it closed the doors of the University on me, it did not open the door of the trades. Entry to these was regulated by their own unions.

In the Trades School I didn't pick up anything at all, useful or otherwise, though I liked Murray, the tall, gloomy, sardonic monk who taught us in an atmosphere of complete hopelessness, as though he knew he had been given the job only because he could not teach and we had been sent to him only because we could not learn. I still read English school stories, and modelled myself entirely on the characters in them, and this continued to get me into trouble because neither Murray nor my classmates had read them, nor indeed anything else that I could ever discover, and continued to treat me as though I were slightly insane. It culminated in a scene when myself and another quiet boy were attacked on our way home from school by a real little fighter. Cowardice was no name for my normal attitude to violence; I slunk home through the streets like one of those poor mongrels that Minnie Connolly sympathized so much with, who flitted from pavement to pavement in an effort to avoid their tormentors, but when I was roused, I had my father's murderous temper, and on this occasion at least, I managed to damage the other boy's mouth and leave him weeping.

I can prove that I was alone in reading English school stories because next morning he complained to Murray – a thing nobody in an English school would do – and when Murray questioned me I told the truth and took the blame, which was an offence in itself, since Irish schoolteachers tend to regard truthfulness as Irish farmers regard the old-fashioned Quaker refusal to haggle – as something unneighbourly. Murray, with his morbid, dyspeptic humour, thought it a neat idea to give my opponent his strap and order him to punish us himself. He did this with my companion, and the class, which was almost as mature as Murray, thought it an excellent joke, but when it came to my turn I told Murray that if he came near me I would knock him down. Murray – not an unkind man –

became a bright brick red and turned nasty, but I was fighting mad and stood my ground. Of course, I paid dear for the pleasure of spoiling his idea of a good joke, but it was one of the few occasions when I had no regrets for having made a fool of myself.

Then my grandmother died. In the early hours of the morning my uncle went for the priest and came in with him looking very pale. As they passed a forge, Father Tierney had said: 'Get off the footpath and let the ghosts go by,' which admittedly was enough to make any man go pale. In the manner of the old country people, my grandmother was well prepared for death. For as long as I remembered her, she had been giving instructions for her funeral, and Father, the tease of the family, had told her he couldn't afford to take her back to her own people, at which Grandmother had told him she would haunt him. In a drawer she had the two bits of blessed candle that were to be lit over her when she died, and her shroud, which she took out regularly to air on the line. She was ill for a week or two and lay upstairs, saying her beads and reciting poetry in Irish. The day before she died she shouted for a mirror, and Mother told her she should be thinking of God, but the old woman only shouted louder. When Mother brought the mirror upstairs, Grandmother studied herself for a few moments in stupefaction and muttered: 'Jesus Christ, there's a face!' before turning to the wall. She had not wanted to rejoin her dead husband, looking like that.

Afterwards we had perfect peace in the house till Father returned from the Army. Mother scrubbed out the bedroom and coloured it a warm pink; she sewed pretty curtains for the attic window and dolled up an old orange-box as a bookcase for me. My books didn't amount to much, but I cheated quite a bit. There was, for instance, the sixpenny Shakespeare which I tore up and rebound as individual plays. There were also tracts you could buy for a penny in the church that made quite impressive titles. My files of boys' weeklies and war papers were ranged along the floor under the attic window. Mother had taught me to make rough binding cases for them, and of course I had a neat catalogue, modelled on the catalogue of the public library, for I was nothing if not orderly, and I never admired anything without trying to imitate it. After some friends of Mother's had taken us to a matinée of *Carmen*, I began another catalogue of operas I had heard, but this never amounted to much. The invaluable boys' weeklies described how to do everything, and being in most ways a very ordinary boy, according to my lights and equipment I did it, from making a model aeroplane (that wouldn't fly) to a telephone (that wouldn't talk), though when I got down to making gunpowder I did blow the eyebrows and eyelashes off the unfortunate boy who was with me. I even made a model theatre out of an old boot-box with a proscenium arch and a selection of backdrops all painted by myself that represented backgrounds in Spain, Italy and other operatic countries; characters traced from illustrations in library books which I coloured and mounted on sticks; and an elaborate lighting system of Christmas-tree candles with coloured slides of greased paper that could be made to produce the effect of moonlight, dawn, storm and every other romantic aspect of nature. I played with this for hours in the dark hallway, singing arias, duets and trios that I made up as I went along.

The boys' weeklies were now the only form of education I had because I had given up school. There must have been some illness to account for this, but I am quite sure that if there was I extracted the last ounce of agony and weakness from it, because I loathed the Trades School and took advantage of every excuse to avoid attending it. Father's absence at the War was a mixed blessing, because it left Mother unprotected against me, and I was every bit as ruthless as he was.

13

In April 1916 a handful of Irishmen took over the city of Dublin and were finally surrounded and overwhelmed by British troops with artillery. The daily papers showed Dublin as they showed Belgian cities destroyed by the Germans, as smoking ruins inhabited by men with rifles and machine guns. At first my only reaction was horror that Irishmen could commit such a crime against England. I was sure that phase had ended with the Boer War in which Father had fought, because one of his favourite songs said so:

You used to call us traitors because of agitators,
But you can't call us traitors now.

But the English were calling us traitors again, and they seemed to be right. It was a difficult situation for a boy of twelve with no spiritual homeland but that of the English public schools, and no real friends but those imaginary friends he knew there. I had defended their code of honour with nothing to support me but faith, and now, even if the miracle happened and Big Tim Fahy returned from Chicago with bags of money and sent me to school in England, I should be looked on with distrust – almost, God help me, as if I were a German who said *Donner und Blitzen*, which was what all Germans said.

The English shot the first batch of Irish leaders, and this was a worse shock, for the newspapers said – the pro-British ones with a sneer – that several of them had been poets, and I was in favour of poets. One of them, Patrick Pearse, on the night before his execution had written some poems, one of them to his mother – which showed him a man of nice feeling – and another, which contained lines I still remember:

> The beauty of this world hath made me sad –
> This beauty that will pass.
> Sometimes my heart hath shaken with great joy
> To see a leaping squirrel in a tree,
> Or a red ladybird upon a stalk . . .

What made it worse was that most of his poetry had been written in Irish, the language I had abandoned in favour of Flemish. And Corkery, who had introduced me to Irish, I had not seen for years. But I still had an old primer that had been thrown into a corner, and I started trying to re-learn all that I had forgotten. A revolution had begun in Ireland, but it was nothing to the revolution that had begun in me. It is only in the imagination that the great tragedies take place, and I had only my imagination to live in. I enjoyed English school stories as much as ever, but already I was developing a bad conscience about them. The heroes of those stories, the Invisible Presences, I knew, must look on me as a traitor. They reminded me of how they had taken me in and made me one of themselves, and I had to reply that if I was different, it was because of what they and theirs had done to make me so. For months I read almost nothing but Irish history and the result was horrifying. I wrote my first essay, which listed all the atrocities I could discover that had been committed by the English in the previous hundred years or so, but it had no more effect than the deceived husband's listing of his wife's infidelities has on his need for her. My heart still cried out for the Invisible Presences.

In the early mornings Mother and I went into town to the Franciscan or Augustinian church where Mass was said for the dead rebels, and on the way back we bought picture postcards of them. One afternoon when we were walking in the country we met Corkery, and I asked him how I could take up Irish again. After that I went on Saturday afternoons to the children's class at the Gaelic League hall in Queen Street. The Irish we spoke was of less importance to me than the folk songs we learned, and these than the kilt that one of the boys wore. I felt my own position keenly. Not only was I suspect to the Invisible Presences; with a father and uncle in the British Army I was suspect to loyal children as well. But no one could suspect the loyalty of a boy who wore a kilt, and I persecuted my mother till she made one for me. She did not find it easy, as kilts were not worn in her young days.

Somewhere or other I had picked up Eleanor Hull's *Cuchulain*, a re-telling of the Ulster sagas for children, and that became a new ideal. Nobody in any English school story I had read had done things as remarkable as that child had done by the age of seven. But for me, even his deeds were small compared with what he said when he actually was seven and some druid prophesied a short life for him. 'Little I care though I were to live but a day and a night if only my fame and adventures lived after me.' No one had ever better expressed my own view of life.

Having exhausted most of the books in the children's department of the library, I had discovered the adult one and, by using a ticket I had got for Mother, I could borrow a school story from upstairs and a book on history downstairs. It took real courage to face the adult library on those days. There was a card catalogue and a long counter surmounted by a primitive device known as an Indicator – a huge glass case where all the book numbers were shown in blue (which meant they were available) or red (which meant they were not). If you were a scholarly person and could deduce from the author and title whether a book was readable or not, it didn't matter perhaps, but if, like me, you knew nothing about books, you might often walk back the two miles home in rage and disgust with something you couldn't even read. Education was very hard.

One of the grown-up books I borrowed was O'Curry's *Manuscript Materials*, which contained a lot about Cu Chulainn. No more than O'Curry himself was I put off by the fact that this was in a form of Irish I didn't know, ranging from the eighth to the twelfth century (I never allowed myself to be deflected by details); and, casting myself in the part of a medieval scribe, I copied it out with coloured initials imitated from the *Book of Kells*.

But though I knew as little about the hero of a modern English public-school story as I did about the hero of a primitive saga, imitating the one turned out to be child's play compared with imitating the other, and I nearly ruptured myself trying to perform the least of the feats Cu Chulainn had performed when he was barely half my age. It seemed I had wasted my time practising with a bow, for the Irish had no use for it, and I had to begin all over again with a slingshot; but though I practised hard, I never came within measurable distance of killing someone in a crowd half a mile away. It was difficult enough to hit a gate post at twenty yards, and even then my heart was in my mouth for fear I should break a window and have the police after me.

Most of my endeavours were wasted on a single episode in Cu Chulainn's infancy. He left home when he was little more than a toddler, hurling his toy spear before him, pucking his hurling ball after that, throwing his hurling stick after the ball, and then catching all three before they alighted. No one who has not tried that simple feat can imagine how difficult it is. There was more sense in the story of how he killed the great watch-dog by throwing the hurling ball down its gullet and then beating it over the head with his hurley, and I practised that, too, beginning with very small dogs; but, knowing my character much better than I did, they decided I only wanted to play with them, and ran away with the ball. When they finally let me catch up on them and grinned at me with the ball between their teeth, I could no more hit them with the hurley than I could do anything else that Cu Chulainn had done. I was crazy about dogs and cats. I saw clearly that the Irish race had gone to hell since saga times, and that this was what had enabled the English to do what they liked with us.

Queer treasures I clutched to my chest, coming over Parnell Bridge in the evening on my way from the Public Library. Once it was a collection of Irish folk music, and I proudly copied the O'Donovan clan march in staff notation, hoping to find someone who would sing it to me. Father had earlier discovered the O'Donovan coat of arms, and I had discovered that there was a village called Castle Donovan in West Cork. The family was obviously something. Sometimes I took out in Mother's name an art book or a novel by Canon Sheehan, who was parish priest of a County Cork town, and had a most unclerical passion for novel writing. He had been greatly praised by a Russian writer called Tolstoy, and later I learned that his clerical enemies had sent one of his novels to Rome in the hope of having it condemned for heresy, but the Papal authorities, mistaking the purpose of the submission, gave Sheehan a DD instead. He shared with the authors of the boys' weeklies a weakness for foreign languages, and printed lengthy extracts from Goethe in the original, and ever since I have been torn between two attitudes to this practice. With one half of my mind I regard it as detestable snobbery, but with the other I think it the only sensible way of influencing young people like myself. If the original monkey had not despised monkeys he would never have invented clothes, and I should not have bothered to learn Goethe's *Symbolen* by heart. Never having anyone to teach me, I learned only by pretending to know. I played at reading foreign languages and tenth-century Irish, at being a priest and saying Mass, at singing from staff notation and copying out pieces of music when I didn't know one note from another, at being a painter and a theatrical producer. It is not a form of education I would recommend to anyone, nor should I ever get a degree in French, German, Latin, music or even Middle Irish, but I still catch myself out at it, playing at scholarship and correcting the experts, and sometimes a little streak of lunatic vanity that runs through it all suggests that I may be right and everybody else wrong.

Mother must have been astonished at becoming a borrower of art books containing pictures of naked gods and goddesses in queer positions, and I had great difficulty in persuading the stupid girls in the Carnegie Library who tried to stop me taking them out that they were Mother's favourite reading, but I knew I should never become a great painter unless I could copy Bronzino and Tintoretto and learn all about the rules of perspective and chiaroscuro, and there is a sort of irresistible force behind a small spectacled boy with an aim in life. At the same time I was astonished at the modesty of the Renaissance artists who painted women different from men, and I still remember the stunned look on Mother's face when I commented on it to her. 'Difference of sex I never knew more than the guardian angels do,' but I was broadminded, and I realized that, for the common run of people, such frankness might not do.

I had my greatest shock in that same year, 1916, when, passing by O'Keeffe's bookshop in Great George's Street one evening, I saw a book called *A Munster Twilight* of which the author was someone named Daniel Corkery. It seemed altogether too much of a coincidence to presume that the author could be my old teacher, and even if I had had a shilling (the price of the book) I dared not have risked it on such a slender possibility. But it stuck in my mind, and when next I waylaid Corkery, he admitted that he was the author. I was instantly struck with awe – not only at the man's ability, but at my own shrewdness in having discovered him before anyone else had done so. Cu Chulainn might have been able to smash bronze chariots with his bare fists and capture whole flocks of birds alive with a single throw of his slingshot – a most difficult feat, as I had discovered by experiment – but there was no evidence of his ever having had an eye for talent.

I borrowed the book from the Public Library and one day when Mother was at work I sat on a warm rock at the foot of the square and read steadily through it without understanding a word. It was not as good as the *Gem* or the *Magnet*, but Corkery certainly had talent. I was interested principally in what it said about me, but, beyond referring to some ancient West Cork poet called Owen More O'Donovan, Corkery seemed to be keeping our acquaintance dark.

And that settled the hash of the English boys' weeklies. I did not know their authors as I knew Corkery, and henceforth their creations would be less real to me than his, little as I might understand them. And one day I woke to find the Invisible Presences of my childhood departing with a wave of the hand as they passed for ever from sight. Not angrily, nor even reproachfully, but sadly, as good friends part, and even when I grew up and had other presences to think of, I continued to remember them for what they had been – a child's vision of a world complete and glorified.

14

By the time I was fourteen it was clear that education was something I would never be able to afford. Not that I had any intention of giving it up even then. I was just looking for a job that would enable me to buy the books from which I could pick up the education myself. So, with the rest of the unemployed, I went to the newsroom of the Carnegie Library where on wet days the steam heating warmed the perished bodies in the broken boots and made the dirty rags steam and smell. I read carefully through the advertisements and applied for every job that demanded 'a smart boy', but what I really hoped for was to find a new issue of *The Times Literary Supplement*, the *Spectator*, the *New Statesman* or the *Studio* free, so that I could read articles about books and pictures I would never see, but as often as not some hungry old man would have toppled asleep over it, and I was cheated. The real out-of-works always favoured the high-class magazines at which they were unlikely to be disturbed, though occasionally some cranky ratepayer would rouse the Lancashire librarian in his rubber-soled shoes, and the out-of-work would be shaken awake and sent to take his rest elsewhere. Then, divided between the claims of pity and justice, I went out myself and wandered aimlessly round town till hunger or darkness or rain sent me home.

'A smart boy's' was the job I needed, because, when it became clear that I would never be a priest, Mother's only ambition was for me to become a clerk – someone who would wear a white collar and be called 'Mister'. Knowing no better myself, but always willing – up to a point – always visiting the Carnegie Library or the advertisement board in front of the Cork *Examiner* office, and answering advertisements for a smart boy, I went to the Technical School and the School of Commerce at night to learn whatever I could learn there in the way of arithmetic, book-keeping and shorthand typewriting. Of book-keeping, all I ever could remember was a saying quoted approvingly on the first page of our textbook – written, of course, by the headmaster himself – which ran: 'In business, there is no such thing as an out-and-out free gift'; and of typewriting, a fascinating example of punctuation that began: 'The splendour falls on castle walls', which I promptly got by heart. Perhaps they stuck so firmly in my mind because they represented the two irreconcilables that I was being asked to reconcile in myself.

In the pursuit of what I regarded as serious education, I also worked hard at a Self-Educator I had picked up, God knows where. From Canon Sheehan's novels I had deduced that German was the real language of culture and that the greatest of cultured persons was Goethe, so I read right through Goethe in English and studied German out of the Self-Educator so as to be able to read him in the original. I was impressed by the fact that one of the pretty songs Mother had taught me as a child – 'Three Students Went Merrily over the Rhine' – turned up in a German anthology as a real poem by a real German poet, so I learned the German words and sang them instead. I also made a valiant attempt to learn Greek, which struck me as a very important cultural medium indeed, being much more difficult than Latin, but as I had never learned the rudiments of grammar in any language I never got far with Greek.

I got my first job through my confessor, a gentle old priest who regarded me as a very saintly boy, and regularly asked me to pray for his intention. If innocence and sanctity are related, he was probably not so far wrong about me because once I confessed to 'bad thoughts', meaning, I suppose, murdering my grandmother, but Father O'Regan interpreted it differently, and there ensued an agonizing few minutes in which he asked me questions I didn't understand, and I gave him answers that he didn't understand, and I suspect that when I left the confession box, the poor man was as shaken as I was.

The job was in a pious wholesale drapery business where every member of the staff had apparently been recommended by his confessor, and I hated my immediate boss, a small, smug, greasy little shopman with a waxed black moustache who tried hard to teach me that whenever he called 'O'Donovan!' I was instantly to drop whatever I was doing and rush to him, crying smartly 'Yessir!' I never minded dropping what I was doing, which was usually folding shirts as if I were laying out a corpse – the two arms neatly across the breast – and I had no objection to calling anybody 'Sir', but it was several seconds before my armour of daydreaming was penetrated by a voice from outside and 'The splendour falls on castle walls' gave place to the stern beauty of 'In business, there is no such thing as an out-and-out free gift', and it was several seconds more before I realized that it was the voice to which I must reply 'Yessir!' so at the end of a fortnight I stopped folding shirts and saying 'Yessir!' and went home to put in some more work at Greek. Then I tried a spell in a chemist's shop that was looking for a smart boy, but I soon discovered that I was only needed to deliver messages and that no amount of smartness would ever make a chemist of me. I still have a vivid recollection of the end of this job. I was still a small boy, and I was looking up at a tall counter, and leaning on the counter and looking down at me through his glasses was a tall, thin Dublinman, just back from a visit to the pub next door. He was telling me in a thick Dublin accent that I had no notion of the sort of people I was working for, and begging me earnestly, for Christ's sweet sake and my own good, to get to hell out of it, quick. I got to hell out of it quick all right.

There was an even briefer spell at a job printer's, because while he was showing me the ropes, the printer asked was I any good at spelling, and I replied airily: 'Oh, that's my forte!' Now, that was exactly the sort of language we used on the heights, and I wasn't conscious of doing anything wrong in using it, but that evening the man who recommended me to the printer met me and repeated the story of my reply with a great deal of laughter, and I realized that, as usual, I had made a fool of myself. It was part of the abnormal sensitiveness induced by daydreaming, and I was so mortified that I never went back. I was sorry for that, because I really was quite good at spelling, and I still feel I should have made an excellent compositor.

Instead, this only became an additional weight in the load of guilt I always carried. It seemed that I could never persevere with anything, school or work, and just as I had always been impressed by the view of other small boys that I was mad, I was beginning to be impressed by their parents' view that I was a good-for-nothing who would never be anything but a burden on his father and mother. God knows, Father had impressed it on me often enough.

I went to the railway as a messenger boy because I despaired of ever becoming anything better, and besides, though the hours – eight to seven – were hard, the pay – a pound a week – was excellent, and with money like that coming in I could buy a lot of books and get a lot of education. It was with real confidence that at last the future had something in store for me that I left the house one morning at half-past seven and went down Summerhill and the tunnel steps to go to the Goods Office on the quay. Upstairs in the long office where the invoice clerks worked under the eye of the Chief Clerk, I met the other junior tracers, Sheehy, Cremin and Clery, and the two senior tracers. Our job was to assist the invoice and claims clerks, bringing in dockets from the storage shed and inquiring in the storage shed for missing goods – hence our title.

All transport companies have colossal claims for missing goods, many of which are not really missing at all but lying about forgotten. Whiskey and tobacco were easy to trace because they had to be loaded into sealed wagons before some old railway policeman who recorded them and the number of the wagon in his little red book. But no one took much responsibility for other articles, and it depended on the memory of the checkers whether or not you could discover what had happened to them. An efficient, friendly checker like Bob St Leger of the Dublin Bay or Leahy of the Fermoy Bay could often remember a particular consignment and, if he were in good humour, could fish it out from the corner where it had lain for weeks, covered by a heap of fresh merchandise. This was a triumph, and you marked your memorandum or wire with some code word like 'Stag', meaning that the thing was at last on its way. But, more often, nobody remembered anything at all, and then you wrote something else, like 'Bison', which meant 'Certainly forwarded please say if since received', to which Goold's Cross or Farranfore retorted 'Moose', meaning that it wasn't, and then you had to go to the storage shed and search through scores of tall dusty wire files to discover the original docket and the name of the checker or porter who had signed the receipt for it.

It didn't take me long to realize that this was only going to be another version of school, a place where I would be always useless, frightened or hurt. The other messengers were railwaymen's sons and understood the work as though they had been born to it. Sheehy was thin, with high cheekbones and an impudent smile; Cremin was round-faced, cherry-cheeked and complacent, and shot about the office and the store almost without raising his feet. Young Sheehy sneered at me all the time, but young Cremin only sneered at me part of the time because he was usually so busy with his own jobs that he hadn't time for anyone else's, but a couple of times when I found myself with some job I could not do, he looked at me for a while with pity and contempt and then took it from me and did it himself. 'See?' he would crow. 'Dead easy!' Cremin was really what the advertisements meant when they asked for a smart boy. Years later I found myself in the same hut in an internment camp with him, and though our positions had changed somewhat by that time, and I was a teacher, he was still the same smart boy, mixing with nobody in particular though amiable with everybody, briskly hammering rings out of shilling pieces or weaving macramé handbags – a cheerful, noisy, little universe of self-satisfaction. Yet the moment I fell ill, he nursed me with the same amused exasperation with which he had found dockets for me on the railway, cluck-clucking with an amused smile at my inability to do anything for myself.

My boss was obviously a man who had also at one time been a smart boy and owed his promotion to it. He had a neat, swift hand, and I imitated his elegant signature as I imitated Corkery's articulation, in a hopeless attempt at becoming a smart boy myself. He had a fat, pale face, a button of a nose with a pince-nez attached that was for ever dropping off and being retrieved just in time; he dressed excellently and swept through the office and the storage shed with an air of efficiency that must long since have secured his promotion to the job of stationmaster in Borrisokane or Goold's Cross. I fancy he was really clever and not unkind, but as the days went by he became more and more infuriated by my slowness and stupidity; and, having readjusted his pince-nez sternly, he would shout abuse at me till the whole office was listening and the other messengers sniggering, and I slunk away, stupider than ever, muttering aspirations to the Sacred Heart and the Blessed Virgin to assist me in whatever impossible task I was being asked to perform. It was one of the senior tracers who, in mockery of my love of Irish and the gilt ring I wore in my coat, nicknamed me 'The Native', but it was the boss who perpetuated it. It was characteristic of Ireland at the time that the mere fact that you spoke Irish could make you be regarded as a freak.

The other clerk for whom I had to do odd jobs was a very different type. He was small, fair-haired, red-cheeked and untidy, and drifted about the office with his hands in his trousers pockets, wearing an incredible expression of sweetness and wonder as though he were imitating some saint and martyr he had heard of in church. Either he would put his arm about my waist and draw me close to him, calling me 'Child', and beg me in a low, quavering voice to assist him – that is if I could spare him a couple of minutes – or else he would call 'Boy!' in a faraway tone, and look at me as though wondering who I was, and rush after me, tearing paper from my hand and scolding and nagging till my nerves were on edge. Then he would sit on his high stool, his fat hands clasped between his thighs, staring incredulously after me.

Not that I didn't do my best. God knows I did. One of my jobs was to answer the telephone, and I did it with such intensity that I could never hear a word the other person said, and so developed a hatred of telephones that has lasted to this day. If there is anything unnaturally stupid or compromising a man can say, I am always guaranteed to say it on the telephone. Sometimes, when I was alone in the Goods Office I listened miserably to some message, too ashamed to admit that I hadn't understood it. Sometimes I summoned up courage and said that I couldn't hear, and then the person at the other end always got furious – a fatal thing to do with me as it drives me completely distracted – and asked if there was no one on the Great Southern and Western Railway who was not stone deaf. Having it put to me like that, I could only reply that there was but he was out at lunch. And whatever stupid thing I said always got back to the boss.

The trouble was that I could not believe in the telephone or the messages that came by it. I could not believe that the missing goods I was supposed to trace had ever existed, or if they had, that their loss meant anything to anybody. Being a naturally kind-hearted boy, if I had believed it I would have found them whatever it cost me. All I could believe in was words, and I clung to them frantically. I would read some word like 'unsophisticated' and at once I would want to know what the Irish equivalent was. In those days I didn't even ask to be a writer; a much simpler form of transmutation would have satisfied me. All I wanted was to translate, to feel the unfamiliar become familiar, the familiar take on all the mystery of some dark foreign face I had just glimpsed on the quays.

I hated the storeroom where the dockets were kept, and when I worked there with Sheehy, Cremin or Clery, I realized that they found six dockets in the time it took me to find one. I had poor sight, and often failed to see a docket properly, particularly as it was usually written in the semi-literate scrawl of carters or porters; and even when I should have seen it, my mind was on something else, and when it was not, it was harassed by panic, shyness and ignorance. Bad as the storage shed was, noisy, evil-smelling and dark except where it was pitted with pale electric lights, I preferred it to the office because a couple of the men were kind and did not lose their tempers with me. But even here I was at a disadvantage. Sheehy and Cremin, being railwaymen's sons, were protected by their fathers' presence from anything worse than good-natured ragging, but I was anybody's butt, and was for ever being pawed by two of the men. One, a foul-mouthed ruffian with streaming white hair, didn't seem to mind when I edged away from him, but the other – a younger man with a thin, handsome, cruel face – resented it and hated me. I was always being mystified by the abrupt changes in his manner, for at one moment he would be smooth-spoken, dignified and considerate, and at the next his delicate complexion would grow brilliant red, and in a low, monotonous voice he would spew out abuse and filth at me, and I never could see why. It didn't even need my timid attempts to dodge his brutal goosing and pawing; anything did it, a word, or a tone of voice, or simply nothing at all that I could observe. But how little there was that I could observe!

There was, for instance, the matter of '1 Bale Foreskins' which appeared on a docket and was invoiced to Kingsbridge by some bored young invoice clerk. Kingsbridge, equally full of bored young men, solemnly replied, reporting that the bale of foreskins had not been received and asking that it should be traced. It was my duty to trace it, and I did so with my usual earnestness, inquiring of every checker and porter in the neighbourhood of the Dublin bay if perhaps a bale of foreskins might not still be lying round somewhere. They listened to me with great attention and asked what I thought it looked like, and I explained that I didn't know, but that it was probably like any other bale of pelts. They assured me that there were no pelts lying round anywhere, and when I had looked for myself I marked the memorandum 'Stag' or 'Falcon' or whatever the code word was. But then the wires began to fly, and I had to visit the storage shed again to make another search and find the docket in the files. To me the docket looked like any other docket, though later I realized that the names of consignor and consignee would have revealed to any smart boy that it was all a practical joke. But, in fact, so far as I was concerned the docket was no more unreal than any other docket, and the bale of foreskins than any other bale, and these than the pawing of the workmen. They were all just a vast phantasmagoria which I had to pretend to believe in to draw my weekly pay, but I never did believe in it, and when I left the building at seven o'clock it faded like clouds in the sky. At the same time I envied people who did believe in it, like young Cremin, and I pitied myself when I saw him, storming through the shed, from one lamp-lit bay to the next, his bundle of documents in his hand, exchanging noisy greetings with the porters, dodging checkers who tried to grab him, and yelling back laughing insults at them – at home with everybody but most of all with himself. In that whole huge organization there wasn't a soul with whom I felt at home, and so I had no self to be at home with; the only self I knew being then in wait for me until seven o'clock in the passenger station at the other side of the tracks, rather as I waited for Father outside a public house.

There was one checker I liked, and though he always nodded gravely to me and was helpful on the very few occasions when I needed his help, he never became involved with me. I think he realized with the force of revelation that I didn't believe in dockets and bales of pelts, and was doomed to trouble and that this trouble would fall on anyone who had anything to do with me. He shuffled through the storage shed with his head buried in his shoulders and a little to one side as though he hoped no one would notice him, his short-sighted blue eyes narrowed into slits. His secret was that he didn't believe in these things either. At the same time the feeling of his own peril gave him a certain guilty feeling of responsibility to me because I was clearly so much more imperilled than he was, and occasionally he stopped to talk to me and shuffled inch by inch out of the way into some corner where we could not be observed. Then, looking furtively over a bale of goods to make sure that no one was listening, he would tell me in a whisper that the country was priest-ridden. I didn't know what he meant by that, but I knew he meant that I had his sympathy. I was for the lions, and family conditions compelled him to burn a pinch of incense now and again, but he and I both knew there was no such God as Jupiter. One day, with a display of caution that would have done credit to an international conspirator, he pulled me aside, opened his blue jacket with the silver buttons, and took out a book which he thrust on me.

'Read that, boy,' he whispered. 'That'll show you what the country is really like.'

The book was *Waiting* by Gerald O'Donovan, an interesting novelist now almost forgotten. He was a priest in Loughrea who had been carried away by the Catholic liberal movement and the Irish national movement. Later, in disgust with his bishop, he became an army chaplain, married, and wrote a number of novels that have authenticity without charm. I read the book with great care, though a boy who didn't know what a foreskin was had little chance of understanding what the country was like. Yet I remember that particular checker for the breath of fresh air he brought for a moment into my life, with its guarantee that the reality of dockets and invoices, smart boys and foul-mouthed workers, was not quite as real as it seemed.

There was one further small reference to the world I really believed in in a kilted man who appeared one day at the office counter, apparently about some missing goods but who refused to speak English. Cremin came back from the counter, looking red, and reported to my boss. Obviously, this was a very tasteless joke, and the boss shot out, adjusting his pince-nez with the air of a man who never stood any nonsense. But it was no joke. French the visitor would speak if he was compelled, but Irish was the language of his choice, and nobody in the office except myself spoke a word of French or Irish. Nobody outside my boss and the other tracers even bothered to jeer me about my weakness for Irish, though one clerk, a small prissy man with pince-nez, did once sniff at me and ask me what literature we had in Irish to compare with Shakespeare. For a few minutes there was consternation as the clerks discussed the irruption. 'All right, Native,' the boss said at last with the air of a man setting a thief to catch a thief. 'You'd better see what he wants.'

Of course, the stranger turned out to be an Englishman, the son of an Anglican bishop, who was enjoying the embarrassment he was causing in an Irish railway station by speaking Irish when the only person who could answer him was a messenger boy. And, indeed, the matter didn't end there, because the Englishman had to put in his claim, and put it in Irish, which I had to translate into English, and the clerks decided to get even with him by making me also translate the official reply into Irish. Of course, he was a sport and I was a fool, but the little incident was a slight indication of a revolution that was already taking place without the smart boys even being aware of it.

It was also an indication of the extraordinary double life I was leading, a life so divided against itself that it comes back to me now as a hallucination rather than as a memory. Usually, there is some connexion between the real and imaginary worlds, some acquaintance in whom the two temporarily merge, but when I left the railway I did not leave a friend behind me and never so much as inquired what had happened to any of the decent people I knew there. One life I led in English – a life of drudgery and humiliation; the other in Irish or whatever scraps of foreign languages I had managed to pick up without benefit of grammar, and which any sensible man would describe as daydreaming, though daydreaming is a coarse and unrealistic word that might be applied by sensible men to the beliefs of the early Christians. That was the real significance of my passion for languages: they belonged entirely to the world of my imagination, and even today, when some figure of fantasy enters my dreams, he or she is always liable to break into copious and inaccurate French – the imagination seems to have no particular use for grammar. Irish was merely the most convenient of these escape routes into dreams, and that was why, on Saturday nights, with a German book from the Carnegie Library under my arm, I attended lectures in the Gaelic League hall in Queen Street, or stood admiringly in a corner listening to my seniors discussing in Irish profound questions such as 'Is Shakespeare national?' and 'Is dancing immoral?' or perhaps 'Is dancing national?' and 'Is Shakespeare immoral?' I still had no education, except such as fitted me for the byways of literature like Shakespeare, or the company of the ordinary girls I met, but these I was too shy or too ignorant to compound for, so I read Goethe a few lines at a time with the aid of a translation, or a page from some obscure novel in Spanish, and adored from afar beautiful university girls I should never get to know. Even Turgenev, who became my hero among writers, I read first only because of some novel of his in which there is a description of the Rhineland and German girls passing by in the twilight, murmuring *'Guten Abend'*.

This, of course, confined my education mainly to poetry, which has a simpler working vocabulary, based on words like *Herz* and *Schmerz*, *amour* and *toujours*, *ardor* and *rumor*, of which I could guess the meaning even when I hadn't a translation. I had taken a checker's discarded notebook from the storage shed and, having patiently rubbed out all the pencil notes, made a poem book of my own in all the languages I believed I knew. Though my love of poetry sprang from my mother, my taste, I fear, was entirely O'Donovan. Nature would seem to have intended me for an undertaker's assistant, because in any book of verse I read I invariably discovered elegies on dead parents, dead wives and dead children and, though my knowledge of poetry expanded, that weakness has persisted, and my favourite poems would be bound to include Bridges' 'Perfect Little Body', Landor's 'Artemidora, Gods Invisible', De La Mare's mighty poem on the suicide that begins 'Steep hung the drowsy street', Hardy's great series on his dead wife, and a mass of Emily Dickinson. And though I was stupid, and went about everything as Father went about putting up a shelf, I did care madly for poetry, good and bad, without understanding why I cared, and coming home at night, still corpse and brass band, I spoke it aloud till people who overheard looked after me in surprise. And this was as it should have been. On the night before his execution at Tyburn Chidiock Tichbourne wrote: 'My prime of life is but a frost of cares,' and on the night before his in Kilmainham Patrick Pearse wrote: 'The beauty of this world hath made me sad.' When life is at its harshest, 'when so sad thou can'st not sadder be', poetry comes into its own. Even more than music it is the universal speech, but it is spoken fluently only by those whose existence is already aflame with emotion, for then the beauty and order of language are the only beauty and order possible. Above all, it is the art of the boy and girl overburdened by the troubles of their sex and station, for as Jane Austen so wistfully noted, the difficulty with it is that it can best be appreciated by those who should enjoy it the most sparingly.

It was a strange double life, and small wonder if it comes back to me only as a hallucination. Each morning, as I made my way across the tracks from the passenger station in the early light, I said goodbye to my real self, and at seven that evening when I returned across the dark railway yard and paused in the well-lit passenger station to see the new books and papers in the railway bookstall, he rejoined me, a boy exactly like myself except that no experience had dinged or dented him, and as we went up Mahoney's Avenue in the darkness, we chattered in Irish diversified by quotations in German, French or Spanish, and talked knowledgeably of Italy and the Rhineland and the beautiful girls one could meet there, and I recited Goethe's poem that in those days was always in my mind – the perfection of the poet's dream of escape:

> Kennst du das Land wo die Zitronen blueh'n,
> Im dunklem Laub die Goldorangen glueh'n.

I know I often hurt Mother by my moroseness and churlishness when some innocent question of hers brought me tumbling from the heights of language to the English that belonged to the office and the store. And between Father and myself there was constant friction. Father was a conservative, and he knew the world was full of thieves and murderers. He wouldn't go to bed like a sensible man and let me lock and bolt the doors and quench the lamp. He and Mother might both be burned alive in their beds. But when I went out for an evening walk I hoped frantically to rescue some American heiress whose father would realize the talent that was lost in me or, failing that, to tag along behind some of the senior members of the Gaelic League and try to talk as grown-up as they seemed, and often I wasted my precious couple of hours, walking up and down the Western Road and meeting nobody who would even speak to me. As I came up Summerhill the pleasure of being all of a piece again was overshadowed by the prospect of the morning when once more I should have to part from the half of me that was real, and it was like a blow in the face when I found the door locked, and Mother came scurrying out to open it for me.

'Don't say a word, child!' she would whisper.

'Why?' I would ask defiantly, loud enough to be heard upstairs. 'Is he on the war-path again?'

'Ten o'clock that door is locked!' Father would intone from the bedroom.

'Ah, don't answer him! Would you like a cup of tea?'

'Better fed than taught!' Father would add, as he had added any time in the previous ten years.

When my first wretched effort at composition appeared in a children's paper and word of it got round the office, everyone was astonished, but most of all my boss. He was a decent man, and a clever one, and he knew better than anyone that I was definitely not a smart boy. I remember him sitting at his high desk with the paper open before him and a frown on his bulgy forehead as he nervously readjusted his pince-nez.

'Did you write this, Native?'

'Yessir,' I said, feeling I had probably done it again. Everything I did only seemed to get me into fresh trouble.

'Nobody help you?'

'No, sir,' I replied warily, because it looked as though someone else might get the blame, and I still clung to the code of the boys' weeklies and was always prepared to own up. The frown deepened on his fat face.

'Then for God's sake, stick to writing!' he snapped. 'You'll never be any good on the Great Southern and Western Railway.'

And that, as we used to say, was one sure five. As usual, looking for models of fine conduct, I had hit on a left-wing time-keeper who knew all the Italian operas by heart and made it a point of honour not to take off his cap before the bosses. Seeing that anyone who knew so much about opera must know the correct thing for other situations, I decided to do the same, with results that may be imagined. Even then, I should probably have been let off with a reprimand, because I had no self-confidence and merely went about blindly imitating anyone and anything, in the hope of blending somehow into the phantasmagoria, but, with my bad sight, I had also fallen over a hand-truck and injured my shin so badly that I couldn't walk for weeks. But on the railway bad sight was more serious than bad manners, because it might result in a claim.

On the Saturday night I was sacked I read my first paper. It was in Irish, and the subject was Goethe, For me, my whole adolescence is summed up in that extraordinary evening – so much that even yet I cannot laugh at it in comfort. I didn't know much about Irish, and I knew practically nothing about Goethe, and that little was wrong. In a truly anthropomorphic spirit I re-created Goethe in my own image and likeness, as a patriotic young man who wished to revive the German language, which I considered to have been gravely threatened by the use of French. I drew an analogy between the French culture that dominated eighteenth-century Germany and the English culture by which we in Ireland were dominated.

While I was speaking, it was suddenly borne in on me that I no longer had a job or a penny in the world, or even a home I could go back to without humiliation, and that the neighbours would say, as they had so often said before, that I was mad and a good-for-nothing. And I knew that they would be right, for here I was committing myself in public to all the vague words and vaguer impressions that with me passed for thought. I could barely control my voice, because the words and impressions no longer meant anything to me. They seemed to come back to me from the rows of polite blank faces as though from the wall of my prison. All that did matter was the act of faith, the hope that somehow, somewhere I would be able to prove that I was neither mad nor a good-for-nothing; because now I realized that whatever it might cost me, there was no turning back. When as kids we came to an orchard wall that seemed too high to climb, we took off our caps and tossed them over the wall, and then we had no choice but to follow them.

I had tossed my cap over the wall of life, and I knew I must follow it, wherever it had fallen.

FOUR

After Aughrim's great disaster

15

Once again I was without a job. Like the old men whose landladies and daughters-in-law turned them out in the mornings, I made the Public Library my headquarters, and continued to read through the advertisements for a smart boy, though I realized that I was ceasing to be a boy and would probably never be smart. Then I went out and wandered aimlessly about the town in hope of meeting someone who would talk to me, and even maybe give me a cigarette. It was a dreary existence, because Father kept on asking what I was going to do with myself, and I had no notion. It was no use telling him that eventually I hoped to find a job that would suit my peculiar brand of education or meet some rich girl who would recognize my talents and keep me in decent comfort till I established myself. She didn't have to be *very* rich; my needs were simple; only a trousers without a patch on the seat of it, so that I could be seen with her without embarrassment, and an occasional packet of cigarettes. Father, having returned from the War with a disability pension to add to his service pension, was past arguing with – a man who had really set himself up for life!

It was a period of political unrest and, in a way, this was a relief, because it acted as a safety valve for my own angry emotions. Indeed, it would be truer to say that the Irish nation and myself were both engaged in an elaborate process of improvization. I was improvizing an education I could not afford, and the country was improvizing a revolution it could not afford. In 1916 it had risen to a small, real revolution with uniforms and rifles, but the English had brought up artillery that had blown the centre of Dublin flat, and shot down the men in uniform. It was all very like myself and the Christian Brothers. After that, the country had to content itself with a make-believe revolution, and I had to content myself with a make-believe education, and the curious thing is that it was the make-believe that succeeded.

The elected representatives of the Irish people (those who managed to stay out of gaol) elected what they called a government, with a Ministry of Foreign Affairs that tried in vain to get Woodrow Wilson to see it, a Ministry of Finance that exacted five to ten pounds from small shopkeepers who could ill afford it, a Ministry of Defence that tried to buy old-fashioned weapons at outrageous prices from shady characters, and a Ministry of Home Affairs that established courts of justice with part-time Volunteer policemen and no gaols at all.

It all began innocently enough. People took to attending Gaelic League concerts at which performers sang 'She Is Far from the Land', recited 'Let Me Carry Your Cross for Ireland, Lord', or played 'The Fox Chase' on the elbow pipes, and armed police broke them up. I remember one that I attended in the town park. When I arrived, the park was already occupied by police, so after a while the crowd began to drift away towards the open country up the river. A mile or so up it re-assembled on the river-bank, but by this time most of the artistes had disappeared. Somebody who knew me asked for a song. At fourteen or fifteen I was delighted by the honour and tried to sing in Irish a seventeenth-century outlaw song about 'Sean O'Dwyer of the Valley'. I broke down after the first verse – I always did break down whenever I had to make any sort of public appearance because the contrast between what was going on in my head and what was going on in the real world was too much for me – but it didn't matter much. At any moment the police might appear, and this time there could be real bloodshed. It was sheer obstinacy that had driven respectable people to walk miles just to attend a concert they were not very interested in, and they paid their sixpences and went home, rightly feeling that they were the real performers.

It was the same at Mass on Sunday. The bishop, Daniel Coholan – locally known as 'Danny Boy' – was a bitter enemy of all this pretence, and every Sunday we had to be ready for a diatribe at Mass. It was as upsetting as discovering that the Invisible Presences still regarded us as traitors for, though I knew that Ellen Farrell and her husband had defied the Church in Parnell's day, I had had no expectation of ever having to do so. The priest would turn on the altar or ascend the pulpit and start the familiar rigmarole about 'defiance of lawful government', and some young man would rise from his seat and move into the nave, genuflect and leave the church. Suddenly every eye would be turned on him, and even the priest would fall silent and wait for the interruption to end. Then there would be a shuffling of feet in one of the aisles, and a girl would rise, genuflect and leave as well. Sometimes this went on for minutes till a considerable group had left. They stood and talked earnestly in the chapel yard, all of them declared rebels, some perhaps marked down for assassination, till the priest finished his harangue and they went back. Naturally, I always joined them, hoping for a nod or a smile from one of them.

It was childish, of course, but so was everything else about the period, like the lttle grocery shop you saw being repainted and the name on the fascia board changed from 'J. Murphy' to 'Sean O'Murchadha'. One can still almost date that generation by its Liams, Seans and Peadars. I suspect that in those few years more books were published in Ireland than in any succeeding twenty years. Not good books, God knows, any more than the little papers that kept on appearing and being suppressed were good papers. But they expressed the mind of the time. One paper I still remember fondly because it proposed that English as a 'secondary' language be dropped in favour of French. In those days it struck me as an excellent idea. The impossible, and only the impossible, was law. It was in one way a perfect background for someone like myself who had only the impossible to hope for.

Then the real world began to catch up with the fantasy. The Lord Mayor, Thomas MacCurtain, was murdered by English police in his own home before the eyes of his wife; another Lord Mayor, Terence MacSwiney, was elected in his place and promptly arrested. He went on hunger strike and died in Brixton Gaol. Mother and I were among those who filed past his coffin as he lay in state in the City Hall in his volunteer uniform; the long, dark, masochistic face I had seen only a few months before as he chatted with Corkery by the New Bridge. Years later I talked with a little country shopkeeper from North Cork who had organized a company of Volunteers in his home town, and been so overawed by the tall, dark young man who cycled out from the city to inspect them that he was too shy to ask where MacSwiney was spending the night. Long after, cycling home himself, he saw someone lying in a field by the roadside and, getting off, found MacSwiney asleep in the wet grass with nothing

131

but an old raincoat round him. That vision of MacSwiney had haunted him through the years of disillusionment.

Curfew was imposed, first at ten, then at five in the afternoon. The bishop excommunicated everyone who supported the use of physical force, but it went on just the same. One night shots were fired on our road and a lorry halted at the top of the square. An English voice kept on screaming hysterically 'Oh, my back! my back!' but no one could go out through the wild shooting of panic-stricken men. Soon afterwards the military came in force, and from our back door we saw a red glare mount over the valley of the city. For hours Father, Mother and I took turns at standing on a chair in the attic, listening to the shooting and watching the whole heart of the city burn. Father was the most upset of us, for he was full of local pride, and ready to take on any misguided foreigner or Dublin jackeen who was not prepared to admit the superiority of Cork over all other cities. Next morning, when I wandered among the ruins, it was not the business district or the municipal buildings that I mourned for, but the handsome red-brick library that had been so much a part of my life from the time when as a small boy I brought back my first Western adventure story over the railway bridges. Later I stood at the corner by Dillon's Cross where the ambush had been and saw a whole block of little houses demolished by a British tank. One had been the home of an old patriot whom my grandparents called 'Brienie Dill'. A small, silent crowd was held back by soldiers as the tank lumbered across the pavement and thrust at the wall until at last it broke like pie crust and rubble and rafters tumbled. It made a deep impression on me. Always it seemed to be the same thing: the dark, shrunken face of MacSwiney in the candle-light and the wall that burst at the thrust of the tank; 'the splendour falls' and 'There is no such thing in business as an out-and-out free gift'. It was like a symbolic representation of what was always happening to myself, and it seemed as though Ireland did not stand a much better chance. The material world was too strong for both of us.

All the same I could not keep away from Ireland, and I was involved in most of the activities of that imaginative revolution – at a considerable distance, of course, because I was too young, and anyway, I had Father all the time breathing down my neck. In the absence of proper uniform our Army tended to wear riding breeches, gaiters, a trench coat and a soft hat usually pulled low over one eye, and I managed to scrape up most of the essential equipment, even when I had to beg it, as I begged the pair of broken gaiters from Tom MacKernan. I conducted a complicated deal for the Ministry of Defence and bought a French rifle from a man who lived close to Cork Barrack, though, when I had risked a heavy sentence by bringing it home down my trouser leg, all the time pretending I had just met with a serious accident, it turned out that there wasn't a round of ammunition in Ireland to fit it. When the British burned and looted Cork and encouraged the slum-dwellers to join in the looting, I was transferred to the police and put to searching slums in Blarney Lane for jewellery and furs. In a back room in Blarney Lane we located a mink coat which the woman who lived there said had just been sent her by her sister in America. Being a polite and unworldly boy of seventeen, I was quite prepared to take her word for it, but my companion said she hadn't a sister in America and, shocked by her untruthfulness, I brought the coat back to its rightful owners. That she might have needed it more than they didn't occur to me; I remembered only that I was now a real policeman, and acted as I felt a good policeman should act. When Belfast was boycotted during the anti-Catholic pogroms, I was sent with one or two others to seize a load of Belfast goods at the station where I had worked a year before. The Belfast goods mysteriously turned out to be a furniture van, but you couldn't take me in like that. Belfast businessmen were very cunning and besides I had my orders. So we made the poor van driver and his horse trudge all the way to Glanmire, miles down the river, and only when he opened it up did we realize that it contained nothing but the furniture of some Catholic family flying from the pogroms.

It was in this atmosphere that I produced my second work, which – as may be understood – was a translation into Irish of Du Bellay's sonnet, 'Heureux Qui Comme Ulysse', well spoken of in George Wyndham's chatty book on the Pleaide. I was probably deeply moved by Du Bellay's sentiments for, being a great wanderer in my own imagination, I took a deep interest in the feelings of returned travellers. It is probably a recurring fantasy of the provincial, for one friend whom I made later – the most conscientious of officials – never read anything but sea stories, and from Corkery's novel, The Threshold of Quiet – itself full of sailors and ships – I can still quote his excellent translation of an inferior French sonnet: 'Returned at last from lands we yearn to know.'

But this sonnet of mine is another triumph of mind over matter and, so far as I know, unique in literature, because it is a translation from one language the author didn't know into another that he didn't know – or at best, knew most imperfectly. This was obscured when the poem was published in one of the political weeklies that were always appearing and disappearing as the English caught up with them because both languages were even more unknown to editor and printer; and the only thing that could be perceived from the resulting mess was that, whatever the damn thing meant, it must be a sonnet; octet and sestet were unmistakably distinguished. However, a journalist in the *Sunday Independent*, mad with patriotic and linguistic enthusiasm, hailed it as a 'perfect translation'. It was a period when journalists could improvise a literature as lightly as country clerks improvised government departments. The occasion brought forth the man – a view of history I have always been rather doubtful of.

I haunted the streets for Corkery till I finally trapped him one day by the Scots Church at the foot of Summerhill and casually showed him the cutting from the *Sunday Independent*. He asked if I had the translation with me, and curiously I had that too. He read it carefully with one eye half closed, not commenting too much on the grammar, which was probably invisible through the typographical errors, and said judicially that it was a beautiful translation. At any rate, he apparently decided that, since what could not be cured must be endured, he had to admit me to his own little group. After all, I was now a published author.

He lived in a small suburban house on Gardiner's Hill with his mother and sister, surrounded by books and pictures. Over the mantelpiece was a large water colour of his own of a man with a scythe on Fair Hill, overlooking the great panorama of the river valley. Inside the door of the living-room was a bust of him by his friend, Joe Higgins, which – if my memory of it is correct – is the only likeness of him that captures all his charm. He presided over his little group from a huge Morris chair with a detachable desk that he had made for himself (he was an excellent craftsman, having been brought up to the trade, and once told me in his oracular way that 'nobody had ever met a stupid carpenter', which I later found to be untrue).

He had a good deal of the harshness and puritanism of the provincial intellectual which I share. As those brought up to wealth and rank tend to under-rate them, people accustomed from childhood to an intellectual atmosphere can take classical standards lightly and permit themselves to be entertained by mere facility; not those who have had to buy them dear. Once, when I was working on the railway, and had spent a whole week's pocket money on Wilde's *Intentions*, I met Corkery and he glanced at the book and shook his head. 'It'll ruin whatever style you have,' he said, and even the suggestion that I might have a style did not make up to me for the realization that once again I had backed the wrong horse.

Most of his friends belonged to a little group that had worked with him when he ran a tiny theatre in Queen Street. The most faithful visitor was Denis Breen, a schoolteacher like himself, who had provided the music and married one of the actresses. He was a big, emotional man with a fat, sun-coloured face, clear, childish blue eyes, and a red moustache that he apparently cultivated for the sole purpose of eating it – a face Franz Hals would have loved. At Gaelic League meetings he roared down patriotic souls who decried English music and talked of the greatness of Byrd, Dowland and Purcell, whom none of us had ever heard of. He also professed to be an atheist, which was rather like proclaiming yourself a Christian in modern China, and the defensiveness this had induced in him was reflected in everything he did and said. He had a great contempt for our little colony of German musicians, whom he spoke of as though they were Catholic priests, as 'bleddy eejits'. They, more objectively, spoke of him as a genius without musical training. It might be fairer to say that his temperament was too immoderate for the precise and delicate work of the artist – the very opposite of Corkery's. The two men were always arguing, Corkery gently and inquiringly, Breen uproariously and authoritatively, something like this. 'Well, on the other hand, would it not be possible to say . . . ?' 'Me dear man, it's possible to say anything, if you're fool enough.' I listened in shame for the whole human race to think that anyone could be so presumptuous as to disagree with Corkery.

I did not like Breen. I was connected with him through two coincidences: one that he had taught me for a couple of days before I left Blarney Lane for good, and even in that short time he had beaten me (Irish teachers, like American policemen, never having learned that to go about armed is not the best way of securing obedience and respect); the other was that my mother and his mother, who kept a little sweet shop at the gate of the University, had been friends. His mother had told my mother that even when he was a small boy no one could control him. He would get hungry at night, go down to the shop for biscuits, sample every tin and leave them all open, so that by morning her stock was ruined. Even when I knew him he would begin his tea by eating all the sweet cakes in case anyone else took a fancy to them. He was greedy with a child's greed, shouted everyone down with what he thought 'funny' stories of denunciations of the 'bleddy eejits' who ran the country or its music, and battered a Beethoven sonata to death with his red eyebrows reverently raised, believing himself to be a man of perfect manners, liberal ideas and perfect taste. All of which, of course, he was, as I learned later when we became friends, for though his wife and my mother would look blank while he ate all the confectionery and then shouted for more; and though afterwards he hammered Wolf's *An Die Geliebte* unconscious; he struck out the last chords as only a man who loved music could do it, scowling and muttering: 'Now listen to the bloody stars!' He quarrelled bitterly with me after the first performance of a play called *The Invincibles* because he had convinced himself that I had caricatured him in the part of Joe Brady, the leader of the assassins – a brave and simple man driven mad by injustice – and though at the time I was disturbed because such an idea had never occurred to me, it seems to me now that the characters in whom we think we recognize ourselves are infinitely more revealing of our real personalities than those in which someone actually attempts to portray us.

But Corkery's greatest friend was Sean O'Faolain, who was three years older than I and all the things I should have wished to be – handsome, brilliant and, above all, industrious. For Corkery, who loved application, kept on rubbing it in that I didn't work as O'Faolain did. Once the three of us met on Patrick's Bridge after Corkery and O'Faolain had attended a service at the cathedral, and when O'Faolain went off in his home-spun suit, swinging his ash-plant, Corkery looked after him as I had once seen him look after Terence MacSwiney and said: 'There goes a born literary man!' For months I was mad with jealousy.

The first book I took from Corkery's bookcase was a Browning. It was characteristic of my topsy-turvy self-education that I knew by heart thousands of lines in German and Irish, without really knowing either language, but had never heard of Browning, or indeed of any other English poet but Shakespeare, whom I didn't think much of. But my trouble with poetry was that of most auto-didacts. I could not afford books, so I copied and memorized like mad. It is a theory among scholars that all great periods of manu-script activity coincide with some impending social disaster and that scribes are like poor Jews in the midst of a hostile community, gathering up their few little treasures in the most portable form before the next pogrom. Obviously I anticipated the disaster of the Irish Civil War, because I never seemed to possess anything unless I had written it down and learned it by heart, and though I scorned what I thought mediocre verse, and never bothered to acquire anything that had not been approved by the best authorities, the authorities themselves proved most unreliable, and for every good poem I learned, I learned six bad ones. Unlike the poor Jew, I could not throw away the imitation pearls, so though my taste in poetry improved, my memory refused to adapt itself, and when it should have been producing masterpieces, it would suddenly take things into its own hands and produce something frightful by some minor Georgian poet like Drinkwater. Describing the death of a neighbour, a small boy in our locality drew his hand across his throat and said darkly: 'De woman went before her God full up to *dat* of whiskey.' I shall go before mine full up to *that* of bad poetry.

Music was different and much more difficult because I had no standards at all. When people played or sang music-hall songs I behaved as I did when they told dirty stories and either left the room or read a book, but I could not go out in the evening without passing a neighbour's house where an old-fashioned horn-gramophone bellowed songs from *The Arcadians* and, in spite of the fact that the Christian Brothers thought I had a defective ear, I picked them up and – like the bad poetry – I have them still. When I became friends with a young fellow called Tom MacKernan, who drilled beside me in the Volunteers and played the fiddle, I got him to play me certified classical tunes from his violin book. I even got him to lend me an old fiddle and a tutor, but I could not make head or tail of staff notation. When I met Jack Hendrick, whose brother was a singer, I got him to teach me the songs his brother sang at musical competitions like *Where'er You Walk* and *Am Stillen Herd*, though I still could not understand key changes and thought he was probably singing out of tune. Corkery took me a couple of times to real piano recitals by Tilly Fleischmann and Geraldine Sullivan, but though I read the programme notes like mad – they were usually by Corkery's friend, Father Pat MacSwiney – and pretended to myself that I could recognize the moment when 'the dawn wind wakes the sleeping leaves, and these, tapping at the window pane, rouse the joyous maiden who has been dreaming of her secret lover', it always turned out that I had just been listening to the climax in which 'Smiling, she leans through the window and plucks a rose for her hair'. It mortified me to see all those educated people who had no difficulty in distinguishing the dawn wind rising from a girl plucking a rose for her hair and made me feel that life was really unfair.

I had no luck with music till Corkery bought a gramophone from Germany immediately after the 1914–18 War, when the rate of exchange was favourable, and with it a selection of records that included Bach's Sixth Cello Sonata, a couple of Beethoven symphonies, Mozart's Violin Concerto in A, Schubert's 'Unfinished' and Strauss's *Till Eulenspiegel*. I gave Strauss up as a bad job because it would clearly not be portable in any future pogrom, but I practically learned the Seventh Symphony and the Mozart Concerto by heart, and for years judged everything by them. I can now read second-rate books without getting sick, but I still cannot listen to mediocre music. I had too much trouble escaping from it.

Corkery took me sketching with him as well, but I was never much good at that, 'it's like me with my game leg entering for the hundred yards,' he said kindly, blaming it on my sight, but it wasn't my sight. It was my undeveloped visual sense. The imagination, because it is by its nature subjective, pitches first on the area of the intimate arts – poetry and music. Painting, which is more objective and critical, comes later. Still, that did not keep him from getting me into the School of Art, where I spent my time copying casts, drawing from the male model, and arguing like mad with my teacher, who said that Michelangelo was 'very coarse'. Apparently, Corkery's idea was that since I could never get into a university, I should become an art teacher, and he even arranged a scholarship in London for me. But I was in a frenzy to earn a little money and, instead, like a fool, I applied for a scholarship to a Gaelic League Summer School in Dublin that had been formed to train teachers of Irish, who would later cycle about the country from village to village, teaching in schools and parish halls. It sounded exactly the sort of life for an aspiring young writer who wanted to know Ireland as Gorky had known Russia.

The Summer School was held in the Gaelic League headquarters in Parnell Square, and the head of it was a sly, fat rogue of a West Cork man called Hurley, who was later Quartermaster General of the Free State Army. I did not like Dublin, probably because most of the time I was light-headed with hunger. I lodged in a Georgian house on the Pembroke Road and, having rarely eaten in any house other than my own, I contented myself with a cup of tea and a slice of bread for breakfast. I decided that the chamber pot in my bedroom was for ornament rather than use. I was even more scared of restaurants than of strange houses. I had never eaten in one except when Mother took me to Thompson's café in Patrick Street for a cup of coffee – her notion of high life – so I lived entirely on coffee and buns in Bewley's. It was to be years before I worked up the courage to go into a real restaurant. Besides, the scholarship did not amount to more than the price of modest lodgings, and I needed every penny I could spare for the books I could pick up cheap at the stalls on the quays. I could not keep away from them. There were books there the like of which one never saw in a Cork bookstore. It was there that I picked up for a few pence the little *Selected Poems of Browning* published by Smith, Elder, which for me has always been one of the great books of the world, and when the hunger got too much for me I would recite to myself: 'Heap cassia, sandal-buds and stripes of labdanum and aloeballs' as though it were a spell.

Far from being recognized as a genius at the school, I was obviously regarded as a complete dud. The reason for this did not dawn on me till years had gone by. All the other students had had a good general education, some a university education. I talked Irish copiously, but nobody had explained to me the difference between a masculine and feminine noun, or a nominative and dative case. Nobody explained to me then either, probably because the problem of a completely uneducated boy masquerading as a well-educated one was outside everyone's experience.

And yet, the whole country was doing the same, and Hurley, who gave the impression of having served his time in a West Cork drapery store, was on his way to one of the highest ranks in the army. My friends in the school were a Dubliner called Byrne and a Kerryman called Kavanagh. Byrne was doubly endeared to me because, though only a boy scout, he had already been involved in a pistol fight with a police patrol. Some hunger striker had died in prison and was being given a public funeral, so the three of us demanded the afternoon off to attend it, and fell foul of Hurley, who objected to what he called 'politics' in the school. When the time for the funeral came the three of us got up to leave the class and Hurley, in a rage, dismissed it. We were expecting trouble, and Byrne had a revolver. The imaginary revolution was taking shape as well.

I was lucky to return to Cork with a certificate that made me a

qualified teacher of Irish – which I was not – and for a few weeks
I cycled eight or ten miles out of the city in the evenings to teach in
country schools by lamp-light. But already even this was becoming
dangerous, and soon curfew put an end to my new career as well.
I seemed to be very unlucky with my jobs.

At the same time I was making friends of a different type. One
evening a pale, thin-lipped young clerk in an insurance office, called
Jack Hendrick, came to see me with an introduction from Corkery
and proposed that the two of us should start a literary and debating
society. Our conversation was rather at cross-purposes, for he did
not seem to have read anything but d'Israeli's *Curiosities of Literature*
and he continued to quote this to me as I quoted Turgenev and
Dostoevsky to him. He didn't seem to know about them, and I had
never heard of d'Israeli, so I agreed to borrow it from him and
meanwhile lent him Turgenev's *Virgin Soil* and Gogol's *Taras Bulba*.
When we met again I admitted that I was bored with d'Israeli, and
he said he thought Turgenev was 'cold'. We didn't seem to be
getting anywhere, but I needed a friend too badly to reject one
merely because he said outrageous things about Turgenev, and
Hendrick was exactly the sort of friend I needed because he had
every virtue that I lacked and was well-mannered, methodical, cool
and thoughtful. He had a neat, square, erect handwriting that I
greatly admired for its legibility, and I set out to imitate it as I had
imitated Corkery's monosyllabic articulation, but I was too restive
to do anything that required exacting labour, and Hendrick's handwriting was a career in itself.

I explained to him that I now had a chance of a teaching job, but
it meant I would have to ride a bicycle, and I had been assured by
the man who had tried to teach me that I had no sense of balance
and would never be able to ride. I had accepted this without question
because it was only one of the dozen things I had been told I
couldn't do. I couldn't sing; I couldn't pass an examination; I
couldn't persevere at a task – naturally I couldn't ride a bicycle.
That evening Hendrick brought his sister's bicycle out the Bally-
volane Road, put me up on it, unclenched my fists on the handle-
bars, and when we came to the first long hill, gave me a push that
sent me flying. I was a mass of bruises when I picked myself up at
the foot of the hill, but when I wheeled back the bicycle, Hendrick,
who by this time was sitting on the grass by the roadside, smoking,
took out his cigarettes and said with a pale smile: 'Now you know
how to ride a bicycle.'

But even this was of less importance to me than the fact that I was beginning to make friends away from my own gas-lamp. It was probably this that Blake had in mind when he said that if only a fool would persevere in his folly he would become a wise man, because sooner or later the imaginative improvisation imposes itself on reality. But it is only then that its real troubles begin, when it must learn to restrain itself from imposing too far, and acquire a smattering of the practical sense it has rejected. That, I think, is where the Irish Revolution broke down. The imagination is a refrigerator, not an incubator; it preserves the personality intact through disaster after disaster, but even when it has changed the whole world it has still changed nothing in itself and emerges as a sort of Rip Van Winkle, older in years but not in experience. This sets up a time lag that can never be really overcome.

Friendship did not make me wiser or happier, for years of lonely daydreaming had left me emotionally at the age of ten. I was ashamed to admit that there was anything I didn't know, and one evening when Corkery talked to me about a story of Gorky's in which there was a eunuch, I was too mortified to admit that I didn't know what a eunuch was. I was morbidly sensitive, jealous, exacting, and terrified of strangers. I did not merely make friends; I fell in love, and even the suspicion of a slight left me as frantic as a neurotic schoolgirl. The attitudes of the ghetto survive emancipation, and I had only to enter a strange house or talk to a stranger to make a complete fool of myself. From excessive shyness I always talked too much, usually lost control of myself, and heard myself say things that were ridiculous, false or base, and afterwards remained awake, raging and sobbing by turns as I remembered every detail of my own awkwardness, lying and treachery. Years later, when I was earning money, I never went to a strange house without first taking a drink or two to brace me for the ordeal. Whether that was much help or not I do not know. It is enough that the things I said when I was slightly intoxicated were never quite as bad as the things I said when I wasn't.

As if this weren't enough, I was also going through the usual adolescent phase of snobbery and was ashamed of my parents, ashamed of the little house where we lived, and when people called for me, I grabbed my cap and dragged them out anywhere, for fear Father should start telling funny stories about his army days or Mother reveal that she was only a charwoman. With me, of course, this was also complicated by the number of things that really humiliated me, like my clothes, which were decent but patched, and the fact that I could never get on a tram without first scanning the passengers to make sure there was no girl aboard whose fare I should not be able to pay. As a result I never got on a tram at all until the moment it started to move, and tried to find a seat where no one could come and sit beside me. Then if I continued to look out at the street till the conductor had gone by, I was safe.

My fight for Irish freedom was of the same order as my fight for other sorts of freedom. Still like Dolan's ass, I went a bit of the way with everybody, and in those days everybody was moving in the same direction. Hendrick did not get me to join a debating society, but I got him to join the Volunteers. If it was nothing else, it was a brief escape from tedium and frustration to go out the country roads on summer evenings, slouching along in knee breeches and gaiters, hands in the pockets of one's trenchcoat and hat pulled over one's right eye. Usually it was only to a parade in some field with high fences off the Rathcooney Road, but sometimes it was a barrack that was being attacked, and we trenched roads and felled trees, and then went home through the wet fields over the hills, listening for distant explosions and scanning the horizon for fires. It was all too much for poor Father, who had already seen me waste my time making toy theatres when I should have been playing football, and drawing naked men when I should have been earning my living. And this time he did at least know what he was talking about. For all he knew I might have the makings of a painter or writer in me but, as an old soldier himself, he knew that I would never draw even a disability pension. No good could come of such foolishness, and it would only be the mercy of God if the police at St Luke's didn't blame him for my conduct and write to the War Office to get his pensions stopped. The old trouble about locking the door at night became acute. Ten o'clock was when he went to bed – earlier when curfew was on – and the door had to be fastened for the night: the latch, the lock, the big bolt and the little bolt. When I knocked, Mother got out of bed to open it, Father shouted at her, and she called back indignantly to him not to wake the neighbours, and whispered in anguish to me: 'Don't answer him whatever he says!' But stung in my pride as a soldier of Ireland, I often did answer back, and then he roared louder than ever that I was 'better fed than taught'. Mother's sympathies were entirely with the revolution, and he would have been more furious still if he had known that not long after she was doing odd errands herself, carrying revolvers and despatches. Or maybe he did know and, like many another husband, decided to ignore her minor infidelities.

I was changing, but though I did not realize it till much later, Corkery was changing, too, in an infinitely subtler and more significant way, and the man I loved was turning into someone I should not even be able to understand. I was merely puzzled and hurt when one night he said: 'You must remember there are more important things in life than literature.' I knew there weren't, because if there were I should be doing them. That change goes farther back than the period I am writing of, and was not perceptible until years later. It is not in his novel, *The Threshold of Quiet*, but it is already adumbrated in the first story of *A Munster Twilight*. In this a worldly farmer wishes to plough the Ridge of the Saints – sanctified ground – but his old farmhand, steeped in traditional pieties, refuses to do it. He taunts his employer by offering to plough the Ridge if the farmer will put his great sire-horse, Ember, to the plough. At the end of the story the old farmhand yokes the sire-horse and the mare, whose name is Beauty, and goes out at nightfall to plough the Ridge, the horses quarrel and horses and man are hurled together over the cliff.

This is a typical bit of symbolism that seems to sum up a deep personal conflict. It describes the suicidal destruction of the creative faculty as an act of revolt against the worldliness of everyday life. 'There are more important things in life than literature.' Scores of other modern writers like Ibsen and James have used such symbolic equations as a way of trying out their personal problems, but this one seems to me to describe what really happened. It is as though the imaginative improvisation of the community had begun to dominate the imaginative improvisation of the artist and make its fires seem dim by comparison. Of course there must have been some more immediate cause, and I sometimes wonder whether it was not Corkery's friendship with Thomas MacCurtain and Terence MacSwiney. MacCurtain's murder aroused the country and MacSwiney's death on hunger-strike was watched by the whole world and cost the British Government more than a major military defeat. It seems to me now that Corkery's admiration for the two men may have made him feel that men of action had more to give than the mere artist like himself. His admiration for the men of action is in *The Hounds of Bamba*, the book of stories he was writing at the time, and there are stories in this that repeat the symbolic equation of the horses. One, for instance, describes how a jockey, who is also a traditionalist, takes up a bet made by his half-witted employer, rides a famous horse along the cliffs, and then wrestles with the horse and throws him bodily over the edge into the sea. Even in the stories where there is no symbolism there is a celebration of imaginary heroes and an attack on imaginary enemies who are not far removed from windmills. And Corkery knew his windmill-fighters, for once when we were looking at a picture called *Don Quixote* he said sharply: 'Those eyes are wrong. They're looking out. Quixote's eyes looked inward.'

I do not blame myself for not understanding and sympathizing with what was happening to him, because it was precisely the opposite of what was happening to me. He was a man who, by force of character, had dominated physical difficulties, family circumstances and a provincial environment that would have broken down anyone but a great man. Breen, who gave the impression of being opposed to him, cursed and raged whenever he described Corkery's suffering in the teachers' training college they had attended together, and I am certain that this sprang from Breen's own clear eye and passionate heart rather than from any self-pity on Corkery's part. Nowadays I remember how his mind seemed always to brood on self-control, as when he described how he had written his novel, getting up each morning at six, or wrote to me when I was in prison, quoting Keats on the beneficial effect of a shave and wash-up when one's spirits were low, or praised Michael Collins, who had made himself leader of the whole revolutionary movement because he was up answering letters when everyone else was in bed. He was as shy and reserved as Chekhov and never asked for sympathy, but behind words like these one could detect a whole lifetime of self-control. Yet he did not, as a lesser man might have done, lose generosity in speaking of an enemy or gentleness in rebuking a friend. He would gaze at me gloomily, and predict in his harsh, unmodulated voice that I would go through life without ever finishing anything, and then add 'like Coleridge', awarding me a valuable second prize. I have described how he ticked me off for reading Wilde, because it would injure whatever style I had. Yeats had exactly the same trick. When he was forming his Academy, even before I had published a book, he and I quarrelled about the constitution of the Academy and he muttered: 'Why worry about literary eminence? You and I will provide that.' Of course it was guileful, and in a lesser man it might have been the basest flattery, but I understood it in him as in Corkery as the desperate attempt of the elderly and eminent man to break down the barriers that separated him from youth and awkwardness. Because of that Corkery developed an authority that was like Yeats's. If, as I now fancy, he was impressed by Mac-Swiney's sacrifice, it was probably because MacSwiney's remarkable self-control and self-denial had given him an authority beyond his intellect and gifts, but Corkery's self-control was of a rarer kind. However little he said, and however insipid what he said might seem, it was on his judgement that we all relied, and I think that in the way of those who combine self-control and humanity, austerity and sweetness, he was full of a consciousness of his own power he would have been much too shy to reveal. Only once did he let anything drop that suggested it, and that was one evening when I suggested that great writers might be more careful of what they did and said if only they remembered the sort of people who would write their lives, and he shrugged and replied: 'Well, I know people will write my life . . .'

That is the period when I best like to remember him. After a cruel day's teaching he would take his paints and sketchbook and trudge miles into the country with me at his heels. I would quote a line or two of Omar Khayyám, and at once he would take alarm lest any fledgling of his should be taken in by something less than a masterpiece. 'What *is* it about Fitzgerald that's not quite right?' he would ask, and I, as well-skilled in the responses as any acolyte, would reply: 'Well, it is a bit sugary, isn't it?' 'It is on the sweet side,' he would say thoughtfully, as though the idea had only just occurred to him, and then, seeing the gable of a cottage in the evening light, he would climb laboriously over a stone wall and search for a dry stone to sit on, cracking jokes about his own softness. 'Turner, of course, sat in a wet ditch to paint.' Then, in the late evening he stood at the door of his little house, leaning against the jamb to take the weight from off his bad foot, his hands in his trousers pockets and his small, dark, handsome head thrown lazily back as he talked endlessly about writers and writing, lost to everything else, a man mad on literature. And remembering him like this I find myself humming the song I made Hendrick teach me: *Herr Walther von der Vogelweid, der ist mein Meister gewesen.*

But self-control like his exacts a terrible price from the artist and already, like the king in his own play, weary of struggle with the world, he must have been brooding on abdication before those who seemed to exercise real authority, even though it could never be more than a shadow of his own.

16

Then came the Truce. It was an extraordinary event that deserves a whole book to itself, though, so far as I know, no one has ever tried to describe it. It had all been announced and prepared for, but it was quite impossible to believe it would really happen. Then, a little before noon on Monday, July 11, 1921, when I was still a few months short of eighteen, a slow procession of armoured cars, tanks and patrols began to move back on Cork Barrack, and I walked along beside it. There were little crowds in every street, all watchful and silent, since everyone realized that anything might yet happen. Then, as the Angelus rang out from the city churches, the barrack gates were thrown open and tanks, armoured cars, officers and men filed in. Here and there a man would turn and give a derisive hoot at the silent crowd. Then the barrack gates closed, and the crowd began to move away quietly with bewildered looks. Did it really mean that it was all over? That there would be no more five o'clock curfew and that one could walk that night as late as one pleased without being shot? That one could sleep in one's own bed? That it really represented the end of seven hundred years of military occupation, the triumph of the imagination over material power, the impossible become law?

All that perfect summer young men who had been for years in hiding drove about the country in commandeered cars, drinking, dancing, brandishing their guns. In the evening the local Volunteers, their numbers vastly increased by careful young men who were now beginning to think that after all there might be something in this for them, drilled openly and learned how to use rifles and machine guns.

And then, in the depth of winter, came the Treaty with England, which granted us everything we had ever sought except an independent republican government and control of the loyalist province of Ulster. The withholding of these precipitated a Civil War, which, in the light of what we know now, might have been anticipated by anyone with sense, for it was merely an extension into the fourth dimension of the improvisation that had begun after the crushing of the insurrection in 1916. The Nationalist movement had split up into the Free State Party, who accepted the treaty with England, and the Republicans who opposed it by force of arms, as the Irgun was to do much later in Israel. Ireland had improvised a government, and clearly no government that claimed even a fraction less than the imaginary government had claimed could attract the loyalty of young men and women with imagination. They were like a theatre audience that, having learned to dispense with fortuitous properties, lighting and scenery and begun to appreciate theatre in the raw, were being asked to content themselves with cardboard and canvas. Where there is nothing, there is reality.

But meanwhile the improvisation had cracked: the English could have cracked it much sooner merely by yielding a little to it. When, after election results had shown that a majority of the people wanted the compromise – and when would *they* not have accepted a compromise? – our side continued to maintain that the only real government was the imaginary one, or the few shadowy figures that remained of it, we were acting on the unimpeachable logic of the imagination, that only what exists in the mind is real. What we ignored was that a whole section of the improvisation had cut itself adrift and become a new and more menacing reality. The explosion of the dialectic, the sudden violent emergence of thesis and antithesis from the old synthesis, had occurred under our very noses and we could not see it or control it. Rory O'Connor and Melowes in seizing the Four Courts were merely echoing Patrick Pearse and the seizure of the Post Office, and Michael Collins, who could so easily have starved them out with a few pickets, imitated the English pattern by blasting the Four Courts with borrowed artillery. And what neither group saw was that every word we said, every act we committed, was a destruction of the improvisation and what we were bringing about was a new Establishment of Church and State in which imagination would play no part, and young men and women would emigrate to the ends of the earth, not because the country was poor, but because it was mediocre.

To say that I took the wrong side would promote me to a degree of intelligence I had not reached. I took the Republican side because it was Corkery's. Breen was going round in a fury, saying we were all 'bleddy eejits', as though we were no better than Catholic priests or German musicians, and O'Faolain shared his views. I still saw life through a veil of literature – the only sort of detachment available to me – though the passion for poetry was merging into a passion for the nineteenth-century novel, and I was tending to see the Bad Girl of the neighbourhood not as 'one more unfortunate' but as Madame Bovary or Nastasya Filipovna, and the Western Road –

the evening promenade of clerks and shopgirls – as the Nevsky Prospekt.

In such a set-up it was only natural that Hendrick and I should be installed as censors of the local newspaper and, as we had no real news, compelled to fill it with bad patriotic verse by our superiors, who had a passion for writing about the woes of dear old Ireland. It was a great triumph when O'Faolain walked in one night and gave us a good poem, for it seemed as if the right people were coming round. It was also only natural that I, on the basis of an intimate acquaintance with Tolstoy's *Sebastopol*, should be cast for the part of war correspondent. It was a shock for us both when one day one of the Dublin publicity people walked into the office and took an agency message we were printing, describing a raid on the house of Mrs Pearse, and re-wrote it under our eyes as: 'Great indignation has been expressed in Dublin at the raiding of the house of Mrs Pearse, the widowed mother of the martyred Irish leader, P. H. Pearse.' It was clear to us that in some ways the Dublin group were much cleverer than we.

This was how we came to meet Erskine Childers, one of the great romantic figures of the period – a distinguished British officer with Irish family connexions who had written a remarkably prophetic thriller that anticipated the First World War and, after it ended, returned to Ireland to serve the Irish cause. Our first glimpse of him was disappointing. He came down the stairs of the Victoria Hotel, limping and frowning; a small, slight, grey-haired man in tweeds with a tweed cap pulled over his eyes, wearing a light mackintosh stuffed with papers and carrying another coat over his arm. Apart from his accent, which would have identified him anywhere, there was something peculiarly English about him; something that nowadays reminds me of some old parson or public-school teacher I have known, conscientious to a fault and overburdened with minor cares. His thin, grey face, shrunk almost to its mould of bone, had a coldness as though life had contracted behind it to its narrowest span; the brows were puckered in a triangle of obsessive thought like pain, and the eyes were clear, pale and tragic. 'All sicklied o'er with the pale cast of thought', Corkery quoted after he met him. Later, Childers's friend, George Russell, asked me if I thought he was taking drugs. I was certain he wasn't, but I knew what Russell meant, for I have seen a look exactly like that on the faces of drug addicts.

We went down Patrick Street towards our headquarters on the

Grand Parade, and halfway there Childers paused and frowned. He had been instructed to register under a false name at the hotel, but had he remembered to do so or given his own name by mistake? I returned to the hotel to check and, sure enough, he had registered as Mr Smith – Mr John Smith, I feel sure. Later, in our head-quarters, we showed him the local political paper that O'Faolain was producing at his own expense, and he passed indifferently over my poem and Hendrick's sketch, and lit with what seemed an inspired lack of taste on O'Faolain's article, 'Khaki or Green?' which, for him, put the whole political situation into a slogan. It was a trick I was to notice in him again and again, and it left me disillusioned. This was a sort of mind I had never met before.

A day or two later Hendrick and I, coming back to work, noticed him drifting aimlessly along King Street, his hands deep in the pockets of his mackintosh. It amused us to watch the way he stopped and started again. Once he stopped to stare in a shop-window that, when we reached it, turned out to be full of women's underclothes. He had a sort of doddering, drooping absent-mindedness that at times resembled that of a person in a comedy. We had been following him for a few minutes when we noticed that someone else was doing the same. This was a shabbily dressed man who seemed to have little experience of following anybody. When Childers stopped and looked in a shop-window he did so too. When Childers went on he went on, following step by step.

Knowing Cork as we did, we had no difficulty in getting ahead of them both, and as Childers passed the laneway into the English Market, we pulled him in, told him what was happening, and asked for his gun. He was very alarmed at our manner, but with old-fashioned politeness he turned aside, unbuttoned one mackintosh, then another, then a jacket and finally a waistcoat. Just over his heart and fixed to his braces by a safety pin was a tiny delicately made gun such as a middle-aged lady of timid disposition might carry in her handbag.

We waited to let the shadow pick him up again, and then we picked up the shadow and took him up another lane off the South Mall. As a spy he was not much good, but as interrogators we were worse, and we let him go when we had taken his name and address and given him a talking-to. Besides, we didn't take it seriously. It wasn't until weeks later we found out that Childers – 'the damned Englishman', as Griffith had called him – was the one man the Provisional Government was bent on killing.

When we returned the toy gun to Childers he looked happy for the first time since we had met him. He had not worried himself about being shadowed but was concerned for the loss of his gun and drove the other people in the office distracted inquiring whether Hendrick and I were responsible enough to be entrusted with it. He pinned it back on his braces as if it was a flower he was pinning to his buttonhole and told us in the dry tone that Englishmen reserve for intimate revelations that it was a present from a friend. Someone told me later that the friend was Michael Collins, the enemy Commander-in-Chief. True or not, that was certainly in character.

I accompanied him soon after to General Headquarters in Fermoy. It was a bright summer morning, and I still remember how I first saw the mountains over Mitchelstown in a frame of wayside trees and felt that at last I was going to see something of Ireland. We stood in the barrack square at Fermoy and saw the generals emerge from a staff meeting, some in uniform, others in civilian clothes with bandoleers and belts. One carried a Lewis gun over his shoulder – a general cannot be too careful. Afterwards we had lunch in the Officers' Mess. Liam Lynch presided in uniform, looking like the superior of an enclosed order in disguise. The meal was a strange mixture of awkwardness and heartiness such as went on in officers' messes on the enemy side when local tradesmen and clerks sat down to dinner in quarters they had once approached by the servants' entrance. That night Childers fixed a bedside lamp for himself so that it would not interfere with the pair of us who shared his room, and when I woke during the night he was still reading and trying to smother a persistent cough so as not to wake us. He was reading *Twenty Years After*. I was reading *The Idiot* and felt sorry that he did not read more improving books. Though I had cast myself for the part of Tolstoy at Sebastopol, I was going through a phase that favoured Dostoevsky and Whitman.

Next night I found myself in Ashill Towers near Kilmallock, a pseudo-Gothic castle that we had taken over as headquarters for our front line. If only I had realized it, it was here that the genius of improvisation had taken complete charge. In Buttevant and Fermoy we had real military barracks, complete with officers' messes; we had an armoured car – a most improbable-looking vehicle, like the plywood tank that captured a Chinese town where a friend was living, flying a large streamer that read 'Particularly Fierce Tank'. We even had a Big Gun that had been made by a Dubliner who had brought it with him to Buttevant along with the nine shells he had made for it and the tenth that was still in process of construction. But the front line was our pride and joy. We had improvised almost everything else but never a front line. The enemy were reported to be on the point of attacking it, and in the library the local officers were hard at work over their maps deciding which bridges to blow up in the track of their advance.

In the long Gothic hall there were fifty or sixty men at either side of the long trestle tables in the candle-light, their rifles slung over their shoulders. The hall seemed to tremble with the flickering of the candles, and tusked and antlered heads peered down from the half-darkness as though even they couldn't believe what they were seeing. Suddenly a young man sprang on a table with a rifle in his hand and sang Canon Sheehan's romantic version of the old outlaw song of Sean O'Dwyer of the Valley. He had a fine untrained Irish tenor, with the vibrant, almost exasperating emotional quality of the pure head voice.

After Aughrim's great disaster,
When the foe in sooth was master,
It was you who first plunged in and swam
The Shannon's boiling flood. . . .

In the early morning, with the news of enemy movements all along the front, I was sent with a char-à-banc to bring reinforcements from Croom. That, too, thrilled me, because I knew that Croom was an old fortress of the O'Donovans from which we had been expelled in the twelfth century by Donal O'Brien. There was a red glow in the sky as I went from house to house in the little town, hammering on the doors with the butt of a carbine which somebody had given me to keep me happy. When I had brought back the reinforcements I was sent to Divisional Headquarters in Buttevant with despatches for the Divisional Commander Liam Deasy, but he disappointed all my expectations by ignoring the despatches, telling me I looked very tired, and putting me to bed in his own room. He was the kindest man I'd met in my short military experience, and to be put to bed by the General was as much as any young Cherubino could ask, but I wasn't satisfied. It struck me that the General wasn't taking the despatches seriously enough, and after a couple of sleepless hours, I went out into the barrack square to look for him. I wasn't the only one who was doing it. There was a column of men lined up there – the angriest-looking men I'd ever seen – and their officers asked me where General Deasy was. I didn't know, I said; I was just looking for him myself. 'Well, when you find him, tell him we're the Limerick column,' the officer said. 'We're after fighting our way down from Patrickswell, and when we got here the Corkmen had meat for their breakfast and we had none. Tell him if the Limerick men don't get meat there'll be mutiny.'

I found Deasy on his way from Mass and he took the news of the possible mutiny as calmly as he'd taken the news of the expected assault on the front line. He gave me despatches for Kilmallock, and warned me urgently to check with the officer in charge of Charleville to make sure there were no enemy troops between me and the front. I took this as a rather fussy precaution dictated by the importance of the despatches, but afterwards I wondered if the General had quite as much faith in our front line as everyone else seemed to have.

It was a sunny summer morning, and on my way I picked up a little hunchback wearing a Red Cross armlet who was making his way to the front on foot, apparently on the off-chance that there might be scope there for an enterprising one-man medical service. At the time that struck me as the most natural thing in the world, whereas nowadays I merely wonder what revelation had been given that little hunchback in whatever back lane he came from to send him trudging off by himself on the roads of Ireland, looking for a battlefield where he might come in useful.

At Charleville I checked with the local commandant. He was still in bed but he assured me that there wasn't an enemy soldier within miles. What he failed to remember was that it was Sunday, and on Sunday the whole Irish race is unanimously moved to go to Mass, so that at that very moment our whole nine-mile front, pickets, machine-gun posts, fortresses and all, had simply melted away, and there wasn't as much as a fallen tree between me and the enemy. In itself that mightn't have been too bad because it might also be assumed that there wouldn't be any enemy pickets either; but a considerable number of the enemy facing us were from the neighbourhood of Charleville, and after his longing for Mass, an Irishman's strongest characteristic is his longing for home and Mother, and anyone who knew his Ireland would have guessed that on that fine summer morning our whole front was being pierced in a dozen places by nostalgic enemy soldiers, alone or in force, all pining to embrace their mothers and discover if the cow had calved.

Just before the real trouble began I saw the people coming from

Mass in a small wayside church. They looked curiously at the car, and I thought how peaceful it all was, the flat, green country and the tall sunshot hedges and the people coming from Mass in their Sunday clothes. And then men in half-uniform emerged from the hedges, levelling their rifles at us and signalling us on. I wasn't worried; I knew they must be our own men, but my driver hissed 'Eat them!', obviously referring to the despatches, and I guessed I must be wrong. He had probably seen despatches eaten in the movies, because even a horse couldn't have got down Deasy's despatches in the minute or two that remained to me, so I tore them up and scattered them. In the high wind they blew across the field beyond retrieving. Then we reached a road block manned by an officer and half a dozen men and were stopped. I had left my carbine in Ashill Towers and had nothing but my camera and *The Idiot*. The camera was taken though the book was returned. The officer was stupid, truculent and argumentative, and my temper was in a shocking state. It had just dawned on me that on my first day in action I had allowed myself to be made prisoner, that a brilliant career as war correspondent had been closed to me, and that the front line might sway to and fro for years in great battles like those of the First World War but that someone else would be its Tolstoy. When he said something nasty I called him and his men a gang of traitors. It was typical of things at the time that I could say it and get away with it. Six months later, it would have been very different. Just then everyone had a slightly bewildered air as though he were wondering how on earth such things could happen to *him*. After all, it is not every day that the dialectic blows up in your face and you, who have always regarded yourself as the victim, wake up to find yourself a tyrant.

The enemy headquarters was in a farmhouse a few hundred yards down a by-road that ran close to the railway, and as I was the bearer of the despatches and obviously a ring-leader of some sort, I was packed off with a soldier at either side and a third man with a drawn revolver behind. He was still smarting under my abuse and he fired at my heel. The little soldier on my left dropped his rifle, threw up his hands, and fell. When I knelt beside him he was unconscious, and the man with the revolver went into hysterics, rushed to the other side of the road, and clutched his head and wept. The third soldier went to console him, so, as it was obvious that no one else would do anything practical for the unconscious man, I opened his tunic to look for a wound. What I would do with it if I found it was more than I had thought of, but at least I was better qualified as a hospital orderly than my one-man medical service, for he only shouted into the prostrate man's ear what he thought was an Act of Contrition but was really the Creed. I had my hand on the soldier's heart when he opened his eyes and said: '—ye all!' It was simple and final. Then he rose with great dignity, dusted himself, buttoned his tunic, shouldered his rifle and resumed his march. Like myself he wasn't much of a soldier, but he had *savoir faire*.

I sat on the floor of the farmhouse parlour with several other prisoners – civilian truck drivers whose trucks had been commandeered for the campaign and were now standing outside in the farmyard. The woman of the house brought me dinner, but the look of the fat bacon made me sick. I wasn't a drinker, but just then I needed a drink badly, and the senior enemy officer, whose name seemed to be Mossie O'Brien, promised to buy me a flask of whiskey at the first pub we passed. He had the same sort of good humour as Deasy, and I liked him as much as I disliked his truculent second-in-command.

At last his column, having collected all the local gossip, prepared to return into exile with their prizes; the engines of the trucks and cars were started, and I was actually being helped into one truck when a couple of shots rang out and we all dashed back to the farmhouse for cover. Our front-line troops had returned from Mass, indignant at what they regarded as a coward's blow, and the enemy were cut off from their base. At least I fervently hoped they were cut off. I was beginning to have my own doubts about our front line.

Back in the front room the enemy soldiers barricaded the little window with bags of meal and a can of pitch. The first blast of machine-gun fire from our Particularly Fierce Armoured Car knocked the pitch right over my driver's head. The realization that we had an armoured car at all depressed the defenders greatly. Except that it was top secret and had been withheld even from me, I should have told them that we had a Big Gun and nine shells as well. There were rifles stacked against the wall behind me, and several times I thought of grabbing one and turning it on the garrison – not because I was particularly brave but because I realized that they were even more scared than I was. At the same time, I knew that there was no help to be expected from my fellow prisoners. They were just saying their prayers. All I could do was to spread alarm and consternation before our men got cross and blew up the house. O'Brien came in and muttered to the other officer that a man had been killed upstairs, and I passed it on. I had to yell it at the deaf man who was reclining on my chest, and he shared my views of the gravity of the situation.

'Will we surrender now, Mossie?' he asked O'Brien, who was going out.

'Not till the last shot is fired,' O'Brien said shortly.

'What did he say?' asked the deaf man.

'Not till the last shot is fired,' I repeated with regret. I liked O'Brien, and I wished he wouldn't be quite so soldierly. I was tired of war and wanted to go home. I felt my first expedition into the heart of Ireland had brought me quite enough material to go on with. I knew that in Cork they would now be coming back down the Western Road after a walk along the river, and I longed to be there with Hendrick, telling him the story without waiting to see what might really happen. The deaf man too appeared to have an urgent engagement, because he began to unload his bandoleer into my coat pockets.

And after all the nonsense I had read about the excitement of one's baptism of fire, I was finding it intolerably dull. It just went on and on. The trucks and cars were still roaring in the farmyard, but one by one, as the petrol gave out or a bullet hit a petrol tank, they fell silent like the instruments at the end of Haydn's 'Farewell' symphony, and at last nothing was to be heard but occasional bursts of fire. It drew on to evening, and with the little window barricaded, we were almost in darkness. The disagreeable officer was firing his revolver dispiritedly out of the window and singing 'You Called Me Baby Doll a Year Ago' in a voice of agonizing tunelessness. The deaf man fell asleep on my chest and breathed nice and evenly at me through it all.

Then came a noise that woke even him, and then a silence, and then a hysterical voice upstairs shouting 'Rifle grenade!' This was followed immediately by another voice shouting 'Mossie is kilt!' and at once everyone began to wail 'We surrender! We surrender!' Someone took out a large handkerchief and pushed it through the window on a rifle barrel, but it went unnoticed and renewed fire filled them all with despair. They were arguing about what they should do next when I grabbed the handkerchief myself and ran out. A soldier opened the door and closed it fast behind me. I waved the handkerchief, but though shots continued to go off all round me there wasn't a soul to be seen. Everything was blended in a rich, moss-green watery light, while from a mile away over the Limerick grasslands came the distracted lowing of cows who had gone unmilked and were sure the end of the world was coming. The first man to climb the fence and approach the house was an old neighbour, Joe Ryan, but the look on his long, pale face was that of a man drunk with noise and tension, and I realized that I was in great danger of being shot myself, through pure excitement. Once more heavy firing began from some distance away, and everyone bolted for cover, convinced that it was all a trap. I had a terrible job persuading both sides of the general good faith, all the time steering round behind me a group of prisoners who were in a highly nervous state and determined on regarding me as an old and intimate friend from whom they could not possibly be separated, and as proof of their affection they loaded me with rifles and bandoleers. Once I did have to intervene when a man with a drawn revolver attacked one of the prisoners whom he had recognized. As an example of the classic peripeteia soldiers after a surrender are remarkable: at one moment lords of the world dispensing life and death, at the next begging for their lives.

At the back of the house O'Brien, who had been shot through the mouth, was coughing up great gouts of blood while an old priest knelt beside him. Two soldiers brought downstairs the body of the young man who had been killed. He had been shot through the nostril, and the dried blood made a mocking third eye across his cheek, so that he might have been winking at us. Someone put a cap across his face; I saw that it was mine but I left it with him. I saw another civilian cap on the ground and I picked it up; caps cost money, and I knew if I came home without one I should hear about it from Father. It was only later that I realized I had picked up the dead boy's cap, which was drenched with blood. An old man and his daughter emerged from a cupboard under the stairs and asked: 'Is it all over now, sir?'

Having seen the prisoners safe into Buttevant Barrack, I made my way home to Cork by the first car. I wanted to get my story into print and, besides, I felt I had seen quite enough of the war for the time being. Nowadays I merely wonder at my own behaviour and remember with revulsion that I once wore a dead boy's blood-stained cap. It was not merely that I couldn't afford to lose a cap. I fancy the truth is that nothing of it was real to me, and it never once occurred to me that the boy whose cap I was wearing had that day been as living as myself, and perhaps loved his mother as much as I did mine. It was all as if I had read about it in *War and Peace*.

I doubt if most other people found it very real either. A few days later I accompanied Childers again to the 'front', as I was now beginning to think of it. At Buttevant Barrack I met his cousin, David Robinson, who was in charge of the cavalry, such as it was. Robinson was another 'damned Englishman', but of the sort I get along with. He was a typical British cavalry officer of the old school with a wide-brimmed hat, a coat that was old but elegant, well-cut riding breeches and top-boots. He had a glass eye, a long, pale, beaky face and the rather languid manner of a hard-boiled, soft-hearted gambler.

Childers wanted statements from our wounded, so he and I and a third man visited the Military Hospital where, as usual, I disgraced myself, for inside the door with his head in bandages was a young enemy officer and I gave one startled look at him and then wrung his hands and said: 'Mossie O'Brien!' I am, as I have said, a natural collaborationist, and O'Brien must have had the same weakness, for when he left hospital it was to join one of our columns. He was captured by his own side and sentenced to death, but escaped from the prison and lived to run a garage in his native town. On the other hand, my driver, for all his old guff about eating the despatches, was reported to have ended up on the other side. That was how things happened. What, after all, do you do when a well-established synthesis blows up on you but wonder whether you are really riding in the right compartment?

Childers also wanted to see the front line for himself. We had to walk along a road and across a railway bridge that was covered by enemy machine guns, and when I saw the officer in charge take cover and run I did the same, but Childers walked coolly across, studying the country and apparently unaware of danger. This, of course, was partly the attitude of the professional soldier who always knows by instinct when and where to take cover, but I felt there was also an element of absent-mindedness about it – the absent-mindedness of the old schoolmaster or parson who is so worried about what to do with Jones Minor's peculiar habits that he has no time to worry about himself. That night I watched him again in Ashill Towers, where the same country boys whose military genius I no longer had faith in occupied the upholstered chairs and studied their maps. There being no chair for Childers, nor anyone who valued his advice on military matters, he sat on a petrol can by the open door, his cap over his eyes and his mackintosh trailing on the floor, and went on scribbling his endless memoranda, articles and letters, like some old book-keeper who fears the new directors may think him superfluous. A tall, good-looking young American war correspondent who interviewed him on the petrol can congratulated him on Corkery's poem 'Old Town of Gaelic Saint', which Hendrick and I had just published.

'Oh, yes,' said Childers with a worried air, 'but have you seen Mr Brennan's poems – "Churchill Gave the Orders but England Gave the Guns"?' He always liked to keep conversation on a serious level.

My last experience of the front was when I was sent back to Buttevant Barrack to collect the Big Gun and the nine shells. The enemy had ensconced themselves in a substantial parsonage and could not be dislodged by rifle- and machine-gun fire. When I reached the barrack, the armourer, who had brought his beloved gun all the way from Dublin with him, was still working on the tenth shell and didn't want the gun fired till the shell was finished. But my orders were peremptory, and we loaded the little weapon and its shells on the back seat of my car. A mile or two from the parsonage we were intercepted by the officer in charge of the attack, and I was sent back to Buttevant with fresh instructions, so that I never really saw the weapon in action. Next day, however, I heard that after the first shell had been fired the enemy rushed out of the parsonage with their hands in the air but, as in Kilmallock, this gesture had gone unnoticed. When the second shell sailed over their heads they came to the conclusion that they were to be massacred whether they surrendered or not, and took to their heels across the country. But this too went unobserved, and the whole nine shells were fired at the parsonage, without hitting it once.

I am not reporting what I saw, merely what I heard, but I do know that stranger things happened.

17

Childers was at the front when Cork was attacked from the sea – a possibility our military geniuses had overlooked. Technically, a landing from the sea is supposed to be one of the most difficult of military operations, but as we handled the defence it was a walk-over. Hendrick and I had just got out our mimeographed news-sheet, describing the total defeat of the enemy; the newspaper boys were crying it through the streets, and Hendrick had fallen asleep on a pile of newsprint when I noticed the victors tearing through the city at forty miles an hour in the direction of the western highlands. We went to Headquarters at Union Quay to find out what we should say in our next number, but when we saw what was going on there we didn't even bother to inquire. There was a crowd of bewildered men in the roadway outside and a senior officer was waving his arms and shouting: 'Every man for himself.' We were both rather shaken. I was quite good on the Retreat from Moscow, but it looked as though the Retreat from Cork was going to be serious. Everybody was in a frenzy; it was no use asking for instructions or trying to bum a lift, so we locked up our office and set off on foot up the Western Road. Corkery had a little cottage in Inniscarra, five or six miles up the River Lee, where he was having a painting holiday, and we made up our minds to walk there and ask his advice. We never doubted but that he would know what to do in any emergency, literary, social or military.

In spite of our bewilderment, it was an enchanting walk on a summer afternoon, climbing gently with the river till we passed the little abbey graveyard where my Grandfather O'Connor was buried, and we didn't mind the cars and lorries that tore past us literally in hundreds. Corkery favoured our pressing on to Macroom to find out if we were still wanted, and after he had given us a meal, we stood in the roadway with him, trying to halt one of the vehicles that went by. Childers was hanging frantically on the running board of one car, and he waved gaily to us as it passed. Naturally, nobody had thought of offering the 'damned Englishman' his seat. Finally a truck came by at a crawl and it stopped at our signal and Corkery saw us aboard. When we had been travelling for a few minutes Hendrick suggested to the driver that he might put on a little more speed. It was only then we realized that we had got on to a lorry of explosives. Hendrick began to sing the poem O'Faolain had given us to print. It was to the tune of 'John Brown's Body' and began: 'In Clareside and in Kerryside we've buried fighting men.' When he finished, the driver asked for another song, and I decided that our situation must be desperate indeed.

Neither Hendrick nor I had been in Macroom before, though it was the capital of the Irish-speaking west, but we got little chance of seeing what it was like because Corkery was there almost as soon as we were. Having seen us off, he had decided in his gentle, fatherly way that we were incapable of looking after ourselves, abandoned his painting holiday, and set off on our tracks. How he got a ride I don't know unless he actually shot one of the drivers, but there he was, and he dragged us back to Williams's Hotel, where he was staying. Childers was there as well. In the middle of the night some noisy men, pleading fatigue, began to hammer on our doors with rifle butts and demand our beds. We told them to go to Hell, but Childers got up at once and spent the rest of the night wandering about Macroom.

Next day the army was disbanded, all but special units like the engineers and ourselves. The staff had apparently realized that keeping an army in the field entailed too much work and had decided to revert to the sort of fighting it was accustomed to, sleeping in farmhouses, dropping down to the local pubs for a drink, and taking an occasional shot at a barrack or a lorry. The army was furious – naturally, since some of the poor devils were faced with an eighty-mile walk home – but Hendrick and myself, regarded as indispensable, felt complacent. David Robinson, who had retreated in excellent order from Ballincollig with horses and field kitchen, gave us lunch on the lawn before Macroom Castle. It was a queer party before the medieval castle with its crude Renaissance doorway; David Robinson putting everyone at his ease exactly as though he owned the place; members of the hungry disbanded army looking on; and exotic-looking women with queer accents arriving from Dublin with despatches warning us that the members of the Free State Government were determined on killing Childers. He was talking to Hendrick and me when one of them came up and said earnestly: 'You know they will kill you if they catch you, Mr Childers,' and he turned away and said wearily: 'Oh, why does everyone tell me that?' Robinson was the only one who took the report seriously. He realized, as we didn't, that in a family row it is always the outsider who gets the blame. He took Hendrick and myself aside and asked if we would join him in hiring a fishing boat at Bantry and putting Childers ashore in France. France! To me it sounded like all the adventure stories of the world rolled into one, and even Hendrick, who made a point of not being demonstrative, looked enthusiastic. But we got a cold reception when we tried to explain Robinson's fears to members of the staff. 'Staff-Captain Childers is under my command,' said one of them, pulling rank on us, and though probably no one but Robinson suspected it, Childers' fate was decided that afternoon. The only man who could have saved him was De Valera, and he was somewhere in North Cork.

Instead, we commandeered a printing machine from the local job printers and had it carried to the schoolhouse at Ballymakeera, an Irish-speaking village in the mountains west of Macroom. To me, who had never seen the wilder parts of Ireland, Ballymakeera looked dry and cold, and the stones stuck up through the soil. Corkery, having seen us settled, went off to finish his painting holiday in the inn at Gougane Barra at the other side of the mountains. He had also probably asked a half-dozen people to keep an eye on us, though that didn't occur to me till I learned he had been hearing slanders about me. I don't deny that I may have given grounds for slander. It was the first time I had found myself in a purely Irish-speaking neighbourhood, and the phonetics went clean to my head. One day I sat for a full hour in the parlour of the little farmhouse, listening to a small boy outside playing numeral games and letting the sounds sink into my memory. My grandmother, of course, had spoken excellent Irish, but her teeth were not so good. I became very attached to the farmer, who also spoke excellent Irish and sometimes sat with me in the front room, talking or tapping out on his knee little rhymes he made up about me, like:

My son, Mick,
My son, Mick,
My son, Mick,
He is a fine man.

As one can see they were not very good rhymes, but they were in good Irish and, anyway, I can stand any number of rhymes in my own praise. I also fell in love with his elder daughter, whose gentle, blond, lethargic beauty was as breath-taking as her Irish, and she spoke that as I had never heard it spoken before, with style. Unfortunately, I had no notion of how to make love to her, because she appeared to me through a veil of characters from books I had read. Most of the time she was Maryanka from *The Cossacks*.

I loved everything else about that family – the warmth of the farmer, the cynicism of his wife, the wit and malice of the younger daughter and the grave humour of the elder. Above all, I loved their perfect manners. They worked about three times as hard as anybody I had ever met, and Hendrick and I must have been pests, but they never showed it, and only afterwards when I learned to speak Irish properly did I realize what it must have cost them to listen to me speaking it.

But neither Tolstoy nor phonetics was in Childers' line at all. He asked petulantly why I went round as a walking arsenal (any fool could have told him I only did it to impress the girl I was in love with) and when his landlady would have her annual bath. He settled down with the printing press we had commandeered and went on with his articles and memoranda, and in his leisure hours sat under the apple tree in the schoolhouse garden and read *Deerslayer*. As I say, his literary standards were not high. One evening a couple of men burst in with the news that Michael Collins had been killed in an ambush near Bandon. I think they had the evening paper with them. Anyhow, they were rejoicing, and Hendrick and I rejoiced as well, and it was only later I remembered how Childers slunk away to his table silently, lit a cigarette, and wrote a leading article in praise of Collins. At the same time the newspapers continued to appear with bloodier stories of the fights and ambushes Childers himself was supposed to have led, and Hendrick and I only laughed at them. We, who didn't even know how to redraft and slant an agency message, couldn't be expected to understand how clever men prepare the way for someone's execution. Now, when I think of all the leads we got, I can only wonder all over again at our innocence.

At the same time, I fancy that Childers would have been very happy with a column to lead. I never for an instant saw under the weary, abstract superficies of a sick and unhappy man, but I could read, and I knew that Dumas and Fenimore Cooper meant a lot to him. One night when a raid was supposed to take place, Childers got leave to join it – purely as an observer, of course – and worked himself into something that in an Englishman almost constituted a 'state'. There was a dance at the village hall, and the men stacked their rifles and danced 'The Walls of Limerick' and 'The Waves of Tory' before leaving for the battle. I couldn't dance, and the daughter of the house looked as though she might be busy for another hour, so I accompanied him back to the schoolhouse where the car was to pick him up. An American journalist went with us.

'Doesn't it remind you of Waterloo?' the American asked gently, referring to the noise of the dance hall behind us. ' "There was a sound of revelry by night" – you remember Byron?' Hendrick and I were not the only ones who worked at improving Childers' taste. Americans did it too, quite a lot, but it never seemed to have much effect on Childers.

'And you will remember the article on "Women in the War", won't you?' he asked anxiously. It wasn't a rebuke, but after all the years it comes back to me as a rebuke, to me rather than the American.

We left Childers at the schoolhouse, and he fell asleep over his trestle table. Nobody bothered to pick him up. After all, he was only a damned Englishman, elderly, sick and absent-minded. Next time he got news of a raid, he took care to be on the spot, and as he unpinned his precious .22 from his braces, he gave Hendrick instructions about what to do with all his papers if he was killed. Next afternoon, Hendrick and I were sitting on the grass in the schoolhouse garden when he stepped out of a car, shrugging his shoulders disconsolately. 'I'll never understand this country,' he muttered. 'I thought I was going off to a bloody combat, and instead, I found myself in Mick Sullivan's feather bed in Kilnamartyr.' The truth is that soldiering as Childers and Robinson understood it was too professional for our lads, who were amateurs to a man. It wasn't that they were less brave; it was simply that they had other things to attend to. Robinson decided to form a column and came to the schoolhouse one day to ask myself and Hendrick to join it, but once again we were blocked, and that was a great loss to literature, because during its brief existence, the column became a legend. Robinson was supposed to have planned one attack on the village of Inchigeela, in which, disguised as a tinker and carrying a baby, he would drive on a ass-cart to the barrack door, shoot the sentry, and hold the way open for his men. It was reported that before the engagement he addressed his troops, warning them that this would probably be the last time some of them would meet, and put such terror into them that they made at once for the hills, while Robinson, going from door to door, trying to borrow a baby, complained of the lack of patriotism in Irish mothers.

I find that difficult to believe, unless Robinson, with his dotty

English sense of humour, was doing it as a joke, but there is certainly some truth in another story, for his column *did* capture the town of Kenmare, and then enemy reinforcements arrived and his troops took to their heels. Someone told me that the last he saw of Robinson was as he knelt in the middle of the Main Street, firing at the advancing troops and shouting over his shoulder in his English public-school drawl: 'Come back, you Irish cowards!' All he would admit to me about the day in Kenmare was that, as a true British cavalry officer, he had made a boatload of men return under fire to pick up the last refugee from the battle. This turned out to be an Austrian Jew, who could barely speak English but, finding himself unexpectedly in the middle of a battle, decided to make off with the silver. I need hardly say that Robinson was delighted with him and that the two became friends.

It was at this time Corkery, deciding that I had seen enough of active service, ordered me home with him. Somebody had told him I was drinking, which was typical of Ireland, where a man can't have a private life and anyway, quite untrue, because drinking, like lovemaking and fighting, was something I still saw through a heavy veil of literature, and all the money Hendrick and I had was the remains of ten shillings we had borrowed from O'Faolain. Now if he had said I was going to hell with phonetics, I should have understood him at once. It was all no good. Corkery was convinced I was disgracing myself and Ireland, and home I must go. I remembered it later as the one occasion when I didn't want to go home, when I might almost have said like Faust to the flying moment: '*Verweile doch, du bist so schön!*'

Because of blown-up bridges, we had a long and wearisome ride home, getting out to let our car go across muddy fields, and we were finally dumped in a village miles from Cork. It was then I saw the Napoleon who was lost in Corkery, for he went straight to the house of a rich farmer and, keeping his hand in his trouser pocket as though he had a gun, commandeered a pony and trap to take us the rest of the way to town.

After this, there was less fighting and less laughter. I slept away from home whenever I could find a bed, as much to escape Father as the enemy. News from the dear country I had left was bad. A whole edition of Childers' papers was thrown into a ditch because it had become too dangerous to transport. His printing press went over a mountain slope into a bog-hole and could not be rescued. Finally, he set off with Hendrick to headquarters and, since there was no further use for him, offered to remain and address envelopes. He was told – rather tactlessly, I thought – that he was a much-wanted man, and his presence was a danger to others.

So he and Robinson set out on a fantastic journey across Ireland, sleeping by day and travelling by night. I hope there is some record of it among his papers, for as Robinson told it to me years later in his light, mocking English way it was like a long section from one of the nineteenth-century adventure stories that Childers loved. One night in North Cork, Robinson, who was cycling beside Childers, skidded into a ditch and broke his shoulder bone. Whe he came to his senses he was in a country cottage and a crowd of people were shouting: 'Take him away! Take him away!' for by this time the two damned Englishmen had become the most unwelcome guests in Ireland. They found shelter in the home of Liam Lynch and, when Robinson's shoulder had healed, resumed their night journeys. Tipperary was so crammed with troops searching for them that they had to cross Slievenamon mountain by night, and in the darkness they tramped up a dry watercourse where a single slip meant death. Dawn was breaking as they got near the top, and there, in the doorway of a cottage, stood a local gallant armed to the teeth, while on the plain beneath them three columns of infantry converged on the mountain. 'Ah, don't be afraid,' the local hero told them. ''Tis me they're after. I went into three towns, and in every town I left a message to tell them where they'd find me.'

Thinking this cottage unsafe, the two hunted men plunged down through a mountain mist to a second cottage, and there they discovered a second national hero in full uniform lying on a sofa while two pretty girls fed him chocolate creams. They finally reached the house of their cousin, Robert Barton – another British officer – in County Wicklow, and were captured there through the treachery of one of Barton's servants. They were given adjoining cells, between which some earlier prisoner had dug a tiny hole. They were both passionate chess-players, so they chalked chessboards on the floor, made chessmen out of newspapers, and played until the morning when Childers went out to die before an Irish firing squad. Robinson's premonitions that afternoon in front of Macroom Castle had been finally justified. The only charge against Childers was the possession of arms – the little toy pistol I had taken from him that day outside the English Market and which he was trying to unpin from his braces when the soldiers grabbed him.

I was in a house on the Wellington Road the morning I read of his execution, and I wrote the date over Whitman's lines on the death of Lincoln in the copy of *Leaves of Grass* that I always carried with me at the time – 'Hushed Be the Camps Today.' Like everything else I did at the time, it reeked of literature, and yet when I recite the lines to myself today, all the emotion comes back and I know it was not all literature. As I say, I am a collaborationist, and Childers was one of the very few people I have met with whom I had no communication of any sort: if, as I hope, his papers of the time have survived, I know that I must appear in them as a sort of Handy Andy, described completely from outside, for there is nothing in nature more removed from the imaginative boy than the grown man who has cut himself apart from life, seems to move entirely by his own inner light, and to face his doom almost with equanimity. And yet again and again in my own imagination, I have had to go through those last few terrible moments with him almost as though I were there: see the slight figure of the little grey-haired Englishman emerge for the last time into the Irish daylight, apparently cheerful and confident but incapable of grandiose gestures, concerned only lest inadvertently he might do or say something that would distress some poor fool of an Irish boy who was about to level an English rifle at his heart.

18

The period from the end of 1922 to the spring of 1923 was one that I found almost unbearably painful. I still had no money nor any way of earning it. Sometimes I slept in the house of Sean French, who was in prison; sometimes I went off with a friend, whom I shall call Joe Clery, and his friend, and the three of us spent the night in a hay-barn or commandeered beds for ourselves in a big house on Montenotte. Clery and his friend fascinated me. Both were swift, cool and resourceful, and seemed to enjoy the atmosphere of danger as much as I dreaded it. Corkery, with whom I discussed them, suggested that the Russian Revolution had shown that, after a certain stage, control of a revolutionary movement passes from the original dreamers to men who are professional revolutionaries.

I am afraid that Corkery saw historical prototypes as I saw literary ones, and that there was more than that to it. The romantic improvisation was tearing right down the middle, and on both sides the real killers were emerging. One morning Clery told me that we were needed for a 'job' that evening. The 'job' was to shoot unarmed soldiers courting their girls in deserted laneways, and the girls as well if there was any danger of our being recognized. I lost my head, and said I would put a stop to the 'job' in one way if I couldn't do it in another. Clery felt as I did and agreed that I should consult Corkery, who was my authority for everything. It was hard luck on Corkery, but he accepted this as he accepted every other responsibility, and advised me to see Mary MacSwiney, Terence's sister and our local representative in Parliament. I went to her house and she received me very coldly. She thought me an indiscreet young man, which, indeed, I was. 'You seem to have some moral objection to killing women', she said disapprovingly, and when I admitted that I had, she added complacently; 'I see no *moral* objection, though there may be a *political* one.' I stayed in her house till a messenger returned from the local commandant to say that the operation had been called off.

It was clear to me that we were all going mad, and yet I could see no way out. The imagination seems to paralyse not only the critical faculty but the ability to act upon the most ordinary instinct of self-preservation. I could be obstinate enough when it came to the killing of unarmed soldiers and girls because this was a basic violation of the imaginative concept of life, whether in the boys' weeklies or the Irish sagas, but I could not detach myself from the political attitudes that gave rise to it. I was too completely identified with them, and to have abandoned them would have meant abandoning faith in myself.

Any moments of relaxation and sanity that came to me were in the few houses I visited, like the Barrys' in Windsor Cottages, the O'Learys' on Gardiner's Hill or the Frenches' on the Wellington Road. The French household consisted of his mother and four sisters. Kitty O'Leary, Hendrick's girl, was a great friend of the family, and when she called, the four sisters mustered about her at the piano and sang all the music-hall songs of the time – 'Oh, It's a Windy Night Tonight, Sally, Sally!' and 'I Left My Love in Avalon' while I listened with the emotions of a seminarist at a ribald party. As a reward, at the end of the evening Kitty played a Schubert Fantasia and sang a couple of seventeenth-century *bergerettes* – *Maman, dites-moi* and *Non, je n'irai plus au bois*. At ten precisely, Mrs French, who looked and talked like someone out of a Jane

Austen novel, asked what I should like to drink, and the 'girls' ranged themselves behind her and laid one finger flat on the top of another to indicate that I must ask for tea. Otherwise they would have to drink hot milk! All these homes were matriarchies. It is an Ireland that is disappearing, an Ireland arranged for the convenience of some particular man, where women – some of whom were more brilliant than any man in the household and risked their lives just as much – worked harder than servant girls and will probably never realize why it is that when I look back on the period, it is of them rather than of their brothers that I think. In those days, when the French girls had drunk their hard-earned cup of tea and gone to bed, and lorries of soldiers tore up the city hills on their sinister errands, I merely read Whitman or hummed:

> Je connais trop le danger
> Ou l'amour pourrait m'engager.

That was a danger that wouldn't really engage me for a good many years, and meanwhile I had other dangers to think of. I was captured effortlessly one spring morning by two Free State soldiers. Fortunately for myself I didn't have a gun. They marched me to their headquarters in the Courthouse.

Imprisonment came as a relief because it took all responsibility out of my hands, and, as active fighting died down and the possibility of being shot in some reprisal execution diminished, it became – what else sums up the period so well? – a real blessing. Not, God knows, that the Women's Gaol in Sunday's Well was anything but a nightmare. The first night I spent there after being taken from the Courthouse I was wakened by the officer of the watch going his round. As he flashed his torch about the cell he told us joyously that there had been a raid on the house of Michael Collins' sister in Blarney Lane and one of the attackers had been captured with a revolver and would be executed. (How was I to know that the irony of circumstances would make me the guest of Michael Collins' sister in that very house before many years had passed?) I fell asleep again, thinking merely that I was very fortunate to be out of the Courthouse where the soldiers would probably have taken it out on me. Towards dawn I was wakened by the tall, bitter-tongued man I knew as 'Mac', and I followed him down the corridor. A Free State officer was standing by the door of one cell, and we went in. Under the window in the gas-light that leaked in from the corridor what seemed to be a bundle of rags was trying to raise itself from the floor. I reached out my hand and shuddered because the hand that took mine was like a lump of dough. When I saw the face of the man whose hand I had taken, I felt sick, because that was also like a lump of dough. 'So that's how you treat your prisoners?' Mac snarled at the officer. Mac, like my father, was an ex-British soldier, and had the old-fashioned attitude that you did not strike a defence-less man. The officer, who in private life was probably a milkman, began some muttered rigmarole about the prisoner's having tried to burn a widow's home and poured petrol over the sleeping children. 'Look at that!' Mac snarled at me, paying no attention to him. 'Skewered through the ass with bayonets!' I waited and walked with the boy to the head of the iron stairs where the suicide net had been stretched to catch any poor soul who found life too hard, and I watched him stagger painfully down in the gas-light. There were only a half-dozen of us there, and we stood and watched the dawn break over the city through the high unglazed windows. A few days later the boy was shot. That scene haunted me for years – partly, I suppose, because it was still uncertain whether or not I should be next, a matter that gives one a personal interest in any execution; partly because of the over-developed sense of pity that had made me always take the part of kids younger or weaker than myself; mainly because I was beginning to think that this was all our roman-ticism came to – a miserable attempt to burn a widow's house, the rifle butts and bayonets of hysterical soldiers, a poor woman of the lanes kneeling in some city church and appealing to a God who could not listen, and then – a barrack wall with some smug humbug of a priest muttering prayers. (I heard him the following Sunday give a sermon on the dangers of company-keeping.) I had been able to think of the Kilmallock skirmish as though it was something I had read of in a book, but the battered face of that boy was some-thing that wasn't in any book, and even ten years later, when I was sitting reading in my flat in Dublin, the door would suddenly open and he would walk in and the book would fall from my hands. Certainly, that night changed something for ever in me.

But I was young, and somehow or other I had to go on living, even in that dreadful place. There were four of us in a cell that had been condemned as inadequate for one, and the one who had orig-inally occupied it had done so in an age when they didn't believe in coddling prisoners. It was seething with vermin. Three of us slept on the floor with our heels to the door and one on the radiator pipes under the window, and that took in the total floor space. My cell-mates were not exactly the type I had been accustomed to, and how ninety per cent of the men in prison had got there at all was beyond me. Cremin was the only one of my cell-mates that I could talk to. He was an ex-British army man with a cruel wound in the belly he had got from the Germans in the First World War. By day he made rings out of shilling pieces impaled on an iron spike while I read *Hermann und Dorothea:* at night, when the other men were kneeling and saying the rosary about the suicide net, he and I sang songs against one another.

The *Hermann und Dorothea* had, of course, come from Corkery, who signed himself 'Martin Cloyne', feeling sure that no one on the enemy side would ever have read his novel or recognized the name of its hero. He complained amusingly of a visit from Clery and his friend, and his sister's discovery of the remains of a half-dozen of stout behind his bookcase – 'These secret, midnight revels, and we in our most innocent slumber!' With the book had come a box of Three Castles cigarettes. Heine, he added, was the proper poet for a man in prison, 'but this, being only a university town, has never heard of Heine.' Characteristically, after this, he sent me tobacco and cigarette papers because, as he said, it might be good for my character to have to roll my own cigarettes. How well that gentle little man understood me!

I replied in the only language I understood. The Women's Prison overlooked the Women's Penitentiary run by the Good Shepherd nuns, and when the penitents walked in the garden in their starched white linen coifs, the prisoners crowded to the tall window recesses and whistled at them through the bars. Someone beside myself was shocked, for after the Rosary on that first night, a small, black, bitter man made an impassioned protest, and I wrote to Corkery to say that the first person I had noticed in gaol was Baburin, the hero of Turgenev's great story. I was still at the stage of seeing Turgenev and Dostoevsky characters everywhere. It was a little closer to reality than Cu Chulainn and Werther, but not much.

Early one morning we were driven through the city to Glanmire Station, and after a long wait in the place where I had already endured so much, we were locked in old-fashioned carriages and the train set off. As it emerged from the tunnel at Rathpeacon we all rushed to the windows to catch a final glimpse of Cork. At Mallow the viaduct was blown up (Childers was supposed to have done it), so we were marched through the town to the railway station. It was April and the whole country looked lovely.

We were locked in our carriages again with nothing but tinned fish to eat, and when the others developed a thirst they could not quench, I was glad I had not been able to eat it. It was dark when we reached Dublin, and after another long halt, we were shunted across the city to Amiens Street and off into the countryside again. The sea was on our righthand side. None of us knew this part of the country, and we had no notion of where we were going. The Free State Government had been negotiating with the British Government for the renting of St Helena to use as a prison, and the general impression was that we were going there. Instead, we stopped at a wayside station in flat pastoral country about an hour's run from Dublin. In the distance a searchlight moved petulantly up and down the sky and over the fields, picking out white-washed cottages and trees in their first leaf and flattening them against the night like pieces of theatre scenery. We marched towards the searchlight, and it flickered along with us, half human in its mechanical precision, till it became a new sensation like hunger and weariness, and gave everything a hallucinatory look.

. At last a group of low, irregular buildings emerged, changing continuously like the images in a kaleidoscope – a long whitewashed hall, a group of dark wooden huts with every board defined by shadow as if by blown snow, a tall gate set in a high fence of barbed wire and lit by arc-lamps. Outside this was another row of wooden huts that seemed to serve as offices and in front of these we were left standing for hours in the cold as the prisoners were checked in, a half-dozen at a time. It was early morning when I was escorted through the main gate. At the quartermaster's store I was given a spring bed, a mattress, blankets and tinware, but when I tried to carry them I fainted. A military policeman helped me to my hut and showed me how to fix my bed, while other prisoners called from their beds to inquire where I had come from and who was with me. All were looking for their own friends and relatives.

Next morning, when I opened my eyes in a real bed, and a man leaving the hut let in a breath of morning air and a glimpse of green fields and blue sky. I felt I was dreaming. That is what I think of whenever I hear the Good Friday music from *Parsifal*:

> Doch sah ich nie so mild und zart
> Die Halmen, Blüthen und Blumen.

It was a long, high, well-lit hut, divided down the middle by a wooden partition that was about as high as a man, and at either side of it and along the walls were rows of beds, metal beds, and wooden beds made of three boards, twenty-five or thirty beds in a row, and all the men were still asleep, wrapped in their brown military blankets. My own bed was against a wall beside a window, and through the window I could see another hut of the same kind across the way. A whistle blew from outside and the little man who had blown it entered the hut and came down between the two rows of beds. When he reached mine and saw me awake, he stopped and instead of blowing on his police whistle he whistled 'Kelly the Boy from Killan', at the same time marking time and miming an elaborate conversation in which he discussed with me the slothfulness of the younger generation, the beauty of the morning, and the delight of one gentleman on meeting another, which was apparently his idea of a joke. I replied in the same way – that morning I was in the mood for seeing jokes – and he raised his hat to march time and went on, blasting away again at his police whistle.

Later came more whistles, and the men dressed hastily and made their beds. Military policemen stationed themselves outside each hut and we stood at ease at the foot of our beds. Another whistle blew outside the door, the hut-leader gave an order, and the men sprang to attention. Then a military officer, accompanied by one of our own staff, entered and passed quickly between the rows of beds, both counting. Nominally we stood to attention only for our own officer. This was part of the camp organization, and I began by admiring it greatly. It duplicated completely the enemy organization so that none of our men ever made contact with their gaolers. Our quartermaster indented for supplies to the enemy quartermaster, our postmaster received our mail from the enemy postmaster; we stood to attention to be counted by our own officer. It was all very dignifed and practical. Or so I thought.

Count, because of the new arrivals, dragged intolerably that morning, and after it came Mass, which was attended only by a handful of men. It was held in the big dining hall, and only the acolyte, a pacifist by conviction, was permitted to communicate. We who were not were not allowed to receive the sacraments. After Mass the whistle blew for breakfast, and I collected my knife, fork, spoon, mug and plate and found my way back to the dining hall. It struck me that the life was going to suit me fine. Within an hour or two I was roped into the teaching staff to teach Irish, for there were an almost unlimited number of students but hardly any teachers. The classes, consisting only of men who attended because they wanted to learn, were excellent, and the teaching standard was high. Spanish was taught by Fred Cogley, who had spent a lot of his life in South America, French by his son. The two of them shared a room with Childers' friend, Frank Gallagher. It was a joy to sit and talk with them and feel that I was back with the sort of people who had really started the Revolution – men who read books and discussed general ideas. They were the type I had looked up to for years and I like looking up to people; it gives me a sense of direction.

All I needed now was to rid myself of the lice I had brought from that foul gaol. Fortunately the weather was fine, and I could wash my clothes and air them in the grass. Besides, the camp was an American aerodrome, dating from the First World War; the American plumbing still functioned spasmodically, and each morning I rose before anyone else was awake, took a cold shower and a brisk walk of a couple of miles round the compound, and prepared my lessons before Mass, and each morning the nightmare of the Civil War grew fainter in my mind, the sleepless nights, the aimless skirmishes and the futile, sickening executions. I loved that early-morning freedom, with the rich fields of Meath all round me and the possibility of silence and recollection before the others came awake, because for the rest of the day the big hut was full of noise and movement, wrestling matches and arguments. Some of the men hammered away at rings, others stood at the partition and wove macrame bags, and there was a continuous coming and going of people mad with boredom, restless, inquisitive and talkative. Now it was a Clare officer with a nervous temperament who wanted to discuss the immortality of the soul, now a West of Ireland teacher who dreamed of becoming a great lawyer and would smile and cry: 'Ah, to be able to sway vast crowds by the magic of the human voice!' The French Grammar I was studying would be sufficient in itself to halt a half a dozen visitors, some with mothers who had spoken French like natives, others who had not availed themselves of the chance of studying it at school and would regret it till their dying day. Anything for the chance of a conversation! It had its advantages, of course, for one's mind was always exposed to the play of new impressions, but it left one crazy for privacy.

The camp was quiet again only on fine afternoons when a majority of the men marched out to the recreation field to play football or watch it. Sometimes I went with them for the sake of the view across the fields to the sea, just to recite to myself: 'It keeps eternal whisperings around desolate shores,' but usually I found it pleasanter to remain behind and work. Apart from the lack of privacy, boredom was the great curse and routine its only alleviation; this was what was so good about the military organization of the camp.

A serious gap in my education was revealed to me during the very first days when I prepared my lessons for class, and the shock nearly killed me. I opened an Irish Grammar for what must have been the first time and read it through with a sinking heart. M. Jourdain's astonishment on discovering that he had been talking prose all his life was nothing to mine on discovering that I had been talking grammar – and bad grammar at that. Even my training as a teacher had been mainly confined to texts and conversation. I don't mean that I hadn't heard of nouns, verbs and adjectives, because obviously I could have learned nothing if I hadn't learned that, but I had not taken it seriously. For me, languages had always been a form of magic, like girls, and I would as soon have thought of taking liberties with one as with the other. Now I started reciting to myself from my little hoard of Irish and German poetry, realizing that if the poet used one form of a word instead of another, it was not because he liked it better but because it was the correct one.

Whatever the importance of grammar in reading or writing, as an image of human life it seems to me out on its own. I have never since had any patience with the apostles of usage. Usage needs no advocates, since it goes on whether one approves of it or not, and in doing so breaks down the best regulated languages. Grammar is the breadwinner of language as usage is the housekeeper, and the poor man's efforts at keeping order are for ever being thwarted by his wife's intrigues and her perpetual warnings to the children not to tell Father. But language, like life, is impossible without a father and he is forever returning to his thankless job of restoring authority. As an emotional young man, I found it a real help to learn that there was such a thing as an object, whether or not philosophers admitted its existence, and that I could use the accusative case to point it out as I would point out a man in the street. In later years George Moore fell in love with the subjunctive – a pretty little mood enough, though, as his books show, much too flighty for a settled man.

Maybe it was the grammar that started me off, or maybe the grammar itself was only a symptom of the emergence from a protracted adolescence, but I was beginning to have grave doubts about many of the political ideas I had held as gospel. One was that the Irish Republic founded in 1916 still existed, that it could not be disestablished except by the free choice of the people – free choice being one exercised in the complete absence of external compulsion; that the shadow government that accepted its principles was the only lawful one and that we could not sit in a usurping parliament. I began to see that the form of choice that was postulated was a rather ideal one, and said that the idea of abstaining from attendance in parliament was absurd. Only one of my new acquaintances agreed with me. He was Tom Walsh, an Irish-speaker from Clare who, when he met me, remembered a poem I had published in some political weekly. It is only in the wilder parts of Ireland, where a newspaper is an event, that a studious, lonely young farmer would remember a poem like that. Walsh was powerfully built; he shambled about with his head down, a lock of dark hair dangling over one eye and with a vague, shy air as though he hoped you would be kind enough not to notice him. But his big features had a shimmering delicacy that revealed an inner conflict; he had a slight stammer that exaggerated his slowness of speech, and when he was at his most earnest there appeared on each temple a slight pallor as though with him thought were something physical, like lifting a great weight. His smile, usually wistful, but sometimes joyous and mischievous, was like sunlight over a western moor. I knew he wrote poetry in Irish but he wouldn't show it to me, and when I pressed him about it, he only became distressed. His diffidence must have run in the family, for he once described to me how his father had caught the local thief at their potato pit by night and, frenzied with embarrassment seeing a neighbour do wrong, could only wave his arms and cry: 'Ah, what will the soul do at the Judgement?' (What the thief said the soul would do was very coarse but probably accurate.)

Walsh was even more disturbed than I was about our political affiliations. His eyebrows would go up into his limp dark hair, and the two white spots would show on either temple as he stammered: 'I believe the bishops are right to excommunicate us. If I was a bishop I'd do the same.'

'Then what are you doing here?' I would ask, and Walsh would throw back his head and laugh softly and secretly at the absurdity of his position. To me it was no laughing matter. I knew that a countryman like Walsh was always slightly abashed before abstract ideas, but if I once convinced myself that the other side was in the right, I should never rest until I had made my position plain. I am sure we were both held back by our admiration for the majority of those among whom we had been thrown. We had our share of fatheads in the camp, and maybe a crook or two, but on an average the prisoners were far finer types than either of us would have met in a normal lifetime in Ireland – better educated, more unselfish, thoughtful and interesting; and though it is all close on forty years ago I still find myself thinking of men I knew there and wondering what life has made of them and they of life. Walsh and I used to study the autograph albums that were always circulating in the camp to see what there was in the quotations to account for our uneasiness. We noticed a preponderance of quotations from Shelley and his followers, like Meredith, with his:

> Our life is but a little holding lent
> To do a mighty labour; we are one
> With Heaven and the stars when it is spent
> To serve God's aim – else die we with the sun!

It wasn't that I didn't admire Meredith, but in quotations like that there was altogether too much about dying for my taste, and it wasn't even the harmless, sugary nineteenth-century dying of Tennyson or Christina Rossetti that always moved me to tears. This was dying for its own sweet sake, and I began to wonder if there was not some relationship between Irish nationalism and the Romantic movement. Gallagher was the great Shelleyan of the camp, and after I had listened to him lecture on Erskine Childers, I complained to him that there wasn't a single characteristic touch of Childers in it. One evening I sat in the hut and listened to a Corkman singing in a little group about some hero who had died for Ireland and the brave things he had said and the fine things he had done, and I listened because I liked these simple little local songs that continued to be written to the old beautiful ballad airs and that sometimes had charming verses, like:

> I met Pat Hanley's mother and she to me did say,
> 'God be with my son Pat, he was shot in the runaway;
> 'If I could kiss his pale cold lips his wounded heart I'd cure
> 'And I'd bring my darling safely home from the valley of Knockanure.'

But halfway through this song I realized that it was about the boy whose hand I had taken in the Women's Prison in Cork one morning that spring, and suddenly the whole nightmare came back. 'It's as well for you fellows that you didn't see that lad's face when the

Lady Gregory outside Hugh Lane's house in Chelsea

Frank O'Connor's mother and father,
Michael and Minnie O'Donovan

The wharves, Cork

A. E. (George Russell)

J. M. Synge

Lennox Robinson

W. B. Yeats

The Tailor and Ansty with Father Tim Traynor; and,
on his left, Nancy McCarthy and Seamus Murphy

Free Staters had finished with it,' I said angrily. I think it must have been that evening that the big row blew up, and I had half the hut shouting at me. I shouted as well that I was sick to death of the worship of martyrdom, that the only martyr I had come close to was a poor boy from the lanes like myself, and he hadn't wanted to die any more than I did; that he had merely been trapped by his own ignorance and simplicity into a position from which he couldn't escape, and I thought most martyrs were the same. 'And Pearse?' somebody kept on crying. 'What about Pearse? I suppose he didn't want to die either?' 'Of course he didn't want to die,' I said. 'He woke up too late, that was all.' And that did really drive some of the men to fury.

I went to bed myself in a blind rage. Apparently the only proof one had of being alive was one's readiness to die as soon as possible: dead was the great thing to be, and there was nothing to be said in favour of living except the innumerable possibilities it presented of dying in style. I didn't want to die. I wanted to live, to read, to hear music, and to bring my mother to all the places that neither of us had ever seen, and I felt these things were more important than any martyrdom. After that, whenever I saw a quotation from Shelley or one of his followers in an autograph album, I usually inserted a line or two of Goethe as near as possible to it. My favourite was: 'One must be either the hammer or the anvil.'

And in spite of all the sentimental high-mindedness, I felt it went side by side with an extraordinary inhumanity. Or maybe angularity is the better word. It was really the lack of humour that seems to accompany every imaginative improvisation, and in other ways I must have been as humourless as everybody else.

The first incident that revealed to me what the situation was really like was funny enough. A man, whose name was, I think, Frank Murphy, had had a disagreement with his hut-leader about the amount of fatigues he had to do, so he refused to do any more. There was nothing unusual about this, of course. In an atmosphere where there was no such thing as privacy and people were always getting on one another's nerves it was inevitable, and the sensible thing would have been to transfer Murphy to another hut. But this was against our principles. We had a complete military organization that duplicated and superseded that of our gaolers, and any slight on this was a slight on the whole fiction it was based on. Murphy was summoned before a court martial of three senior officers, found guilty and sentenced to more fatigues. Being a man of great character, he refused to do these as well. This might have seemed a complete stalemate, but not to imaginative men. The camp command took over from the enemy a small time-keeper's hut with barred windows to use as a prison, and two prisoners, wearing tricolour armlets to show that they really were policemen and not prisoners like the rest of us, arrested Murphy and locked him up. That night Walsh and I, who both liked Murphy, visited him in his prison and talked to him through the bars of his window, while I looked round me at the tall sentry posts and beneath them the camp command taking its regular evening walk as prisoners of the men in the sentry posts, while *their* prisoner stared at them through the bars of his window and talked bitterly of justice and injustice. I felt the imaginative improvisation could not go farther than that, but it did. Murphy still had a shot in his locker, for he went on hunger strike, not against our gaolers but his own and – unlike them when they went on hunger strike soon after – he meant it.

This was too much even for men who affected to believe that the Irish Republic was still in existence and would remain so, no matter what its citizens might think, so a mass meeting was held in the dining hall, and the various officers addressed us on the wickedness of Murphy's defiance of majority rule. From people who were in prison for refusing to recognize majority rule and who had even been excommunicated for it, this was pretty thick. When it was proposed to release Murphy and boycott him, and all those in favour were asked to raise their hands, nine hundred-odd hands were raised. When those against were called on, one hand went up, and that was mine. Later in life I realized that it was probably the first time I had ever taken an unpopular stand without allies.

19

All the same, that summer was exceedingly happy. When the weather was fine, I held my classes on the grass outside some hut. In fact, since Father had gone to the War in 1914 I had never been so well off. I was still only nineteen; thanks to the American plumbing, I lived a healthier life than I could have lived at home; I had regular and pleasant work to do – I was now teaching German as well as Advanced Irish – and I knew I was doing it well. For me, who had lived all my life by faith, it was an exhilarating experience to know that I was doing something well by objective standards. Above all, I had friends I liked and admired. Apart from Walsh, there was Cathal Buckley, the youngest of us, who had a fat, pale, schoolboy face and a quiet clerical manner, and Ned Moriarty from Tralee, a British ex-soldier, who was tall, thin and Spanish-looking and whose hands were more expressive than other people's faces. Apart from these, my immediate friends, there were others from whom I learned a lot like Gallagher, Cogley, Sean T. O'Kelly (later President), who lent me Anatole France in French, and Sean MacEntee (later Minister for Finance), who gave me the Heine I had coveted so long and proved that Corkery was right and that Heine was the proper poet for a man in prison.

But there was no lack of interesting people. There was the quartermaster, for instance. He was a North Corkman, small and thin, with a thin, desperate face, burning blue eyes, and a tiny moustache which he tugged as though the tugging provided all the energy he needed. He needed plenty, because he seemed to go by clockwork, swinging his arms wider than anyone else, and he had a capacity for swearing and bad language that beat anything I ever heard. All the North Corkmen swore well, but he swore artistically, so that you immediately forgot whatever he was swearing about and merely admired the skill with which he did it. And after he had cursed you through every byway of his fancy, he would grab you by the collar and mutter: 'That suit is in rags! Bloody fellow that can't even look after himself! Come over to the store till I make you look decent!' I think he had a sneaking regard for me too, for he once told me I might become a great man myself if only I imitated a certain politician in the camp who practised oratory before the mirror every day. 'And I once heard him give a lecture on Robert Emmett before a thousand people and there wasn't one that wasn't sobbing. That's what you should do!'

In fact, it was the nearest thing I could have found to life on a college campus, the only one I was really fitted for, and I should have been perfectly happy except that I was still doing it at my mother's expense. It was all very well to be teaching German and Irish, but I still had no clothes and no boots except what I got from the quartermaster's store, and the overcoat I used as an extra blanket was an old belted blue coat with a fur collar that somebody who was throwing it away gave to Mother. It looked absurd on me, but it was the only warm thing I had. I knew what those weekly parcels from her cost – the cake, the tin of cocoa, the tin of condensed milk and the box of cigarettes – and I felt sure that she was going out to daily work to earn them for me. That was true. One day one of the soldiers, who had served with Father in the old Munster Fusiliers, got himself transferred to the garbage collection and brought me a letter from her. She had got work in the house of a plumber on Summerhill who was supposed to have 'influence' and would try to get me released. In an emotional fit I replied that when I got out I would not be a burden to her for long, and she replied in a sentence that I knew did not apply particularly to me and was merely part of her attitude to life – 'If there were no wild boys there would be no great men.'

But towards the end of the year things began to go to hell. Fighting outside had definitely ended; De Valera had issued a cease-fire order but had refused either to surrender or negotiate (the Government of the Irish Republic, being the only lawful one, could not possibly negotiate with impostors), and we were left to play football and study Irish behind barbed wire. The Free State Government was incapable of letting the prisoners go as a generous gesture. But all the same, people were being released, in ones and twos and on no basis that anybody could understand, so that it became harder to concentrate and plan. Classwork had suddenly become very difficult, and the certificates I signed for successful students had an air of finality about them.

Then one day a disciple of Gallagher's called Joe Kennedy and myself heard that a group of prisoners who had made themselves objectionable had been evicted from their room in the Limerick hut. We were both studious and suffered greatly from the noise in the bigger huts. The Limerick men, when we went to interview them, turned out to be a splendid crowd, and they urged us to come in with them. We applied and got the room.

Only after we had done so did we realize that we had committed the unforgivable sin. If we had not applied, no one else would have done it, and in a couple of days the original occupants would have crept quietly back. That is how things happen in Ireland. We were in the middle of a land war, and we were grabbers too proud to withdraw. I coveted that room almost to the point of insanity. I wanted a place to myself where I could go and read. I had written an essay on Turgenev which I had submitted to a national competition, and for some reason now known only to God, I was translating *Lorna Doone* into Irish. I had never seen the book before, and have never looked at it since, so I cannot even guess what attraction it had for me.

Walsh helped us to carry our beds and mattresses into the new hut under a fire of taunts and threats from the dispossessed and their friends, and Kennedy, a tall, handsome man, with a long, bony shaven skull and a squint, turned and denounced them in a cavernous voice that made me think of Savonarola. That should have been sufficient warning to me, because I am sure that Savonarola and I would never have got on under the one roof. The Limerick men dropped in to make us feel at home and they and I became fast friends. They were a curious lot, quite different from any other county group I had met in the camp, independent and apparently indifferent to what anybody thought of them. This was curious, for Limerick had always been a hot-bed of fanaticism, the only place in Ireland to tolerate anti-Semitic riots. I can only suppose that after the public opinion of Limerick, any other seemed a joke.

The arrangement worked excellently as far as they and I were concerned. They were the only group who sang in harmony, and I had a passion for part-singing though I didn't know enough about music to join in it. Every night we met in their big room and brewed our tea and cocoa, and I got them to sing, and they dragged me into arguments. Here again, they were different from all the other groups, for though they shouted and gibed and laid down the law, they didn't seem to resent my heresies in the least. But Kennedy did. He was chock-full of mystical nationalism which I found much more exasperating than mystical religion, though I often felt they were the same thing: the only difference was that along with an invisible God who was the fourth wall of our earthly stage the mystics wanted an invisible Ireland as well. Living in the presence of God was one thing; living in the presence of Ireland was more than I could tolerate, Kennedy began to sound more and more like Savonarola, and soon our cosy, quiet little room no longer attracted me. I know now that the fault was mine, because I was young and desperately trying to think things out for myself for the first time. Soon we were barely talking, and he made a public profession of faith by pinning over his bed a manuscript poem of Gallagher's with the stock reference to martyrdom – 'Death's iron discipline', if my memory of it is right. With youthful contentiousness I wrote over my own bed my favourite lines from *Faust – Grau, teurer Freund* . . . ('Grey, my dear friend, is all your theory and green the golden tree of life'). The word 'Life' seemed to affect Kennedy as the word

'Death' affected me, and he accused me of 'beastly, degrading cynicism' and took off his coat to fight me. After that we didn't speak again till the tragi-comedy ended in the national hunger strike, and he took up his bed and returned to a hut where he could endure 'Death's iron discipline' among loyal comrades. Fortunately, he thought better of it and lived to be a distinguished parliamentarian of whom I could say complacently: 'Yes, he and I were in gaol together,' which is rather like the English 'He and I were in Eton together' but considerably more classy.

At the same time an incident occurred that probably made me more tolerant than I might otherwise have been. The Free State authorities gave parole as the Catholic Church gave the sacraments – in return for a signed declaration that one would behave oneself for the future, and opinion in the camp was dead against this, though in fact, there was no fighting and nothing was to be lost by signing. The mother of one of the Kerry boys in the hut where I visited Moriarty was ill, and the neighbours had written begging him to come home and see her before she died. His mother was a widow, and there was a large family to be looked after. Finally there came a wire that said: 'Mother dying come at once,' but he still refused to sign, and his decision was regarded as a proper one. It caught me in my most vulnerable spot. I knew if Mother were dying and that this were my only opportunity of seeing her, I would eat the damn declaration if necessary. I kept on asking everybody I met: 'Would you do it?' and found very few prepared to say they wouldn't sign. I appealed to a friend in the camp command to get an order issued that the boy should sign, so as to clear him among his friends, but, like transferring Murphy from one hut to another, this was contrary to principle. I said bitterly that it was a great pity God hadn't made mothers with the durability of principles.

The mother, being of softer material, died, and her younger children, left homeless, were taken in by the neighbours. Now, it was not the possible death of my own mother that I was thinking of so much as that other day when she and her little sister were thrown on to the roadside by bailiffs. I cursed the inhumanity of the two factions with their forms and scruples. At the same time the boy's companions apparently began to realize that his refusal to sign the form and their encouragement was not altogether the grandiose gesture they had thought it, because they concealed from him what had happened. One day as he was wandering down beside his hut and the windows were open, he heard his name mentioned and stopped to listen. He waited until the conversation ended and then, without hesitation, walked straight across the compound towards the barbed wire. A sentry in one of the tall watch-towers had his rifle raised to fire when a military policeman ran up, shouting at him. The policeman put his arm about the boy and brought him back to his hut. When the policeman had gone the boy said: 'They wouldn't even shoot me,' and began to drop into silence and melancholia; and still, no one had sense enough to make him sign the declaration and go home before it was too late. No wonder I hadn't much patience with my room-mate.

And then the whole business turned sinister. It was announced that all prisoners in the country would take a pledge not to eat until they died or were released. I didn't know whether the morality or the expediency of this scheme was the worse. We professed to be prisoners of war, but the government to which we gave allegiance would accept no responsibility for us, either by surrendering or coming to terms with the enemy. The idea that thousands of men would keep such a pledge to the point at which mass deaths would threaten the existence of the Free State Government seemed to me absurd. Mass martyrdom was only another example of the Shelleyan fantasy, though there were plenty on our side to whom it wasn't even a fantasy but a vulgar political expedient to break the stalemate caused by De Valera's Ceasefire Order.

Walsh, Buckley and myself let it be understood that we would not take part in the hunger strike. We did not like doing this, because we knew that our position among a thousand men who were hunger-striking for their freedom would be much worse than that of the average blackleg in a plant of the same size. Though we had the blessing of Moriarty and the Limerick men who were joining the strike, we knew it would not be much use to us if things got really dirty. A meeting of the men would have to be held to confirm the decision, and we announced that we should all speak at this, purely to put our purpose on record. This apparently caused some alarm, for at the last moment we were told that the resolution initiating the strike would not be put before a general meeting but before meetings of county groups, so that between us we would only be able to address the Cork, Clare and Kildare men, leaving ninety per cent of the prisoners unaware that there were objections to the strike. Then Buckley was served with an order exempting him from the strike because of his youth. I am sure it was done merely with the purpose of protecting him if we were attacked, but he thought otherwise, and replied that he did not propose to avail himself of it and would not join the strike for conscientious reasons. I was impressed by his presence of mind. If it had been I, I should not have seen the consequences of the order until it was too late to clarify my position to anybody.

To make things worse, I was ill with bronchitis, and our own doctor – one of the prisoners – had advised me to go to the hospital. Before I went I attended the Cork meeting and made my speech. I was listened to in silence, and the resolution was passed with only my vote against it. The other two had the same experience. They took me to the main gate on my way to the hospital at the other side of the wire. I was sorry now that I had agreed to go, because I felt I was deserting them.

That night in the hospital a military policeman led in a tall country boy with a vacant expression who had to be undressed and put to bed. Even before the policeman said anything I knew it was the Kerry boy whose mother had died, and that already his mind had begun to give way. I did not sleep much. I would hear a heavy sigh and a stir of clothes and then the Kerryman would slip quietly out of bed and pad across the floor to a window. He climbed on the sill and stood there in his short shirt, his arms outstretched, his face crushed between the bars. He would remain like that for several minutes, and then give another deep sigh and return to his bed. A couple of times when I woke it was to see him there like that, caught in the blaze of the big searchlight, his arms outstretched, and I could not help thinking of the crucifixion.

I knew nothing about mental illness, but I understood that boy's as though I had been responsible for it myself. I felt that if I had done to my mother what he had innocently done to his, I should be unable to think of anything else and be searching frantically for any dark corner of my mind where I could take refuge from the dreadful gramophone record that went on repeating itself as though it would never stop. For hours next day I sat by his bed, trying to talk to him. I found that with persistence I could get him to follow a simple conversation in a fairly lucid way, but the moment the conversation veered even for an instant towards his home and family he slumped into vacancy again, and each time it was harder to rouse him. Next day they took him away – to a mental hospital, I was told.

Meanwhile I could get no treatment nor even a discharge. Only a military doctor could discharge me, and he rarely appeared. When he did drop in a couple of days later I was mad with frustration and insisted on going back to the camp. It was a bitter, black day; the compound was a sea of mud and apparently deserted, since most of the hunger-strikers had taken to their beds to keep warm. I had a message from one of the hospital patients for a friend in the Cork hut, and I was shocked at the changes in it. Partitions and doors had been torn down to keep the stoves going, big cans of water were steaming on the stoves, and the men were lying in or on their beds unshaven, with mugs of hot salt water beside them. This was supposed to stay the craving for food. Those who were still up and dressed were shivering over the stoves, dishevelled and gloomy. But it was the silence that struck me most – all that busy hammering, singing and chatter ended. The men avoided my eyes, and as I went out I was followed by a general hiss. I had apparently got back in time to see things turn really ugly.

There was no change in my friends of the Limerick hut. Nothing seemed able to suppress their high spirits, and when I came back from the dining hall with my tinware under my blue coat to avoid giving offence, they yelled for a full report on the meal and started to plan ideal menus for the evening of their release and ideal girls to share them with. But though I didn't realize it, there was already a change. Next day a small group of Corkmen – some of whom had hissed me the previous day – gave in, and when I reached the dining hall there was an ugly scene as they pleaded for food, and the kitchen staff told them arrogantly that they must give twenty-four hours notice. Walsh, Buckley and I gave them our food. One of them asked shyly: 'Do you remember the day we rescued you in Kilmallock?' It was his way of reminding me that he had not always been so abject a figure and had done his stint of soldiering as well as the rest. He did not have to justify himself to me. I felt like killing somebody.

I was blamed for this collapse, quite without justification, because Walsh, Buckley and myself had already agreed that once the strike began we should say nothing to influence anybody. I got the *Irish Statesman*, which was sent me by a Quaker friend, and that week it contained one of the most furious articles that its editor, George Russell, ever wrote, denouncing the hunger strike. This, too, we decided to keep to ourselves, though Moriarty always got the paper after me.

That evening an order was issued that I must leave the Limerick hut, live by myself in a room sealed off from one of the bigger huts, and not enter any other. The Limerick men wanted me to ignore it, and offered to deal with any force that was sent to eject me, but I felt they already had enough trouble on their hands. Buckley insisted on moving in with me and, when I protested, said: 'Oh, no, they're trying to break us up.' The baby of the group was growing up with great rapidity.

There was nothing in the order to prevent me speaking to my own friends, so that evening at dusk I went to see Moriarty and talked with him through the window. He and his three room-mates were in bed, drinking salt water. I sat on the windowledge in the rain, and he began to complain of the delay in bringing him the *Irish Statesman*. I told some lie about having left it behind me in the hospital, but he didn't believe me.

'You didn't bring it because there's an attack on us in it,' he said, and I had to admit he was right.

'Is it bad?'

'Pretty bad. Cathal and Tom also thought you'd better not read it.'

'Oh, we'll read it,' he said in his gentle lazy way. 'We're four sick men, but if you don't bring that paper down tonight, we're going up for it.'

Just then a file of soldiers passed behind me in the rainy dusk with a military policeman at their head. Two burst in the door of Moriarty's room, took the mugs of salt water from beside the beds, and threw the contents past me into the compound. Then they filled them with hot soup from a bucket. Before they could leave the room, Moriarty, mad with rage, jumped out of bed and emptied the soup after the salt water. I went back to my room, took the *Irish Statesman* and tossed it in the window to him.

Next morning, as Buckley and I were on our way to the dining hall with our plates under our coats, Moriarty and his three room-mates staggered out to join us with their plates and mugs in their hands. One of them told me that Moriarty had read the article aloud to them without comment and then asked: 'Are we as mad as this fellow thinks?' 'We are,' said one, and the other two agreed. I knew then that the strike was over. The others who had given in were only poor, shamed and frightened boys to whom nobody paid attention, but Moriarty was a natural leader, and no one who followed his example need regard himself as a weakling. The strike had now become a mere endurance test, and already there was a different tone in the dining hall. The kitchen staff, who fed like restaurant cats, had maintained a tone of chilly disapproval to conscientious objectors and contempt and scorn to defaulters, but now they were on the defensive, waving their arms and shouting that they couldn't produce food without notice. The defaulters had ceased to be mere individuals and become a class.

But the strike dragged on for days before the master-minds of the revolution saw that their organization was bleeding to death under their eyes and issued a hasty general dispensation. Immediately the whole camp became hysterical. Even the sentries dropped their rifles and dragged buckets of soup to the barbed wire, and the prisoners tore their hands as they thrust their mugs through it, pushing and shouldering one another out of the way. Some got sick but came back for more. A tall, spectacled man who had not been invited to join the strike came up to me with an oily smile. 'Well, professor,' he said gleefully, 'the pigs feed,' and I turned away in disgust because that was exactly what the scene resembled, and I knew it was the end of our magical improvisation. Buckley, Walsh and myself looked on as though it were the funeral of someone we loved, and when we could bear it no more we went off by ourselves to the other side of the camp. We had reason for complacency, but there was no complacency in us. We knew we should never again find ourselves with so many men we respected and we felt their humiliation as though it were our own. In the years to come, travelling through the country, I would meet with the survivors of the period – some of the best, like Walsh, I should not meet because they took off early for America. 'The Lost Legion' I called them. There they were in small cities and towns, shopkeepers or civil servants, bewildered by the immensity of the disaster that had overwhelmed them, the death-in-life of the Nationalist Catholic establishment, and after a few minutes I would hear the cry I had so often heard before – 'The country! Oh, God, the bloody country!'

The same day another mass meeting was held. This time there was no nonsense about individual county meetings because one of them, out of sheer cantankerousness, might have voted to continue the strike, and the strike was over. I didn't bother to attend it, but Walsh brought an account of it. Everyone congratulated everyone else on the superhuman endurance and discipline that had been displayed and exonerated those who had abandoned the strike on their own responsibility. But this was anti-climax, and everyone knew it. The camp was a grave of lost illusions; amid the ruin of their huts it was impossible to get the men to take pride in their duties, and the school practically disbanded for lack of students. Nobody thought any longer but of how soon release might come for himself.

We had had a foretaste of what that meant. Two audacious girls, realizing that fighting was over and that no one was likely to kill them in cold blood, walked coolly across the fields one evening from the main road and stood outside the wire by the Limerick hut, asking for some relative. In their high tower the sentries fumed, waiting for a military policeman to escort the girls away. In no time a crowd gathered, and two or three men who knew the girls stood on the grass bank overlooking the wire and talked to them. The rest of us stood or sat around in complete silence. It was years since some of the group had heard a woman's voice. Nobody cracked a dirty joke; if anyone had, I think he might have been torn asunder. This was sex in its purest form, sex as God may perhaps have intended it to be – a completion of human experience, unearthly in its beauty and staggering in its triviality. 'Mother said to ask did you get the cake. Jerry Deignan's sister asked to be remembered to you.'

One bright cold November day after I had been in prison for almost a year, I was sitting in Walsh's room when the Limerick hut-leader burst in and said: 'Come on, Michael! You're being released.' He was a small, brusque, slightly pompous and very kindly man. I didn't move. It was a favourite joke, though not one I should have expected from him, and I felt I must not give myself away. 'Come on, I tell you! The officer is waiting,' he said impatiently, and Walsh went pale and smiled and said in a low voice, 'That's right, Michael. You're wanted.' I still could not believe it. Walsh accompanied me to my room, but the officer had gone, and suddenly I did believe it and wanted to cry. 'Oh, he'll be back,' the hut-leader said testily. 'Why don't you get your things together?' My shirt and underpants were drying on a line outside the hut but I could not be bothered to take them. Shaking all over, I made a parcel of my little library – my sixpenny anthologies of German and Spanish poetry, my anthology of Gaelic poetry, my beloved Heine, *Hermann und Dorothea*, and a school history of the Crusades in French – all that had kept me in touch with the great world of culture that I hoped I might some day belong to. Suddenly the door opened and a green-clad figure asked: 'Is O'Donovan here?' That was how they came to call you before a firing squad, and I fancy the sensation was very similar. Too big to be apprehended, it left you stunned and weak and wanting to cry.

I was too bewildered to feel anything at parting from Walsh, who carried my parcel to the front gate, and I felt ashamed. After the usual signing of forms in the front office, I was given the travel vouchers for the little group that was being released with me, and as the camp gate opened and let us through on to a narrow country road with high hedges that led to the station, I realized that it was something of a responsibility, for I could feel in myself the same hysteria that swept through my little group. When they heard the sound of a car they looked round and cracked morbid jokes about being re-taken, and I could see them measuring the hedges at either side, wondering if they could run for it. I understood it perfectly because I wanted to get into the fields and then run like mad. Run and run and run and never stop! For the first time I felt the presence of that shadow line that divides the free man from the prisoner.

I had difficulty at the refreshment centre our women had set up in a little cottage by the road. Though I explained that there would be no train for an hour, the men did not want to go in. They wanted to go back on to the main road and bum a lift. Two of them actually did. When the rest had been reassured, we had sandwiches and tea, and the girls who ran the refreshment centre escorted us to the little seaside station. The small local train from Drogheda came in and, seeing a young woman with a baby in one carriage, I climbed in beside them, and all the way to Dublin I scarcely took my eyes from the baby. Even the lovely open sea in evening light did not distract me. I am bad with men, indifferent with women, but I can no more pass a baby than a bookstore. All that year I had been missing what Pearse was to remember on the eve of his execution, 'Things bright and green, things young and happy'.

The girls had arranged rooms for us in a hotel in Parnell Square because there was no train to Cork. It was late when I reached home next day and, after the first excitement of homecoming was over, Mother suddenly burst into tears and said: 'It made a man of you.' It was one of those remarks she often dropped that puzzled and upset me, because the context was always missing, and I had noticed no change at all in myself unless it was the urgent realization of the importance of grammar, particularly the accusative case. Now I know that she saw some change in me and was glad that I was at last a man, though she could not help grieving for the awkward adolescent who had been so helplessly dependent on her. All that really mattered to me was being home again, where I could see her and talk to her about my plans for the future, and sleep in the little pink-washed attic she had made so neat for me, and sit by the orange-box that served me for a bookcase and flick through the pages of books I had been separated from so long that I had forgotten their very existence. It did not even matter to me that while I was in gaol I had won the first prize in the national competition for a critical essay on Turgenev in Irish – a prize that Corkery had won a couple of years before – which was just as well, because that year the national festival went bust, and I never got the seven pounds that would have meant so much to me. Anyway it pleased Father because it meant that sooner or later the writing might bring in some money.

But the following Sunday I found I did not want to go to Mass, and at the first and only political meeting I attended, Corkery had to rescue me from a young man who called me a traitor. After that, it was friends who believed I had done wrong in opposing the hunger strike, and a girl who said bitterly when I met her in the street: 'I hear you don't believe in God any longer.' Though this wasn't true, it took me some time to realize what Mother had seen in that first glimpse of me, that I had crossed another shadow line, and made me wonder if I should ever again be completely at ease with the people I loved, their introverted religion and introverted patriotism. I suspect she saw it all, in the way that mothers do, and understood the consequences for me better than I have ever been able to do. Thirty years later, when she was not far from her death, I spoke to her about the possibility of my having to leave Ireland and – knowing her hatred of leaving home – suggested that I might get a place for her in Cork. 'Of course I'll go with you,' she said without a moment's hesitation. 'I know you must be free. Life without freedom is nothing.' To her, of course, 'freedom' did not mean freedom to do what one pleased – that was a conception that never crossed her mind – but freedom to do what one thought 'right', whatever the consequences. She left me bewildered then, as she had so often left me bewildered before. It was strange to hear an old woman of eighty-five, an orphan, a servant girl who had never had anything she could really call her own, speak with the very voice of Antigone.

All our arguments about the immortality of the soul seem to me to be based on one vast fallacy – that it is our vanity that desires eternity. Vanity! As though any reasonable man could be vain enough to believe himself worth immortality! From the time I was a boy and could think at all, I was certain that for my own soul there was only nothingness. I knew it too well in all its commonness and weakness. But I knew that there were souls that were immortal, that even God, if He wished to, could not diminish or destroy, and perhaps it was the thought of these that turned me finally from poetry to storytelling, to the celebration of those who for me represented all I should ever know of God. My mother was merely one among them, though, in my human weakness, I valued her most, and now that I am old myself, I remember the line of a psalm (probably mistranslated) that has always been with me since I read it first:

'And when I wake I shall be satisfied with Thy likeness.'

New York, 1958–60

My Father's Son

Contents

When Frank O'Connor died on 10 March 1966, he had not completed this second volume of his autobiography, *My Father's Son*. Much of it existed in early drafts, some of it in separate pieces. We are indebted to Dr Maurice Sheehy of University College, Dublin, for comparing the different drafts and producing the present text.

ONE

Rising in the world

1

At the age of twenty I was released from an internment camp without money or job. The Civil War had just ended, and since I had taken the loser's side I found that ex-jailbirds like myself did not get whatever positions were available under the new government. But all teachers were now required to learn the Irish language, so for a few months I taught Irish to the teachers at the local Protestant school in Cork – St Luke's. This brought in only a few shillings a week, but I now knew how to teach and I liked the work.

I also liked Kennelly, the headmaster, an irascible little Kerryman who wore pince-nez. I suspect he was a fearful bully and disciplinarian because he always snapped at everyone who came near him, including his pretty daughter, and snapped loudest of all at the school manager, Canon Flewett.

'All clergymen are the same, Mr O'Donovan,' Kennelly would say as he saw me part of the way home. 'Catholic, Church of Ireland or Presbyterian, you can never trust any of them.'

It was part of his innocent vanity that I could never teach him Irish because he remembered it all perfectly from his childhood in Kerry. But he was a man with a real flavour, and I enjoyed watching him when someone got him mad, keeping what he thought was a perfectly expressionless face, though his little nose took on an autonomous life and expressed a whole range of emotions that no pince-nez could stand up to. In spite of his snappiness he was extraordinarily gentle with me; he even brought me home once or twice to supper with his wife and daughter, but I was so embarrassed that I do not even remember what nonsense I talked; and when he saw me home it was to advise me in a fatherly way to have nothing more to do with politics.

'With you it's not a question of politics,' he said, referring delicately to the fact that I was still wearing Father's old trousers. 'It's a question of how much a man can take, and you've taken enough. You can't afford to take any more.'

One of the pleasantest revelations that life has offered was that on his retirement that stout anti-clerical rushed himself into Holy Orders and worked gallantly as a missioner in the East End of London through the blitz. All Irish anti-clericals are spoiled priests, and you must never trust any of them.

Late in 1923 my old teacher Daniel Corkery told me that Lennox Robinson, the dramatist, who was now Secretary of the Irish Carnegie United Kingdom Trust, was organizing rural libraries and looking for young men and women to train as librarians. The moment he said it I knew that this was the very job for me and that I was the very type of person Robinson was looking for. It was not so much that I wanted to be a librarian, or even knew what being a librarian meant; it was just that never in my life had I had enough books to read and this was my opportunity.

I met Robinson in the restaurant of the Cork railway station at Glanmire, where he was waiting for a train to Dublin and drinking double brandies. He always looked like someone's caricature of him, long and mournful and disjointed, as though at some time he had suffered on the rack, and he had a high-pitched, disjointed voice that sounded like someone's reading of an old maid's letter from Regency times, with every third word isolated and emphasized.

The only sort of job he could offer me sounded hopeless. I should have to spend a year or two studying librarianship somewhere in the north of Ireland, and the salary would be thirty shillings a week, though at the end of my training I should qualify for a librarian's post at two hundred and fifty pounds a year. The latter figure, of course, was fantastic; I couldn't imagine what anyone would do with five pounds a week, but even in the twenties I knew that nobody could live away from home on thirty shillings a week. I could manage it at home, but not in lodgings.

I have met some tough bargainers in my life, but none quite so ruthless as Robinson. He merely looked ineffectual and sad, and God did not choose to reveal to me that within a few years *he* would be begging for a job from me and I would not have the sense to look ineffectual and sad, so I went home in great distress to my mother.

She, poor woman, did not have much sense either, but she saw clearly that a job in a library was about the only job I was qualified for, and she timidly offered to add half a crown, or even – if she was lucky – five shillings to the salary till something better turned up. I hated to accept her offer because I knew how she would have to earn it.

But, shortly after, she got a loan to buy me a decent little cardboard suitcase and packed it with my spare shirt and underpants and a few pairs of stockings she had knitted herself. I have a strong recollection that she packed a holy picture as well, for fear I might not find one in an out-of-the-way place like Sligo, and I set out for Dublin on my way to the west, like Cu Chulainn setting out for Armagh at the age of seven, though I was fourteen years older and had nothing of the heroic spirit.

2

I found lodgings near Sligo Cathedral at twenty-seven and sixpence a week and had a whole half-crown for laundry, cigarettes and drink. Mother had it worked out that it would be cheaper to post my laundry home than to get it done locally, and every week I posted home my shirt, my underpants, a pair of stockings and some handkerchiefs.

My room was in the house of an ex-officer in the Free State Army who had been a private soldier in Churchill's campaign against Russia and taught me my first words of Russian. When he was on the drink he was very like Father, and I slept with his rifle under my mattress because his wife was afraid he might use it. One night when he took it out and loaded it, she begged me to stay up and watch with him. It seemed that somebody had been sleeping at the bottom of his garden. Early next morning we stole out of the house and crept down the garden in approved army style to surround and overwhelm the trespasser. She turned out to be a poor country girl from near Collooney who had been thrown out by her parents and had nowhere in the world to go, so my landlord let her off with a caution.

There were other troubles as well. Across the road lived a loyal Protestant, and occasionally in the evening the passions would rise in him at the thought of all the dirty disloyal Catholics about him, and then he would throw open the window and play 'God save the King' on the gramophone. At the first notes of the insulting melody my landlord, an equally staunch supporter of the other side, would drop whatever he was doing and race for my room with a portable gramophone, rest it in the windowsill and play 'The Soldier's Song'. His wife, a decent Cork woman, said that the Sligo people had 'no nature', but I wouldn't have gone as far as that. They struck me as very patriotic.

Robert Wilson, the librarian, was a small nervous man with an irregular face, flushed with whiskey, thick sensuous lips and delightful brown rogue's eyes set a little to the side of his head. By the time I got there Lennox Robinson was on the point of being compelled to resign from his position as Secretary. He had written what had been denounced as a 'blasphemous' story in a little paper called *To-Morrow*, and what Lady Gregory tartly called 'a storm in a chalice' followed. The story concerned a simple country girl who believed she had been visited in the same way as Christ's mother and, as if to ram the point home, Yeats contributed his sonnet on Leda. When we heard of Robinson's resignation, Wilson buried his head in his hands and moaned, 'O Ireland, how thou stonest thy prophets!', which struck me as excessive.

Wilson was neat and dexterous, and though after a week or two of my clumsiness he gave me up as a bad job and began to introduce me as his 'untrainable assistant' he was extraordinarily kind, drove me to every spot Yeats had written about, and stopped the car while he chanted poems with tears in those gentle, beseeching rogue's eyes; took me home to dinner in his flat and played me Vaughan Williams, and lamented the ugliness of Irish Catholicism (to which he was a convert) and the beastliness of the cathedral music. I liked him and I liked his poems, but I wished he wouldn't bring me home, because at the age of twenty I had never dined out anywhere, and his English society wife could make me mix the cutlery and gag over my dinner like no hostess I ever met after. Years later, it was of her I was thinking when I made a young policeman say of his sergeant's wife that God Almighty had put her in the world with the one main object of persecuting him.

Long after, Wilson and I met when she was dead and he had left the library to return to schoolmastering. Over a drink he told me shyly that he had changed his name to 'Robin', and then produced photographs of the beautiful schoolboy with whom he had just spent a Continental holiday. I understood then, too late, the brave face he had been putting on things in those Sligo years and the thick crust of innocence and ignorance that had made it impossible for me to return his kindness.

I wasn't really 'untrainable', as he jokingly complained, but I was not very happy either. Partly I missed Cork, but partly there was a certain air of futility about the work of the library that reminded me a little of the railway.* We had village and small-town branches throughout the country, and every three months we sent them each a box or two of books by rail. We had a printed catalogue of the 'Three Thousand Best Books', and the local secretary made his choice from this, though as we had only one copy of each book, he rarely got what he asked for. The catalogue of the 'Three Thousand Best Books' had been compiled by an unbookish Belfastman, who was rarely sober and, like the 'Hundred Best After-Dinner Stories', his choice plunged whole provinces in gloom.

The Belfastman's notion of rural libraries was based on city libraries of the Victorian era, and these in their turn had been based on university libraries. Hence the importance of having only one copy of a book instead of the twenty or thirty copies that were really needed – this would decrease one's 'basic stock'. A library with forty thousand titles was more useful to an imaginary research student, and nobody explained to us that we were not dealing with research students.

All the same, I wasn't entirely unhappy. For the first time in my life I had books at my disposal. Whenever a box was returned from some country centre I fell on it, hoping for treasure – a book of poems or a Russian novel I had not read. I took away the library's *Collected Poems* of Yeats and practically learned it by heart. The local assistant, Bob Lambert, who was almost as hard-up as I was, came on long lonesome walks with me, out to Strandhill or Rosses Point, and we carefully spaced the poems and the cigarettes. Long as the walks were, I do not remember that either of us ever had enough to pay for two bottles of beer. And besides, after I had been in Sligo only for a month or two, the Carnegie Trust summoned Wilson and myself to a conference in London, with all expenses paid, and I dreamed of it for weeks. It was to be my first trip out of Ireland.

And a terrible trip it was. We took ship in Belfast; I was seasick the whole time and thought I was going to drown, so I comforted myself by reciting 'Lycidas' the whole night through. When Wilson

*See *An Only Child*, chapter 14.

came into my cabin next morning I smiled bravely at him and said,
'For Lycidas, your sorrow, is not dead.'

Encouraged, no doubt, by this, he insisted on taking me to Matins
in Liverpool Cathedral, having first explained to me in his kindly
way that the Irish bishops' ban on attending Protestant services did
not apply in England – as though that worried me. Poor Wilson!
In his genuine desire to make an educated man of me he was always
going out of his own way to put things in mine – Yeats, Vaughan
Williams, English villages and now Matins.

On the boat we had been joined by MacIntyre, the Donegal
librarian, an untidy, harassed little man in glasses, who had been a
village postman. Wilson had told me about MacIntyre's visit to
Sligo, when he had hung over the bridge, looking at the foaming
waters beneath and said solemnly, ' "I would that we were, my
beloved, white swans on the foam of the sea!" – God, there's enough
water here to wash all the watter-closets in Sligo.'

Mac, who was a native Irish speaker, did not like the idea of
travelling alone in a foreign country, so he attached himself to us,
more particularly to me because I spoke Irish almost as well as he
did, though he would not have admitted this. Neither, of course,
did he like the idea of attending a heretical service, and the moment
a prayer began he ran quivering to the west door and stood there
till the organ began again.

'Och, such a nice cathedral!' he clucked at me. 'Such a pity it
isn't our own!'

At the other side Wilson turned beseeching brown eyes on me
whenever he particularly wanted me to admire the service; and at
last he could stand it no longer and joined in himself. As a Catholic
he should not have done this, but as a parson's son he simply could
not resist. Between the two guilty creatures I felt like Goethe's
description of himself – *Propheten rechts, Propheten links, das
Weltkind in her Mitte.* I was inconceivably worldly.

MacIntyre attached himself to me all the time in London and
insisted not only on staying in the same hotel, but on sleeping in
the same bedroom. He also refused to speak anything but Irish,
which was a sore trial to me as I spoke Munster Irish, which has
been infected by the accentuation of Norman French, and he spoke
Ulster Irish, which has been affected by Scottish Gaelic. It was only
a question of the tonic accent, of whether you said '*P'cheen*' or
'*Potin*', but oh, dear God, the trial that tonic accent could become

when MacIntyre became glued with fright in the middle of Piccadilly Circus and would neither come on nor go back.

He had tried to buy for Donegal Country Library a book which he thought was very devotional – it was Joyce's *Portrait of the Artist as a Young Man* – and had actually bought an anthology of contemporary French poetry. One night at bedtime he begged me to read to him from this. From listening to Wilson's French I knew how deplorable my own French accent was, but he was so much in earnest that I read him Jammes' 'Prayer to Go to Heaven With the Donkeys'. It put MacIntyre into a state of ecstasy.

'Och, man dear,' he said at last, 'isn't it a terrible pity you can't speak Irish as well as you speak French!'

Ulstermen are the nicest people in the world except in the matter of religion and dialect.

I am sure he saw little of London because my London was not one that anyone else would recognize. We must have seen Westminster Bridge because it would have been an excuse for my reciting 'Earth has not anything to show more fair' to him, but I doubt if we ever saw Westminster Abbey. On the other hand I rapidly made myself an authority on London bookshops, and knew the shortest possible route from anywhere through Charing Cross Road to Mudie's or the Times Book Club, and I moved in a lover's trance through the wet twilight, clutching under my arm some treasure I had gone without lunch to buy.

And under the lust for books and pictures was another lust – the provincial's for the strange book or print or packet of cigarettes or bottle of wine that may bring back into the gloom of some provincial town a flash of glory from the world outside. He imagines he can open the book, and there will be Charing Cross Road, or light a Gauloise and back will come the Boulevard St-Michel, but the glory fades; the book becomes like any other book, the print like those he bought in Patrick Street; the cigarettes and wine lose their flavour, which was never theirs to begin with.

Nevertheless the trip had its compensations. A few weeks later I returned to Cork for the Christmas holidays and a little crowd gathered in Corkery's front room on a Sunday night. He was discussing modern architecture and sculpture and spoke severely of Liverpool Cathedral. I protested, and said it wasn't as bad as all that, and Corkery turned on me with unusual severity. I think by this time he felt I was getting notions. 'What do you know about it?' he asked. 'The photographs are there. The detail is *very* bad.'

I was embarrassed, because though I might high-hat the neighbours, it would never have occurred to me to be anything but deferential to him, so I said feebly. 'Oh, nothing, but I was there at Matins a few weeks ago, and I thought it very impressive.' It was only in the silence that followed that I realized that, quite without intending to do so, I had left my old master with nothing at all to say.

3

After six months in Sligo I was sent as assistant to Wicklow, where a new library was to be opened. With me went a second assistant called Brennan, an ex-seminarist who later in life abandoned his literary career and went back to the priesthood.

I lodged in a little huxter shop kept by a widow named Soames on the main street. The house itself seemed to be slipping gently away down from the street into the river. When you opened the unlocked half of the glass front door, there were steps down into the shop, which never seemed to have anything but a few packets on its quite substantial shelving. Then a bell rang and Mrs Soames, with an old coat thrown round her shoulders, came grousing and moaning up another step from the kitchen, which was on the right. She had a long, bloodless white face and the air of an old witch. Behind the shop was the sitting-room, also down a step, but this did little to reduce the house's urge to subside, for the floor sloped alarmingly towards the little window, and the midday soup usually overflowed on to the tablecloth.

I had the room to myself, except for one night in the week when a travelling teacher came. He was small and neat and fussy, with a rosy face and bright blue eyes. He had a poor opinion of Ireland, and when this made him too depressed, he took a couple of drinks. They only made the depression worse, and he kicked his school-books round the room and broke into a nasal wail.

'I'm a child of the sun, and what am I doing with my life? Teaching Eskimos up at the bloody North Pole. This is an awful country!'

Then he took up a Greek play and started to read it to me. When I said I didn't understand it, he became impatient.

'But can't you feel it, man? Can't you feel the Greek sunlight?'

Bill Soames, the only son, was about thirty-five. He was an agricultural labourer, and every morning, wet and fine, cycled miles out into the country to earn his miserable wages. For close on fifteen years he had been keeping company with a servant girl, and each week on her free night they went for a walk or to the cinema. In due course – maybe, if God was good, within the next ten years – his mother would die and leave him the little shop and Bridie could make a few shillings selling cigarettes and keeping a lodger as his mother did.

It was a house of character, and very pleasant on those winter evenings when the rain lashed the window and you heard the roar of shingle from beyond the Murrough, the curious bar of land that divided river from sea.

Geoffrey Phibbs, my boss, was tall and thin and dark, with a long lock of black hair that fell over one eye, a stiff, abrupt manner, a curt, high-pitched voice and a rather insolent air. There was something about him that was vaguely satanic, and he flew into hysterical rages about trifles. Within the first few minutes of our meeting he made it clear that he despised Brennan and myself and proposed to have as little as possible to do with us. He was the eldest son of a Sligo landowner, and had the natural contempt of the educated man for the self-educated. He under-valued his own education; I over-valued mine, and the laboriously acquired bits and scraps of Goethe, Heine, Musset and the Gaelic poets which with me passed for culture seemed to him mere country pedantry.

Our very first attempts to organize a library in Wicklow ran into bad trouble. Before the library committee had met at all, the priest who represented the Catholic Church on it told us that he intended to propose at our first meeting that the committee adjourn *sine die*. There would be no library at all if he could stop it, and he would. The reason for his opposition was still the fuss over Lennox Robinson's 'blasphemous story'. Although Robinson had been forced to resign and Tom McGreevy* had resigned with him, the entire library foundation came under suspicion. Clearly, the Carnegie United Kingdom Trust was involved in a vast conspiracy to deprive the poor Irishman of his faith.

Phibbs, an Irish Protestant with an English education, was incapable of understanding a situation like this, much less of dealing with it and, left to himself, he would probably have delivered a few

*Robinson's assistant. He later became Director of the National Gallery, Dublin.

well-chosen blasphemies and retired in a huff. I knew that in Ireland you can oppose the clergy only with nationalists, so I introduced Phibbs to another ex-jailbird, Seamus Keely, who taught Irish in the local technical school, studied law in his time off and was on his way to a judgeship.

Keely was a handsome man, though you could hardly see the good looks for the cloud of melancholy that surrounded him. Even the pince-nez on the end of his nose looked as if it were on the point of committing suicide. When I proposed that he should present himself at the committee meeting as a representative of the Carnegie United Kingdom Trust, he shrieked with outraged legal virtue; but when I explained that the alternative would be the abolition of the library, the humour of the suggestion dawned on him and he began to giggle. I also warned Phibbs, who would chair the meeting, to insist on a vote *ex officio*, which seemed to me a match for *sine die* any day of the week.

But it was not necessary. The mere presence of Keely, handsome, modest and fresh from an internment camp, and an exemplary Catholic besides, was enough to assure everyone that the Irishman's simple faith was in no immediate danger. I should add that afterwards Keely, the priest and I became great friends, but the Wicklow County Library owes its existence to a shameless piece of gerrymandering by an Irish judge who was probably even less ashamed of it than I was.

After that, Phibbs treated me with considerably more respect. What was more important from my point of view was that he showed his gratitude to Keely, though none of us knew that this gentle teacher of Irish would become a judge. Phibbs realized that in our ignorant way we knew things about Irish life that he had never been taught. It was the first time I realized the isolation of the Anglo-Irish, which Elizabeth Bowen once compared to the isolation of an only child. At home, all he had known of Irish literature was Miss Hutton's version of the *Cattle Raid of Cooley* – in which he had studied the youthful feats of Cu Chulainn, who drove a *sliotar* down the hound's throat and then beat it over the head with a hurley stick, and a patriotic novel by Canon Sheehan called *Lisheen*, which always lay on the living-room table, because the house was called 'Lisheen'. He began to sign himself 'Seathrún MacPhilip'. But he also had the Anglo-Irish incapacity for language, and after attending a few of Keely's Irish lessons at the technical school, he resigned himself to monolingualism.

Phibbs became the dearest and best of my friends, and I have had many. I don't think I ever even showed Wilson a poem, but I showed all my work to Phibbs. He read my poems, which I hammered out on the office typewriter after hours, and marked them all 'Rubbish' except a few translations from the Irish, which I felt he accepted more because of the material than the treatment. He called for me each day at my lodgings on his way to work, but Mrs Soames soon stopped this. One day she came into the sitting-room, wailing and wringing her hands, and told me that she was delighted to welcome my friends at the house, but she had to make an exception of Mr Phibbs; he was the Devil. I told this extraordi-nary rigmarole to Phibbs, who was impressed rather than angry. He may have had a genuine interest in satanism and regarded her as a witch.

After this, we met at his rooms on the Murrough and drank small glasses of cheap sherry. He had a passion for the destructive criti-cism of religion, which I did not understand, and I still have his Bible with his exclamatory comments on the improbabilities and improprieties of the first few books – I doubt if he ever read further. He believed that marriage in the modern world was an outmoded institution. He forced Havelock Ellis' *Psychology of Sex* on me and was exasperated when I returned it unfinished and commented that it bored me. 'It is permissible to say one is shocked by such a book,' he said curtly. 'It is unforgivable to say one is bored.' He really enjoyed pornography, and when someone irritated him – which was often – he promptly got his own back by writing some murderous and bawdy satire. I still remember his poem on Robert Wilson's English wife:

The night that she, just newly wed,
Was brought, a blushing bride, to bed
Hers was so stout a maidenhead
That all his passion, all her will,
Left her at dawn a virgin still . . .

Yet I, who was so puritanical that I left a room rather than listen to dirty stories, never resented either his blasphemy or obscenity. I think I understood them as the play of a powerful and utterly fearless mind, and to me they were as interesting as the antics of a tiger. I was fascinated by the sheer mental agility that went with his physical agility, which was considerable. Despite his height he walked with short quick steps, changing step frequently to adjust himself to my own long, slow stride. Sometimes I just sat and watched him as though he were something in the zoo.

He had a sort of animal beauty and a touch of animal cruelty. He had been trained as a zoologist, but his only interest was poetry, and since he simply could not grasp the idea of a foreign language, this meant English poetry. He had joined the British Army as soon as he was old enough, but when a drill sergeant shouted at him: 'Hi, you! Take that damn thing out of your pocket!' he had shouted back with equal truculence, 'What do you mean, calling this book a damned thing? It's Shelley's *Collected Poems*.' If the war had continued, he would probably have made a very fine officer.

When he was self-conscious, as he usually was for the first quarter of an hour, particularly if there was someone else in the room, he was stiff, curt and mechanical; but when he relaxed he had all the grace of a thoroughbred. The long lanky hair hung over one eye; the thin lips softened, and you saw the thick, sensual lips of the poet, and he paced round the room with his hands in his trousers pockets, bubbling with boyish laughter. Later, when I read Proust, I knew exactly what Saint-Loup must have looked like.

He was an Irish country gentleman; so he regarded himself and so he behaved – in the way in which an Irish country gentleman believes an English country gentleman behaves. He gave great thought to questions of precedence, and one night he asked me in great perturbation the meaning of a passage he had been reading in some eighteenth-century book, which laid it down that no gentleman sees his guest to the door. Being a boy from the Cork slums I had no difficulty in explaining to him that this is a butler's job, and this gave him much food for thought.

He loved poetry as no one else I have ever known loved it, and he rapidly turned me from a reader of anthologies into a reader of poetry – a very different thing. He loved all poetry, good and bad, famous and forgotten, but he loved the forgotten best, and would come triumphantly back to Wicklow with *Poems of Puncture* by Amanda McKitterick Ros or the works of Thomas Caulfield Irwin. He had an unerring eye for books, and he must have spent a small fortune on them. Once, in later life, he spotted the Kilmarnock edition of Burns on the shilling shelf and, true to character, instead of buying it he brought the error in valuation to the bookseller's attention. Once, maddened by people who borrowed books from him and did not give them back, he had defaced them all with a rubber stamp – 'This Book Has Been Stolen from Geoffrey Phibbs'

– a typical, impulsive bit of vandalism that he must soon have regretted.

He read everything and studied everything that could conceivably have been called 'modern' or 'advanced': ballet, painting, sculpture, poetry and (even though he was tone-deaf) music. His favourite modern poet was an American woman of whom we were both to learn a great deal more. In reading, he preferred the difficult to the simple: it suited his agile, inquisitive mind, while I, of course, preferred the simple, above all if it was sufficiently gloomy. We were never in step: he loved bright modern pictures, Braque and Matisse, while I liked Rembrandt: he listened to Stravinsky or Bach on the gramophone, and I hummed the slow movement of the Beethoven *C Sharp Minor Quartet;* and when he quoted Carew:

To be a whore in spite of grace,
Good counsel, and an ugly face,
And to distribute still the pox
To men of wit . . .

I replied with Landor's 'Artemidora, gods invisible . . .'

His own verse was comparatively straightforward, and he wrote it every day – sometimes three or four poems at a time – and always off the cuff, sometimes within an hour of whatever incident had excited him. One evening, when we were out walking on the hills over Wicklow, he killed a rat, and the poem followed that very evening; another day, when he was alone, he met Austin Clarke's wife, Margaret Lyster, and in due course, I got the poem:

Mister Lyster
Gave it to me the day she had the blister
Between Jack's Hole and Five-Mile Water
And introduced me to her landlord's daughter.

With him, verse was always immediate and spontaneous, and, so far as I could see, complete. The pains and aches of composition, which with me went on year after year, did not seem to exist for him. We would be working together in the office and suddenly he would reach out, grab an old envelope from the wastepaper basket and begin to scribble furiously. Then he would go to the typewriter and type it before he read it to me. I corrected the spelling and grammar, a process that amused and exasperated him: sometimes I thought he mis-spelled deliberately to keep me occupied. 'You will die of sintactical exactniss of the mind,' he once wrote to me. 'I believe it is a very slow and paneful death.'

Nowadays I wonder if those early poems were not much better than I thought them. Now, at least, I realize how brilliant he was, but then, with my large appetite for melancholy music, I thought the poems too flashy, too topical and, above all, too slapdash; and I longed for the moment when the wit and topicality collapsed and let through the pure lyric tone:

Now lets laburnum loose all her light golden locks –

Or –

O solemn slope of mighty limbs so long accustomed to
  Arcadian rams!
'But I'm not much of an antiquary,' she said. 'Oh, no,' I said,
  'you're still quite young and nice.'

It doesn't matter. We were two young poets in love with our trade, and though I wasn't a real poet I enjoyed it as though I were, and not even one's first experience of love-making is quite as satisfying as that.

4

Thanks to my friendship with Phibbs my position in life suddenly changed for the better. I had to borrow the library bicycle one night each week to cycle seven miles out into the mountains and teach Irish for the sake of the five shillings. My pupil was an old school-teacher who had to learn Irish to keep his job; he was a kind old man and always saw that I had drunk well before he sent me home. But Phibbs grew very angry when he understood at last how hard up I was, and he wrote a cruel and witty letter to the Carnegie Trust about it. The Secretary replied handsomely by return, apologizing for Lennox Robinson's meanness, increasing my salary to two pounds ten a week and promising a further increase to three pounds ten when the trustees met.

Even in Big Business overnight increases of more than a hundred

per cent do not often occur, and when they do they do not involve
the same distinction between poverty and wealth. I became reckless,
and when I went home on holiday got my aunt's husband, Pat
Hanlon, to make me a suit – the first I had owned since I was a
small boy – and a shirtmaker to make me two green shirts. These
were a tribute to Phibbs, who, as a serious poet, always wore green
shirts and a black bow-tie. The problem of how to get a broad-
brimmed hat like his had to be deferred till I reached a country
where poets were respected and hats made to suit them, but I
opened an account at Bumpus of Oxford and ordered a pocket
Dante and a pocket Landor. The Dante was my own long-cherished
wish, but the Landor was pure Phibbs.

Naturally I agreed to sign with him a manifesto against Yeats, to
whom he had a great aversion, first because the Yeatses had been
'in trade', and second because Yeats (who, as I later realized, was
half blind and had offended half Dublin by trying to be polite and
call people by their names) had addressed him as 'Coulter'. George
Russell, the Editor of the *Irish Statesman*, made some slighting
reference to our manifesto, and Phibbs and I called to protest.
Russell did his editing from an attic room in a Georgian house in
Merrion Square, which he had papered in brown wrapping-paper
and decorated with gods and goddesses in dark browns and gold.
He sat behind a large desk to the side of the fireplace – a big, burly
North of Ireland Presbyterian with wild hair and beard and a pipe
hanging from his discoloured teeth. He usually sat well back in his
chair, beaming benevolently through his spectacles, his legs crossed,
and his socks hanging down over his ankles. Sometimes in an earnest
mood he leaned forward with his two fat hands on his knees, his
head lowered as he looked at you over the specs, giving his appearance almost an elfin quality. He was an extraordinarily restless,
fidgety man, forever jumping up to find some poem he was about
to print (usually lost in the heap of papers, prints and manuscripts
in his desk) or some book he was reviewing. With him was his
secretary, Susan Mitchell, a deaf woman with a sweet, faded face,
who was supposed to have loved him platonically for the best part
of her life.

Phibbs, like many of the younger writers, despised Russell, whom
he regarded as an old windbag. I was prepared to do the same, but,
while we were still arguing, Phibbs said, 'The difference between
your generation and ours is that we have had no youth.' 'Oh, really!'
Russell replied with an air of great concern, and I disgraced myself

by a roar of laughter in which Russell joined. One of his favourite quotations was a phrase from the *Three Musketeers* – 'I perceive if we do not kill one another we shall be good friends': and I think at that moment Russell and I decided we should be friends, for as we were leaving he put his arm round my shoulder and said, 'Send me something for the paper.'

I did, and he printed it, and another source of income became open to me. Admittedly it was small, but when one has never had anything the occasional guinea or two guineas seems like wealth. I could now spend a night in a hotel – though six and sixpence for bed and breakfast struck me as wicked – so I went to Dublin, mastered even my timidity, and visited him in his house in Rathgar on Sunday evening. I went through the performance I went through so often in later years, climbed the steps, pulled the bell, heard the smelly old dog begin to yelp; and then Russell, shouting and kicking excitedly at the dog, pulled me in by the hand. He had the usual Dublin combination of living- and dining-room, filled with paintings, mostly by himself, and all in glaring colours that matched the glaring overhead light. Corkery, who had once visited him, had told me that the pictures were 'like Hampstead Heath on Sunday night'.

For the first hour he sat uneasily in his big chair in the middle of the room, intent on the doorbell, which was always anticipated by the infernal dog. It was like sitting in the middle of Grand Central Station. Visitors to Dublin – American, Japanese and Chinese – were always dropping in, as well as a gang of adoring old ladies whom I called 'The Holy Women'. He lectured to them all, telling American agriculturists how to organize co-operatives and Indians how to understand Gandhi, and suggesting new themes to poets and storytellers. He talked in set patterns and phrases which had endured for years, some indeed of which could be traced back to his boyhood.

'You know, A.E.,' I said to him years later, 'back in 1904 Joyce has you saying: "The only question about a work of art is, out of how deep a life does it spring." '

'Well, that's clever of him,' Russell replied. 'That's true, you know. I may have said that.'

He said it at least once a day. What was more he did not realize that I was joking him.

He was a creature of habit, and his conversation, like his life, like his pictures, ran in patterns; well-formed phrases, ideas, quotations and anecdotes that he repeated year after year without altering an inflection. He was unskilful in the way he introduced them, and they were usually so general in their application that they had a tendency to obliterate the point in discussion. 'Leonardo advised young painters to study the stains in old marble to discover compositions for their own paintings' was a standard phrase that was exceedingly difficult to relate to any subject one was considering. After a time you got to see Leonardo hovering in the air a mile off and found yourself trying to ward him off as if he were a wasp.

It was this repetitiousness that got him the reputation of a windbag among people like Phibbs, and I understood the criticism even when I disagreed with it. In fact, Russell was a man of intense intellectual vitality; ideas came to him almost too readily, and his experience, when he chose to draw on it, was profound and varied, particularly when he remembered it casually as a result of something someone had just said and it came to him with the freshness of a theme rediscovered.

When the occasional visitors left to catch the last tram, and two or three regular ones like Osborn Bergin the philologist and C. P. Curran the lawyer remained behind, Russell ruffled out his beard as though he were expelling the smoke of generalization from it, and the talk – political and literary gossip – improved enormously. When we rose to go Russell cried, 'Oh, books! You must have books!' On the left-hand side of the wall between sitting- and dining-room there was a tall shelf of religious books that no one was allowed to borrow; but a big, low bookcase against the wall beside it was free to everybody. Russell, a poor boy himself, had picked up an occasional book in a second-hand store and made his soul on it, learning whole pages by heart (his verbal memory was fabulous), and he knew everyone must love books as he did. He would squat cross-legged before the bookcase, grab a new book and lift his glasses to read from it, his short-sighted eyes skipping from line to line, and then look up at you happily, drooling and beaming.

'Isn't that good? Isn't that clever? Don't you like that? Doesn't he interest you? Ah, but here's something you will like.'

I don't think I ever left that house or the office without an armful of books, good, bad and indifferent, and later, when I was in hospital, Russell continued to send me regular parcels of them – 'to raise your soul above the troubles of the flesh' as he would explain.

He was that sort of man. Within half an hour he enveloped you in universal curiosity and affection in which shyness was forgotten.

It was like an old fur coat, a little bit smelly and definitely designed for someone of nobler stature, but, though it might threaten you with suffocation, it never left you feeling cold. He would find you a new doctor, a new wife, a new lodging or a new job, and if you were ill would cheerfully come and nurse you.

I did not quarrel with friends like Phibbs who resented the old fur coat, but I, who found it hard enough to write a letter and almost impossible to wrap up a parcel, appreciated the fury of affection that went into all that vague letter-writing, picture-giving and parcel-sending. It all came out of a great emotional abundance like that of one of the nineteenth-century writers he loved so much – Hugo or Dumas – and it was always a mystery to me how that emotional volcano poured forth only little twelve-line lyrics in which every second word was vague and literary.

As all Russell's discoveries had to be pronounced on by Yeats, Russell ordered me to visit him on one of his Monday evenings. In those days Sunday was Russell's night, Monday Yeats', Tuesday afternoon Sarah Purser's, Sunday afternoon Seamus O'Sullivan's. Yeats' Mondays were peculiar because they were all male; on Monday nights he discussed sex, except when Lady Gregory was staying, and, of course, it would be my rotten luck to be ordered to the presence when she was staying and no one else came, so that I had to face Yeats and herself alone. At that time I did not know Mrs Yeats, who could manage to make even me feel at home. To complete my confusion, Lady Gregory wore a mantilla as though for an audience with the Pope.

It was all too much for a raw youth who was terrified of social occasions anyhow. Yeats' study was kept deliberately dark, and everything in it was expensive and beautiful; the masks from his dance plays, the tall bookcases with the complete sets of the classics, and the long, orderly table with the tall silver candlesticks. Even Corkery could not have said that the pictures were 'like Hampstead Heath on Sunday evening'. And nothing less like Russell could be imagined than the tall man in the well-cut blue suit with the silk shirt and bow-tie who came shuffling in, holding his hand out high as though he expected you to kiss his ring – a beautiful ring, as it happened. Never could you imagine an Irish countryman giving Yeats an approving look and shouting, 'Bring in the whiskey now, Mary, and be *continually* bringing in the hot water', which was how Russell was received in one Irish town. Later, the very sight of Yeats at the door would send Mother scuttling to her bedroom.

There was something ecclesiastical about the blind man's stare, the ceremonial washing of the hands and the languid unction of the voice. That night I noticed that he said 'weld' and 'midder' for 'world' and 'murder'.

There was a touch of the bird about him as well; the eyes, like those of a bird, seemed to be at the sides rather than the front of the face, and his laugh tended to be harsh, abrupt and remote – a caw, as Moore called it. When he was happy and forgot himself, animation seemed to flow over him. He sat forward, arms on his knees, washing his hands over and over, the pose sometimes broken by a loud, harsh, throaty laugh and the tossing back of the big bird's head while he sat bolt upright in his chair gripping his lapels and raising his brows with a triumphant stare; sometimes he broke it by tweaking his nose; most characteristically perhaps by raising his index finger for attention. But when he was really excited his whole face lit up as from a light inside. It was astonishing, because even in old age when he was looking most wretched and discontented that blaze of excitement would sweep over his face like a glory, like a blast of sunlight over a moor, and from behind the mask a boy's tense eager face looked out at you. I had already noticed with Lennox Robinson the way you could see under the mask to the boy beneath. In Robinson the boy was a practical joker; a brat who had already done something terrible to your bed; but the boy behind Yeats' mask was one who had been kept in on a summer day and looked at you, trapped and despairing, from his bedroom window.

It was a while before I realized that Yeats was a desperately shy man who had the effect of driving other shy people slightly dotty as he drove me that night and many a night after. I am not saying that Russell was not shy – poets, after all, are not made of brass – but shyness was forgotten in the folds of the old fur coat, which, I fancy, was the thing about him that Yeats hated most. To Yeats, Russell was as much mob as man. Yeats loved the half light, Russell the full light, though Yeats was an infinitely more observant man than Russell; and if you had the misfortune to bore him you were perfectly well aware that he had marked you down as an enemy and would remember it against you in time to come.

In spite of the blindness, in spite of the shyness that made it impossible for Yeats to use Christian names, he was extraordinarily watchful and observant. Within the first half-hour George Russell would smother you with curiosity, affection and kindness, but I never felt that these bright, kind, honest eyes saw me at all; while Yeats, apparently blind, bored and bad-tempered, astonished me by his apparent familiarity with my life, my work and my friends.

'I know Strong is a great friend of yours, O'Connor,' he said one night many years later, 'but he *bores* me.'

The important thing to me was not that Strong bored him, but that he remembered that Strong was a friend of mine and was quite ready for an argument. On another night he said, 'I see the Censorship Board has banned the book by So-and-So – the fellow who stole your story.' I didn't know that anyone had stolen that particular story;* it has been stolen so often since that even the newspapers comment on it, but Yeats was the very first to notice the plagiarism.

There was no doubt as to which was the easier to make friends with, Russell or Yeats. That first night Lady Gregory and himself were putting me through my paces. Lady Gregory asked me to say some modern Irish poem, and I said Father Paddy Browne's translation of a poem of Gogarty's, which is better than the original. Then I spoiled it all by telling how another travelling teacher of Irish like myself – Dick Murphy – whose small salary often went unpaid, tried to eke it out by producing his own translation of Lady Gregory's *Workhouse Ward*, but, being too poor to pay the royalties, re-titled it *Crime and Punishment. Translated from the Original Russian of Fyodor Dostoevsky*. I know it was not a tactful story to tell before the author, but I was embarrassed, and anyhow I still like 'from the Original Russian'.

'And didn't he know it was wrong?' Lady Gregory asked bleakly, in that flat, peasant accent of hers, and this ruined the rest of the evening for me.

It was no comfort to learn a few days later that Lady Gregory was re-telling the story all over Dublin or that Yeats had said my conversation was 'profound'. What I needed was that big, smelly old fur coat.

*'Guests of the Nation'.

5

I was now comparatively well off, but the job of librarian in Cork County was coming up, and I dreamed of it. To my surprise Russell was violently opposed to my taking it at all. There were other jobs I could get within twenty or thirty miles of Dublin and he wanted me to apply for one of these: then I should be on the spot if a job turned up in Dublin itself, and meanwhile could spend my weekends in town. He simply could not understand that I did not particularly want to live in Dublin, and he had the lowest view of Cork.

'My dear fellow,' he said dogmatically, 'you wouldn't be able to stand that hole for six months.'

What astonishes me now, looking back on the period, is that I did not even understand what he was getting at. Is it that young writers have no sense of fear? I was prudent enough. When I used the pseudonym 'Frank O'Connor' (my second name and my mother's maiden name) I left myself a loophole against the sort of mistake Lennox Robinson had made when he published his silly little story under his own name while still Secretary of the Irish Carnegie United Kingdom Trust, but the real dangers I did not see at all, then or for years later. Cork was to me merely my material, the place I knew best, and it never occurred to me that that particular material could ever have any effect on me, or that I might eventually find myself in the position of Heine's monkey chewing his own tail – 'objectively he is eating, subjectively he is being eaten.'

And yet, during my time in Wicklow, I could see the consequences of this restrictiveness all round me. There was the problem of getting local sanction to establish our libraries, which was not made any easier by Robinson's 'crime'. Some of the priests would allow no libraries at all. In Rathdrum, a town up the country from us, the parish priest initially resisted all our efforts to start a branch library. At last I decided that the time had come to visit him. Phibbs and I called first on the curate, a splendid young fellow who was in despair with the parish priest and with Ireland. A couple of nights a week he went off to the local technical school and took off his coat to practise carpentry so as to encourage the unemployed lads of the town to learn a trade, all to no purpose.

'You'll go up to that parochial house,' he said, 'and see the old man at the table with his dinner gone cold and a volume of Thomas

Aquinas propped up in front of him. And between you and me and the wall,' he added, 'Thomas Aquinas was a bloody old cod.'

We found the parish priest exactly as the curate had predicted, Aquinas and all, but there seemed to be nothing of the obscurantist about the delightful old man we met. On the contrary, when we introduced ourselves, he beamed and regretted that we hadn't come to lunch. He took a particular fancy to me because I spoke Irish, and he was devoted to Irish and Irish literature. In fact, one of his dearest friends had been George Moore. Poor George. Of course he had been greatly wronged in Ireland, where people did not understand his work, but George had been a really dear and good man.

I didn't, of course, believe for an instant that he had been friendly with George Moore, but if the illusion made him more tolerant of our business it was all right with me. But when I introduced the subject I saw at once what the curate had meant. Oh, libraries. Libraries, hm! Well, libraries, of course, were wonderful things in their own place, but town libraries were a great responsibility. It was all very well for sophisticated people like ourselves to read the works of dear George, but could we really thrust them into the hands of simple Irish townspeople?

I damn near told him that from the little I knew of simple Irish townspeople they could give us all odds, but I knew this would get us nowhere. Charm was the thing, and charm won us permission at last, but only if the curate took full responsibility and satisfied himself of the innocuousness of the books we sent out. Swift wondered how it was that every virtuous English bishop translated to Ireland was murdered on Hounslow Heath and his place taken by a highwayman, but I wondered what happened to those nice, broadminded young curates one met after they became parish priests.

Nevertheless I was beginning to suspect that as an authority on Irish ways I was a wash-out. And now I had another shock coming to me, because, as we left, the parish priest said to me, 'I know you'll be interested in this,' and handed me a presentation copy of *The Untilled Field*, in Irish, with an affectionate inscription by George Moore.

'It's all very well for you, O'Donovan,' the travelling teacher said testily one night as we were standing on top of the stairs together, holding our candles and speaking in low voices so as not to disturb the Soameses. 'You don't know what life in this country is like. I can keep it up for a few years more, but I know damn well the way

I'm going to die. I'll be dodging up to the church three or four times a day to say a prayer, and looking at the other side of the street when I meet some old friend that might be a temptation to me.

'That's the way my father died, and my father was a very intelligent man. He was one of a crowd in Limerick, and none of them believed in anything either. One of them – a fellow called Cremin – went to the States. They were all very fond of him. But you know the sort of thing that happens. One by one they got married and settled down and went to Mass, and they were ashamed of their old friends too, the way I'll be.

'And then, long after, Cremin wrote to say he was coming home. He was after making a bit of money and he wanted to retire to Limerick. Father was delighted. He couldn't believe that the good old days weren't going to come back. They were all delighted; they all liked Cremin, so they arranged for a big car to take them to Queenstown and meet the liner.

'Well, Cremin came ashore as sprightly as ever. They'd arranged for a dinner at the Commodore, and they made speeches about Cremin and their youth, and he got up to reply, and, begod, didn't he drop dead across the table!

'They brought him home that night and buried him, and after the funeral Father invited a Redemptorist back to the house, and from that day till the day he died we were never without a priest in the house. And I tell you, O'Donovan, that's the way I'm going to die too. You mark my words!'

But why should I mark them when the very same thing was taking place under my eyes in the Soames household? Neither Mrs Soames nor her son was very pious. In fact, Mrs Soames was a most superior woman. I think she had been parlour-maid in some Wicklow big house and married the coachman. In spite of her rigmarole about Phibbs being the Devil, she had a good natural intelligence, and hers was the only Catholic lodging-house I ever knew that wasn't cluttered up with holy pictures and statues.

Then we had a Redemptorist mission in the town. The women's turn came first, and each night Mrs Soames hobbled off to the church and she confessed and communicated like everybody else. She was no zealot, but like any other woman she did not want to be different.

But before the women's mission ended at all it was clear that there was trouble in the house. From the sitting-room I could hear

herself and Bill arguing in the kitchen, her voice shrill and querulous
and Bill's deep and mournful. When she brought in my glass of
milk she was full of complaints. Bill refused to go to the mission at
all. According to himself – and, knowing Bill well, I believed it –
he had done no harm to anyone and had nothing at all to confess.
What harm could he do, cycling out at the crack of dawn, wet or
fine, miles out in the country and only seeing Bridie for one evening
a week? Besides, it was too bloody silly. That was more or less the
way I felt myself, but Mrs Soames seemed to feel that it was a
matter of maternal discipline and that he mustn't make a show of
her before the town.

The night the men's mission opened I heard the row going on in
the kitchen. Bill, with his deep husky voice, sounded like a cow
that was being driven to the knacker's. His mother scolded and
hounded him out, and then watched from the front door to make
sure he did not bolt down some lane to the quays.

I followed to see the fun, but it wasn't very funny. The Redemptorist had one of those thick pulpit voices that bellowed till it
bounced and then dropped to an awed whisper. He described to us
what he obviously thought was how Voltaire died, knowing he was
damned, and screaming, screaming for the priest who never came.
As I emerged from the church the town atheist approached me.

'How did you like God's representative telling those damned lies?'
he hissed angrily.

'He probably believed them himself,' I said.

'He never read a line of Voltaire's in his life,' said the atheist in
a fury.

Then I saw Bill, and his whole face was lit up.

'How did you like that, Bill?' I said.

'Finest bloody sermon I ever heard in my life,' Bill said enthusiastically. 'Aha, that fellow knows how to talk.'

For the rest of the week his mother had no trouble in getting Bill
shaved and dressed for the show. As a disciplinarian she might have
taken alarm at this, but we are always blind when our temperaments
are rushing us to a crisis. Nothing dawned on the poor woman until
Saturday night, when Bill came home and told her he was getting
married at once. The priest had given him a terrible time in
confession, and asked him what he meant – a grown man with a
steady job – indulging in occasions of sin with poor Bridie for fifteen
years. Finally he had threatened Bill with a terrible death – by
drowning, no less, though how Bill could get drowned in his daily

excursions to the farm was not clear. Down, down, down he could go, and then rise again for a moment with outstretched hands, gasping for air – Voltaire himself had nothing on Bill. After a dreadful fifteen minutes Bill had slunk out of the church, convinced that everyone was looking at him and blaming him for some terrible crime he had never committed.

At first Mrs Soames was her usual sarcastic self and asked whether he had told the priest that he only earned twelve shillings a week – it may have been fifteen or eighteen, but it was in that neighbourhood. Bill replied that he had and the priest had said it didn't matter. Only then did the immensity of the disaster become clear to Mrs Soames. Her Boy, whom she had looked after and bullied and defended from designing women, had slipped out of her hands into those of a priest, and not even the poor decent Kerry priest she could pin the blame on, but a nameless Redemptorist who was here today and gone tomorrow.

For hours I heard the voices going on in the kitchen and felt ashamed to pass them on my way up the stairs. Finally, when Bill had gone to bed, Mrs Soames came in with my glass of milk and wept and wrung her hands. She had met the fate of every strong-minded woman and found an adversary stronger than herself. When she had tried to talk to Bill about money, all he had been able to do was to cover his eyes and describe the horrors of drowning.

'And when I asked him how they would live, he said Bridie would have to go on working. And when the children start coming? I said, and all I could get out of him was "God will provide". He will, I hear! I know who'll do the providing, Mr O'Donovan. I will. I'll have to take them in, and give them your room, and then the children will come and I'll have to mind them as well.'

She left me in a state of distraction, and God knows I was sorry for her – the saddest woman who had ever done her duty by attending a Redemptorist mission. But I saw it from outside – my material, as you might call it. It never occurred to me that anything of the sort could happen to myself.

6

Notwithstanding Russell's forebodings, I accepted the job of librarian in Cork County with a salary of two hundred and fifty pounds a year.

It was great money; more than anyone in Harrington's Square had ever earned, so far as I knew. Indeed, I suspect that Father's imagination refused to grasp it at all, and that it only worried him. It even worried me at times, because I had more in common with Father than I liked to admit; but Mother, with her placid, sanguine temperament, knew it was the will of God and a proper reward for my years of hardship, so she rented a gas stove to cook properly and had gaslight installed in the kitchen and the front room so I could write without straining my eyes.

To furnish the front room she bought a second-hand carpet, a round table that was a little unsound on its one leg, two dining-room chairs and an armchair. I bought myself a Morris chair – a poor commercial substitute for the fine chair that Corkery had made for himself – a second-hand typewriter for seven pounds, a print of Degas dancers (as a student in the School of Art I had quarrelled with my teacher, who said that Degas could not paint, and later I quarrelled with Yeats about him), a gramophone and a few records of Mozart and Beethoven. I also got the local carpenter to make me a fitted bookcase that ran the length of one wall. As well as that I bought a black suit to go with the green shirts and the black bow-tie. 'We writers, ma'am', as Disraeli said to Queen Victoria.

But beyond this my imagination, which was strictly conditioned to the interior life, did not function too well. Indeed, it would not be too much to say that it did not function at all. Anyone with a glimmer of worldly wisdom would have bought himself a comfortable modern house with a bathroom; and indeed some glimmerings of this I must have had because Father and I argued over it for years.

He was an emotionally generous man and did not hold it against me that – so far, at least – I had not turned into the liability he had prophesied. Among his old comrades of the Munster Fusiliers it flattered him to see my name in the papers and know I was in a public job – pensionable, of course; anything else would be valueless. He even came to see the advantages in the gas stove and the aluminium kettle. He liked to get up early and make the tea. 'Star of Life's Ocean!' as Minnie Connolly said, 'If a man brought me up tea at seven in the morning I'd plaster him with it.'

All the same I suspect that he was never without a secret feeling that there was something flighty and insecure about it all, even about the gas stove; something that lacked the Roman calm and permanence of his own two military pensions and the reliable old iron kettle. With these a man knew where he was, so he advised caution. If I had a little bit of money over and above (between grown men he realized that neither of us could afford to admit anything of the kind or people would start trying to borrow it from us) the thing to do was to put it in the bank. And seeing how difficult I found it to dispose of my money in any practical way, the bit of me that was Father inclined to the same view.

Besides, he would add with great resignation, one of these days I should be wanting a home of my own. This again was an appeal to my non-existent manliness and a gentlemanly assumption that I was not in love with my mother. What would he and she do then? The picture of my throwing out the pair of them for the sake of any woman struck me as merely laughable, but he nodded his head gravely and assured me that Life was like that.

And when this argument was not enough he had a real clincher. The son of an old friend had become a famous boxer and had immediately bought his parents a fine house in the suburbs. Father and the boxer's father, who adored his son, met occasionally after Mass and went for long walks together, usually to some new building development on the outskirts of the city, but always ending up outside his friend's old house in the poorer part of the city where the old friend had lived when he was poor and innocent and happy; and his friend would say, 'God, Mick, I'd hate the Boy to know it, but I never had a day's happiness in that other bloody misfortunate hole!'

Anyhow, Father's reasons for not wanting to move went deeper than that – much deeper, and if I could plumb them I could reveal every detail of his character and much of my own. He didn't own our house; he had to pay four and sixpence a week for it; but he identified himself completely with it and would have died for it if necessary. Children playing ball outside his gate plagued him – they might break a window – and he would stand in ambush behind the lace curtains in the front room, watching them, while Mother sat in the kitchen, sewing or reading.

'Min!' he would whisper in a tone of high tragedy.

'Wisha, what is it now?'

'It's that little pup of the Horgans again!'

'Ah, wouldn't you forget them and read your paper?' Mother would ask in a complaining tone.

'How can I read my paper?' Father would hiss back. 'My goodness, what sort of parents do them children have?'

He was waiting for the supreme moment when one of them would jump over the wall from the next garden after his ball, or take a swing on the squeaky gate with the broken latch. Then he would rush to the front door, fling it open and glower and mutter at the children, who would run madly to the top or the bottom of the square and stand there, daring him. Father was too good a neighbour to make scenes that would involve him with the parents, and this left him in a permanent state of frustration, for after a couple of minutes of outraged dignity he would stamp back slowly to the kitchen, brooding on firing parties, the cat-o'-nine-tails and other neglected forms of military discipline.

At the same time though, like any true artist scornful of general criticism, he could admit to small weaknesses in his masterpiece and remedy them in his own way. When I pointed out that the wall and gate-pillars were disintegrating, he studied them at length with pursed lips, working out how they could be repaired at little or no expense. He had noticed a pile of quite good discarded bricks on some building site and brought brown-paper parcels of them home after dark. pleased as an old dog who has disinterred a juicy bone. Mother, accustomed to his treasure trove, gave them a curious eye and asked, 'What are you going to do with them?' 'You'll see,' Father said complacently. We saw. He knew a builder's labourer who could wangle him a bit of cement and some sand, and after evenings of labour during which trowel, cement and bricks had all turned and bitten him, he asked me to admire brand new gate-posts, not perpendicular, of course, and very rough on the top, but still substantial, and now if God would only throw in his way a latch he could mortar into it and prevent those ill-mannered kids from using his gate as a swing, we should have a better house than any on the College Road and for a mere four and six a week. Father's attitude to new building developments was mixed, to put it mildly. As a Corkman with a low opinion of all other nationalities, particularly Dubliners, he was fascinated by the expansion of the city, but as a potential victim he was highly critical of it.

So I could not have a house, and I was scared at the prospect of trying to keep a car in Harrington's Square – 'them kids' would take it asunder – but I was determined that at least I should rent a cottage by the sea for a few weeks in summer as others did. Father humoured me and even agreed to come down and join Mother and myself for a couple of days himself. Anything longer would be impossible, and even the couple of days involved something like preparations for a siege of the home. It was not enough that neighbours guaranteed to watch it; bolts and window fastenings had to be renewed and strengthened, and when he left the house the gate was tied to the gate post with coils of barbed wire.

I enjoyed having him with us because he was an even better walker than myself, though a more perfunctory one. On a visit to the country his trained military eye sized up the number of roads, and he liked to inspect each once, and when the inspection was complete to go home. The fact that a road was attractive did not mean it needed a second inspection.

One of these walks in Courtmacsherry is very vivid in my memory, and I wrote a story about it long after. We had climbed a hill overlooking the sea, and on the horizon, apparently moving across it in a series of jerks, like the swan in *Lohengrin*, was an American liner on its way into Cobh. A farmer working in a field by the road joined us; he too had been watching the liner and it had reminded him of his son who had emigrated to America when he was quite young. After a few years the boy had married an Irish-American girl whose family had come from Donegal, and soon after ceased to write home, though his wife continued to write. Then she fell ill and her doctor suggested a holiday in Ireland. She had arrived one day on a liner like the one we were watching, and her father-in-law had met her at the station with his horse and cart. She had stayed with them for weeks, regained her health and gradually won the affection of the family. After that she had set off to visit her parents' family in Donegal, and it was only then that the old Cork couple had learned from a letter to a neighbour that their son was dead before ever she left America.

Up there on the hill in the evening with the little whitewashed farmhouse beside us and the liner disappearing in the distance, it was an extraordinarily moving story, all the more so because the farmer was obviously still bewildered and upset by it.

'Why would she do a thing like that to us?' he asked. 'It wasn't that we weren't fond of her. We liked her, and we thought she liked us.'

Clearly he suspected that some motive of self-interest was involved, and I was afraid to tell him my own romantic notion that the girl might have liked them all too well and kept her husband alive in their minds as long as she could and – who knows? – perhaps kept him alive in her own.

I knew that some time I should have to write that story, but Father only listened with the polite and perfunctory smile that he gave to the scenery. Both, no doubt, were suitable for people living in backward places, but did not call for closer inspection, and next morning he was up at six to make sure of catching the noon bus for Cork.

He was the most complete townie I ever knew.

7

Once, summing up what she owed to Father, Mother said that since the day of their marriage he had never looked at the side of the road another woman walked on.

She was probably right. Father was a one-woman man, and in the same way he was a one-town man, and one might go even further and say he was a one-house man. In some extraordinary way she and Cork and the house in Harrington's Square (not to mention the pensions) were all fused together into a vast complacency that hid whatever fundamental insecurity drove him to his terrible drinking bouts. Clearly I had something of his weakness to go back to Cork in defiance of Russell's warnings. Mother worried and fretted even more than I did, but I feel that inside she was quite free of the tyranny of objects, and I sometimes wonder if she was not half-suffocated by the close texture of Father's world – and my own.

It was pleasure enough for me to be back with money in my pocket among those, some of whom had regarded me as a half-wit and a ne'er-do-well and some who had wished me well and thought I had something in me if only I got a chance. Even Mother, ordinarily so humble, had her little moments of satisfaction, as when the ambitious woman who had refused to salute me when I was poor took her aside to ask if the books I was always reading when I was a boy were all about being a librarian. 'I didn't bother to enlighten her,' Mother said stiffly, knowing that poor Mickie Joe, the ambitious woman's son, would at once be sent to the library to borrow books on librarianship.

But I also had enough of Mother's intellectual inquisitiveness in me to make me aware within a month that Russell had been right. I couldn't stand the damn place. It was one thing to be in exile from it compelled to make friends of Phibbs and Russell and rely on brief visits to report on them to Jack Hendrick*, and Corkery, and another thing entirely to be in Cork with Hendrick and Corkery, waiting for the post to bring me news of Phibbs and Russell. This was a reversal of parts which I hadn't expected at all, because it had simply never occurred to me that I could feel as deeply about new friends as about old ones. One night when I met Corkery in King Street, I said it to him quite innocently, and afterwards felt that things were never quite the same between us.

At last I was beginning to get a picture of Ireland, the real Ireland, lonely and dotty. This was no longer the romantic Ireland of the little cottages and the hunted men, but an Ireland where everyone was searching frantically for a pension or a job. I also found that my ability to handle a priest in County Wicklow was no qualification for handling the Cork County Council.

On my first morning at work I came to interview the Secretary of the County Council. I had a cheque in my pocket for what was to me a vast sum from the Carnegie United Kingdom Trust, and I needed instructions as to where I should lodge it. I had also to select premises for my library and insure them. Under such circumstances it was the business of the senior County Council official to advise, and it was our business to regard the advice as instructions. The final decision rested with the Library Committee of the County Council when it was formed, but it was also common form that the Committee should not interfere with the Council on whom they would eventually have to rely for funds.

But, of course, nothing like this happened to me. I knew my Turgenev and Tolstoy, but they were useless when applied to local authorities. What I needed was a strong dose of Gogol, an author whom I had never studied.

I arrived at the Secretary's office at ten o'clock in the morning and was told he was at Mass. This sort of message is one that every Irishman automatically accepts. The Secretary may even have been

*See *An Only Child*, chapter 15.

at Mass. About eleven-thirty he came strolling in, a tall, gangling man with long white hair and a white moustache and a wonderful air of inconsequent buccaneering. A number of people seemed to be waiting on him, and he shouted at one, became involved with another, and whatever the subject was he seemed to change it.

He did precisely the same thing with me. For the best part of half an hour I tried to get from him the instructions I would have got from the Secretary of the Wicklow County Council in five minutes, but every time he evaded me. Finally the Angelus bell rang from the Franciscan church behind the court-house, and he slowly clambered on to his desk – a tall, old-fashioned desk like a lectern – joined his hands and closed his eyes. When I interrupted him again, he snapped at me angrily.

'Ah, let me say my prayers!' he said. And that was all the advice I ever got from the Secretary of the Cork County Council. I doubt if even Gogol would have been enough.

I went from him straight to the manager of the County Council bank and modestly asked to be allowed to open an account with the large cheque in my pocket.

'When you produce a resolution signed by the chairman of your committee, Mr O'Donovan,' the manager said coldly, practically implying I had stolen it.

I was distracted. Never in my life had I had a bank account or more money on a cheque than would pay my own small salary, but I did know that people deposited such cheques in a personal account, collected the interest and then later wrote a cheque for the original amount, and I was sure that sooner or later someone would accuse me of having stolen it. I knew one member of the County Council who had voted for my appointment, so I went to see him in his office in Patrick Street. He was a big fat man who had told me the story of his life – the publishable portions at least – when I went to solicit his vote, and I had liked him for it. As a boy his dream had been of becoming a great violinist, and he had practised in his room till he was found out and beaten by his mother.

Normally he moved slowly and apparently with great difficulty, but he moved like a bird when I told him my sad story.

'Leave it to me, boy!' he said in a sad, booming voice. 'Leave it to me!'

He took me straight to his own bank and repeated the story to the manager. The manager, who obviously admired Mr Buckley, as I may call him, received me with Christian understanding and said there would be no difficulty; he would take it on himself; and when I left an account had been opened on behalf of the Carnegie United Kingdom Trust. I was very relieved and thanked my friend Mr Buckley. He told me that whenever I was in difficulty again I had only to call on him.

I suspect now that Mr Buckley knew very well the difficulty I was in and intended that I should remain in it. Before a week was over I had visits from a score of councillors who complained of my opening an account for a sub-committee of the County Council in an unauthorized bank. Obviously they did not believe my version of the incident.

By the time the County Council Secretary had done with organizing my sub-committee it consisted of a hundred and ten members, and anyone who has ever had to deal with a public body will realize the chaos this involved. Finally I managed to get my committee together in one of the large council rooms, and by a majority it approved my choice of bankers. There was, I admit, a great deal of heat. Some of the councillors felt I had acted in a very high-handed way, and one protested against my appearing in a green shirt – a thing which, he said, he would tolerate from nobody.

A general meeting of the County Council was being held at the same time in another part of the building. During the discussions I was exasperated by people banging on the doors at one side of the chamber we occupied.

Later I learned that (through an oversight no doubt) all the doors leading into the committee room from the Council Chamber had been locked, so that councillors who wished to oppose my choice of banker had been locked out and only those who knew the architecture of the building were in their seats on time.

By the time the next meeting was held the supporters of the County Council bank were staging a revolution. They accused me publicly of having had the doors of the committee room locked so that they could not arrive at the meeting on time. I was out of my wits, trying to understand. Several councillors tried to explain to me, but I didn't understand their explanations. 'You see,' one would say in a whisper, 'poor Murphy has an overdraft in the Banba Bank', but I did not see why that should make him so angry with me. Another said that 'Buckley is under the thumb of the Eire Bank', but that did not make any sense to me either. It was all very confusing.

By that time other events had me more nonplussed than ever.

The manager of the insurance company that handled the Council's business had called. He was a very nice man, and he made no objection at all to insuring the library premises and stock. Here at last, I felt, was a really sensible man. But a week or two later I received by post a substantial cheque from the insurance company, and it was made out to me personally. I telephoned and was assured that it was perfectly all right. This was the commission on the insurance, and it was correctly made out to me. When I suggested that it should be made out to the Secretary of the Cork County Library Committee, the manager hastily said he would come over and explain it to me.

I have said he was a nice man, and he did his best for half an hour to make things clear to me, but that day I was denser than usual. The one thing I did gather was that the insurance company could not make out the cheque so that it could be lodged to the credit of the committee because this would be a great embarrassment to other officials. Considering the amount of property that other officials had to insure compared with the library premises, I saw that this might be so, but it didn't help me about what I was to do with the cheque. The damn thing pursued me for years, and so did the insurance company, begging me either to cash the cheque or give it back. When I left the public service for ever twelve years later I still had it with me.

I really should have studied Gogol.

But if I didn't know what was going on, other people did, or at least affected to do so. There was a small but determined group of old-fashioned Republicans on the Council which did its damnedest to have the Secretary fired, but whenever the battle was pitched the Secretary always won. I saw him at work myself, and his technique was fantastic. He could be dignified. When that failed he could clown, and there is nothing that the majority of men prefer to a clown. When the hunt became too fierce he would grab at a pile of correspondence and say, 'Gentlemen, in connexion with what we are discussing, I have before me at this minute a letter from the Minister of Local Government', and then proceed to read a letter which dealt with drainage in Ballymorebingham, and before anyone knew what was happening the representative from Ballymorebingham would be on his feet denouncing the Department of Local Government and taking the heat off the Secretary, who sat listening with an attentive air.

Then there was the County Council clerk, a small, gentle, inoffensive man, who had appointed himself Grand Inquisitor of Cork County Council. 'I watch everything they do, Mr O'Donovan. Someone must clean out the Augean stables.' Once a small businessman rang me up to ask when his account would be paid, and I replied that it had already been approved for payment a month before and sent to the Secretary for endorsement. He asked if I couldn't get it speeded up, and I asked what the difficulty was in collecting it. He said in that hopeless Irish voice, 'Look, I'd better come round and explain it to you' – exactly as the insurance man had said. He came round to see me and I liked him at once though I didn't know what he was talking about. He said that in order to get his cheque he would have to give somebody a hand-out. I didn't know what he was talking about even then, and inquired why. He replied that every shopkeeper in Cork had to do it. At this I lost my temper and said I would ring up the Secretary's office, and if his account was not paid within a week I would report the matter direct to the Department of Local Government. For a while he looked at me incredulously, and then he said, 'Mr O'Donovan, if you could do that you would have every small shopkeeper in Cork on his knees before you.' I did not have to do it, because immediately after my first telephone call the account was paid, so I never had the spectacle of the small shopkeepers of Cork on their knees before me to contemplate.

So naturally I didn't pay too much attention to the little clerk, though he always managed somehow or other to meet me outside the office with fresh denunciations and fresh threats of reporting it all to the Minister. Perhaps it was just as well that I hadn't had to protest to the Minister myself, for when the little clerk did report direct to the Minister for Local Government, he was promptly dismissed by sealed order. Left in middle age with nothing, the Grand Inquisitor set out for Dublin to live with his sister and devote his gentle, God-fearing life to showing up the Minister. When I moved to Dublin myself, he came along regularly to tell me how his great case against the Minister was going. Usually he came when I finished work and walked home with me, the happiest man in the world because he was sacrificing himself for the only thing he cared about – France. 'Ever since I was a boy I have loved France,' he would proclaim dramatically, stopping on the pavement and beaming at me. It was France he was dreaming of when he tried to tidy up the tangled affairs of the Cork County Council, France he was dreaming of when he switched his attention to the whole country.

I sometimes wanted to hug him as he trotted along beside me with his glowing face, happy and doomed. For I, too, wanted to do something about the country.

When at last I had got the library organized I realized that I had to have closer contact with the country branches. I bought a van to carry the book boxes about – I did not realize the necessity for a proper travelling library until this was under way – and Cronin, my assistant, and myself drove all over the country in it. This was another eye-opener. It made me realize that I was a townie and would never be anything else. In the best of the houses I visited – usually the houses of people who had been prominent in the Troubles – the people were better related to the wild country about them than I was to the tame city about me. Seeing them in Cork in their uncouth clothes with their uncouth accents was one thing; seeing them on their own farms was another thing entirely, and it made me conscious of my own uncouthness rather than theirs. But those families were few, and the total effect of the country on me was one of depression.

It was as much to escape from the unreality of my work as for any other reason that I started a dramatic society in the city. There had been no such thing since Corkery had organized his little theatre twenty years before. There was the Cork Operatic Society, which in the usual way of provincial societies performed a Gilbert and Sullivan opera once or twice a year, with the aid of an English producer. There was also a local Shakespearean Society, run by a priest, which performed Shakespeare with the dirty words left out. We held our drama meetings in the old Women's Prison where Sean Neeson gave us space.

I knew even less about the theatre than I did about being a librarian, but I read and re-read every textbook on the subject and learned how to make scenery and organize the lighting – that is, if you could get a proper lighting set, which I never could, so that even today the one part of a production which I shall have nothing to do with is the lighting.

Our first production was to be Lennox Robinson's *Round Table* – one of his functional comedies, which could be transferred to an English provincial production by the change of a few town names – his personal names were strictly inter-racial. I found suitable actresses very hard to get. The heroine is a determined bossy type, but that type seemed to be quite unknown to Ireland. The moment you put an Irish girl on the stage and told her to say: 'Now, have you all washed your hands?' she instantly realized that there was something slightly improper about addressing men in this tone and became either coy or wheedling. I did it for them, but that only made them more embarrassed than ever and they became practically tearful. I had just decided to give it up as a bad job when someone tapped me on the shoulder. It was a good-looking girl with an atrocious stammer. 'W-w-w-would you m-m-m-m-mind t-terribly if I t-t-tried that part?' she asked with a determined air. I decided that she was pulling my leg and said without looking round, 'Well, you can't be worse than the one that's doing it.' She got up and did it as though all her life she had been doing nothing else. Nancy McCarthy became my leading actress.

After this we produced *The Cherry Orchard*. I think I had been toying with *The Playboy of the Western World* because either then or soon afterwards we rehearsed it, but the results were too horrible. I realized during these rehearsals that a writer writes not only for a particular group; he writes for a particular accent. Everybody in Dublin suffers from adenoids, so Synge had no difficulty in finding actors who could sustain a long, unbroken line through speeches in the manner of Racine, but the Cork accent goes up and down, up and down, and I could find no actor or actress who could sustain a note even during a brief speech.

I had to be content with naturalism and even naturalism involved me in difficulties. One of the lessons I learned during *The Cherry Orchard* production was that my translation of the Russian names had not taken me far enough into the whole business of theatre. There were '*versts*' and '*roubles*', and, just as I did not know from my training as a librarian that the one thing I needed was to get into immediate communication with my readers, so as a budding man of the theatre I didn't know that there is no way of getting an actor to say '*verst*' and '*rouble*' as though he knew exactly what it meant, nor is there any way of making contact with the audience except through its own knowledge of life. I saw it all quite clearly in that wonderful scene of the two sisters chattering in the dawn with the shepherd's pipe sounding in the distance. The only trouble was that I had no method of making a sound like a shepherd's pipe or, even if I had, of getting an audience to identify it as a shepherd's pipe. I could not believe but that I could master that pipe and give the same unearthly effect to a Cork audience that it must have had for a Russian one. I still did not realize what I was to argue later, against Yeats and everyone else in Dublin, that theatre is a collaboration between author, actors and audience, and when that collaboration ceases to exist, theatre ceases to exist.

It is clear I didn't recognize it then, because I went on with *A Doll's House*. But from other things I was beginning to realize that Cork standards of literature and my own could not exist for long side by side. I had got a hint of this when our Ranevskaya confessed she couldn't say the line 'At your age you should have a mistress'. Then the young newspaperman who was playing the part of Firs supported her with his own argument. This was that, as the nephew of the Dean, he could not possibly tolerate such a line being spoken. I should have given up at that point, because the priest who conducted the Shakespearean Society was also attacking us in print and complaining that instead of the uplifting plays of Shakespeare we wanted to produce the filthy works of Sean O'Casey. As a result our leading man failed to turn up at the dress rehearsal. He sent a message that he had a toothache, and when one of the group went to his lodgings, it seemed that the toothache was so bad that he couldn't come to the first night either. Hendrick had to postpone the show until Tuesday and that night he and Nancy worked for hours trying to teach me the part.

In those couple of years I published two or three stories, one of them, 'Guests of the Nation', in the *Atlantic Monthly*. Nevertheless, as I have said, I did not enjoy my years in Cork, because it was no longer the place I had known. O'Faolain was in America and I found it impossible to talk to Corkery. He was too gentle and considerate to be rude, but he made it plain that he was taking sides and that I was on the wrong one. I was restless and felt that Cork was threatening to suffocate me. I suffered from a sort of intellectual schizophrenia, living for the few days in the year when I could get up to Wicklow, talk literature and art to the Phibbses, and go on to Dublin and see Russell and Yeats. Russell could give me all the latest books and gossip, and of a Sunday evening I could go to the Abbey Theatre, where the Dublin Drama League was putting on a remarkable series of continental plays, Chekhov, Strindberg and contemporary German plays in which Phibbs' friend, Denis Johnston, was a leading figure.

I had also fallen in love in a completely hopeless way with my leading lady in the dramatic society. I had been reading Chekhov's love letters to Olga Knipper and probably felt I needed an actress of my own. Nancy was not in the least like Knipper. She was a pharmacist and very conscious of her responsibilities, and as well as that she was a very pious Catholic. When people complained of prescriptions she went to St Peter and Paul's to pray. When they took legal proceedings she made a novena. For a year or more I always seemed to be meeting the girl outside St Peter and Paul's. I gave her Chekhov's letters to Knipper, but they seemed to have no effect. She just wouldn't marry me.

Even so, when I applied for a job as municipal librarian in Dublin, I still had the notion that I should do it only as a temporary expedient until a similar job turned up in Cork. Nothing could cure me of the notion that Cork needed me and that I needed Cork. Nothing but death can, I fear, ever cure me of it.

TWO

The provincial in Dublin

8

I had been ill in Cork, and Russell, distrusting all Cork people, including doctors, had made me come to Dublin and get examined by his own doctor, Frank Purser, the only medical man he trusted. 'He cured Stephens. Stephens was dying when Frank saw him first, and now he can eat beef-steaks.'

When Russell heard that a new appointment was to be made in Dublin, he went wild and besieged a couple of government departments, assuring them that I was the only possible candidate, though whether this did me good or harm I never knew. but I got the job – organizing the library at Pembroke. When I saw the new library I was to work in, I cursed. It was a miniature Georgian version of a Dublin library of 1880, which in its turn had been copied from some English library of 1840.

Pembroke, like Rathmines, was one of the old townships that disappeared a few years later in Dublin city; it had a substantial Protestant population, and I found myself with a committee which was neatly balanced but small enough to be practical. I made my first friend in a boy who came to me looking for a job, supported by the local Labour Party. I sent him to see my chairman, who ran an automobile business in Dublin. 'But don't you realize that he's a Freemason?' the boy asked. 'Never mind what he is,' I said. 'I want him to support you when the committee meets.' He went off in the spirit of the Light Brigade, but next day the 'Freemason' came in and said, 'I thought that was a fine lad you sent to see me yesterday. He's getting my vote.' He did get the chairman's support, which was just as well for me and the library, as the Labour vote happened to go elsewhere. By a bare majority vote Dermot Foley became my assistant.

After Cork it was wonderful. Dermot was a musician, and we built up a music library that we could be proud of. I was a language enthusiast, and we built up a foreign library which attracted those French, Germans and Italians in Dublin who could find nothing in their local libraries. We bought an epidiascope and a cheap gramophone, and each week we talked to the children about pictures and classical music until the Dublin Corporation took over, removed our epidiascope and gramophone and sent Gaelic League lecturers who talked about Red Hugh O'Donnell and life in the Gaeltacht until they drove the kids away.

I had a room in Sandymount Green in a big house kept by a Donegal man and his sister who had retired to enjoy themselves in the great city. I do not think they enjoyed themselves much, because all their talk was of Donegal. I was never much in love with Dublin, but I thought they were unfair to it and said so.

'Ah, but you still have your dreams, Mr O'Donovan,' said the sister, her eyes filling with tears.

I liked them, but I adored my fellow lodger. He was an engineer, tall and dark and handsome, with grave manners and an enchanting smile. He was a saint as Mother and Minnie Connolly were saints, but a masculine version of the type.

I am a heavy sleeper, and I had an arrangement with him to wake me each morning on his way to Mass, but I slept so heavily and he woke me so gently, touching me with his fingers and then smiling into my face to reassure me, as one wakes a baby, that I did exactly what a sensible baby would do and went off to sleep again.

This caused him great scruples of conscience, because he had trained himself to leap out of bed at the first sound of the alarm clock by imagining that the bed was on fire. He was now training himself to wake immediately before the alarm clock went off, which he assured me was not so difficult as it sounded; and he felt sure that by waking me in this childish manner he was sapping my will-power. Everybody, from Corkery on, seemed to be concerned about my will-power.

He then made me prepare a card reading 'Please Wake Me at 7.30', which I had to hang on the door handle before going to bed. He said that this made all the difference between a real act of the will and an automatic gesture, but I could not see that it improved my character in the least. All that really happened was that I usually forgot to hang it up.

Everything in the Saint's life had been reduced to schedule, even the walk from Sandymount Green to the Star of the Sea church, which was so many hundred steps and took so many minutes and seconds, measured by the watch on which everything was tested – exactly the complaint that a writer of the early Middle Ages makes of the Irish monks and their arithmetical piety. When we went for walks, I was a sore trial because I stopped to speak to anyone I knew, but those foolish, social conversations interrupted the flow of the Saint's thought, and he walked on to the next corner. Waiting for me while I chattered worldly irrelevancies was almost as bad as listening to them, because it threw out the whole mathematical quality of the walk, and after a while he explained to me that he would continue his walk at exactly the same pace – so many steps to the minute – and by quickening my own pace slightly, say by three steps to the minute – I could easily catch up on him. Running, of course, he neither expected nor approved of. Running and thinking were incompatible.

Any money left over from his rather good salary was available without interest to anyone who wanted it, and as I was short of money during the first few months of my stay in Dublin, I borrowed from him as well. But he was always getting into trouble because so few of the people who borrowed from him paid him back at the promised time, and sometimes new borrowers appealed to him when he himself was short.

No watch could control this, and once he came to me in great distress. I owed him a couple of pounds which I should pay when I got my first month's salary, and someone had asked him for money in a hurry at a time when he did not have it. He came to my room, blushing, and asked if I could lend him a pound that evening. If I could he promised to pay it back when he got his own pay on Friday night. At first I thought he was joking and laughed, and this distressed him even more. He swore that only dire need could make him borrow from a friend like myself, and then I realized that he was really in earnest so I only laughed louder than ever, while he went through every gambit of the confirmed panhandler; and the more he tried to persuade me that he was not the sort of person who normally did this, and that he really would pay me back on Friday, the louder I laughed. Nobody else had ever made me laugh so much or with so good a conscience.

But no more than Mother or Minnie Connolly was the Saint anyone's fool. Like them he was simply a person of spiritual genius who treated money in the proper way. He was always in trouble with his infernal Loan Office, and one day he came to me with a circular which he was proposing to send to all his ancient debtors.

It ran something like this, though I suspect the original was much subtler and funnier:

> Dear—, I don't know if you will remember that on . . . 19. . . . you borrowed from me the sum of . . . This letter is not intended as a request for payment, but it would help my book-keeping if you would kindly reply to two questions –
>
> (a) Do you acknowledge the debt?
>
> and
>
> (b) Do you propose to repay it?

It was the most effective dunning letter I had seen, and I am sure the money came pouring in, but the Saint could get his own back on me in exactly the same gentle, subtle way. He kept on trying to persuade me to come to Mass with him, and was not in the least concerned when he did not succeed. God, he explained, knew that I was a very good Catholic – even if I did not know it myself – and would accept a reasonable compromise. So the Saint went to two Masses on Sunday, one for himself and one for me, and on the second occasion explained to God that he was representing me.

This was moral blackmail, but he went one better. He decided that, as one of the few really good Catholics he knew, I should contribute to the Society for the Propagation of the Faith, a cause in which I had no interest whatever. We had a thundering row about this in which I accused him of every form of complacency and arrogance, but he won, as usual. He explained quietly that God, knowing me as He did, expected me to contribute to the Society for the Propagation of the Faith, so he would add my subscription to his own.

What can you do with a saint? Heine once said that the Celts were the only real believers because you could borrow money from a Celt money-lender and arrange to pay it back in the next life. Maybe in the next life I shall pay back what I owe the Saint, including my subscription to the Society for the Propagation of the Faith – blast it!

But sanctity was not the origin of the trouble I was having with my other dear friend. When he was an assistant like myself, Phibbs had fallen in love with another assistant, whom he had wanted to marry, but since then he had fallen in love with a Dublin painter. It is not an unheard-of situation among poets and, indeed, among others.

He and I had been coming back from a long walk over the

hills by Rathnew when he told me. He might have chosen a more
experienced adviser. At that time I had kissed three girls, but, after
the first, who had splendid Irish, I had found it a rather wearisome
occupation. On the other hand, from my considerable reading of
French and Russian novels, I felt I had a complete theoretical
knowledge of the subject.

'Tell the first girl to go to hell,' I said firmly.

'You cannot do that sort of thing to a girl,' said Phibbs.

'In that case you're going to be pushed into a marriage you don't
want,' I said.

'I know that,' he said irritably. 'But I don't know the best thing
to do.'

'The best thing is to ask the second girl to marry you at once,' I
said.

'Now?' he asked incredulously.

'If you really want to marry the girl you may as well do it now
as any other time,' I said, still rejoicing in my infallibility.

'Oh, of course I want to marry her, but she has to work for a
year in London. It seems silly to ask her to marry me just because
of another girl.'

'Try her,' I said. 'I doubt if she'll think it's so silly.'

I could usually sound very wise, and I must have done so then,
for Phibbs went to London over the weekend, and apparently Norah
saw things much as I did. When she returned to Wicklow as his
wife I was not so sure of my own wisdom. On the first Sunday
when I went to lunch there were no potatoes, and I was scandalized
when she went on with her painting and allowed Phibbs and myself
to go into town for them. I had never met a girl who forgot things
like potatoes, and if I had I should have expected her to repair her
omission in silence. I thought Phibbs was too easygoing. Besides,
Norah got between him and me in ways I had not anticipated at
all. I was as jealous as a schoolboy, and sometimes thought that
love and marriage had been greatly exaggerated by the poets and
dramatists.

The loneliest creature on God's earth is a young writer trying to
find himself, and every few months I took a few days off to stay
with the Phibbses, where we talked our heads off into the early
hours of the morning about books, pictures, music, religion and
sex. I was able to report the arrival at my home in Dublin of the
Other Girl's Brother at about seven in the morning. By this time I
had bought myself my first dressing-gown and slippers, and when

my visitor proceeded to read Phibbs' letters to his sister I was able
to strike an attitude and say that I did not wish to listen to my
friends' private correspondence. 'But this is about you!' he had
cried, and went on to read all the witty and malicious things that
Phibbs had written of me in the first few weeks of our acquaintance.
I thought they were very funny, but managed to remain severe and
withdrawn, and the Brother had then set off to drive all day to read
to Wilson the references to *him* – not, I hoped, to read the poem
on Wilson's wife. In fact, I had liked the Brother and wished I
could be more openly sympathetic, because secretly I pined for the
days when brothers were brothers and an insult to a woman's honour
could only be wiped out in blood.

The Phibbses had rented a little bungalow on a hill over Wicklow
town with a garden and a fine view of the sea. Phibbs was happier,
more contented, than I had known him, and very proud of Norah
– prouder of her than she of him, I sometimes felt resentfully. I
was still jealous, and besides I felt he needed a good deal of the sort
of admiration that I quite naturally gave him. When we met, there
was always an hour or two when he was stiff and perfunctory, but
as discussion went to his head the mechanical man dropped away
and again he was a creature all fire and air, much as I imagine
Shelley to have been.

I had gone after the job in Dublin largely on their account. I
planned to have a little flat where they could stay at weekends, and
I could join them in Wicklow. When I left Cork for the last time I
took the long train-ride round by Waterford so as to spend a night
with them. Phibbs met me at the station and we went up the hill
to the bungalow together. He was abstracted and short in speech,
but I put it down to the usual awkwardness we felt on meeting
again, and I was sure that before the evening was over it would
wear off. It wasn't until Norah had gone to bed that Phibbs told
me why he was upset. There was Another Man.

Exactly why he chose me for confidant in his love affairs is
something I have always wondered about. Ten years later I would
have laughed him out of it, but in those years of insecurity light
love was as much beyond me as light verse. Naturally, having
listened to his iconoclastic conversation for years, I knew in theory
that these things happened, and as a student of the nineteenth-
century novel I realized that they were more liable to happen in
France and Russia than in England – witness Mme Bovary and
Mme Karenina – but, so far as my knowledge went, they did not

happen in Ireland at all. Sometimes I suspect that this was precisely why he did confide in me, because, 'advanced' as some of his attitudes were, he had others that were not so advanced.

'Oh, I know what you think,' he said bitterly. 'You think I should have shot them both, and that's how I felt. I walked over the hills like a madman for two days. But that is all only nineteenth-century romanticism. There must be absolute freedom in marriage. That's all.'

'Oh, Geoffrey, you bloody fool!' I said.

I think I began to see then what became clear to me years later, that he was a man who was trapped by his own nature. We are all trapped, of course, sooner or later, but he was more inescapably trapped because in him the gap between instinct and judgement was wider than it is in most of us, and he simply could not jump it. With the two-thirds of him that was air and fire he adopted new attitudes and new ideas, without ever realizing how they contradicted conventions that were fundamental to himself.

Norah was accompanying me to Dublin next morning, on her way to art school in London, and on the train she talked to me about her English friends, each of whom seemed to have Another Man or Another Woman in the background, and I did not wish to say that they all sounded to me as dry as cream crackers. Cream crackers are all very well with morning coffee, but cream crackers for breakfast, lunch and supper as well seemed to me to lack nourishment. So I suffered and sulked the whole way. We went to a party together and said goodbye, she to catch the morning boat to England. By lunch-time I knew she had changed her mind and gone back home, for they both wired me to come down on the evening train. I went round the office singing with sheer relief. The whole thing had been like a nightmare to me.

I suddenly found my whole attitude to Norah changed. Up to this I had been jealous and resentful of her, feeling that she didn't really value the Ariel she had married. Now I saw that she had done what Phibbs could never do, and I could perhaps do, but only after a long struggle, and jumped the gap between instinct and judgement. Women, I think, can do that sort of thing better than men, but not without a considerable amount of self-knowledge and courage. At this point I began to shift my allegiance; for the first time I began to think as much of her as of him.

By evening there was another wire to say that all had been arranged and that both were leaving for London. I was innocent enough to be glad of that too. But a couple of days later I got a distracted letter from Norah to say Phibbs had gone to live in a flat with two other poets, a man and a woman, both of whom he admired. I also admired the man, but the woman was too modern for my comprehension. To add to the peculiarity of the situation from my point of view, the man had a wife and children who lived on a barge on the Thames.

I could not make head or tail of it. Norah returned, and she, too, seemed to be at a loss. It was part of the cult in this unusual London *ménage* that Phibbs' correspondence with me should be supervised as in a seminary, and his letters, which had been explosive and malicious, took on a tone of unction more suitable to a hysterical ecclesiastical student. They were sprinkled with words like 'right' and 'wrong', but the moral context was missing. Yeats came back from London with a highly coloured version of the story, and Russell was furious with me for having kept it from him.

This wasn't discretion – nobody has ever accused me of discretion, and that long silence was a strain – but I could not tell it without making it sound like farce, and to me it was not farce, but tragedy, in a language and convention that I did not understand. In my own letters I accused Phibbs of satanic pride and longing for revenge and, though he mocked at me for it, I am sure I was right. He had been hurt and now he wanted to hurt back beyond the point at which revenge is still feasible and one can hurt without injuring oneself more.

Because I knew he was hurting himself, I decided to intervene. I arrived at the flat that the three poets shared one cold and grey Good Friday. I was shaken when Phibbs told me that the Woman poet was at work and must not be disturbed, because even I was observant enough to see the unfinished sentence in her handwriting on the paper before me, with the ink still wet. I was even more disturbed when I lit a cigarette and he told me that she did not like smoking. She disapproved of ashes – and of crumbs, so we should smoke and eat on the barge. The Woman poet later wrote a novel about it in which I appear as Handy Andy, in love with Norah – Yeats, if I remember rightly, being my rival – but Handy Andy would have been sophisticated compared with me at that Mad Hatter's lunch on the Thames. We drank absinthe and ate salad, and I admired the poet's wife, so when Phibbs walked with me later to the main road I asked in exasperation why, if he was tired of the perfectly good wife he had, he hadn't run away with the poet's wife.

I knew nothing of light loves, but I simply could not resist giving my view on them. This, mark you, was the third time I involved myself in Phibbs' love affairs!

I was in a suicidal mood of loneliness as I walked back down the river to London. The public-houses were shut, so I could not even have a drink. There was a pavement artist on the Embankment who, instead of drawing pictures, wrote out little verses, and it was not till I had passed him that I remembered that one of them was the first of the Irish rebel song, 'The Croppy Boy':

> It was early, early in the spring
> The birds did whistle and sweetly sing,
> Changing their notes from tree to tree,
> And the song they sang was 'Old Ireland free'.

I was so homesick that I went back, to give him a shilling and talk to him about Ireland, but I gave up in disgust when I saw that he had changed the last line to 'And the song they sang was "Old England for ever the Land of the Free" '.

I left for Paris that night, and two days later Phibbs bolted after me, but he was so panic-stricken that he immediately set off for Rouen with Norah. They were followed by the two poets and the poet's wife, urging him to return; the hotel manager asked them to leave and they continued the scene in a cab which drove round and round the town. By this time I was getting bored. Norah and I with our combined puritanisms wanted it to be serious, but it would not stay serious.

And then, to culminate everything, Phibbs went back to London to say he could not go back, and the Woman poet threw herself out of a third-storey window and was visited in hospital by Phibbs and the poet's wife, and Phibbs – always attentive to my good advice – set up house with *her*. In protest against his father's inhuman behaviour in not having invited her beyond the verandah of 'Lisheen', he changed his name by deed poll to Taylor, much in the spirit in which he defaced his books with a rubber stamp. He seemed incapable of withdrawing from a situation when it had become impossible.

After this he taught English for a while in Cairo, but this did not last long either. He found himself at a cocktail party beside a nice man who listened with great interest to his blasphemies and obscenities and asked politely if he was a Communist. 'Good God, no!' said Phibbs. 'I'm an Anarchist.' The nice man did not say, 'And I am the Secretary of State for Education', but he was, and

Phibbs had to find himself a job washing dishes in a Cairo hotel. His neighbour and friend in this occupation was the ex-Civil-Hangman of Baghdad, who duly turned up in the batches of poems that reached me.

The poems were not quite so good, and they got decidedly worse after his return to England.

Changing his notes from tree to tree
And the song he sang was 'Old England for ever the land of the free'.

The atmosphere was too tolerant for his angry, individual humour, or so at least I thought, and he drifted without effort into the attitudes of a mildly eccentric English liberal. As for me, I had made the change to Dublin for no reasonable cause. Dublin without him was empty; there was no writer of my own age to whom I could say the things I said to him, and when I wrote I seemed to be writing only for myself.

9

Phibbs' defection made the problem of where and how I was going to live worse. There was no longer a bungalow in Wicklow where I could go for weekends and talk literature, and it seemed pointless for me to rent an apartment, having no one to share it with. Nancy was in Cork, and she was even more evasive on paper than she was in the flesh. Mother was there, and I had more or less determined that I should return there too in a couple of years' time and do what I should have done in the beginning, buy that house that Father and I argued about.

I was fortunate in my lodgings, and Mother came on visits and became friendly with my landlady, but I was still dissatisfied. I was rising in the world, but I saw no point in it unless I could have the visible signs of it about me – my own furniture and pictures, my own books and records. I still could not see beyond chattels, and I came some terrible croppers in apartments before I realized that they had to have things like bathrooms, kitchens, light and air, and here Mother could not help me at all because she had as little experience of creature comforts as I had.

I wanted to buy a house for the three of us somewhere on the coast, but Father exploded at the very idea of it. He had agreed to everything else, hadn't he? He had let Mother come and stay with me as long as she pleased. She could go on doing it; he had no objection, but live in a place like Dublin he would not. No more would he come and stay with me for any extended period just to see how he liked it. How could he, with the sort of children that were growing up nowadays, who would wreck his house the moment his back was turned?

It was all true, and I felt guilty about it and sympathized with them in the intolerable separations I inflicted on them; for it would have taken six police to remove Father from his house and more than that to prevent Mother from coming to see that I was all right. Of course, Father was an old soldier and could make himself comfortable in circumstances where another man would perish, but he was even more dependent on her for society than I was. I never had any difficulty in imagining what he felt, having made one of his long pedestrian excursions round the city and filled himself with what for him was hot news – such as how poor Mickie Mac was getting on without the dead sister and what new devilment Gauger in Barrack Street had thought up to plague his respectable daughter-in-law – when he came home to a dark and empty house and had to light the fire and boil the kettle and then read his *Evening Echo* without a soul he could discuss it with.

But I was as helpless against his complacency as he was against my restlessness, and for a month or six weeks at a time Mother would come and stay with me in Dublin, and Minnie Connolly, the saintly old maid at the other side of the square, would trudge over to listen to Father's news and report to Mother on how he was doing; and when he wasn't 'keeping too good' – her euphemism for going on a drinking bout – Mother would grow fretful because she felt that no one else could understand him or deal with him in that state, and she would go home before her visit was up.

Father and I shared her in the way that men in Phibbs' circle in England were supposed to share some woman while remaining fast friends, but my experience with him had not persuaded me of the possibility of such friendships, and anyhow Father and I were not in the least sophisticated. He was just patiently waiting for some nice girl to marry me and get me out of his hair so that he could have Mother in peace for the rest of his days, while I was hoping by firmness (insisting on my own share of her) and kindness (showing him the considerable advantages of living with me) to wear him down. We were both tolerant, considerate and even generous, but each of us knew that this particular doll belonged to him, and, indeed, it seems to me to say a lot for us that we never really came to blows over her.

At last he agreed to come to Dublin for a few days. He was generous; he did, once started, enjoy free excursions, particularly to a place such as Dublin, where he had been stationed as a young soldier, and he would have a great story for the other old sweats who gathered for Mass on the Sand Quay, but he wanted to make it clear from the start that these would be only excursions and would involve no liability to buy.

He arrived in Dublin with his itinerary in his head. As I remember it, it did not include any tourist monuments and was confined to five military barracks and one cemetery. Each day he set off to perform it on foot, a fine-looking old six-footer with his cap pulled over his eyes, striding along like a boy, interested in every detail. One barrack he visited because he had been stationed there himself, another because my Uncle Tim had been stationed there, a third because some girl he had once tried to pick up in O'Connell Street had said, 'They're a nice lot in the Wellington Barrack', a very ordinary remark which he had trotted out for forty-odd years as though it were a gem of wit. Glasnevin Cemetery he revisited because as a young man he had attended a funeral there and been interested in the graves of the Irish leaders O'Connell and Parnell.

For some reason I decided to go to Glasnevin with him – possibly because he had tried to get there and lost his way. As we came to the Crossguns Bridge he identified the Brian Boru bar with a grin. Obviously he knew it of old. On the way back he stopped outside it.

'You'll have a little drink?' he asked uneasily.

He might well be uneasy, because he knew what I thought of his drinking bouts, and I might have been angry or rude, but there was something wistful about his tone which suggested to me that this might be an occasion.

'Very well, we will,' I said, and we went in and stood at the bar. Father continued to make the pace.

'What will you have?' he asked in a lordly way. 'You'd better have a bottle of stout' – meaning that with a father as broadminded as himself I need not pretend that I did not drink, and I had the impression that if I refused the stout he would be bitterly hurt.

'Stout will be fine,' I said nervously.

'A stout and a bottle of lemonade, miss,' he said to the barmaid and then over our drinks he talked to me pleasantly as man to man. Curiously, the conversation has completely left my mind, which shows how disturbed I was, but I fancy he was giving me advice on how to handle Mother – a subject on which, like all husbands, he considered himself an expert. It may have been then that he broke the news to me that Mother was a good deal older than himself and very close to qualifying for the old-age pension.

Being an orphan, she hadn't the slightest idea of when her birthday was or even what her age was. If she was pressed, she would describe her age as 'about sixty', leaving it to mannerly people to say they would never have believed it. But Father was convinced by something my Uncle Tim O'Connor had let drop – no doubt in his well-meaning effort to keep the two of them apart – that Mother was close on seventy and would sacrifice a perfectly good pension of ten shillings a week from mere vanity.

Father, as I have explained, had an absolute mania about pensions. He had wangled two out of the British Government, one for long service and another for a non-existent disability. My Uncle Lar, of course, being the smart man he was, had wangled a total disability pension for asthma, which he had always suffered from and which he could re-energize immediately before a Board by running up Patrick's Hill where the doctors' houses were, but Father always admitted that his brother was a cleverer man than he was. He was looking forward to doing a bit of wangling on the Irish Government as well; he would not, of course, get the full ten shillings, but every little helped. It was the nearest thing he knew to an unearned income and the status of a gentleman, and there was much in his attitude to remind me of the retired businessman with his securities. It was not all jam, of course; it had its little tragedies. Lar could get total disability when there was nothing whatever wrong with him, but Father would come back from one of his sessions outside the Sand Quay church, gloomy and disturbed because some old soldier had got total disability, and the other old sweats recognized that he would not be with them for long.

But mainly it was the decency of the British Government that he recognized. Here he was, in his sixties, and he could make his daily tours of new building sites and talk patronizingly to the labourers, who would never be able to do the same, but would have to work until they dropped and died in the workhouse. And – as with the retired businessman – there was something ambivalent about

Father's friendliness towards the labourers. He was genuinely sorry that they had to go to the workhouse, unlike himself, who could go up to the British Army Hospital in Shanakiel; but he was also proud and pleased that it was they and not he who had to do it.

He had done his best to implant the same sound Conservative principles in Mother, and he simply could not understand that no good-looking woman, however intelligent, wants to be seventy, merely for the sake of ten shillings a week. Now if Father had explained that he only wanted to prove she was fifty, she would have entered into the search with the enthusiasm of a girl, but, as it was, she just listened inattentively to him and continued to look a good ten years younger than himself.

When I tried to pay for the drinks he said nonchalantly 'No, let me do this', and I realized that this, too, was part of the ritual, and probably rehearsed days before. He returned home with me that evening, full of high spirits. He didn't, of course, tell Mother about our little adventure. It was also part of the ritual that you did not tell women what men did when they were out together. It was perfectly easy to rationalize. It was a warm day, and The Boy was thirsty. Ritual is only a linking of the dead with our daily actions, but whom among the dead he was trying to impress that afternoon is something I shall never know – his own father, perhaps, or someone he had drunk with there when he himself was The Boy. I only know that I was deeply moved because the little scene had shown me all that had been missing in our relationship and how inspiring it might have been.

It did not, of course, mean that he softened in the least in his objection to living in Dublin with me, or even to staying one day longer than he had bargained for. Sometimes I wonder if he was not afraid that – as with the drink – the first surrender would turn him into an abject old man.

What he felt like at being separated from Mother I could imagine because I had felt it myself, but it never occurred to me that he could feel the same about Cork till one evening when he was staying with us in Glengarriff. For some reason he had been quite reckless and agreed to come for a fortnight, but on the third evening, when he had inspected all the roads out of the little seaside village, I heard him muttering to Mother, half in amusement, half in chagrin:

'My God! Another ten days in this misfortunate hole!'

10

For the first two or three years in Dublin, I organized my library and wrote two books: *Guests of the Nation*, the book of Civil War stories from lodgings in Ranelagh; the novel, *The Saint and Mary Kate*, from my first flat in Anglesea Road, which was neither cheerful nor comfortable, but where at last I had my own books, records, pictures and furniture about me. I still considered myself a poet, and had little notion of how to write a story and none at all of how to write a novel, so they were produced in hysterical fits of enthusiasm, followed by similar fits of despondency, good passages alternating with bad, till I can no longer read them.

All the same, for all its intolerable faults, I knew that *The Saint and Mary Kate* was a work of art, something I had never succeeded in producing before, and as I wrote it, I read it aloud to Mother, who either went into fits of laughter or looked puzzled and said restlessly, 'Well, aren't you a terrible boy!' It became the principal argument of the pious Catholics against me, and at one library conference in Cork I had to sit and listen to a denunciation of it as a scandalous and heretical work by the editor of the 'Three Thousand Best Books', who was so drunk that he could not stand straight on the platform.

George Russell enthused about it, not with the enthusiasm of a schoolteacher whose favourite pupil has passed an examination with honours, but with that of an inhibited man who rejoices in any sort of emotional outpouring – the excitement he displayed over Hugo and Dumas. He was passionately inquisitive about the character of the heroine, and a dozen times at least brought the conversation round to what she would be like to live with. This was something I didn't know myself, because I wasn't really writing about any woman in particular – I didn't know enough of them for that – but about that side of women that appealed to me – the one that has no patience with abstractions. I, of course, was full of abstractions.

Russell was extraordinarily inquisitive about women, and with an ingenuousness that even I found upsetting. Though he never talked to me of his wife, and only rarely of one of his sons, I had the feeling that he was unhappy in his marriage and inclined to think that women were a plague.

'Do you have flirtations with pretty girls?' he asked me one night.

'Sometimes,' I admitted – I should have hated to confess how rarely.

'And do they get you to write poems for them?'

'Yes.'

'That's fine,' he said happily. 'Write them all the poems they want, but take care they don't marry you. That's the devil of it.'

When he came back from his first American tour he was in a wild state of excitement about American girls. He had spent a birthday in Vassar or some other women's college and the girls had made him a birthday cake with a great mass of candles. Afterwards, one of them had come up and kissed him, and when he started, said, 'Oh, boy, do be your age!'

'They must be the most beautiful girls the world has ever seen,' he said to me. 'If only you could get them to sit in a corner and keep quiet, you could admire them for hours. But they *will* talk!'

At the same time he tried to arrange a marriage between Simone Tery, a beautiful French journalist, and me. He showed his love for Simone as I never knew him to show love for anyone, but knowing his passion for generalization I assumed – quite correctly, I think – that I was not the only young Irish writer he had chosen as a husband for her. He merely adored her, and wanted somebody in Dublin to marry her so that he could be sure of entertainment one evening a week. He got off on the wrong foot with Simone and myself, because when we met for dinner he looked at me and said, 'Isn't she nice?' and then at Simone and said, 'Isn't he nice?' and for the rest of the evening we sat and glowered at one another. He made it worse by congratulating her on not using 'any of those horrible cosmetics that American girls ruin their beauty with', and she, made up as skilfully as only a Frenchwoman can be, modestly lowered her eyes and said, 'I only use them on particular occasions, A.E.'

He was very impressed one night when I repeated a bawdy story a girl had told me and said with great solemnity: 'That is a wonderful example of the economy of Nature which I am always impressing on you. Nature intended me to be a lyric poet, so I *never* met a girl who told stories like that. She intended you to be a realistic novelist, so she just throws girls of that sort in your way.'

I might have said that one reason I did not meet more girls like that was that I saw too much of people like himself. It is the real weakness – if it is a weakness – of the Mother's Boy. It is not that he is not attracted to women, but that he is liable to get into emotional relationships with older men. And Russell suffered as well from a frustrated paternalism towards younger men that was strange in one who had two quite attractive sons of his own. I thought I observed it one night when I got him to talk of the youth of Padraic Colum. Usually he talked in set speeches, which could be very boring, but occasionally, when his memory was jogged by love or hate – or disappointed love, as when Yeats had got beneath his skin again – there was an astonishing change, and you realized that you were dealing not with a pathetic old man, but with a first-rate mind. I had never known him more master of his own cool and sympathetic intelligence than that evening when he sketched for me the picture of an enchanting boy who rushed up to meet you, his overcoat unbuttoned, the pockets of it stuffed with railway waybills and handbills all scribbled over in the intervals of work in the railway offices, and began to read you his latest masterpiece – the great play in which the thud of hoofs continued from first curtain to last – till he suddenly discovered he had the wrong waybills and was really reading from his great epic on St Brendan the Navigator.

I suspected that night that he looked on Colum as his son, and he developed something of the same possessiveness towards me. One night I said something that pleased him and he replied, 'I should have had a son like you, Michael. Don't you think I'd have made a good father for a poet?'

I said something about Diarmuid's being a good substitute, but he laughed it off.

'Oh, Diarmuid has the makings of a very good businessman. Did I tell you I discovered he'd been emptying my wastepaper basket and selling drafts of my poems to an American collector?'

One night a year or two later he called and discovered I had been in bed for a week with bronchitis.

'You should have sent me a wire, you know,' he said with tears in his eyes. 'I'd have come and looked after you. I'm quite a good plain cook, you know. I can cook chops very well.'

Every week he came to my lodgings or flat, on the same evening and at the same hour. Every time he said the same thing, 'My dear fellow, I hope I'm not interrupting you', tossed his coat and hat impatiently on the sofa (once when I took them out to the hall he looked at me slyly and asked, 'Was that necessary?'), combed out his hair and beard, and settled himself in my favourite chair. He was a creature of habit, the sort of man who all his life will sit at the same table of the same restaurant to eat the same meal, and be ill at ease when waited on by a waitress he is not acquainted with.

First, he wanted to know how the writing was going. Usually it was going badly. In those days I wrote in brief excited fits that might be followed by months of idleness and depression, or – what was worse – of fruitless and exhausting labour on some subject I was not mature enough to tackle. A book on Irish literature, which Yeats and he had urged me to write, was not written until thirty-five years later. Sometimes he lectured me on the Dark Fortnight and the Bright Fortnight, one of those generalizations like Leonardo and the Economy of Nature that wore me out. At other times he was really intelligent.

'You know, my dear fellow, a man cannot be so dissatisfied with his own work unless he has much better work to come.'

Once I must really have exasperated him, for he said: 'You know, you remind me of an old hen who has just laid an egg and is going round complaining. Did you ever hear a hen that has laid an egg? She says, "Oh, God! God! God! God! There are going to be no more eggs!" That's what she says, you know.'

He took a cup of tea, clutching the cup and saucer close to his beard, refused a second cup, always in the same dim, hasty way – 'No, thank you, my dear fellow' – while looking at you unseeingly over his spectacles. Precisely at twenty minutes to eleven he glanced at his watch and gasped, 'I must be going', leaped up as though on wires and fumbled his way downstairs for the last tram. He always stood right in the tracks, signalling frantically with both arms to the driver, and then, without a backward glance, bundled himself on and was halfway up the stairs before the tram re-started. There were no regrets, no backward glances or waves of the hand. His mind was already on something else, like Father's when he was leaving for Cork.

Any break in the habitual round, as when I went home to Cork for the Christmas holidays, irritated him and caused a minor convulsion in his life, and he hit back by complaining that I was 'imperilling my immortal soul by guzzling and swilling'! He was left with a whole evening on his hands that he did not know what to do with, and if he chose to go to someone else's house on that particular evening, there was a reasonable chance that he would continue the practice for the rest of his life, unless they, too, with the incurable instability of human beings, decided to take a holiday or get sick.

For months after I got back I would not see him at all. It was not that he was punishing me for my infidelity, but that he had got himself entangled in some new routine and, since he was completely unaware of it himself, could not get free of it. Then one night I would hear the peremptory, irritable rat-tat-tat that I could tell from hundreds of others, and there he would be tranquilly waiting at the door, stroking his beard, and as he strode impatiently in, without waiting for an invitation, he would say with a sort of happy sigh, 'My dear fellow, I hope I'm not interrupting you.' Another cycle was under way.

He liked fixed days for doing fixed things, and fixed ways of doing them. At one period of his life he painted every Sunday, and the Dublin story was that when he counted his pictures at the end of one year he said in great distress, 'There's something wrong. There are only fifty-one.'

One Monday evening, when the pattern was running smoothly in Mondays, he came in and said without even waiting for an opening: 'I was in Howth yesterday afternoon. I hadn't been there for twelve years. It's very beautiful, you know.'

The face and tone were stoical, but I had the feeling that he was desperately unhappy. I could not imagine why. I have a very slow mind, and it was not until half an hour later that I recognized what it was about the phrase that sounded wrong.

'But isn't Sunday your day for going to Seumas O'Sullivan's, A.E.?'

'Seumas was very rude to Stephens at the Academy dinner on Thursday night,' he said gravely. 'You weren't there. He called Stephens a poetaster. I didn't think that was very nice. I don't think I could ever be friends with Seumas again.'

I was deeply touched by his grief at the loss of an old friend and even more by his loyalty to James Stephens, whom he loved in the almost immoderate way he loved Colum, but I was completely shaken by his next phrase. He gave me a piercing look and asked, 'Michael, has it ever occurred to you that Seumas tipples?'

Literally, there was nothing anyone could reply to that because O'Sullivan's drinking was on the High Court scale. I did not quote Yeats' remark that 'The only trouble about Seumas O'Sullivan is that when he is not drunk he is sober'. I merely felt as I had when Russell had explained that I met girls who told bawdy stories because Nature intended me for a realistic novelist. I could hardly believe that any human being could be so utterly unobservant.

But all ended happily, for the following Monday evening he arrived at my flat at the usual time and – well on in the conversation – remarked casually, 'I was at Seumas' yesterday', and I knew that habit as well as old affection had triumphed again.

Russell's old friends loved the creature of habit, the well-tried phrases on the regular evening visit: his enemies detested them. What fascinated me then, and fascinates me still, is the wild creature behind them – the Portadown Presbyterian with his ingenuousness, his loneliness, his unforgettable flashes of genius. And it was hard work to get at it: talk, pictures, poems, everything he did was generalized into insignificance.

Once he asked me to select one of his pictures for my flat, and I chose a painting of a tree by a lake – chose it because it was the only picture in the room that did not contain those dreadful children who appeared in almost every picture he painted and whom he had seen originally in some landscape of Corot's.

'By the way,' I asked, 'what *is* that tree?' I did not mean to be impertinent, but at once I knew I had been.

'Oh, no particular tree,' he replied with a hurt expression. 'Just a tree!'

Everything with him was 'just a tree', not an oak or an elm or an ash; above all, not one with a character or pattern of its own. Habit had obliterated all distinctions.

Even his poems, as often as he repeated them – and he repeated them endlessly – never changed a word or an intonation. He said he knew by heart every line he had written, and this I found hard to understand, because he was the first person to point out to me that language is finite and that its beauty wears away by repetition. But even Yeats' early poems, for all the work Yeats had put in on improving them, never altered by a word or a tone on Russell's lips. He remembered them as they had been written, and though he knew perfectly well when Yeats had improved them, he hated the alterations. If he is the 'old school friend' whom Yeats accused of liking the early poems merely 'because they reminded him of his own youth', that is altogether too simple-minded. Russell was a fine critic, and he knew an improvement the moment he saw it, but the habit-forming complex, like a hardening of the arteries, never allowed him to see Yeats' early work as he saw mine and Higgins' and Kavanagh's, and, though Russell was kind to the point of fatuity, you simply could not take him in. However bad a poet he may have been, he was a poet, and he simply knew.

11

Russell, who was full of Hegelianism, used to argue that Irish literature developed in pairs. There were himself and Yeats, then Stephens and Colum, then Austin Clarke and F. R. Higgins, and now Geoffrey Phibbs and I.

But Russell was an example of another sort of Hegelianism, which he did not observe at all. The rediscovery of Old Irish, on which the whole literary movement was based, had been made by German scholars. When the discovery spread to Ireland the remarkable group of philologists, Irish and German, who worked here was probably the best group of scholars the country had known in modern times, and isolated by their very eminence. When Irish writers such as Yeats and Synge began to make use of the material they unearthed, and wrote as nobody in Ireland had written since the ninth century, they in their turn were isolated, and the two groups were drawn together and existed in an extraordinary love-hate relationship. There were the highly improbable friendships of George Moore and Kuno Meyer, of George Moore and Richard Best, of John Synge and Best. 'Moore didn't know the English language at all,' Best said. 'Moore pointed to a passage in a book and said, "Best, this man is very ignorant. He writes, 'It were better to say'." I said, "Moore, that is *not* bad English. That is merely the subjunctive mood." "Best," he said, "what is the subjunctive mood?" I explained it to him, and he said, "But, Best, how wonderful! I shall never again use *anything* but the subjunctive mood." '

Best also explained that Synge didn't know English, but I have forgotten what it was that Synge didn't know. All I do remember is that Synge did not know how to make tea. 'So I said to him, "Synge," I said, "I will buy you a teapot," and Synge asked, "Best, what *is* a teapot?" ' It would be fascinating to know what other strange discoveries great scholars and writers made about one another.

The truth is that they were friends without knowing why and without understanding the fierce resentments that sometimes blew up between them. They were the nearest thing in nature to the two sexes, for ever scouting about one another's encampments and bringing back horrible tales of what went on in them. Best had the last word on 'that fellow, Joyce', whom everyone talked about. 'He borrowed money from everyone in Dublin, but he never got a penny out of me.'

So it was quite natural that Russell should come to my flat with Osborn Bergin, the greatest of Irish scholars; that we should all meet on Sunday evenings at Russell's and that Russell and I should drop in on Bergin. The only difference was that Russell and I both made tea, but Bergin provided no refreshments. Either he was too much of an ascetic or he was too afraid of his housekeeper.

On the river under the windows of my library at Ballsbridge I used to watch the romance of a swan who had lost his mate and had struck up an immoral relationship with a fussy little duck who was obviously thrilled to death by such a large, strange, beautiful husband. Whenever I watched that strange pair I used to think of Russell and Bergin.

Bergin was a prince of scholars, and the figure I think of whenever I re-read *A Grammarian's Funeral* – who 'gave us the doctrine of the enclitic *De*, Dead from the waist down' – though Bergin wouldn't give you anything, not even a doctrine. 'Bergin's Law', known to all serious philologists, was identified and named by his pupil D. A. Binchy, but Bergin himself never really believed in it. He was a small man with a neat brown beard and a face that varied between the stern and precise and the vague and vacuous. He usually wore a costume that had been fashionable among Irish nationalists at the time I was born – a tweed jacket, pantaloons and long cycling stockings – and he usually sat with his legs crossed and one eye half closed, making patterns in the air with his pipe. I used to follow the patterns with my eyes, feeling sure that his subconscious mind was writing messages of great significance in the air, if only I could interpret what they meant. Where Russell burbled, Bergin rasped. When he had a story to tell you he would pull his legs in under his chair, point at you with his pipe, and screw his face up. When we were alone in his house he would put down his pipe, pick up his old fiddle and play and sing *Gaudeamus Igitur* and other songs from his student days in Germany. His fiddling was worse than his voice, which was terrible.

On one subject he knew more than anybody in the world, and he could not bear to discuss it with more than perhaps five people – rather in the manner of the Lowells and Cabots, and if the God's truth was known he probably thought the Cabots very unreliable. Robin Flower, a really fine scholar, he could not tolerate because

Flower spoke Irish with an English accent – forgivable enough in an Englishman, one would have thought.

Nothing would persuade Russell, who knew no language but English, but that I was a formidable scholar too, since I had once, to his own knowledge, caught T. F. O'Rahilly out. O'Rahilly, second only to Bergin in scholarship, though not in crankiness, had a great grudge against Edmund Curtis, the historian, who reviewed books in Irish for Russell's paper, the *Irish Statesman*, and he wrote abusive letters to Russell, suggesting that Curtis couldn't read a page of Irish without a dictionary, till poor Curtis gave up. Russell conscripted me in his place, and in the first review I wrote I came a cropper that wouldn't even have occurred to Curtis, and O'Rahilly wrote his usual letter of complaint, but with what for him was urbanity. He probably felt that if you must have devils you had better have them of your own making. By a coincidence, the very same week that O'Rahilly's letter appeared I got one of his two beautiful anthologies of love poetry for review, and there was a mistake that even a child wouldn't have made. I struggled hard with my conscience, because the book was so beautiful I merely wanted to enthuse and not bother with what to me was nonsense, so I finally ignored it. But I couldn't resist writing to Russell to prove how noble I was, and Russell, walking forth (it was one of his favourite examples of the Economy of Nature that he was always talking about), met Bergin, who read my letter with the air of a Lowell being told of a Cabot solecism by a Boston Biddy. 'Nature' must have been working overtime that day because the first person Bergin ran into was O'Rahilly and, in the true Lowell spirit, he showed O'Rahilly the note he had taken. That night, coming on to midnight, O'Rahilly was pounding on Bergin's door, almost in tears, with the cry of 'But I had it right in proof, Bergin! I had it right in proof!' Bergin went round next evening to tell Russell, and Russell wrote to me next morning.

Ah, me! But after that O'Rahilly sent me his works, and was delighted when Thurneysen and I in acknowledging one of them used exactly the same words, Thurneysen in German and I in English. Is it any wonder I enjoyed scouting round the scholars' encampments for what I could bring home in the way of gossip?

But Bergin could not trust a man capable of making a mistake like that. One night, he and I were walking home from Russell's, and I told him I was uncertain of the meaning of one verse in O'Rahilly's second anthology of love poetry. I got a very short answer: 'Couldn't say without seeing the text.' But I was getting used to Bergin's 'Don't knows' and 'Can't imagines' and I produced the book. Bergin took it with great politeness and loathing and stopped under the nearest gas-lamp to read. Having read the verse I didn't understand, he turned the page to the beginning of the poem and read it right through. Then he turned back the page and did it again. Finally he closed the book and handed it back to me. 'I'm always telling O'Rahilly not to publish manuscripts he doesn't understand,' he said in a dead voice, and after that he said no more.

He had such a horror of inaccuracy that he avoided the risk of it by never speaking anything but English, except when he was reminiscing, and had it all, as you might say, pat. Once in explaining to me his dislike of the Germans, he described an incident of his student days when he and a French student named Etienne went to register as aliens. 'Osborn Bergin' sounded a good Teutonic name, so he had no trouble, but when it came to the French boy's turn the policeman said flatly, '*Etienne, das ist kein Name.*' According to Bergin, this had given him a hatred of Germans that had lasted throughout his life. When I protested, he said gloomily, 'There are only two tones in the German voice, the whine and the bellow. They're whining now; the bellow will come later.' (This was before Hitler.) I, having no culture at all except what I had picked up from German, protested again, but he crushed me brutally. 'Binchy' (then our ambassador in Germany) 'says the Germans are a people you keep on trying to like.' That settled that, too. God alone knows what Binchy did say, but this is what Bergin felt he should have said, and it was said on his behalf.

When Bergin and Best went to Germany in later years, Bergin refused to speak German at all, and he let the unfortunate Best struggle with the problem of transport and currency without once opening his mouth. But when Best in Cologne station, having asked Bergin for some small change and got nothing but a scowl, told the railway porter, '*Ich habe nicht Geld*', outraged majesty recovered sufficiently to rasp '*Ich habe KEIN Geld!*' Everybody in Ireland knew the story of how, when he stood over the grave of his old friend Father Peter O'Leary, he glanced at the breastplate of the coffin and muttered '*Four* mistakes!' but I suspect I was the only person ignorant or innocent enough to challenge him with it. When I did, he merely cocked one eye, made figures on the air with his pipe and muttered. 'Well, I didn't make the mistakes, did I?'

He was rather friendlier to the French than to the Germans, and

I suspect that if only he could have spoken their language in a way that satisfied his own standards he would have enthused about them. He used to tell with glee a story of Meyer's, who had been with some other scholars at the house of a French philologist and discussed the disappearance of final consonants in the language. The host's old father listened with horror to those blasphemies about his native language, because he knew that final consonants had not disappeared, and at last he whispered in anguish to Meyer, '*Ne le' croye' pa', m'sieu! I' ne sav' pa' ce qu'i' di'.*'

And yet, because I loved him, I knew Bergin was a fiercely emotional and possessive man, consumed with obscure abstract hatreds. I know now what I did not realize at the time – what it was that Russell and he had in common. Both were European figures who in their hearts had never ceased to be anything but small-town boys. When Russell was moved he reverted to the Lurgan Orangeman, and when Bergin was moved he reverted to the Cork Gaelic Leaguer. It was an experience to lunch with him and Tadhg O'Donoghue of University College, Cork, who didn't seem to me to have an idea in his good-looking head, though Bergin put on more of a performance for him than he did even for Russell. Bergin had once been Secretary of the Leeside Branch of the Gaelic League in Cork, which had had a disagreement with the Governing Body in Dublin, and when Bergin talked of his disagreement, then forty years old, he became almost incoherent with anger. I never discovered what the Governing Body was supposed to have done, though I listened to the story several times.

Another of his hatreds was George Moore, who, in his usual petulant way, had said to him one night at Best's, 'Oh, Bergin, you bore me!' to which Bergin had retorted, 'I am as much entitled to bore you, Mr Moore, as you are to bore me.' When a man repeats years later the crushing retort he has made, you can be sure that he was badly hurt, and judging by the way Bergin repeated it he must have wanted a writer of his own as badly as Moore wanted a scholar, and felt about Moore's behaviour as a man feels when told by a girl he had been in love with that he was no good as a lover.

His third detestation was Yeats, who, according to Bergin, had insulted him during a meeting of the Dublin Literary Society. 'Dr Bergin, are there any astrological manuscripts in Irish?' Yeats had asked, and Bergin had replied, 'Not to my knowledge, Mr Yeats.' Yeats had then deliberately turned away in his chair. It was no good telling Bergin that Yeats had probably turned away to meditate on the question of whether the British Government or the Catholic Church had destroyed the manuscripts. Bergin knew it was an insult intended for him.

But his greatest rancour was reserved for his old friend Joseph O'Neill, a good Celtic scholar, who had been a fellow student of his in Germany. O'Neill – one at least of whose donnish romances will be remembered – married a literary woman, who – again according to Bergin – was always talking of 'Peguy and Proust' and getting the pronunciation wrong – a major offence in anyone but an intimate friend. (When I quoted in German or French Bergin contented himself with following me soundlessly on his lips.)

The O'Neills dropped Bergin, 'a man who couldn't dance either literally or metaphorically', and he resented it fiercely, all the more because Russell replaced him as the O'Neills' best friend, and over the years he made O'Neill the butt of scholarly jokes and poems. The verse squibs began with their student days in Germany and O'Neill's passion for stories of the Wild West:

> Buffalo Bill war ein Mann, he read,
> In des Wortes bester Bedeutung, oh!

They described O'Neill's days as a school inspector – 'Holy nuns would give him tea, priests would give him dinner' – and described him at his first public function:

> When Gally was young he had more sense
> Than to follow the fiddler and waste his pence.
> Dancing reels on a Galway strand;
> He was saving his feet for a Free State band.
> Heyho, Gallio dancing,
> Slithering, sliding, prancing!
> Heyho, Gallio dancing,
> Dancing at a Free State ball.

And when Russell (who lived round the corner from both O'Neill and Bergin) reached San Francisco, there was a savage little note waiting for him that read: 'Please remember me to Joseph O'Neill.'

Russell and Bergin were both lonely men, and there was nothing to indicate that one was a widower and the other a bachelor but the fact that the bachelor's house didn't look as though it needed cleaning. Each week they went together to the local cinema and they carted detective stories to one another's houses. In his days as editor Russell could glut himself on whodunits, but now he was often hard up for something to read, and as a librarian I was able to help. Lit up by the discussion of some new gimmick in Agatha Christie or Dorothy Sayers, Russell would expand on the great detective story he would write, called 'The Murder of a Celtic Scholar', with Bergin as principal suspect, though the victim might be Agnes O'Farrelly, Douglas Hyde or even Eoin MacNeill, a fine historian, but 'quite unscrupulous with his sources', according to Bergin. Those were delightful evenings, though when they came to me it took a full week to get rid of the stink of their tobacco. Each year they got someone to drive them into the country, collected masses of coltsfoot, dried it on trays before their windows and then ground it up to mix with their tobacco.

They were always making mystifying little jokes at one another's expense. If it wasn't 'The Murder of a Celtic Scholar', it was Bergin's 'If A.E. had written the Odyssey', a neat little twelve-line lyric in Russell's vaguest manner, which summed up the epic. then it was Russell writing to Bergin as he crossed the Mississippi, 'which at this point is a mile wide', and Bergin's reply, 'Aristotle says an animal a mile long could not be beautiful, but please don't quote me because I haven't the text before me.' This was reported back to me by Russell with the comment, 'Isn't that just like dear Osborn?'

But in spite of all the joking Russell was very perturbed by the rumour that dear Osborn had written love poetry in Irish which, some friends had told him, was very passionate indeed. I tried to reassure him, but he wasn't satisfied. Russell had wanted a scholar for a friend, and if it now turned out that Bergin was really a wild romantic poet whose word no man could rely on it would be worse than not knowing what to do with his Sunday afternoons. One night he came to my flat, bristling.

'I was at Curran's last night,' he began, without preliminaries, as he did only when he was upset. 'He says Bergin has a poem in all the anthologies which is very passionate. Have you got it? Could you translate it for me? I want to know what it's like.' Of course, I knew it by heart. It was part of the anthology of bad verse I had memorized in the days when I couldn't afford books. It was the plague of Bergin's life, because nobody reprinted it correctly, and it had almost begun to seem that nobody could, as though it had a jinx on it. Bergin had had a circular drawn up, embodying the correct text and demanding a proof.

I translated out of my head for Russell, and after the first few lines he began to stroke his beard and beam like a lover being reassured of his girl's fidelity. 'All literary convention!' he murmured joyously. 'I knew it! I knew our Osborn had never been in love!' (In which, of course, he was wrong, because our Osborn had been very much in love with one of his students; an American girl he had pursued, even abroad; but we cut our friends to suit our needs, and Russell needed a scholar rather than another poet.) So the two elderly men went on happily adoring one another.

Yeats was madly jealous of Russell's scholar and would have given anything to possess one of his own. Nothing would have pleased him better than to be able to say, 'My friend Bergin, the greatest living philologist, tells me . . .' But, anyway, Bergin wouldn't have told him the time of day. Except among the Lowells and Cabots he never talked of his own subject except to say, 'Don't know', 'Can't tell', or 'Too obscure for me'. He knew I was crazy to learn Old Irish, but the only contribution he ever made to my knowledge of it was when he took Strachan and O'Keeffe's edition of *The Cattle Raid of Cooley* from a shelf one night and murmured, 'Em. Very clean!'

He wasn't at all the dry stick one must make him appear if one is to get the real biscuity Bergin flavour. As with Russell, there was under the urbanized exterior the emotional volcano of the provincial town. Mother adored him, and used to sit at the window, watching for his arrival, so that she could be the first to welcome him. He told her stories of Cork and liked listening to her stories of it. Yeats, of course, either hadn't heard of Cork or didn't think much of it. One night when Bergin was in the flat with us a knock came at the door and she went to answer. A moment later she appeared in the room, looking like a ghost and with her hands in the air. 'Michael!' she cried. 'Yeats!' Then she rushed off to her bedroom, where Yeats couldn't get at her. Yeats, embarrassed by his extraordinary reception, came in looking shyer than ever, and Bergin completed his confusion. Bergin had only to see Yeats to remember that monstrous scene at the Dublin Literary Society.

Yeats and I talked for a few minutes and the name of George Moore came up. Bergin grunted, and Yeats' spirits began to rise, because he began to discern that however much Bergin hated him, he hated Moore worse; and many a dear friendship has begun on nothing more substantial than a common enmity. I could see he was thinking that he might yet acquire a scholar of his own, for he burst into the wonderful series of malicious anecdotes that later appeared in *Dramatis Personae* along with a number of scabrous ones that haven't appeared anywhere yet.

Bergin was exceedingly vulnerable in his sense of humour, particularly when it concerned a man who had the audacity to say that Bergin bored him. First he chuckled, then he laughed, and finally he was rolling round on the sofa, hysterical with laughter. I had never seen Yeats put on such a performance for anyone before, and I accompanied him to the tramcar in a glow of love and admiration for both of them.

But when I returned, one look at Bergin was enough to dissipate the charm. He was sitting on the sofa, scowling, despising Yeats, despising me for permitting a man like that into the house, but most of all despising himself for the weakness of character that had made him sacrifice his dignity for the sake of a few funny stories. He was already casting himself as Browning's 'Lost Leader' – 'Just for a handful of silver he left us'.

'Isn't he a great old card?' I said as enthusiastically as I could.

'He's a great old cod,' Bergin snapped, without looking at me, and for the rest of the evening I couldn't even get a civil answer out of him.

A scholar's work is often as much a self-portrait as a writer's. Osborn Bergin loved Irish professional poetry of the late Middle Ages, and to those who knew him the poems give back a reflection of the man. Many of them belong to the Elizabethan period, which was the last great period of Irish love poetry, but it was characteristic of Bergin that he left all that to O'Rahilly. He edited only Cu Chonnact O Cléirigh's *Ní mé bhur n-aithne, a aos gráidh*, and that only because he found it 'mysterious', which it is not, except for the fact that the passion becomes lost in the conceit.

One cannot imagine his friend Kuno Meyer editing them. Meyer was the romantic scholar, and he fell upon the earlier poetry with a freshness and joyousness that can still be felt in his translations, which are all the more remarkable because they are translations from one foreign language into another. According to Bergin, Meyer carried his translations round with him, ready to read to anyone of literary sensitiveness who could produce the perfect word for him. One cannot imagine Bergin doing that. His scholarship was superior to Meyer's and his translations are more exact, but it is the exactness of prose rather than verse. D. A. Binchy tells the story of an English student of Bergin's who once asked in exasperation, 'But what is it all about?' Bergin replied evenly, 'I will give you an exact translation of the words.' And that, too, is characteristic. Even in his choice of words Meyer tries to tell you 'what it is all about'; Bergin gives you the exact prose equivalent and allows you to work out the rest for yourself.

As a result his prose is sometimes more difficult than the verse he is translating. In that beautiful poem on the death of his wife, Muireadhach O'Daly wrote:

Beag an cion do chúl na ngéag
A héag ó a fíor go húr óg.

Bergin translates: 'Little was the fault [or affection] of the branching tresses that she should die and leave her husband while fresh and young.' But whether *cion* means 'fault' or 'affection' it would be more polite to translate: 'It was no blame to the girl of the branching tresses' or maybe even 'It was small desire the girl of the branching tresses had to die'.

It was not that Bergin was insensitive to what the Irish said. On the contrary, he merely believed, as he said himself, that they were as untranslatable as an ode of Horace. When I took him up on this, and translated 'A Winter Campaign' into the pseudo-Horatian metre of Marvell, he ignored both the compliment and the criticism, and I gathered I had committed *lèse-majesté*. He was touchy about any slighting remark regarding the poems themselves. Once, when I had mentioned them in the same breath with the verbose eighteenth-century poets, he replied stiffly, 'Those men were aristocrats and scholars.' He liked the aristocratic flavour, but even more he loved the neatness, the order, the scholarship, and the feeling of an Oxford common-room.

That strongly donnish note existed in Irish poetry from the beginning, but in these poems it is at its strongest because the world they knew was collapsing in ruin about its authors. I think Bergin liked to remember that even in the days when earth was falling, 'the day when earth's foundations fled', these Irish professional poets continued to count their syllables, and admitted no word, no grammatical form, which their masters of two hundred years before would not have approved. Like other artists, he identified himself with his subject, for he was one of the last of a great generation of scholars in a country where scholarship was no longer regarded.

12

What Yeats had come to see me about was his Academy of Letters, which still drags out some sort of shadowy, precarious existence. The idea of it was sound enough – a solid body of informed opinion that might encourage young writers and discourage the Catholic Church from suppressing them; but for both purposes it suffered from the fact that, apart from Yeats, its most important members lived in England and had no notion of what conditions in Ireland were like.

The Dublin committee was Yeats, Russell, Higgins, Robinson, O'Sullivan, Gogarty and myself, 'two of whom', as Yeats said in his oracular way, 'make themselves drunk and a third who came drunk from his mother's womb'. The two who made themselves drunk were O'Sullivan and Robinson and, as he explained to me later, Yeats had to invite Robinson to tea before every committee meeting in order to supervise his drinking and make sure he reached the meeting in a sober state. The one who came drunk from his mother's womb was Oliver Gogarty, 'the kindest heart in Dublin and the dirtiest tongue', as a friend of his described him. I knew the kindness. I had been only a short time in Dublin before a surgeon ordered me into hospital for an operation on my throat. A friend of mine told Gogarty, and he said, 'Tell him to come round at once.' I went, and Gogarty, who did not know me at all, began by apologizing for the creator of the universe in a way that endeared him to me. 'You know you're in the cancer group,' he said gently, and then spent ten minutes looking at my throat. 'Jesus Christ!' I heard him muttering. 'There are doctors in this town that don't know the difference between cancer and a sore toe.' After that, he sprang into rambunctious life. 'There's nothing wrong with you, only Indian tea. I'll write it out for you – you can get it at Roberts' – Lapsang-Soo-Chong. I'm like Yeats; "I have forgotten all my Hebrew." ' I couldn't help liking Gogarty, though he did make a vicious attack on me later at an Academy dinner, describing me as 'a country boy with hair in his nose and hair in his ears and a brief-case in his hand'.

However, Yeats was a natural organizer, never happy unless he was organizing something or somebody – a great bully, as I discovered later, and an outrageous flatterer. When I, who at the time had not even produced a book, questioned the inclusion of St John

Ervine in the Academy, Yeats did not say, as he should have said, that Shaw insisted; he merely asked mellowly, 'Why worry about literary eminence? You and I will provide that.'

When he began to bully me I always gave him lip, almost on principle. After my father, I never quarrelled so much with anyone, and even if one allows that I am a bit in the same line myself, it takes two to make a disagreement last as long as ours. One might say that I was discovering my real father at last, and that all the old attitudes induced by my human father came on top. Yet I can truthfully say that when, towards the end of his life, I became his devoted slave, it was entirely due to his generosity, because with no one else was I so crude and uppish.

His principal weakness was that he was easily bored, and L. A. G. Strong was not the only one who bored him. George Russell bored him too, and many others, and he made no effort to conceal it. This, I think, cost him the affection of a number of people who would have been better friends than some of those he made.

Apart from these things, I think of him as a shy and rather lonely man who desperately wanted to be friends, and was utterly loyal to the friends he made. It took a long time to appreciate that shyness in him because it tended to make him portentous and overwhelming in society and even in the home. Once, when Michael Yeats was pulling his sister's hair and Mrs Yeats failed to separate them, Daddy was summoned. He stalked slowly and solemnly to an armchair, sat down and recited, 'Let dogs delight to bark and bite', and then stalked out again, apparently feeling he had done all that was expected of a father. The children never became intimate with him: even the marvellous 'Prayer for my Daughter' was written while Anne was safely in another building. Michael once got his own back by asking in a piercing voice as his father went by, 'Mummy, who is that man?' and Yeats was deeply hurt.

Mrs Yeats was my favourite among authors' wives. This was an old romance, dating from my earliest days in Dublin, when again and again she had covered up my shyness and awkwardness. One evening someone had lured me to a fashionable party at Gogarty's. I was sitting on the floor wishing I was dead when the door opened and George Yeats came in. She gave one look round the room and then came and sat beside me.

'How did you know the way I was feeling?' I asked.

'You looked exactly as Willie does when he gets shy,' she said with a grin. 'You were running your hand through your hair.'

I used to think no one in the world suspected my attachment, least of all George Yeats, though nowadays, I wonder if Yeats himself did not suspect it.

The only person I ever heard him speak of with real malice was George Moore, and that still puzzles me a little, because he was a remarkably tolerant man. I have a suspicion that it was because Moore had hurt Lady Gregory by describing herself and her family as 'soupers'. You could say anything you liked about himself, or even his family, but his toleration never really extended to people whom he thought had injured either Lady Gregory or Synge. He was generous enough in his public references to Arthur Griffith, but there is submerged ice in that line that describes 'Arthur Griffith staring in hysterical pride', and Padraic Colum once said to me, 'Yeats never had any time for me after the *Playboy* row.' More than anything else that happened to him I suspect the quarrel about Synge's great play really hurt him.

We had our first big showdown at an early meeting of that wretched Academy when Yeats demanded that Russell, the Secretary, should change the minutes of the previous meeting. Yeats had apparently said something he should not have said and wanted it omitted. As a public official I knew that the minutes were perfectly correct, and since everybody else was afraid to oppose Yeats I said so. As a friend of Russell's I also knew that he was terribly hurt, and when Yeats persisted in his rigmarole I flew at him.

The minutes remained as they were, and when everybody else had gone home I stayed to comfort Russell, who was close to tears.

'Yeats has always been like that,' he said bitterly. 'Always unscrupulous and always dishonest.'

Naturally I believed him without wondering why on earth he had let me defend him instead of standing up for himself. It was only later, when I got to know both men better, that I noticed more and more in Russell the oscillation between love and hatred of Yeats. It worked both ways, of course. Yeats was intolerable with Russell, and one of my most shameful evenings was when I joined Yeats in baiting him; but, on the other hand, Russell was never so dull with anyone as he was with Yeats, who, when he became embarrassed, could be outrageous. Russell complained to me that when cornered in an argument, Yeats would wave his hand and say loftily, 'Yes, Russell, but that was before the peacock screamed' or some other bit of nonsense. This was exactly what Yeats was likely to do when he was bored, but, on the other hand, Russell did bore him. He even bored me occasionally.

Once, when I arrived at Russell's house in Rathgar before he was ready to receive me, I noticed the proofs of *Song and its Fountains* on his desk with a dedication to Yeats, 'Rival and Friend'. (The dedication has since been printed in a different form, but I think I am right about the one I saw.) The revealing phrase was deleted from the printed book. Russell was not only too modest a man, but too good a critic not to know that there could be no rivalry between himself and Yeats, and somewhere in him there was a sense of failure that came out in his evenings with Yeats. Behind it all, I think, was Yeats' resentment at Russell's not having taken Synge's side in the *Playboy* controversy and letting his house be used as a headquarters by the anti-Synge faction, but this was all so long before my time that I could not have been sure of identifying it. What I am sure of is that Russell needed Yeats' pity, and Yeats had no pity. He could give you things that I think now were more worth while – admiration, tolerance and absolute loyalty, but he was as pitiless with others as he was with himself.

By this I do not mean that Russell was his inferior, if such judgements have any meaning. He was one of those people, like Desmond McCarthy, whom I later became friendly with, who love writers and books for their own sweet sake, have no apparent jealousy and who, though first-rate men themselves, will appear hardly at all in literary history.

A week or so after the quarrel I have described, Russell resigned from the secretaryship of the Academy, giving as his reason that he 'would have nothing to do with us or with a country so given over to the devil', as Yeats quoted him in a letter to me. The quotation is probably correct because, as I shall have to explain, during his last year in Dublin Russell was exceedingly depressed. Yeats thought he was just afraid of a row.

'Russell is always timid before a row begins,' he wrote to me, 'though when it does he fights like a madman.'

This was true enough, but I suspected that it was not Russell's real reason, and I told Yeats he had been insufferably rude. He took this reproof from a young and unknown writer with extraordinary graciousness. 'I must smooth him down,' he said mildly, washing his hands with an episcopal air.

He had been reading a novel by Austin Clarke, one of the young writers Russell felt he had discovered, and reading it with genuine admiration, but instead of writing to Clarke as he would normally have done, he wrote to Russell, congratulating him on being the first to appreciate Clarke's gifts. 'As usual, you were right and I was wrong,' he wrote.

Russell, who was always pathetically grateful for any little tribute from Yeats, rushed round to my house to show me the letter. 'I think that's very noble of him, don't you?' he asked ingenuously and, pleased to see him happy, I agreed. Of course he wrote at once to Yeats, withdrawing his resignation, and things went on as before. I could not resist making fun of Yeats about it, and told him I was writing a book of stories in which all my acquaintances would appear in the historic circumstances that suited them best, and that he was being described as a Renaissance cardinal. He chuckled, because he loved to be thought a really smooth intriguer, which he wasn't. 'Ah, we know one another so long,' he said modestly.

The Irish Government had just banned Shaw's *Black Girl in Search of God* as being 'in its general tendency indecent and obscene'. It was a crude effort of the Censorship Board to prevent the teaching of Rationalism, and the one small peg they had to hang the charge of obscenity on was the woodcuts of a naked girl. There was no clause in the Act which permitted the Minister to ban any pictures, even if they were obscene, and I wanted to use the book to fight the Censorship Board. I argued that if Shaw, Yeats and lesser writers like myself took the Abbey Theatre for one Sunday in the month, lectured and sold copies of the book, we could force the Government to withdraw the ban because even Mr de Valera's government would hardly be idiotic enough to prosecute Shaw and Yeats, but Yeats felt he was too old and ill to face a public campaign, so we compromised on a deputation to the Minister of Justice, Patrick Rutledge.

It seemed to me important that we should not offer Rutledge the excuse of having banned the book on account of the pictures, because only if we could get him to state this himself could we show that the order was illegal. Accordingly the deputation – Yeats, Russell, Higgins and I – agreed that we should confine ourselves to the text and make no mention of the pictures unless the Minister mentioned them himself.

But next morning when I arrived at Government Buildings, there was Yeats with a suspicious-looking folio under his arm. 'What is that?' I asked, and, with the air of a small boy caught at the jam, he said angrily. 'These are reproductions of the frescoes by

Michelangelo in the Pope's private chapel.' I said that we might as well go home, but it was no use. Yeats had made up a beautiful speech on the Sanctity of the Nude and he intended to deliver to to somebody.

He did, and Russell added a few useful observations about Victorians who put trousers on table-legs, while I fumed and Higgins chuckled. As an old trade-union official he knew as I did exactly how much the Sanctity of the Nude troubled the sleep of an Irish politician. That night in the foyer of the Abbey Theatre the Minister grabbed Higgins by the arm and said, 'Yeats thinks I'm going to use what he said about the dirty pictures in the Pope's chapel. What a fool I am!'

All the same, Yeats refused to quarrel with me. He published two books of my translations from the Irish and rewrote them in the process. Gogarty once invited me to come to Yeats' flat with him – 'He's writing a few little lyrics for me, and I'd like to see how he's getting on.' It *was* rather like that. I went one night to Yeats' for dinner and we fought for God knows how long over a single line of an O'Rahilly translation I had done – 'Has made me travel to seek you, Valentine Brown.' At first I was fascinated by the way he kept trying it out, changing pitch and intonation. 'Has made me – no! Has made me travel to seek you – No, that's wrong, HAS MADE ME TRAVEL TO SEEK YOU, VALENTINE BROWN – no!'

Long before that evening I had tired of the line, and hearing it repeated endlessly in Yeats' monotone I felt it sounded worse.

'It's tautological,' I complained. 'It should be something like "Has made me a beggar before you, Valentine Brown",' and he glared at me as if he had never seen me before.

'No beggars! No beggars!' he roared, and I realized that, like other theatre men I have known, he thought the writer's place was at home.

All the same, it was as interesting to work over poetry with him as it was later to work over plays. He was an absolute master of both, and his principal virtue was his principal defect. He had absolutely no ear for music that I could discern, though this, of course, never shook his faith in his own musical genius. He told a story of how he had gone to Dr Sigerson's one day when Sigerson had an old countrywoman in a hypnotic trance and made her feel Yeats' face. 'Poet,' she had said, then 'great poet', then 'musician'. 'And then I knew she was a genuine medium,' Yeats declared.

He was pleased when someone said he had a 'natural' ear, and, for all I know, this may have been true: he certainly had not a cultivated one. When I returned from a holiday in Italy and told him of the folk-singing I had heard on the canals in Venice, he asked me modestly if it was anything like his own. Nevertheless, it saved him from the sort of jingle that poets with too sensitive a musical ear fall into, and the harder he worked at writing words for music, the more unmusical they became. Even when he revised the O'Rahilly translations I had done, which were in alexandrines, he treated them as though they were in iambic pentameter, unaware that he had dropped a beat.

His musical adviser was F. R. Higgins, another old friend of Russell, and up to a short time before Yeats' death his most intimate friend in Ireland. For years the one fathead wrote what he thought were songs, the other fathead fitted them, as he believed, to old Irish airs, and they got a third fathead to take down their nonsense in staff notation. If Russell and Bergin were a queer pair, Yeats and Higgins were queerer still. Higgins was huge, fat and handsome, with a red face and black lank hair that tumbled in a lovelock over one eye and tiny feet that would not support his Falstaffian frame. He was emotional, indiscreet and generous, and, after talking to him for an evening, you were left with the impression that you had made a friend for life. But he left you, and within ten minutes was giving himself with equal generosity to your worst enemy and, before even he knew what he was doing, was betraying you all over the shop.

I once said of him that he was a Protestant with all the vices of a Catholic, but *because* he was a Protestant, and had set up a little trade journal of his own and lived off the small proceeds, and had bought himself a little bungalow on the Dodder, and was a kind and considerate husband, he kept building up in himself an enormous feeling of guilt, so that when you next met him he was merely wondering how much you had heard of his witty description of you and what plots you had thought up to get your own back on him, till at last you felt he was no friend at all, much less a friend for life.

Once, after a meeting of Yeats' moribund Academy, when O'Faolain and myself had been trying to get Ernie O'Malley elected, we had a drink with Higgins and then went out to Yeats' house. Yeats greeted us with his Renaissance cardinal's chuckle and asked: 'What do you two young rascals mean by trying to fill my Academy with gunmen?'

We realized at once that Higgins had been on the telephone to report everything we had said in the most disparaging way, and I said in exasperation, 'Trust you to make a friend of a man who is uneducated, intellectually and emotionally!' Yeats gave a great guffaw, but, as always happened when he felt he had been rebuked, he must have brooded on it, because he replied to it a year or so later.

'You don't understand my friendship with Higgins, O'Connor, but when you reach my age you will find there is one thing a man cannot do without, and that is another man to talk to him about women.' To someone else he said, 'X comes here and talks to me about women, and it is all invention. Higgins comes sweating from his whore and every word rings true.' But there was much more to his friendship with Higgins than that. It was characteristic of Yeats to deprecate the genuine warmth of his own attachments. He needed Gogarty and Higgins as he needed the women he talked to them about, because they broke through the barriers he could not help erecting about himself.

Higgins never knew when he had been rebuked. Yeats felt he had been rebuked even when – as on that occasion – no rebuke had been intended.

But God help Yeats if he really listened to Higgins' romances! At regular intervals he fell in love as we all do, always madly and for the first and last time, and Dublin resounded with his confidences distributed generously like everything else he had and always under a vow of secrecy; and when his unhappy passion reached its inevitable tragic conclusion he fell ill, always with cancer or something equally incurable. He knew that no ordinary doctor would be heartless enough to break the news to him, but he knew how to beat that too. He applied for a life insurance policy, had himself examined by the insurance company's doctor, and when the policy was accepted tore up the papers and rushed into town to drink with his cronies.

Unfortunately, it was to Higgins that Yeats found it easy to confide all his little domestic difficulties. It was typical of Yeats' capacity to size a man up that with me, on the contrary, his references to sex were usually almost boyishly modest and even made me impatient. He knew, too, though I never told him so, that I did not share his interest in spiritualism. One night I asked him bluntly if he ever had had an experience that could not be explained in strictly rational terms. He thought for a while and grew embarrassed.

'Yes, once. I think I can tell you. You are, after all, a man of the world. I was having a love affair with a certain woman and she said she was pregnant. I was very worried because I felt that if she was, I must marry her. I came home to Ireland and confessed to an old aunt. "Don't believe her," she said. "She's having you on." So I went to a certain famous medium and asked for her help without telling her what my trouble was. She went into a trance and produced some writing that neither of us could read. Finally I took it to the British Museum and they told me to come back in a week. When I went back the head of one of the departments said, "Mr Yeats, this is a most remarkable document. It is written in the form of Hebrew taught in the German universities in the seventeenth century." '

Then Yeats looked at me triumphantly, his head tossed back, the big, blind eyes behind the spectacles challenging me to explain that one if I could.

'Never mind what sort of Hebrew it was written in,' I said. 'Did it tell you whether you were the father of the child or not?'

The practical Corkman! He sat back wearily – rationalists are so hard to argue with.

'Oh, no, no,' he said vaguely. 'It just said things like "O great poet of our race!" ' Clearly he thought this important, but I didn't. As a storyteller I felt that the point had got lost.

'Well, there wasn't any necessity for saying that in Hebrew,' I said, and this too, like the business of Higgins, rankled because I got the usual well-thought-out retort a couple of years later.

What Yeats did not know was that his harmless little crushes on younger women and every small disagreement in the home would be repeated by Higgins within an hour in an exaggerated and witty way in some Dublin public-house. This embarrassed me, not because I am not indiscreet myself and don't enjoy gossip like the next man, but because Higgins' gossip had an element of intrigue in it. It was almost as though by telling you funny stories about your friends he was ingratiating himself with you and lining you up against them. Gogarty's gossip, which was much more slanderous and a breach of professional confidence besides, since Yeats was his patient, was so disinterested that it seemed to get lost in its own malice, and you could laugh at it without feeling that you were betraying anybody or anything. To stop him in a story would be like stealing a bottle from a baby, but it was almost like doing a kindness to Higgins.

Once when he was telling some story about the Yeatses that embarrassed me, I got up in a hurry and said, 'And yet I never leave that house without feeling like a million dollars' – a queer phrase for me to use, and one that shows how uncomfortable I felt. But the effect on Higgins was even stranger. There were tears in his eyes – tears of real affection – and he replied, 'And I feel exactly the same.'

Of course he did, but he simply could not resist a good story when it aligned you against someone who was involved in his intrigue – innocent intrigues enough, God knows, because he was fantastically generous. There was the occasion, for instance, when Yeats was reported to be dying in Majorca. I can still remember the lights flashing it out over O'Connell Bridge and feeling sick at heart. Robinson and Higgins, in a state of maudlin emotion, arranged for the lying in state in the foyer of the Abbey Theatre with a wreath of laurel over Yeats' head – 'not *plain* laurel, Fred,' Robinson sobbed, 'but the small-leafed poet's laurel.' When Yeats recovered and came home, this was much too good a story for Higgins to keep from him – since it showed Robinson in a ridiculous light. It never once crossed Higgins' mind that an old and sickly man might not appreciate the comedy of his own death.

'You needn't go on,' growled Yeats. 'It reminds me of my two uncles, one of whom was drunk and the other mad, quarrelling over my grandfather's open grave as to which of them was to inherit Grandfather's musical box.'

Yeats' comment was so much better than the original story that Higgins had to come and tell me about it, and I don't think that even then it occurred to him that it contained a rebuke. Which, of course, was also what was nice about Higgins, even when he did not know that he was being nice.

In his last phase, when I knew him, Yeats was by way of being a Fascist, and a supporter of O'Duffy. He wrote unsingable Fascist songs to the tunes of 'O'Donnell Abu' and 'The Heather Glen' and caused me acute embarrassment by appearing at dinner in the Kildare Street Club in a blue shirt. At the same time there never was anyone with less of the fanatic in him. He took a mischievous delight in devilling anyone who took politics too seriously. One evening in the club he insisted on introducing me to an old Unionist, and then, when I'd left, made the old man's life a misery by telling him that I was a notorious gunman and a supporter of de Valera. He told of a London party where a duke had come up to him and said, 'I suppose you support Dr Cosgrave?' 'Oh, I support the gunmen – on both sides,' said Yeats. 'And what did he say?' I asked. 'Oh, the damn fool turned his back on me and walked away,' Yeats said in disgust.

I had to threaten to resign before I got him to drop the proposal to produce *Coriolanus* in coloured shirts at the Abbey, and even after that he deliberately provoked me by coming out to dinner with me again in a brilliant blue shirt. Mrs Yeats, who was English, was a strong supporter of de Valera and hated all Fascists, including her next-door neighbours, who were Blueshirts also. Now Mrs Yeats kept hens and the Blueshirts kept a dog, and the dog worried Mrs Yeats' hens. One day Mrs Yeats' favourite hen disappeared, and she, according to W.B., said, 'It's that damn Blueshirts' dog', so she wrote a very stiff letter to the neighbours accusing the dog of having made away with her hen. 'But you see, O'Connor, the neighbours are Blueshirts, with a proper sense of order and discipline, and within an hour or two back comes the reply, "Dear Madam, Dog Destroyed." Now George is English, and like all English people she has a great tenderness towards animals, and I felt her almost in tears for the death of the Blueshirt dog.'

The second part of the story came a few nights later when Yeats said to me, 'O'Connor, you remember the story I told you about the Blueshirt dog and the democratic hen? The democratic hen has come back. George is overwhelmed with guilt. She wants to write an apology to the neighbours, but I say to her, "It is too late for apologies. No apology is going to bring the Blueshirt dog back to life." '

Both the Yeatses are in that little story; the sincere and sometimes cranky public man, and the tolerant and affectionate husband and friend who, like the plain girl at the party, does not miss a single move.

13

By 1932 I had begun to notice that Russell was becoming more and more emotional. This was the year of his wife's death, and he could not manage the unnecessarily large house with just the aid of an old housekeeper.

I was unwell, and my doctor, Richard Hayes, ordered me away for six weeks, so I took a seaside house in Glengarriff for myself and Mother. Father came down for a fortnight, but it nearly broke his heart.

The Eucharistic Congress was being held in Dublin, and during the preparations Russell got himself involved in a newspaper controversy with a Jesuit whom he slaughtered. The Jesuit complained to me about his conduct. 'There were three courses open to Mr Russell: he could have denied my major, denied my minor, or said that my conclusion did not follow. What did Mr Russell do? He ignored my syllogism entirely. That is not the conduct of a gentleman.'

Russell came to spend the week at the Congress with me, and Osborn Bergin accompanied him. On the way down he was interviewed by a reporter from the *Cork Examiner* and not only denounced the Eucharistic Congress, but recited in full Oisin's great tirade against St Patrick. Bergin discovered a mistake in the recitation, but he told me admiringly that he could not have believed in such a perfect verbal memory. After having let off all that steam Russell was in high spirits and his conversation was full of mischief and invention. While Bergin and I swam, he sat on a rock, sketching and commenting to the Celtic gods on the thunder that rolled promisingly in the distance.

'Oh, come on, come on, Mananan! You can do better than that. All I want you to do is to wash out those damned Christian idolators.'

Bergin's swimming was like his scholarship. He could only do the breaststroke, but he did it perfectly and effortlessly, and when I attempted the crawl he trod water and glared at me, even without glasses. 'What's all the splashing about?' he asked.

I rowed them to Bryce's island, where Russell had stayed as a young man. 'I gather I should encourage you with a boat song,' he said. 'As I can't sing, I'll recite instead.' And he did. His high spirits were dimmed when Mrs Bryce took us to a corner of the island and said, 'Don't you remember this, A.E.? This is where you saw the vision.'

'There are places like that, you know,' he said curtly to me, but I saw that he was glad to escape from her and suspected that he was just a little tired of elderly ladies reminding him of the mystical experiences of his youth, particularly when he had managed to forget all about them himself.

Each day as we went walking we found a young painter stationed in the roadway with his easel, painting like mad and pretending that he did not know who Russell was, until Bergin and I flatly told Russell he would have to talk to the young man. He was genuinely shocked. He may have seen the vision, but he did not see the painter. Next day he went straight up to the easel and gave his views with his usual frankness and kindness.

'Young man, I think you've been painting in a rather dry climate?'

'Yes, sir. I've just come from Spain.'

'Well, this isn't Spain, you know. This is a very damp climate. Between us and those mountains there are half a dozen planes of moisture. Those are what gives it its luminousness.'

After supper the three of us went up the hill to the field where the young painter was camping out, and as Russell squatted happily on a rock to look at his pictures a country girl rose, like an apparition against the sky, above a loose stone wall with something large clapped to her backside.

'Well, Nellie?' the young painter said, and she held up a portrait of herself as though dissociating herself entirely from it.

'Dey say 'tis AWFUL!' she said.

The poor young painter was getting a bad time that night, for as we left I heard Bergin chuckling happily to himself.

'What's that?' I said.

'Twenty-two per cent,' said Bergin.*

Next evening another painter – a much more famous one – dropped into the hotel to see Russell, and he was in a state of intense misery. He had studied Glengarriff closely, and except for one old wooden pier by the hotel there was nothing at all to paint.

'Nothing?' Russell said delightedly. 'All those mountains and woods and water?'

'Nothing,' said the painter. 'It is all too saturated with the essence of what it is.'

It was a delightful holiday, but it was the last flash of the gay and youthful Russell. He was becoming more and more angry and afraid before the new Establishment of priests and politicians, particularly Sean MacEntee and de Valera. One night he really frightened me by cursing de Valera in the way I had seen old women in Cork curse – raising his arms above his head and giving himself up entirely to his emotion.

* Bergin's judgements, based on his own set of criteria, were frequently expressed in percentages.

'I curse that man as generations of Irishmen to come will curse him – the man who destroyed our country!'

One night that winter he came to my flat, bewildered and distraught. He told me that he had just received a warning that he had only a short time to live. I knew he did not mean that he had seen a doctor: he was much too plain-spoken to conceal a fact like that, and besides, when his illness really became a subject for doctors he was the first to accept their optimistic prognosis.

'I wasn't told how soon,' he said. 'I dare say it could be a month or a year.' He was not afraid of death, but he was afraid of the pain and the humiliations that would precede it – 'the immortal soul being kicked out of the world like an old sick dog with a canister tied to its tail'.

I did my best to comfort him, but it was not very successful, partly, I suppose, because I did not really believe in his premonition, but largely because I had little or nothing of the genuine religious feeling of himself and Yeats. It was not for lack of good will. I knew that their search for religious truth, no matter what absurdities it had led them into, had given them an intellectual richness that I had not got; I had let them argue with me and had read the books Russell lent me, but it hadn't affected my own way of thinking in the slightest.

'Why do you shut your eyes to those things, O'Connor?' Yeats stormed at me once when I told him the story of an old priest in Ballingeary who was supposed to have been shot by the Queen of the Fairies. 'You know perfectly well that things like that were once the religion of the whole world.' On another occasion, when I had to tell Russell that I had got nothing from a reading of Mme Blavatsky, he replied angrily, 'Oh, you needn't tell me! Like all Irish Catholics you are just an atheist at heart.'

That night, after we had discussed his premonition of death, Russell and I talked of the immortality of the soul, and he gradually began to brighten up.

'Socrates is the fellow I want to meet,' he said, laughing. 'I have lots of questions to ask him about some of the things Plato makes him say. Who do you want to meet? Tolstoy, I suppose?'

'No!' I said. 'Certainly not Tolstoy.'

'I couldn't stand Tolstoy either. I don't mind being told about my faults by people who like me, but Tolstoy didn't like anybody.'

And curiously, when he left and I accompanied him home, he was in the highest of spirits again. He had talked himself happy.

But a week or two later I was seeing him home again and quoted a poem I had just written which began:

A patriot frenzy enduring too long
Can hang like a stone on the heart of a man,
And I have made Ireland too much of my song;
I will not bid those foolish old dreams to begone.

He stopped dead at the corner of Appian Way and threw his arms in the air in a frenzy.

'That's exactly how I feel,' he cried. 'I have to get out of this country before it drives me mad.'

Soon afterwards he told me that he had made up his mind to give up his Dublin house and take a flat in London. He also talked of going on a world cruise and visiting his son Diarmuid, who had married in America.

Yeats was puzzled, and as always when there was something that he did not understand, inclined to mockery.

'Indian saints give up the world when they reach a certain age,' he said to me. 'Russell is a saint, but he is also a great journalist, so he's giving up the world to go on a world cruise.'

Nothing could have been wider of the mark. Of all the men I have known, Russell was most a creature of habit, and for him to give up everything – his house, his books, his pictures, his friends – was already a sort of death. Unless, indeed, it is that these were the death he wished to escape from, the inextricable patterns of habit that encompassed his fiery soul. Whatever it was against which he had erected them had breached them at last. I would have done anything to comfort him, but how can you comfort a man who does not weep, who perhaps himself does not know what it is he wants to weep about?

He asked me to come to his house the week before his departure and take whatever I wanted of his things, but I could not endure the thought of taking things that had been dear to him, and I did not go.

Then one evening Higgins came to my flat with peremptory instructions from Russell to bring me along with him. Higgins himself was close to tears, and I had never liked him so much as I did that evening.

'You'll have to come,' he said. 'A.E. will be hurt if you don't come, the man is hurt enough.'

'How can I go to the house of a man who's hurt like that and take his things away?' I asked.

'How do you think of it?' Higgins asked. 'I've had to sit there and listen while they said, "Oh, A.E., I wonder if you could let me have that nice little drawing by So-and-So?" You should see the greed in those fellows' eyes.'

I went back with him. Russell's face was like a tragic mask as he showed other friends about the rooms and let them take his little treasures. By this time I was as emotional as Higgins, and the longing to weep only made me angry. I told Russell that I did not want to take anything of his, and he said in a broken voice, 'You mustn't leave without taking something. I put aside a set of Jack Yeats' broadsheets for you. I know you admire Jack Yeats. Do please take them.'

I stayed on and Higgins stayed with me and we made casual conversation as we might have done at a wake, only that on this occasion the corpse made one of the company. When we left, the pubs were shut. Otherwise I think we would have got blind drunk.

Russell left for London, and for the first few months our friendship remained as close as ever. As anyone might have predicted, London was a disappointment to him.

'It is really a dead country,' he wrote to me, 'but there are very nice people among the dead, and if they were only alive they would be the best people in the world.'

He wrote to me that he was unwell and that his London doctor had diagnosed colitis. That evening, when I was walking on Sandymount Strand with my own doctor, Richard Hayes, I showed him the letter.

'I am very sorry to say that is not colitis,' he said after a moment. 'That is cancer.'

I did not take this any more seriously than I had taken Russell's own premonitions, but I was deeply upset by certain caustic remarks Higgins reported him as having made, and our friendship cooled off. It was only long after, when I got to know Higgins better, that I wondered whether those unpleasant remarks had ever been made outside the excitable, devious imagination of Higgins himself, because that Till Eulenspiegel of a man delighted in nothing so much as embroiling mutual friends and then grieving uproariously over the sufferings of both.

When Russell died, he grieved louder than ever, because Yeats refused to speak over the grave. 'If I spoke I should have had to tell all the truth' is the excuse Higgins reported his making, but what that meant I do not know – unless, perhaps, Higgins had made mischief between Russell and Yeats as well. I made the speech, and Yeats stood behind me, an old man who looked as though he had not long to live himself, and opposite me, at the other side of the grave, was de Valera (in those days it was not considered a sin for a Catholic to attend a Protestant funeral). When I had finished, Yeats in his generous way stepped forward and took my hand, saying in a loud voice so as to be heard by everybody, 'Very fine! Very noble!' and then, in a whisper, 'Have you copies for the Press?'

Of course I hadn't, which is probably as well because in those days I could be both pompous and silly. What I should say now is, 'This was the man who was father to three generations of Irish poets, and there is nothing more to be said.'

Later, when I told Yeats how strange it was to speak about Russell, with all his enemies round the grave, he grumbled, 'I know. I saw them too. I'll beat them yet, though. I've arranged to be buried in Sligo where nobody but my friends will follow me.'

Poor man! That was all he knew.

14

Richard Hayes, the man who had spotted what was wrong with Russell, was the local dispensary doctor. I had gone to him in the ordinary way as a patient, and we had become friends. He was a tall, thin man with a melancholy face, a big nose and prominent chin that made you think of a punchinello. In the evenings he called for me and we went for walks along Sandymount Strand, dropping into his house on Guilford Road on the way back for a cup of coffee or a drink. Years before, in the internment camp, I had noticed how uninquisitive and unrevealing men friends can be, and it was only after I had known him for some time that I realized that he was one of the heroes of the 1916 Rebellion and had been sentenced to death by the British. His brother, a delightful old priest from County Limerick to whom he introduced me, had also distinguished himself by defying some British general. As Irish people put things, the Hayeses were a 'decent' family.

I discovered it only by accident and by what later seemed dramatic irony. One evening when he was coming to my flat I invited James Montgomery, the film censor, and his wife. Montgomery was one of the greatest of the Dublin wits and, though I had no great liking for wit and detested the Dublin brand, I was very attached to Montgomery. He was a natty little man with a red face and a Roman nose and an extraordinary sweetness of character, as though he had been steeped for a decade in a vat of port wine. He is the man I think of in the part of Mr Bennet in *Pride and Prejudice*, and a prig like Darcy might account him a failure, because his talent, which was cynical, was at war with his temperament, which was humble and given to hero-worship.

Like Mr Bennet, Montgomery had his domestic troubles, for he was married for the second time to a great beauty, much younger than himself, and their verbal tussles were part of the Dublin legend. She indulged in palmistry, and that night she read Hayes' palm and said, 'There's some terrible crisis here. It's as though you'd died, and then started to live again.' Hayes was slightly shaken and left early, and Montgomery said excitely to me, 'You realized what the crisis was, didn't you? He was sentenced to death and then reprieved. Ethel hasn't a notion who he is.'

A day or two later Hayes said to me, 'You didn't know the crisis Mrs Montgomery was referring to. It was true enough. I was only once in love, and then it was with a girl who had tuberculosis. I was a doctor, and I knew how long she had to live. I couldn't bear the thought that my children might be the same way, so I gave her up.'

Hayes' main interest was the Irish on the continent in the seventeenth and eighteenth centuries. He had admirable manners; a trifle too elegant – even pompous – but no more disconcerting than those of the few French aristocrats I have met. I felt sure that the poor people of Ringsend adored him, because, though he stormed and screamed at them when they got him out of bed or interrupted him late at night when he was reading, he always went to them, always on foot.

His scenes with them were also very French. 'What are you saying? Why don't you speak up, man? How do you expect me to hear you? I asked what your name was . . . Murphy? Never heard of you, my good man. Your wife is poorly? I don't know your wife, and I don't know you. How long has your wife been "poorly"?'

'Well, she was took bad this morning, Doctor.'

'She was took bad this morning! And you wait until midnight to drag me out of my house in the pouring rain! What sort of conduct is that?'

'Well, Doctor, I only got in myself at half six.'

'Oh, so you got in at half six. Your day's work is over at six o'clock and nobody can disturb you. But when will I get in? You make me sick! Where did you say you live?'

They knew he got into such tizzies, and if the truth was known probably enjoyed them as much as I enjoyed the other sort of tizzies he got into. He would fly into sudden, old-maidish fits of self-righteousness when he felt that the memory of some famous Irishman was being slighted. O'Faolain and Frank MacDermott, working on the manuscript of the Wolfe Tone autobiography, had discovered a passage that Tone's son had omitted which showed that Tone, the great lover, had had a mistress, and Hayes pleaded with me to persuade O'Faolain not to publish it. I laughed so hard that he complained of me to a group of his old political associates at Sean MacEntee's, and they laughed even louder.

'You may laugh,' he said pompously to me, standing up before the fireplace. 'But you remember what Goethe said – "The Irish are always like a pack of mongrels dragging down some noble stag." '

'You got that quotation from Yeats, Dick.'

'Never mind where I got it. It's true!'

'And neither you nor Yeats ever read a word of Goethe in your lives. If you had, you'd know that the "noble stag" was the Duke of Wellington and the mongrels were O'Connell and his party.'

'Oh, what rubbish!' he snorted, all his indignation diverted for the time being on to Goethe.

I enjoyed those evening strolls with him because he raised his hat and bowed very low to every poor slum woman he knew, and saluted every man, and sometimes would stop to introduce them and make them show off. He bent his long frame in two like a jack-knife, his walking stick thrust out from behind his back like a tail and his punchinello face distorted with amiability, and said in that angular way of his, 'Oh, Jim, I wonder if you would mind telling my friend that shocking experience of yours with the Black and Tans – you remember, that night they threw you into the river? I often wonder how you survived it.'

He even brought me with him on his visits to the slums and introduced me as a young doctor, inviting my opinion on certain marks and symptoms, but after the first time I refused to go. I thought it might be dangerous for himself and felt it was humiliating to patients. As a doctor he did not see it in that light at all. He liked them, and he gave them better service than they would have had from most doctors they would have had to pay.

I am not observant, and for a long time it did not strike me as strange that this distinguished man should be in such a modest job, for even at medicine, which he usually merely made fun of, struck me as brilliant: I have described how he had diagnosed Russell's disease from a few lines in a letter. It took me even longer to realize that, far from having been slighted, Hayes had refused every sinecure he had been offered. It was when we argued about this that I came across the other side of the man – the side that did not ring altogether true – a mock modesty that amounted to arrogance.

Then one day the British and Irish Press were full of the story that he was to be made Governor-General – representative of the British King in Ireland. I thought he would be an admirable choice. That night, after he had dodged the reporters, we went for our walk as usual and argued all the way. He protested rhetorically and insincerely that it was not a position for someone like himself, an obscure dispensary doctor with an amateur's interest in history. Suddenly the humour of it seemed to strike him and he stopped and laughed loudly and heartily.

'You needn't tell me what you really think, O'Donovan,' he said. (He called me O'Donovan only when he wanted to mark the distance between us.) 'I can see the very thought in your mind.'

'What's that?' I asked.

'I'll tell you,' he replied, bending double and thrusting his jaw forward with a glitter of daft humour in his eyes. 'You're thinking that never before in your life have you had to deal with a man of such insane vanity.'

Almost literally this had been what I was thinking, and my protest did not come quick enough.

'I knew it,' he said with a crow of triumph. 'And you're right, of course. I am mad with vanity.'

For several years he was my dearest friend, the man who replaced Corkery in my affections, to whom I went in every difficulty and who gave me advice that was always disinterested and sometimes noble. This, of course, was not all clear gain. This dependence on older men was part of the price one had to pay for being a Mother's Boy. It was not he who suggested that I should write a play about the Irish Invincibles or a biography of Michael Collins, but I doubt if without him I should have written either. That might have been small loss, but without him I should have had no help from any of Collins' friends. Some had not even helped Beasley,* who was himself one of Collins' associates, but they were prepared to do anything for Hayes. It was the first time I realized the extent of his influence.

We had one extraordinary experience while I was writing the book. The hardest man in Ireland to get at was Joe O'Reilly, Collins' personal servant, his messenger boy, his nurse, and nobody – literally nobody – knew what O'Reilly could tell if he chose, or could even guess why he did not tell it. He was then Aide-de-Camp to the Governor-General; a handsome, brightly spoken, golf-playing man who could have posed anywhere for the picture of the All-American Male.

Hayes' invitation brought him to the house in Guilford Road one evening, and for a couple of hours I had the experience that every biographer knows and dreads. Here was this attractive, friendly, handsome man, completely master of himself, apparently ready to tell everything, but in reality determined on telling nothing.

Hayes was puzzled – after all, he was a historian – and he took over the questioning himself. He was a much more skilful questioner than I, but he too got nowhere.

And then, suddenly, when I was ready to give up and go home, O'Reilly collapsed – if the word even suggests what really happened, which was more like a building caving in. Something had gone wrong with him. Either he had drunk too much, which I thought unlikely because he was perfectly lucid, or, accidentally, either Hayes or I had hypnotized him.

I can remember distinctly the question that precipitated his collapse. I had asked, 'How did Collins behave when he had to have someone shot?' and O'Reilly began his reply carefully, even helpfully, in such a way that it could be of no possible use to me. Then he suddenly jumped up, thrust his hands in his trousers pockets and began to stamp about the room, digging his heels in with a savagery that almost shook the house. Finally he threw himself on to a sofa, picked up a newspaper, which he pretended to read, tossed it aside after a few moments and said in a coarse country voice, 'Jesus Christ Almighty, how often have I to tell

* General Piaras Béaslaí wrote the first biography of Collins, *Michael Collins and the Making of Ireland* (Dublin and London, 1930).

ye? . . .' It was no longer Joe O'Reilly who was in the room. It was Michael Collins, and for close on two hours I had an experience that must be every biographer's dream, of watching someone I had never known as though he were still alive. Every gesture, every intonation was imprinted on O'Reilly's brain as if on tape.

I had seen that auto-hypnotism only once before. That was in 1932 when Mother and I were travelling by bus from Bantry. One of the passengers was a violent, cynical, one-legged man who began to beg, and the conductor was too afraid to interfere with him. I took an intense loathing to him and refused to give him money, but he was much less interested in me than in some members of a pipers' band who were also travelling. He demanded that they should play for him, and when they merely looked out of the windows he began to imitate the bagpipes himself. After a time I realized that the bagpipes he was imitating were those he had heard during some battle in France fifteen years before. The bagpipes hypnotized him, and now he began imitating the sound of a German scouting plane, the big guns, the whistle of the shells, and as they fell silent he began to mutter in a low frenzied voice to someone who was beside him. 'Hey, Jim! Give us a clip there, Jim! They're coming! Hurry! Jim, Jim!' He reached over to shake someone and then started and sighed. Then he took an ammunition belt that was not there from the shoulders of someone who was long dead and slung it over his own, fitted a clip – that gesture I knew so well – into the heavy stick he carried and began to fire over the back of the seat. Suddenly he sprang into the air and fell in the centre of the bus, unconscious it seemed, and for some reason we were all too embarrassed to do anything. After a few minutes he groaned and reached out to touch his leg – the one that wasn't there. Then he got to his feet and sat back in his seat perfectly silent. I have rarely been so ashamed of myself as I was that day.

But the scene with O'Reilly was almost worse because you could see not only Collins, but also the effect he was having upon a gentle, sensitive boy, and it made you want to intervene between a boy who was no longer there and a ghost. I did it even at the risk of breaking the record. He was sobbing when he described how Collins had crucified him till he decided to leave. 'Here!' was all Collins replied. 'Take this letter on your way.'

'But didn't anybody tell him to lay off you?' I asked angrily.

'Yes, the girl next door,' he said. She said, 'Collins, do you know what you're doing to that boy?' And Mick said (and suddenly Collins

My Father's Son

was back in the room again), 'I know his value better than you do. He goes to Mass for me every morning. Jesus Christ, do you think I don't know what he's worth to me?'

When O'Reilly left, the handsome, sprightly young man had disappeared. In his place was an elderly, bewildered man, and you could see what he would be like if Collins had lived. Hayes detained me, and as he refilled my glass he asked, 'Have you ever seen anything so extraordinary?' We both doubted if O'Reilly would turn up next evening.

He did; but this time he looked like the ghost. He gave me a pathetic, accusing look.

'I don't know what you did to me last night,' he muttered. 'I couldn't sleep. I never did anything like that before. I can't stop. It's going on in my head the whole time. I have to talk about it.'

He did so for the rest of the evening, and once again Collins was there. Nowadays a tape-recorder in the next room would probably catch most of it, but I had no way of getting it down because I did not dare take out a notebook.

The sequel to that was interesting too, for when the book on Collins was published O'Reilly was reputed to be going through Dublin like a madman, threatening to shoot me. One day, he and I met in the middle of Grafton Street. There was no escaping him and I stopped. 'I've been trying to see you,' he muttered. 'Come in here for a cup of tea.' I went along with him, wondering what I had started, but all he wanted was to tell me the book had already gone out of print and he wanted a half-dozen copies to send to friends. Reality, I suppose, is like that. One looks at it and turns away, appalled by the Gorgon's head. And then one realizes that one has lived with it, that one has no other reality than the fact that one has once looked at it with naked eyes and survived.

Some years previously Hayes had published a couple of books on the Irish in France, which had had a sort of local success, but had scarcely paid for the cost of their production. He was now writing a book on the French Invasion of Ireland. I accompanied him on some of his trips in search of material. Again, his wide influence worked wonderfully. Sean McKeon led us to one old man whose grandfather had told him the story of the invasion. It was an extraordinary experience because the old man was a character out of Thomas Hardy, a mere vehicle. He pronounced the name of the French General, Hoche, in the French way, and then added apologetically, 'That's how grandfather used to say it, Oche.'

Although I had done some work on that book, there was no reason for my name to appear in it at all. Yet in the final draft, Hayes intended to print a few lines of a '98 song which I had translated for his amusement. But after an interview with his publisher he came to my flat while my mother was staying with me. Everything else the publishers would stand – but not my name on the title-page. According to Hayes' version of the interview, I had mistranslated the lines, misinterpreted the sentiments.

The lines, for all the little importance they have, were:

The sturdy Frenchman, with ships in order,
Beneath sharp masts is long at sea;
They're always saying they will come to Ireland
And they will set the poor Irish free.

Rather than sacrifice the book, he had sacrificed the lines, and I had heartily agreed with him. At that time, rather than see that book unpublished, I would have eaten everything I had ever written. But years later this event was sharply brought back to my mind when Dick Hayes himself was the author of an attempt to censor my writings.

15

The other friend of those years in Dublin was the curate in the Star of the Sea church in Sandymount, Tim Traynor. I had met him first through Sean O'Faolain when he was curate in Adam and Eve's church. He brought us down to the vaults to see the coffin of Leonard MacNally, the informer who betrayed Robert Emmett, and as we left he gave the coffin a thundering kick. He did the same with all visitors, and it was something you liked or did not like as the case might be. It was so typical of Traynor that I liked it.

We became friends only when he came as curate to Sandymount and lived in the presbytery in Leahy's Terrace – beautifully described by Joyce. It was almost the fashion to say that he was an interesting man who should never have been a priest, and Hayes – the seed and breed of priests and himself everything I admired in certain priests of the older generation – said it to me several times.

I knew he was warning me against Traynor, and if he had seen me at a country race-meeting, putting on bets for Traynor, who was not allowed to bet himself, he would have said it even louder. They disapproved of one another, and Traynor in his conspiratorial way told me that Hayes owned slum property.

He had the sort of face that I now see oftener in New York and Boston than in Ireland – the pugilistic Irish face, beefy and red and scowling, with features that seemed to have withdrawn into it to guard it from blows; a broad, blunted nose and a square jaw. Except for the good looks, it had a lot in common with the face of Fred Higgins, as his character had a lot in common with Higgins', for when I described Higgins as a Protestant with all the vices of a Catholic I might, but for the one small difference, have been describing Traynor. He was as conspiratorial as Higgins and much more malicious. If you were injured by one of Higgins' intrigues there was nothing much to blame for it but the will of God, but Traynor, in pursuing some imaginary grievance, would invent and carry through cruel practical jokes. When he swaggered into my room of an evening I would sometimes ask, 'Well, which is it to be tonight, Nero, Napoleon or St Francis of Assisi?' Most often it was Nero.

'It's that fellow Jenkins. Wait till I tell you!'

Yet I never really felt that he was not a good priest, and he gave me an understanding of and sympathy with the Irish priesthood which even the antics of its silliest members have not been able to affect. It was merely that his temperament and imagination constantly overflowed the necessary limits of his vocation as they would have overflowed the limits of almost any calling, short of that of a pirate. Yet they also enriched his character, so that you felt if he lived for another twenty years he would be a very fine priest indeed. It was significant to me that our old friend, the Tailor of Gougane Barra, who had a trick of nicknaming all his acquaintances in ways that stuck instantly, christened Hayes 'The Old Child' and Traynor 'The Saint'. There *was* an element of childishness in Hayes, and you always underestimated Traynor if you paid attention only to the devil and forgot the saint.

It was characteristic of him that he became really friendly with me only when he discovered that as boys we had both had a romantic crush on the same girl. He had had better fortune than I, for one night he had seen Natalie home from college up Summer Hill, and all the way they had held hands without exchanging a word. When the man she was proposing to marry had held back, she had complained of him to Traynor; he had advised her and they had remained friends until her death.

It was also characteristic of him that when I left his rooms that night he insisted on my taking the only picture he had of her. That was not only the new friend and the outburst of generosity; it was also the priest who knew he should not brood on a dead girl's picture.

But, of course, he brooded just the same. The emotional expansiveness that overflowed the limitations of his profession made him brood on all the might-have-beens of his life, and they were endless. I used to make fun of his rooms, which were a museum of all the might-have-beens: books on science, history, art; paintings, sculptures, a shotgun that needed cleaning and a cinematograph that wouldn't work – all passions pursued with fury for a few weeks till each in turn joined the exhibits on view. It was not only Nero and St Francis who alternated in his strange, complex character, but Einstein, Michelangelo and Gibbon as well.

Sometimes, when I visited him he would come to meet me with the big fist out, swaggering with excitement.

'How are you? You're looking fine. You'll have a drink. Listen! I have a great wine here. This is something special.' (Just like a boy with a new gadget.)

'How much did it cost, Tim?'

'Five and six,' he would say wonderingly, turning back from the drink cupboard. 'He had only a case of it left. Wasn't I lucky? Wait till you try it!'

Wine was only a sketch of an escape route, because Traynor was no drinker. Another, and more profitable one, was a career in the world. One evening, when he came to me, acutely depressed about some frustration, I asked, 'Tim, why the hell don't you cut your hook and get out?'

Traynor had no intention of cutting his hook, and he knew me too well to imagine that I was slighting his vocation; it was the chance of exploring another might-have-been that attracted him.

'Why?' he asked shamefastly. 'What could I do if I did get out?'

'You wouldn't starve.'

'Maybe I wouldn't, but what could I do?'

'If you'd gone to America five years ago you'd probably be a millionaire by now.'

'Do you think so?' (By this time he was beginning to light up again.)

'I'm damn sure of it. I can easily see you in a big office, giving everyone hell.'

'You might be right,' he admitted wistfully. 'I'd love to be able to get things done.'

He was always trying to get things done, and he wasn't always as successful as he was with St Brigid's thighbone. This was a marvellous story, and all the more remarkable because he did not realize how funny it was. He was curate of a new church in Killester which was being dedicated to St Brigid, and in one of his manic phases Traynor imagined how wonderful it would be if the church contained a genuine relic of the saint. The only reported relic was a thighbone, which was in a convent somewhere in the Peninsula – Portugal, I think, or it may have been Spain. He got round his parish priest – parish priests are the bane of an active curate's life – received the blessing of the kindly old archbishop, Byrne, and set off armed with letters of introduction to the Portuguese Department of Antiquities, the Portuguese Foreign Office, and above all to the Cardinal who controlled the contents of churches, monasteries and convents throughout the country.

The trouble was he could not get anywhere near the Cardinal.

Day after day he haunted the Cardinal's palace, and the greasy Monsignore who acted as his secretary said regretfully that the Cardinal was away, that he was opening a convent outside the city, was at lunch with some gentleman from the Curia, or was merely taking his siesta and could not be disturbed. Meanwhile Traynor's leave of absence had almost expired, and he dreaded the thought of returning to Dublin without having accomplished anything whatever.

'I was desperate, I tell you,' he said, scowling with remembered panic. 'That last day I went up I saw the same greasy brute. No, the Cardinal was lying down. No, immediately he got up he would have to leave for an important engagement. So I said to myself, "There's nothing those dagos can do to me. I'm not in my own diocese." And I just took out my wallet and handed the Monsignore a pound note. "For your charities, Monsignore," I said, and he glanced back over his shoulder and said, "Wait a moment, Father. I think I hear His Eminence's footsteps. Perhaps he hasn't retired yet. Do come in."

'He showed me into a bloody enormous waiting-room with folding doors, and he left me there for about five minutes. Suddenly the folding doors were thrown back and in came this wizened-looking old woman of a man and sat down in a big chair. I knelt and kissed his ring, and then I told him what I came for. He put on a sad air.

' "But you see, Father," he said, "this convent is in a very remote area. The people are poor; they are rather simple-minded and they have a great veneration for St Brigid. I am afraid, Father, that if there was any question of interfering with the relic there would be danger of violence. In my position I cannot risk the possibility of riots and publicity. I am sure you will understand." "I understand, Your Eminence," says I.

'And then the same idea crossed my mind and I nearly laughed into the old ruffian's face. "I'm not in my own diocese. There's nothing whatever he can do to me." So I put my hand in my pocket and took out my wallet – did you ever see a film called *The Clutching Hand*?'

'No.'

'Well, you should. Because it happened to me. Suddenly I saw the Clutching Hand reaching out for my wallet – like a bird's claw with the long nails on it. Before I could take it out he had the five-pound note out of my fingers. "One moment, Father, and I'll see what I can do," he said and left the room. In another ten minutes back comes the greasy Monsignore with the written authority for me to break the thighbone of St Brigid and bring it back to Ireland with me.'

And then, because he was proud of his Church, he gave me a dirty look and said, 'You can say what you like about the Irish priests, but you couldn't buy an Irish bishop for five pounds.'

But, of course, marriage was the greatest might-have-been of all, and on that he could talk for hours. Like most priests (and indeed lawyers and doctors), he had seen its shady side. When my own marriage (which he had opposed) broke up, he stopped all traffic at a busy intersection to come out of his car and shout at me, 'I *told* you she was too tough for you!' Even Natalie's marriage he felt bitter about because she had talked too freely of the man she had married; and when he was telling me about some particularly sordid episode he had encountered in his parish, he comforted himself with the usual seminary sour grapes. Once he told me about a parishioner who was convinced that his wife was trying to poison him, and another night about a man and wife who occupied separate rooms and communicated only by notes in the hall-way.

'There's marriage for you now!' he said with gloomy pride.

'Oh, for God's sake, that isn't marriage,' I replied.

'It could have happened exactly the same to me,' he said.

'It couldn't,' I said. 'It could happen only to someone who had the capacity for behaving like that. You haven't.'

'What do you think I'd have done?' he asked, delighted to explore imaginatively that land which for him would for ever be unknown.

'Nothing, probably,' I said. 'You'd have been too busy, worrying about the kids.'

'You might be right there,' he said scowling. 'I often wonder what sort of father I'd have made.'

'You needn't worry,' I said. 'You'd have been a very good one, only a little bit too conscientious. You'd have fretted yourself into the grave about their marks at school.'

'That was the way Mother was with us,' he said.

He had a peculiarly intense relationship with his mother, who, after his father's death, had brought up and educated two fine sons entirely by her own efforts as a dressmaker and small shopkeeper. He was too clever not to have observed all her little foibles and vanities. He had been compelled to wear an Eton collar, which distinguished him from the toughs of the neighbourhood, and he had not quite forgiven her that. She had had him trained to play the violin, and a neighbouring shopkeeper with a son who was to be a priest had taken up the challenge and had her son taught to play the piano. As the other shop had a narrow stairway the piano had to be lifted by crane to an upper-storey window, which had caused the Traynors great satisfaction.

But when he had to play at a convent concert and the rival shopkeeper had arranged that his name would be omitted from the concert programme, she had stalked out of the concert hall with Traynor at her heels and refused to allow him to play at all. ('And you were perfectly right, Mrs Traynor,' her friend among the nuns had told her.)

'Once, when I was at University College, Cork,' he said to me, 'I made an excuse not to come home for the weekend. I pretended I had a lot of work to do, but, really, all I wanted was to get off with a couple of fellows for a weekend in Youghal. When we were walking along the promenade, who do you think we met, but Mother? She'd got lonely at home and come down for a day excursion. When she saw me she smiled and bowed and said, "Good evening", and all I could do was to raise my hat. But after that she wouldn't even let me talk about it. "Ah, you have no word!" she said. Wasn't that a terrible thing for her to say – "You have no word"?'

It was a phrase my mother used to me. 'Word' meant 'honour', and I knew exactly how he felt.

At the same time he was too imaginative a man not to realize the full extent of her sacrifice for himself and his brother. When she died, he felt it was his duty to read the burial service.

'Don't do it, Tim,' another priest warned him. 'You'll only break down.'

But Traynor felt he owed this last duty to his mother. He didn't even need to read the service: he loved the poetry so much that he knew it by heart and recited it to me, but the poetry was too much. After a few moments he burst into helpless sobbing, and his friend took the book from his hand and finished it for him.

All the imaginative improvisation was only the outward expression of a terrible inward loneliness, loneliness that was accentuated by his calling. In that sense only could I ever admit that he was not a good priest – he should have had a tougher hide. Priests in Ireland are cut off from ordinary intercourse in a way that seems unknown in other countries. Once when we were arguing he made me impatient and I said, 'Ah, don't be a bloody fool, Tim!' His face suddenly went mad, and for a moment I thought he meant to strike me. Then he recollected himself and said darkly, 'Do you know that nobody has called me a bloody fool since I was sixteen?' Then the humour of it struck him, and he described how, once, when he was home on holidays from the seminary he was pontificating at the supper table and suddenly caught his uncle winking at his mother. Then he grew angry again.

'People like you give the impression that it's our fault if the country is priest-ridden. We know it's priest-ridden, but what can we do about it? I can't even get on a tram without some old man or woman getting up to offer me his seat. I can't go into a living-room without knowing that all ordinary conversation stops, and when it starts again it's going to be intended for my ears. That's not a natural life. A man can't be sane and not be called a bloody fool now and again.'

That, of course, was my function, though we both knew that his friendship with me was highly dangerous to him. One night after dark, when he was sitting with the other two curates on the sea-front, I passed and he hailed me. Immediately the others rose and strode off without an apology, while Traynor sat there, mad with chagrin, muttering, 'Dirty ignorant louts!'

Before I knew him he spent his holidays as a stretcher-bearer in Lourdes: somehow the contact with people who were ill and dying satisfied the gentleness and protectiveness in his nature. There was an enormous amount of this, but it never went on for long because when he felt rebuffed, brooding and anger took its place. In those years he took every chance of spending a few days in Gougane Barra in the mountains of West Cork. He stayed at the inn, abandoned his Roman collar and served at the bar, went fishing and argued with the visitors and (if I knew him) got involved personally and vindictively in every minor disagreement for miles round. His loneliness was of a sort that made it difficult for him to become involved with anything except as a protagonist. Most of his evenings he spent with Tim Buckley, the Tailor, who had nicknamed him 'The Saint'.

The Tailor was a very remarkable man, a crippled old man of natural genius, with a wife as remarkable as himself. Ansty was thin, tragic and sour; the Tailor was plump, wise and sweet-tempered. He sat on a butter-box and blew the fire with his old hat, and carried on an unending dialogue with his wife about the fire, the cow and the Cronins who kept the inn, but their real subject was always human life. He was one of the greatest talkers I have known; and if in the way of great talkers he did occasionally hold the floor too much, it was never because he was self-assertive, but because he had a sort of natural authority that asserted itself without assistance. He suffered from the fact that his cultural tradition was an oral, and hence a very fallible one, so that faced with the unfamiliar it always rationalized, turning everything to folklore. For instance, nothing could persuade him but that the Boer general, De Wet – one of the heroes of his youth – was not a County Cork man who had introduced himself to the black men with a '*Dia dhuit*', the Gaelic 'Good day', and much of what he took for granted was of the same order of knowledge. But he knew almost all that was good in the oral tradition, and because he was a man of natural genius was never completely contained in it, and like Traynor himself he overflowed.

Literally he was a man who did not know which century he lived in. He lived it intensely in his own as perceived from a little cottage above the mountain road to Gougane Barra, with Hitler, St Patrick and Danny Cohalan, the Bishop of Cork, as strict contemporaries. His favourite song in English was 'The Herring', which Cecil Sharp collected also in the Appalachians, but any story or verse he quoted might be of the nineteenth or the fifteenth century, or indeed, from the world of prehistory, and he used it all to serve his own Johnsonian purpose of commenting on the vagaries of human existence. When Ansty tried to rouse him to a state of activity which he found unnatural, he blew the fire with his hat and commented on her folly in the words of the Gárlach Coileánach – 'My mother was drowned a year ago; she'd have been round the lake since then'; and it was only after his death that it dawned on me that the Gárlach Coileánach was only a corruption of Gárlach Ioldánach, the Youth of Many Arts, which is one of the ancient names for the Celtic god Lug who gave his name to such faraway places as Lyon and Laon. 'Take life easy and life will take you easy,' he used to say, and life had taken him fairly easy up to that: he had never seen a volcano or a bishop in eruption. His time was coming.

I spent one delightful Christmas with Traynor in Gougane, because I knew that he was feeling restless and lonely. There was no one else at the inn but a middle-aged lady who had known Sir Basil Zaharoff intimately from childhood and had come to spend a few days of perfect peace in the mountains. Traynor, who was gloomily convinced that she was having us on or someone was having her on, had her luggage examined and it contained two dance frocks that Ansty made great play of. 'Jesus Christ!' she would mutter mournfully, returning from one of her excursions after the cow. 'Two young strong men and no wan at all to give the poor woman a tickle!'

The Tailor knew that I was searching for a song called 'Driving the Geese at Evening', which was too broad for the local folklorists to record, and he had ordered down old Batty Kit from the hill to sing it for me. At the sight of Traynor Batty dried up; it was not only in the towns that the conversation changed when a priest came into the room, but the Tailor would have none of this. ''Tis a bit barbarous,' Batty said. 'Even so, even so,' said the Tailor. 'It wasn't you who wrote or composed it.' Actually, Batty was crazy to sing. He was a melomaniac and in spite of his great age had a beautiful voice. He lay in wait for the children from the local national school to learn their latest songs, and it was extraordinary to hear that remarkable old man, whose sense of music and language were impeccable, imitating the metronomic beat and the synthetic accent that the schoolchildren had picked up – a horrifying example of what we do to ancient cultures when we try to revive them.

However, he did sing the song, and I got it down as well as I could, while he interrupted me to point out some verbal felicity. The first verse begins 'One lovely evening at the yellowing of the sun', and he stopped and cried, 'There's a beautiful phrase for you – "the yellowing of the sun". There's a cartload of meaning in that – *Tá lán trucaill de bhrí annsan.*'

I had brought whiskey and the Tailor provided beer, and as we left Batty Kit threw his arms round my neck and sobbed, 'Thanks be to God, Frinshias, we had one grand dirty night.' Then, as we went up the mountain road in the moonlight, Traynor stopped and looked back.

'Now they're beginning to talk about us,' he said darkly.

'Let them,' I said, but I knew that he was haunted by the thought that whenever he was not there Life in some unimaginably interesting way was going on.

Then came a tragedy that none of us had expected. A young chemist from London who was camping in Gougane Barra became friendly with the Tailor and made an enchanting record of his conversation and stories to which I wrote an introduction. Mr Edward de Valera's government immediately banned it as being 'in its general tendency indecent and obscene'. It was a staggering blow for that kind old couple, who had no notion of how their simple country jokes and pieties would be regarded by illiterate city upstarts. The scores of students who had accepted their hospitality affected never to have heard of them. Their neighbours boycotted them; all but the sergeant of the local police, who cycled out regularly to see that they were not interfered with. Three louts of priests called and forced the old man to go on his knees before his own hearth and burn his copy of the book.

The Tailor found one defender in a Protestant landlord, Sir John Keane, who spoke of him in the Senate. But the Government henchmen would have none of it, and Mr de Valera's friend, Senator Bill Magennis, made a speech in which he referred to Ansty as 'a moron'.

It was almost as hard on Traynor as it was on the old couple, for his position as a priest made it impossible for him to speak out. He and I visited them together. Nobody from the neighbourhood called, but the Tailor made light of it all. In fact I rarely heard him talk so well. When we rose to go, we found that some local hooligans had rammed the branch of a tree between the latch and the wall so that we were imprisoned until someone got through the little cottage window and released us. Ansty, dreading that the hooligans intended to burn them alive in their home, began to sob, and the Tailor patted her gently and said, 'There, there, girl! At our age there is little more the world can do to us.'

Years later, the Irish Government appointed an Appeal Board, which instantly discovered that *The Tailor and Ansty* was neither indecent nor obscene, but by that time the book was out of print and the Tailor and Ansty were dead, so it was all quite proper and perfectly safe.

Traynor died while I was in America, and somehow or other his priest friends managed to bury him where he had always wished to be buried, in Gougane Barra: how, I don't know for, being Traynor, he died penniless and intestate; the rules dictated that he should be buried in the town, and the island cemetery he wished to be buried in had been closed by order of the bishop.

But even in death he was a romantic, bending circumstances to his will, and his old friends brought him there on Little Christmas Night, when the snow was on the mountains, and the country people came across the dangerous rocks and streams with their lanterns, and an array of cars turned headlights on the causeway to the island church where he was to spend his last night above ground.

At the other side of the causeway lies the Tailor, under the noble headstone carved for him by his friend Seamus Murphy, with the epitaph I chose for him – 'A star danced and under it I was born'. I was glad that Traynor permitted that, though he refused to allow Murphy to do what he wanted and replace the cross with an open shears. He himself has no gravestone, but the country people have not forgotten him and on his grave his initials are pricked out in little coloured stones. Even in death the things that Traynor would have most liked to know have been hidden from him.

16

In 1937, two years after Russell's death, I had a dress rehearsal of the death that had haunted me from the time I was a child. For years Father had been nagging at me in his own quiet way to get hold of Mother's birth certificate. At last, he wrote me a peremptory letter, and off I went, half angry, half amused, to the Custom House and wasted time searching for the entry of her birth where I felt it ought to be until I found it more or less where Father said it should be – seventy years back, all but a month or so. I was slightly shocked and very sad, because I had never thought her old at all, but she didn't seem to take it personally. 'Your poor dad will be so pleased,' she said thoughtfully, evoking a very clear picture of Father's boyish pride and the excitement with which he would report it to the family and friends.

She was staying with me at the time, and for the first birthday party she would remember I brought home a bottle of champagne. I should have had sense enough to realize the effect that even a glass of sherry could have on her. After supper I went for my usual walk. When I came home she was in the kitchen and she rushed out to greet me. Between the hall door and the kitchen there were seven or eight steps and before my eyes she tripped and tumbled down into the hall-way at my feet. When I tried to lift her she moaned, and I realized that she was badly injured. The McGarrys, who owned the house I lived in, carried her to bed and telephoned for Hayes. I was no help to them because I was hysterical. It seemed to me unbelievable coincidence that she should die after her first birthday party, and I blamed myself and my damned champagne.

Hayes arrived soon after and spent nearly half an hour in her room. I waited in the hall, and when he came out I saw from his look that he had no hope. He put his arm about me and drew me into the front room, shutting the door behind him. 'It's easier for you to hear this from me than from someone else,' he said gently. 'I'm afraid she isn't going to live. Her shoulder and pelvis are broken, and I've never known an elderly person who survived it. Even if she did, she'd never walk again. All the same, she is a remarkable woman, and I'd be happier if we could get a specialist to see her. It's late, but if I can get Charlie Macauley on the phone he may come. Charlie was very attached to his own mother.'

Macauley was at home and came out immediately. While we waited for him, Hayes said: 'It's extraordinary. Do you realize that that woman has had chronic appendicitis since she was a girl, and never even told a doctor about it.' Macauley confirmed Hayes' opinion and advised me not to expect the impossible. He insisted on getting her into a nursing home immediately, and about midnight the ambulance took her to one in Eccles Street. I walked home through the dark streets, knowing I should not sleep. I had to break the news to Father yet, and I knew he would blame me, as I blamed myself. And what made it hardest was to think of the stoicism with which she had all her life borne the pain of chronic appendicitis, knowing she could not afford to go to a doctor or take the time to enter a hospital.

When I saw her next day Mother was still resigned to death, but she got some very interesting stories from the nurses. On the following day she complained that she looked a sight and that the nurses could not do her hair, so I combed and brushed it for her. 'A private room in a nursing home,' she said, closing her eyes, 'sure it must be costing a fortune,' and anyhow, even from bed, she could look after me better than I could do for myself. I met Macauley outside her room and told him. 'The funny thing is, she probably will go home,' he said. 'At this very moment I'm looking after a girl patient who did exactly the same thing to herself on the hunting field, and she'll never walk again.' It was ten days before Mother did come home, and then the McGarrys gave up their beautiful drawing-room on the ground floor to her. But she was very embarrassed at having to wear a dressing-gown when she went to and from the bathroom. 'My goodness,' she said, 'you could meet anybody in that hall.' After that, the dressing-gown was put away, and I had to dress and undress her as well as brush and put up her hair.

Meanwhile I had arranged to take my holiday in Switzerland, to see a specialist on my own account – a famous doctor who had been a friend of Thomas Mann at Davos – but Minnie Connolly's letters from Cork were alarming. Father, well-informed by me about the gravity of the situation, had chosen it as an excuse for an uproarious drunk. I knew what life with him would be like while Mother couldn't even climb a stair, much less go out to the pub to 'get in' for him. Instead, I took her with me to Switzerland. The journey, of course, was an intolerable chore. Mother was much too modest to look for the 'Ladies' herself; I had to find it and lead her to it. And, like all chores for her, it turned into joy. Mother made an intimate friend of the chambermaid in the London hotel, and got her life story from a nice girl she had chummed up with in Trafalgar Square. She disliked Paris, because no one could tell her any interesting life stories. Besides, she hated French coffee and broke into tears on me when I took her up to the Basilica in Montmartre and bought her some. However, Switzerland made up for it, and she liked to sit on the terrace of the hotel and listen to the crowds yodelling on the little pleasure boats passing up and down from Geneva and to go on the funicular to some little mountain chapel where she could say her prayers and listen to the cow-bells tinkling in the evening. She also made friends with a Swiss lady who spoke excellent English and was good enough to tell her the story of her life. It was all much more like home.

She cramped my style, for I had intended when I was finished with the doctor to tramp over one of the passes into Italy as Irish pilgrims had done in the seventh and eighth centuries, but still I felt a sort of enchantment in the holiday. It was like the fulfilment of a prophecy, the accidental keeping of promises made to her as a small boy, when she came in exhausted by a hard day's work and I airily described to her – all out of a guide-book and a couple of phrase-books – the wonderful journeys we should make when I was older and had come into my own. And the enchantment was only sharpened by the feeling of guilt we both had when we worried about my foolish father staggering home in Harrington's Square when the public-houses shut.

Father survived Mother's absence, but on her return he made it clear that he thought I had had more than my share of her. Life in Harrington's Square was restored to its rigid pattern more firmly than ever, despite Mother's wistful reminiscences of the Continent. It was some years before the occasion Father had been looking forward to for so long occurred, and I found myself responsible for a woman and her son, waiting for the end of ecclesiastical and divorce court proceedings so that I could marry. Of course, I had been asking for that. You can't live on two levels – the level of the imagination in what concerns yourself and the level of reason in what concerns others – for sooner or later the two will change places; and no consideration of expediency had ever really deterred me from getting into situations which my experience did not qualify me to deal with. Every humiliation that can be inflicted on a man who tries to live by his imagination and doesn't know the rules of the group to which he aspires I had gone through, and this was merely the greatest of them.

Mother came to stay and was reassured, as I knew she would be, for she could deal with any situation, no matter how preposterous from her point of view, so long as she could size it up for herself. After she went back, it was Father's turn, because somehow or other my life would not have been complete unless he had seen me in my new part as a father myself. I think now that perhaps I built too much on that; perhaps I always built too much on his visits, hoping each time that at last things between us would be as they should have been from the start and that I could confide in him things I could not have confided even in Mother. When I rushed to open the carriage door for him, he staggered out, very drunk. He must have been all right before he left home or Mother would have kept him there, but he had had a long wait at Waterford for a connexion, and boredom or nervousness had proved too much for him.

I got him home and put him to bed, but not before the child had seen him. I knew the boy's look because it had been my own at his age, and faced with this disaster I wasn't a day older than he. I knew I couldn't control Father; nobody could control him when he was like that, and I lay awake, shivering as if in a fever and going through the whole nightmare of my childhood again. I must have fallen asleep, for in the early hours of the morning I found he had got out, and knew what had happened. He was rambling mad through the countryside, looking for a public-house and hammering at the door for drink. Later I went to search for him and when I found him said, 'This can't go on. I have trouble enough in this place already.' 'I know, I know,' he muttered stupidly. 'I shouldn't have come. I'll go back by the next train. I'll be better at home.' 'I'm afraid you will,' I said, and later that day saw him off from the little station. My heart was torn with pity and remorse because I knew that was no way to behave to a dog, let alone to someone you loved, and yet I could not control the childish terror and hatred that he had instilled into me so long ago when he threw us out in our nightclothes on the street, or attacked Mother with an open razor.

I never saw him again. A few weeks later war broke out and communications collapsed. What was worse for people of Father's generation, tea was rationed to a fraction of what people in Britain were allowed, and when he wasn't on the booze he had nothing else to drink. It was part of the poverty of our class that we grew up literally on bread and tea and never really felt hungry if we had enough of both. Mother and Father did what the rest of their generation did and left the tea-leaves in the pot to be watered again and again till the last colouring had gone from them. When I worried about it, it wasn't of Mother but of him I was thinking, for apart from liquor he had no other resource.

He died as he had lived, blundering drunk about Cork in the last stages of pneumonia, sustained by nothing but his giant physique (my cousin Christy, who looked after him, told me at the funeral about the big black stain that appeared about his heart when he died). Mother refused to tell me anything until he was dead. This was something I found hard to forgive, because though with half her mind she felt she was saving me anxiety, deep down there was something else, not far removed from resentment – the feeling that I wouldn't understand and that I never had understood. She was like a loving woman who, when her husband has been unfaithful to her, blames not the husband, but the other woman. 'That damned drink!' she would cry bitterly, always implying that it was the drink that followed Father, not Father the drink, and in this she was probably wiser than I. But she felt that only she could have the patience to deal with him when he was dying and to realize that he must be allowed to die in his own way, not mine, as in later years she followed him with Masses and prayers, knowing as no one else could know, how lost and embarrassed that shy, home-keeping man would be with no Minnie O'Connor to come home to, no home, no Cork, no pension, astray in the infinite wastes of eternity.

THREE

The Abbey Theatre

17

Lennox Robinson, who at Corkery's request had given me my first job, had been a director of the Abbey Theatre since Lady Gregory's day. It was against Robinson that F. R. Higgins intrigued so passionately, although Robinson was a much better intriguer than Higgins himself and, in the beginning at least, much closer to Yeats. When I knew Yeats first and would visit him at his home, Robinson frequently strolled in towards the end of an evening to report on how the play at the Abbey was doing and how much had been taken at the box office. Usually the children refused to go to sleep until Robinson had come to say goodnight to them, and children do not feel like that towards a man unless he is a good one.

Robinson was very good to me. Although he had been tight about my wages when he took me on as an assistant librarian, he made up for it when I came to Dublin almost a stranger. He took me to the Abbey with him, let me sit in on rehearsals and introduced me to the players. Occasionally he invited me to spend the night with him. He lived in a small house on the shore of Dublin Bay with his mother, a sweet old lady from County Cork, who was glad to talk, even to a Papist, about places and people she knew there. She called Robinson 'Stuart' (his real name was Esmé Stuart Lennox, in memory of some remote Scottish ancestor), and it was clear that Stuart to her was an entirely different person from this lanky, remote, melancholy man who kissed her goodnight at ten o'clock and then brought out the whiskey decanter and drank himself stupid before morning.

He had been something of a musician, and when the whiskey was lowered and the french window open on the rocks over the strand, he would play his gramophone. He mocked me in his brilliant, bitter way, because I was uneducated and did not really admire any music but that of the three or four composers I knew well. He would deliberately play music he knew I would not like, but sometimes we came to an understanding over *Der Rosenkavalier* or American folk songs, to both of which he introduced me. I was unaccustomed to alcohol and completely unaccustomed to late hours, and often the dawn was breaking over Dublin Bay when the pair of us staggered up to bed.

I admired him enormously, but never became fond of him. I could not understand the sudden, extraordinary changes of mood, when the kind adviser turned into a mean, sardonic enemy, determined on making every word rankle. With Phibbs I could answer back, and our quarrels only resulted in a deeper friendship, but I stood too much in awe of Robinson to answer him back.

I had admired his later work and produced it in Cork without realizing that a footnote like 'If this play is produced in England read Birmingham instead of Cork' was not really a Kafkaian generalization of the theme, but a desperate appeal for a London production. I had not learned then that in literature X never marks the spot.

When I knew him first, Yeats had what I can only call a 'crush' on Lennox Robinson, whom he insisted on calling 'Lennix'. One of Robinson's 'functional' plays – 'a table, two chairs and a passion' as the author described it – had been slighted in England, and Yeats insisted on reviving it in Dublin, with a programme note by himself, trouncing the English critics. 'Within five years Lennix will be a European figure,' Yeats assured me with a wave of his hand, and I was glad to report the confidence to Robinson. I had not counted on the depth of despondency in him, because he merely looked away and said drearily, 'He might as well have said five hundred.' One morning, before we went to bed, we strolled down the garden to look at the first streaks of dawn on Dublin Bay, and Robinson said with his usual Regency emphasis: 'One *night* I shall swim out into *that*, and swim and *swim* until I give up.' It sounded to me like the whiskey, and unfortunately for himself it was the whiskey.

My memory seems to have made a blank of all that conversation of his, sometimes silly, but often delightful. Even free whiskey doesn't make bores tolerable, and Robinson had his own profundities. Once, when we had the usual argument about the early and late O'Casey, in which I must have been at fault, he suddenly burst out, 'I don't *mind* how many bad plays Sean writes for the rest of his life. What*ever* they may be like, they will be the plays of a happy man.' That stuck in my memory, not only because of its relevance to O'Casey – and it is very relevant to O'Casey – but because of its relevance to himself. It is the remark of a man who will never be happy again.

Yeats was for ever probing me about him. He knew that I admired Robinson as he did, and felt that I was keeping from him things he should know. There was that dedication of a book to Iseult Gonne, which suggested an unhappy love affair, but by this time we both felt that Robinson was only pretending to be in love with Iseult because Yeats had been in love with her. 'What *is* wrong with Lennix?' he asked me point-blank one night and, remembering the conversation overlooking Dublin Bay in the dawn, I said, 'Dissatisfaction with his work.' Yeats looked at me shrewdly over his glasses and said, 'I was afraid you were going to say dissatisfaction with something else.' I think he knew what the something else was and, while resenting my refusal to confide in him, liked me just a little bit better for it. I felt that he thought for the most part that Catholics were not to be trusted, but on the odd occasion when we hit it off he began to develop a theory that I was really the illegitimate son of some Protestant big house.

Meanwhile, the Abbey Theatre was going rapidly to the dogs. After the death of Lady Gregory, Yeats had allowed it to pass entirely into the control of Robinson. After her first experience of him as a young man Lady Gregory allowed him no control whatever, because she thought him irresponsible about money and morbid in his attitude to life. She made no bones about her dislike of him, and he would hardly have remained on as a director of the theatre if it had not been for Yeats. He took his revenge by editing her journals and choosing all the biting things she said of him for quotation to his friends. But that brilliant, moody, despondent man was a dead weight on the theatre. It wasn't only that he drank himself, he encouraged the younger actors to drink with him. He not only approved of dreary farces, but when a fine play came in he would fasten on some fault and try to have the play rejected. As his own circumstances grew worse, he grew more and more obstructive.

The theatre was heavily in debt. It was keeping open only on the strength of a group of favourite knockabout comedies by Robinson himself, Brinsley MacNamara and George Shiels; excellent comedies some of them, but all produced in the same slapdash hearty manner as though they were all written by the same author. If it had not been for the players – and there was hardly a weak actor in the group – the Abbey might not have survived. In Barry Fitzgerald (William Shields) it had a great comedian, in Maureen Delaney a great comedienne; F. J. McCormick and Eileen Crowe were two of the best actors I have ever seen. Any play that suited their genius did not even have to be completely written. They could do almost anything they pleased with a part. I once saw Fitzgerald set a scene of astounding bitterness in a comedy of Sheils and turn it into an uproarious farce. Usually the players directed themselves – sometimes they even selected the plays that were to be performed – and one got the impression of a garden gone wild, of every player grown so tall that it was all but impossible to tell what a play was really like. It was not the players' fault. I have never forgotten one performance of Synge's *The Playboy of the Western World* in which all the wild Connemara girls appeared in permanent waves.

According to Robinson, the old plays had to be put on all the time because there were no new ones. I didn't believe him, because in a theatre, as in a magazine, you get exactly what you look for. Theatre directors, like editors, must go out and find their writers, and W. B. Yeats was too old not to forage on his own. Yet, although he didn't want to let Robinson down, Yeats was not happy with Robinson's excuses. Once, when I was talking with Yeats about *The Saint and Mary Kate*, which I was writing at the time, he said wistfully, 'I wish you would write that as a play for me.' Had he been George Russell I probably would have tried to, for I realized a great editor like Russell would have handled the situation so differently. 'My dear boy, that is a play, not a novel. Now the first date available is November 10th, which means that we have to start rehearsals not later than October 15th, so if you can let me have a script within the next month I can guarantee you a production.'

And yet I am sure that Robinson was quite sincere. Though his inertia and indifference meant that his own harmless plays were kept permanently in the repertory, and though later I saw him try to ditch the work of better writers, either by faint praise or by criticism that smacked of dishonesty, I think his real weakness as a director was that he was himself in a state of despondency, and no despondent man can do work that requires endless improvisation. That was the 'morbid' streak in him of which Lady Gregory had been afraid. When Fred Higgins took his place as Yeats' best friend, Robinson's position became pitiable, and by 1935 Higgins had already achieved the first stage in his attempt to dislodge him.

Meanwhile, across the street from the Abbey two enthusiastic penniless young actors from London, Mícheál MacLiammóir and Hilton Edwards, were filling their little theatre, the Gate, with productions of European classics like *Brand*, *Peer Gynt* and *Anna Christie*. When anyone mentioned their success, Yeats was furious. 'Anything Edwards and MacLiammóir can do, Lennix and Dolly' (later Mrs Robinson) 'can do better,' he told me, but he didn't really believe it. He reconstituted the Board of Directors of the Abbey and brought on Higgins, Brinsley MacNamara and Ernest Blythe, the ex-Minister for Finance to whom the theatre owed its little subsidy of eight hundred pounds. The last appointment was typical of Yeats, who never forgot a rebuke or an obligation.

But the eight hundred pounds a year gave the Irish Government the right to appoint its own representative on the Board. The Cosgrave governments had exercised this right discreetly by appointing people like George O'Brien and Walter Starkie, of whom Yeats approved; but de Valera's government refused to reappoint Starkie and appointed instead a notorious and unscrupulous politician named Magennis. Yeats, who knew the man of old (everyone in Dublin seemed to know Magennis of old), reappointed Starkie as an ordinary member of the Board, refused to sanction the Government nominee and threatened to close the theatre instead. He then learned that before being offered to Magennis the seat had been offered to and refused by Hayes in his usual petulant way. Yeats rushed round to my flat to ask me to intercede with Hayes to withdraw his refusal. By this time I knew enough about Hayes' vanity to realize that the appeal would be much more effective if Yeats himself made it, and we took a taxi to Hayes' house in Sandymount.

Hayes' manners were even more formal than Yeats', and when I introduced them there was a pretty competition in elegance, which I enjoyed. Yeats made a brief passionate speech, appealing to Hayes on behalf of his theatre. It was only one of the many I heard him make, yet it was only when he was dead that I realized how urgent they all were. He was appealing for something that to him was perhaps the most important part of his life's work, something that must be passed on to future generations as he, Synge and Lady Gregory had fashioned it.

Hayes rose and stood before the fire with his hands behind his back.

'Mr Yeats,' he said loftily, 'I have no interest in the theatre. I have no knowledge of the theatre. I can be of no help to you there, but if I can be of any assistance to you in keeping that ruffian out, I shall be glad to accept.'

So 'that ruffian' was bought off with a seat in the Senate, which carried a salary, where later he was de Valera's principal spokesman in the attack on the old Tailor of Gougane Barra and his wife. Through my friendship with Hayes I became an intimate observer of the workings of a theatre which I had attacked again and again and whose policy I disapproved of.

I had also, without realizing it, put a large nail in the coffin of Yeats' life work.

The new Board, to show how up-to-date it was, decided to compete with Edwards and MacLiammóir by producing European classics also. I doubt if it ever crossed their minds that what attracted younger people like myself to that pair of rascals was not that they had discovered the key to wealth, but that they were nearly as crazy as Yeats himself had been in his youth and produced what they wanted to produce regardless of anyone's opinion.

So the first thing the new Board did, just as Hayes joined it, was to import a young English director named Hugh Hunt and a young English stage designer called Tanya Moiseiwitsch, to balance Edwards and MacLiammóir, and set them to producing a rigmarole of 'European' plays like *Noah, Coriolanus* and *Dr Faustus*. Meanwhile, Robinson went on with his productions of Irish plays, though he did take over from Hunt a scurvy piece of French religiosity about St Ignatius Loyola. The division shows a split personality on the Board, though I suspect that the split was in Yeats rather than in the Board, which did not seem to have any particular personality to split. Yeats prided himself on his subtlety, though as theatre manager he was very unhappy. If the current of opinion was in favour of European masterpieces – which bored him – he would have European masterpieces, but he would not have any damn English director tinkering with the sort of plays that had been written by himself, Synge and Lady Gregory, and producing them in a theatrical idiom he did not like. Though he was responsible for Mrs Pat Campbell, his whole attitude to English directors and players could be summed up in Synge's comment on Mrs Pat as Deirdre of the Sorrows: 'She'll turn it into The Second Mrs Concho-bhar.' The theatre now had two producers, though it could not afford to pay the salary of one.

However, the new policy had scarcely been announced than Brinsley MacNamara, in a fit of pique, issued a personal *pronunci-*

amento against O'Casey, the greatest of contemporary Irish dramatists, and the other members of the Board in another fit of pique
demanded his resignation. They invited me to take his place, and
though I admired MacNamara as the ablest of the directors, after
Yeats, and thought the Board's attitude to him absurd, I agreed. I
entered the boardroom for the first time, seeing nothing but the
figures of John Synge and Augusta Gregory, and trusting they would
inspire me, but their inspiration was similar to that of the Sacred
Heart and the Blessed Virgin in earlier days when I couldn't do my
lessons or my work.

I knew nothing about the theatre, and so asked the advice of my
best friend among the players, Arthur Shields, as to what I should
do, and his advice was so extraordinary that I took it as a good joke
until I noticed that I was creating chaos in the theatre. 'Treat us as
though we were children,' he said shortly. 'Nice children, of course,
children that you're fond of, but not as grown-ups. And for God's
sake, whatever you do, don't praise us. That drives us mad.' It is
the best advice that was ever given to a man of the theatre, if only
he could be intelligent enough to appreciate it. I wasn't; not for a
long time. Arthur never made a great reputation as an actor; he was
far too discerning for that; and it was only when I had almost
wrecked the company that I realized how discerning he was.

18

For much of the time during his last years Yeats did not attend
meetings of the Abbey Board at all. Either he was abroad or he was
at home and didn't feel strong enough to face the trip into town.
Initially, not being observant, I got the impression that he was only
vaguely interested. I should have remembered the evenings at his
home when Robinson dropped in late to report on the takings and
the other evening when Higgins had telephoned him after the
meeting of the Academy of Letters to report on what O'Faolain and
I had said. The old watchdog never relaxed his vigilance, and after
every Board meeting Higgins called, telephoned or wrote to recount
every word that had been said – rarely in a favourable way, if I
knew Higgins.

Yeats was one of the most devious men I have ever known, and

I deliberately mocked at his deviousness as he mocked at my simple-mindedness, probably with equal justification. He was taken aback at the trustfulness I showed towards my fellow-directors, and he once hinted as much to me. 'Well, I can't treat them as if they were a gang of masked conspirators,' I said irritably, and he replied with great unction, 'No, you remind me of a character in a Victorian novel by a lady that I once read – someone who believes that for most of the time the vast majority of people do not intend much harm to the others.' That description of my own character delighted me so much that I didn't even notice the pinch till I got home. In the light of later events he was putting it mildly.

The best example of his deviousness I remember was in the last years of his life, at a time when I felt that at last he and I were on the point of an understanding. By this time, like the two kings in *The Herne's Egg*, we had fought so long and so hard that there didn't seem to be much left to us except to become close friends. Paul Vincent Carroll had written a play which offended some members of the Board and, instead of sending it along to Yeats and me in the ordinary way, they had returned the play to the author with an exceedingly insulting letter. When the Secretary showed me the letter I grew furiously angry. Quite apart from the fact that Carroll was a distinguished playwright who had earned a good deal of money for the theatre, I felt that no writer should be treated with such discourtesy, so I wrote to Carroll, asking him to submit the play again to Yeats and myself. He did so, and Yeats and I did not meet again until the Board meeting at which our two reports were read out. Yeats said, 'All the characters in this play are corrugated iron', but he went on in his noble way to praise Carroll's work and volunteered to contribute fifty pounds from his own pocket (a lot of money for an old man who made manuscript copies of *Innisfree* for American booksellers at five pounds a time) towards its production by Edwards and MacLiammóir at the Gate or any other theatre that wanted to produce it. My report read, 'All the characters in this play are cardboard', and Yeats started and stared incredulously at me. Then, as my negative report went on, he began to chuckle grimly, and when it concluded he said, 'O'Connor, I owe you an apology. I thought you'd asked the play back because Carroll was a friend of yours. It had not occurred to me that you had asked it back because you thought he had been unfairly treated. It serves me right! I've lost my fifty pounds.' How could anyone not love the sort of man who said a thing like that?

Still, in the matter of deviousness, he was a child compared with Higgins. Even as I wrote down this fairly straightforward story I found myself wondering, 'Who or what gave Yeats the notion that I was a friend of Carroll's; above all, a friend who, right or wrong, would insist on the production of his play?' Twenty times at least I had evidence that Higgins told Yeats things that simply weren't true. Why had it not occurred to me that this might be another of them? The truth is that Higgins created such a miasma of intrigue about him that I look back on it as I used to look at Abbey plays of the period, wondering what exactly was going on behind it all.

Most of the time Hayes made an admirable director, warmhearted, appreciative and intelligent. I paid no attention to the oldmaidish tizzies into which he worked himself occasionally about a scene or a word – generally concerning politics or religion. Usually he could be kidded out of them. Walter Starkie, the ex-Government representative whom Yeats had brought on under his own steam, was a fat amiable man, as amiable as Higgins, but with none of Higgins' intolerable treachery. Starkie took little part in meetings or discussion, although once – it was the time of the Civil War in Spain – when I came into the boardroom late with an evening paper and said, 'Well, boys, we've got the Alcazar,' he became very voluble. 'Really,' he said, 'I cannot understand how people who knew nothing of Spain can speak like that of this terrible Civil War.' (He later became the British Council representative to Madrid.) Robinson had what no other Board member had, an immense capacity for silent, despondent resistance. He merely sat back in his chair, sucked his pipe and replied in monosyllables. If I had known that Ernest Blythe was the man who would outlast us all I should have paid more attention to him than I did. He looked like a Buddha in grey plaster, and spent most of his time doodling on his pad. Then someone would use a specialized polysyllabic word and immediately a great change came over Blythe. Pencil poised on paper, he waited for inspiration, and then would write down a Gaelic equivalent. Then there was a further pause and he wrote down an alternative. He was genuinely attached to the Irish language and anxious to revive it, but in his wise way he realized that it was lacking in polysyllabic words. He believed that the language could be revived if only people could be induced to sing popular songs in it. His collected poems contain his translation of 'The Beautiful Isle of Capri' and American songs like 'I Got a Gal in Kalamazoo' in his peculiar version of the Irish language. One might call Blythe a single-minded man if the adjective did not raise the question of whether or not it was a contradiction in terms.

Hugh Hunt got off on the wrong foot by wearing a red, white and blue rosette in the theatre on some English state occasion (King George V's jubilee I, imagine), which infuriated Higgins. Higgins' dislike of Hunt had turned to a persecution mania when Hunt gave an interview to some English weekly paper in which he spoke of his difficulties and described Higgins and myself as Red revolutionaries, determined on turning the theatre towards our own political aims. Higgins, having at last unmasked a genuine plot, demanded his immediate dismissal; Hayes was fearfully upset because he didn't want 'that charming boy' dismissed over an indiscretion. I had conceived an admiration for Hunt that has outlasted our theatrical relationship, and was delighted at Hunt's display of independence. When he came before the Board to explain that he had never said those dreadful things – and I'm sure they were exaggerated in the news report – I interrupted to say that of course he had, but in future would he mind not saying them before newspapermen.

At the same time I found myself engaged in a long battle with Robinson which was to go on until I resigned. I had come on the Board as his friend, but it didn't take long to realize that the theatre had been mismanaged for years and that most of the mismanagement could be traced to him. When the bank threatened to close down the theatre, he merely shrugged and said, 'Every theatre in the world carries an overdraft.' We had two producers, Robinson for Irish plays and Hunt for European ones, and two secretaries, Eric Gorman for correspondence and Robinson's brother, Tom, for accounts. The presence of Robinson's brother at Board meetings made another difficulty, for it meant that even when Robinson was absent there could be no confidential criticism of his work. The directors groused among themselves, but nothing was ever said at meetings. I asked for the exclusion of Robinson's brother from Board meetings. Soon afterwards his appointment was terminated. I regretted it, but it was difficult to see how else we were to save the Abbey. Then the company shares were redistributed to deprive Robinson of the controlling interest he would have when Yeats died.

Higgins, of course, was the most pugnacious member of our Board and criticized me to Yeats and Yeats to me and Robinson and Hunt to anyone who would listen; but he could not fight. He saw secret agents everywhere, but the vivid imagination that had created them collapsed the moment they presented themselves before him in ordinary human shapes, and at the least sign of opposition his astute criticisms turned into jokes. His very amiability prevented his fighting. I had no ability as an intriguer and could be fooled by appearances most of the time, so I had no shyness about fighting for any reasonable cause. Higgins made no secret of the fact that he used me as his muscle man – just as the Board used me in that capacity to have the shares redistributed and have Robinson's brother removed from the room during meetings. Once, reporting in shouts of laughter to the Board how he got rid of some importunate playwright, he said, 'I use O'Connor all the time as an excuse. You have no idea of the character that man has in Dublin! Murphy showed me his play and I couldn't read it, so I told him it was a masterpiece, and then, when he kept persecuting me, I said O'Connor had turned it down. They'll believe anything of him.' He enacted these scenes with such laughter and devilment that only an out-and-out egotist could have complained, but now I wonder whether the joke was not on me and Yeats.

The New Abbey Policy of competing with Edwards and MacLiammóir I disagreed with on two grounds. One was that it seemed to require two producers when we couldn't afford one. The other and more important reason was that, in my view, it was wrong. For years the directors had been unable to find new Irish plays, or so they said, or so Robinson had persuaded them, and later, when really interesting new plays were submitted the Board had practically decided beforehand that the plays could be no good. Even when it was working at full capacity the theatre never managed to produce more than a half-dozen new plays a year. I felt that this could be increased to nine or ten, but, allowing for the fact that some of them would have to be popular plays by established playwrights like Robinson himself. Shiels and MacNamara, the production of four or five European classics like *Coriolanus* and *Dr Faustus* would mean that there would be no opportunity for young serious dramatists. This would mean the end of the literary movement, for magazine and book publishers we had none.

As for the European classics, I had seen them performed as well as I was ever to do and had decided that they might not be as classical as they were generally supposed to be. Shakespeare could be boring, so could Sheridan; one could even get too much of Ibsen and Chekhov. I had not yet classified them as 'Museum Theatre', and in those days would probably have disputed the theory. The theory I later evolved to explain my own disillusionment I have expounded so often that I have almost ceased to believe in it myself. It seemed to me that the theatre is by its nature a contemporary art, a collaboration between author, players and audience, and once the collaboration is broken down by time it cannot be repeated.

There are exceptions, of course, particularly when an old text is rehandled by a modern writer and the staging recreated in terms of a contemporary society. Even with *Hamlet* one can still enable the audience to walk on the razor's edge of real drama, but in my experience it was much easier to make them walk it with some little play by a contemporary author in a local setting. The lightest of Robinson's own comedies had an immediacy of effect that Goethe's *Faust* or Ibsen's *Peer Gynt* at the rival theatre did not have. If I was to work for it, the Abbey had to be an all-Irish theatre.

Yeats, too, of course, wanted a living theatre. If he had been younger and in better health he would have come to the theatre himself and insisted on it. It was he who in the middle of the New Abbey Policy was desperately holding on to Lennox Robinson and a few rough-and-ready comedies, so that when he died he might transmit some part of what he and his friends had achieved in the creation of an original repertory and an original style of acting. Nowadays when I think of what the situation really was, it is not of my work and feelings that I think, but of his. Like many a lesser man who has created some unique institution, he wanted to guarantee its continuance when he himself was dead, and did not realize that what he wanted was a miracle. His sense of urgency is evident in the dispute over the production of *Coriolanus*. It had just been produced in Paris in coloured shirts and caused a riot. Yeats demanded that we produce it in coloured shirts among our European classics, in the hope that, as in France, a Dublin audience might riot and he could defend the message of the play as he had defended the message of *The Playboy of the Western World* and *The Plough and the Stars*.

I don't think he understood that I admitted the tradition as much as he did, but in the circumstances of the theatre I thought he was going the wrong way about saving it. *Coriolanus* might be a dramatic gesture, but there is a difference between that and drama. Besides, with Spain bleeding to death, my judgement as a theatre man was influenced by not wanting to have any part in Fascist propaganda. I refused to agree to its being produced in coloured shirts, so Hunt finally produced the play in Renaissance costume. This saved a riot maybe, but it lost the theatre a lot of money, and I practically finished the job of bankrupting it.

After that, the New Abbey Policy was not heard of again till I went to the first performance of a nice little play about the poet James Clarence Mangan, and saw a Masque of the Seven Deadly Sins, which had not been in the original manuscript. I realized that Hunt simply could not stand those beautiful and expensive masks that had been made for *Dr Faustus* lying around unused, and had induced the author to write a scene about them. Poor Mangan! Later, when I came to write a study of *Macbeth* this enabled me to understand why Macbeth's death scene had been omitted and his head brought in on a pole instead. The stage director of Shakespeare's company had a head available, as we had masks for the Seven Deadly Sins. Theatre people are like that – even Hunt. Not economical – definitely not economical – but very conscious that use can be made of the stuff that is lying about the theatre.

Meanwhile, though Robinson had blown cold on our two best plays – Carroll's *Shadow and Substance* and Teresa Deevy's *Katie Roche* – we produced new plays and recovered lost ground. I had gone the rounds begging for plays and had a few promises, one from Sean O'Faolain and another from Brinsley MacNamara. Then Hunt had the idea of dramatizing a story of mine called 'In the Train', and, with the threat of *Dr Faustus* hanging over me, I jumped at the chance. I disliked Hunt's method of dramatization, which had choruses in the manner of a German impressionist play, with invisible groups chanting in the rhythm of the train. 'To Stop the Train Pull Down the Chain – PULL – DOWN – THE CHAIN – *Pull Down the Chain.*' But the performance proved that Hunt was the very man we needed to put new life into the tradition. The curtain went up and there was an Irish railway carriage, lovingly re-created in every particular, and a group of Irish villagers – not Abbey comics – who were involved in a murder trial the significance of which they could not apprehend. The whole performance was drawn to a fourth of the scale usual in Abbey productions, but every detail was in focus and exquisitely rendered, and one could hear from the audience little chuckles of delighted recognition, as when one of the policemen pulled down his greatcoat to use as a card table. The most beautiful performance was that by Denis O'Dea, whose voice and build have kept him cast as the stage Irish policeman, and who there, for a few minutes, created a gentle timid country boy in uniform that I have never been able to forget. I knew that night that Hunt could give us the thing I had dreamed of for years, a theatre that could express the poetic realism that I admitted in Liam O'Flaherty, Sean O'Faolain and Peadar O'Donnell.

As I rushed round to the green-room to congratulate the players I bumped into Yeats, who was equally excited, but for a different reason. 'O'Connor, you have made a *terrible* mistake. You should have explained in the first scene that the woman was the murderess. You must never, NEVER, keep a secret from your audience.' He said it in the tone of an American television announcer telling you you may never drive a car without consulting your local agent, but though I fancy I swore under my breath, I knew he was right again. Fictional irony and dramatic irony have nothing in common. It was one of the occasions when I got a hint of what a really great man of the theatre Yeats was, far greater than Robinson, who had the reputation.

Yeats had a fixation on the well-made play and the functional type of production which he passed on to Robinson. 'A play is two chairs and a passion,' Robinson would quote, and Yeats went one better by quoting enthusiastically a story of Salvini. Salvini was rehearsing on a stage that was empty but for one chair, and finally he could stand it no longer and asked, 'When do I break the chair?' I saw Yeats' original production of his own translation of *Oedipus Rex*, in which Oedipus hardly changed his position from beginning to end of the play, and for once I wanted to scream. Years later I saw Laurence Olivier's production of the same version, and Laurence, remembering that 'Oedipus' means 'clubfoot', demonstrated the fact by jumping nimbly up and down boxes until I wanted to cry: 'Is there an orthopedic surgeon in the house?' That, it seems to me, is the weakness of the Shakespearean convention; it runs to irrelevant bits of business that merely distract attention from the eternal words.

Admittedly, if he was bored, Yeats could be worse than useless as a critic, and even dangerous. Once he went to see *Cartney and Keaveney*, a popular play of George Shiels, which had been in the repertory for several years, and insisted on its being removed. His reasons might have been those of Dr Johnson; the principal characters in the play glorified idleness and irresponsibility, and this was an improper moral lesson to teach our audience. Long before I joined the theatre we had an argument about Teresa Deevy, whose plays I admired. 'She might have been a good playwright if only she let me reconstruct her plays,' said Yeats, and even for Robinson, who was listening, this was too much. 'A play of Teresa Deevy's reconstructed by you would be rather like a play of Chekhov's reconstructed by Scribe,' he said tartly.

But when Yeats was excited he never missed a point. Once – it was the time after Higgins had already ousted Robinson from first place in Yeats' confidence and esteem – we did a revival of Robinson's early play *The Lost Leader*. It dealt with the idea that Parnell, the greatest of Irish leaders, had not died, but, suffering from amnesia, had lived on as porter in a small West of Ireland hotel. A hypnotist from London breaks down the old man's secret. It is a good dramatic gimmick, and, as usual with gimmicks, there was a masterly first act, a weak second act and a silly third act – in which Parnell, having delivered a typical Robinsonian appeal to love and good fellowship in Ireland, is killed by a stone thrown by a blind man. Hunt made a beautiful production of it, and the opening of the third act is the only occasion I recall of a décor being applauded in its own right.

The lead was played by an established London actor, and, as usual, Yeats couldn't stand him. We spent the interval together, and Yeats embarrassed me in the foyer by illustrating how he felt the Englishman acted. 'When he should have been calling down the thunderbolt,' he said, reaching towards the ceiling, 'he was picking up matches,' and the tall figure bent and groped on the floor. But during the last act Yeats' imagination was working overtime; he had his old affection for Robinson, and nothing could keep him from rewriting the works of people he liked. When I went up to the boardroom later, Robinson was sitting with his head in his hands while Yeats strode up and down in a frenzy, lecturing him. 'Tell him, O'Connor,' he snorted at me when I entered. 'When Parnell has to tell the mob what to do, he must tell them only what has already happened. There must be no abstractions. Everything must be concrete. He must tell them to do only what the audience knows they themselves have already done.'

'I'm sorry,' Robinson said, looking at the floor. 'I disagree.'

God knows I sympathized with Robinson, being lectured like a schoolboy on his first night, because I had been lectured myself in my time and hadn't liked it, but I knew Yeats was right again. Nothing could have rescued that feeble last act but some such impudent piece of theatrical dexterity.

It was a grave mistake not to take up Yeats on those wild ideas of his, for, apart from anything else, if you couldn't do the job yourself, he was only too pleased to do it for you. He had the ultimate brazenness of the great performer, the man to whom the audience was merely an instrument, and any refusal to use the instrument he regarded as 'barren pride' – the phrase he used when dismissing a friend of mine who had refused to accept any suggestions for the improvement of his play. He was not afraid to accept suggestions himself – 'She might be that stately girl that was trodden by a bird' is supposed to be the suggestion of a poet he particularly disliked – though he did kick up a great pother before accepting them. He hissed with rage when I told him that 'Made Plato's tolerance in vain' was not English, but all the subsequent editions have 'Made the Platonic tolerance vain, and vain the Doric discipline', in spite of the nasty assonance.

In plays that nominally are not his, one can sometimes see his workmanship in the 'properties', the things that are actually on the stage when the play opens – Salvini's 'chair'. In *On Baile's Strand* they are the cooking-pot and the stool. Once he told me how he and Lady Gregory had worked on *The Rising of the Moon* until he was exhausted and sank on to a piano stool. That gave him the idea. 'A barrel!' he cried. 'We must have a barrel!'

Towards the end of his life a young dramatist submitted a bad play on a theme that seemed inspired. A party of pilgrims is setting out from an Irish provincial town on foot to an Italian hill-shrine when the father of one of the girl pilgrims falls ill and she has to stay behind to nurse him. She makes the pilgrimage, walking about the sickroom, but when the pilgrims reach the shrine they find her there before them, kneeling at the altar. Yeats was ill at the time, so I went to his house to talk the play over with him, and as we talked the old man's mask was dropped and I saw the face of the boy behind. It was astonishing to see the reserve of energy he could throw into any literary project: of course the energy was nervous, not physical, and left him exhausted, and one felt guilty at having excited it, but less guilty than when, as sometimes happened, one felt one was boring him. The finest scene he planned took place outside the heroine's house while she made her pilgrimage round the room, unaware of being watched, while the awed villagers interpreted every movement of hers in terms of a real landscape. 'Now she's climbing a hill. It's a steep hill. Now she is stopping and pulling up her skirt. It must be a mountain stream she is crossing.' As he described it, I could even see an Italian landscape emerging.

Though I didn't realize it at the time, it was the only sort of play that made any profound appeal to Yeats. It was a mystery, and all the great early plays of the Abbey Theatre – with the solitary exception of Colum's – were mysteries.

Now I am sorry that after that evening, with a masterpiece 'ready made to my hand', I got cold feet. I had a vague feeling that Yeats and I had been able to construct that scenario easily only because a better dramatist had done so already. He was so convinced of the overall importance of the fable that he once said to me, 'When you want to write a play, write it on the back of a postcard and send it to me. I'll tell you whether you can produce it or not.' I had the feeling that that particular postcard had already been written and mailed. I lunched with the author and begged her to tell me whether she might have read it. She couldn't remember, but thought it might have been in a book of Chinese fairytales she had read when she was a child. This gave me new hope and I read every book of Chinese stories I could lay my hands on without finding it. Indeed, it was only long after I had left the theatre that I found it described in a book of Nora Waln's as one of the masterpieces of the Chinese theatre. The curious orientalism of the whole Abbey Theatre movement was visible that evening when an Anglo-Irishman and a mere Irishman tried to compose the scenario of a great modern Irish play round the theme of a great ancient Chinese play whose existence we didn't know of.

19

By this time, I am afraid, I had been led into spiritual pride, as Catholics like myself called it. I had always known that with economy and hard work the theatre could be made self-supporting, but even then we should have nothing to set against a run of bad luck. In a bad week we could lose a couple of hundred pounds, but in a good one we could rarely make more than twenty-five. All that could be changed if only we had a hundred extra seats, and the only hope of fitting these in was to buy the hardware store next door.

I explained to the Board that if the proprietors of the hardware store knew that instead of their going into bankruptcy, the theatre was proposing to buy them out, they would raise the price beyond anything we could afford to borrow from the bank. Then one evening I went to a Board meeting and saw Higgins with a long face. Robinson had sent the stage carpenter round to the hardware store to inquire the price.

I think it was that evening that I lost my head and stamped out of the boardroom to the little office where Hunt was nervously waiting his summons and asked him angrily, 'Will you accept a contract as manager for the next two years?' He blushed and stammered, 'I suppose so, if it's offered to me.' I said, 'Don't worry; it will be', and I returned to the boardroom and drafted the resolution appointing him. It is one of the few decisions I have never regretted, because for two years he ran that theatre as it had not been run since Lady Gregory's day. Soon we had new plays and money in the bank. Though Yeats gave me the credit, it was mainly Hunt's doing.

One evening, when Yeats was in attendance, the Secretary, before reading out the bank statement, grinned and said, 'Well, gentlemen, I have some good news for you. For the first time in years the theatre has a credit balance.' The credit balance was only three shillings and sixpence, but it meant we need not worry about letters from the bank, threatening to close us down. The directors applauded, and as we left the meeting Yeats asked me to walk with him. When we were approaching O'Connell Bridge, where he was to get his bus, he stopped and made one of his formal little speeches. These, like his reminiscences of people he hadn't met for twenty years, were part of his dramatic stock-in-trade, and had the same childlike quality. I wish I could recall its perfection of phrasing; it had obviously been thought out, because as so often with that strange, romantic man, self-accusation blended with congratulation of someone else. It was something like this.

'There's something I wanted to say to you, O'Connor. You may not have realized that I was watching what you did, because I have had to oppose so many of the things you have done, but all the same, I knew they had to be done. Thirty years ago I should have done them myself, but now I am an old man and have too many emotional associations. Thank you.'

But I had my emotional associations as well as Yeats. I knew that Hunt was the one man who could save the theatre at the time, but I also knew that giving him the opportunity had left Lennox Robinson as jobless and penniless as he had found me in Cork a few years before, and it was too neat an example of the classical peripeteia to cast myself for a part in it. I also remembered that when I came to Dublin Robinson was the first to invite me to his house. After a sleepless night I took him to lunch. It is a task I would not wish on anybody. To speak about his drunkness to an older and more distinguished man is a task for one who in Standish O'Grady's phrase is 'not only brazen-faced, but copper-bottomed', and I am lacking in brass. I asked what I could do to help him and he replied quite simply, 'Get me a job.' That was a tall enough order in itself, for the theatre does not run to jobs in which a man can drink himself to death without doing any harm to the institution. 'And if I can get you a job, will you agree to go to a specialist – the theatre will pay.' 'Yes, yes, anything you like,' he said wearily, 'but I must have work.'

There the man was in all his strength and weakness – he could not fight back. If I offered him a job as uniformed doorkeeper he would have accepted it – and later shown me off the premises with perfect courtesy. What I did not recognize then, what Yeats never recognized (though I suspect that Lady Gregory had her suspicions), was the immense power behind that inertia, fed as it was by masochism and accepting without complaint, rebuke, humiliation and even insult. For even if I had understood it then as I understand it now I should still have lacked the ability of the old society woman to shut it out altogether from my mind.

There was only one thing for me to do. A few days before the scene at the Board meeting I had pressed for the appointment of Shelah Richards as Director of the Abbey School of Acting, so I went straight to her and asked to be released from my offer. 'If you want the job for Lennox Robinson, you're welcome,' she said without hesitation. The theatre is a cut-throat business, and actors are of necessity a thankless lot, but not, it seemed, where Robinson was concerned. I only wished I could attract the same sort of devotion. Unfortunately, within a month or two Robinson was turning up drunk to classes, or not turning up at all, and the School of Acting was in as big a mess as the theatre had been.

Meanwhile the final quarrel in the theatre was being staged between Yeats and Higgins on the one hand and Hunt and myself on the other. 'Why do you support Hunt?' Yeats asked me bluntly one night. For want of anything better to say I replied, 'Because we must have a competent man in the theatre.' Yeats drew himself together like an old grandfather clock preparing to strike, and, as he always did whenever he wanted to say something crushing without being personal, told a story. 'My mad brother' (sometimes it was 'my father' and sometimes 'an old aunt of mine') 'once said to me: "What does an artist have to do with competence?" '

I knew that about the main issue between us – the style of acting which Yeats called the Abbey tradition and Higgins called 'porthery' – Yeats was absolutely right, and I preached the same doctrine to Hunt at every opportunity, but not being a theatre man I felt it was my immediate responsibility to get the theatre on its feet, with a repertory of modern Irish plays and a style of acting that suited them. Yeats wanted a continuation of the Senecan style of acting, common in the universities in Shakespeare's day, in which words were all-important, nobody spoke while moving and nobody moved while someone else was speaking for fear of distracting attention from the words – the opposite of the later English naturalistic convention in which beautiful speeches are chopped up and fitted into bits of stage business – picking up matches, for instance. It is like a duet in which two instruments never play together. But the Senecan style must have been out of date even in Shakespeare's day. In one of the *Parnassus Plays* there is a scene in which Shakespeare's friends, Burbage and Kemp, give an audition to some university lads trained in the Senecan tradition, and they describe it as resembling a walk with someone who speaks only when he comes to a stile. The Senecan is a purely rhetorical convention and admirable for poetry; the other, the Shakespearean convention, is purely dramatic, and sometimes plays hell with poetry, even Shakespeare's. And how easily I could have got round Yeats if only I knew then what I know now and could have given him the word 'Senecan' to brood over! He was a man who loved pedigrees, even for his canaries, and would have been so happy murmuring to visitors, 'Our convention, the Senecan, which preceded the convention of Shakespeare . . .'

But Hunt had been brought up in the Shakespearean convention, and he couldn't take the Senecan style seriously, so that when he produced the plays of Lady Gregory and Yeats he did have a tendency to squeeze the poetry out of them to make room for dramatic effects. Our biggest disaster was with *Deirdre*, and for this I was largely to blame. I wanted to produce *The Player Queen*, my favourite Yeats play. As Hunt wanted occasionally to work with an English actress, we suggested Jean Forbes-Robertson, who had the fairylike coloratura quality that the imitation queen must have. But Yeats had promised the part to an actress with whom he was friendly at the time. She was inexperienced, and since I had heard no favourable account of her I refused to invite her to Dublin. After that, all Yeats would give us was *Deirdre*. Apart from the fact that we didn't like the play, it was quite unsuitable for Jean Forbes-Robertson. It was like asking the perfect Zerlina to play Isolde. I felt even more unhappy when I took Jean out to lunch and she said gaily, 'Well, I don't understand a word of the part, but I've made up a little story of my own that covers it pretty well.'

So, on the first night I gave up my seats to friends from the country and went to the theatre only to check the takings. They were good and the reception – to judge by the prolonged yells that could be heard in the foyer – was overwhelming. I was in the box office when Yeats came staggering up the stairs from the stalls, clutching his head. 'Terrible! Terrible! Terrible!' was all he could bring out. I was certain he was exaggerating, so next evening I went by myself and sat in the back of the gallery. It was even worse than Yeats and Higgins had led me to believe, because they at least had liked Mícheál MacLiammóir as Naisi and I could see no merit in anybody. I felt that all the actors must have heard Jean Forbes-Robertson's 'little story'. None of them could keep still for two minutes, and the play needed all the Senecan starch. Higgins' 'porthery' simply couldn't exist in that Shakespearean atmosphere. Unfortunately it was a great popular success, and its expensiveness forced us to continue it after MacLiammóir left, so Hunt took on the part himself. It should be enough to say that Hunt was half MacLiammóir's build and with less than half his voice, and that it was no use trying to explain to him how an actor in the Senecan convention can build a tremendous climax merely by using fractions of semitones.

Naturally Yeats was furious, and Higgins stormed against Hunt, without, however, having the faintest idea of how to produce the poetic effects he talked of. Instead, he had invented something called 'Peasant Quality' – which the players turned into 'PQ' and used the slogan 'Mind your PQ'.

And yet neither Yeats nor Higgins could see that the English naturalistic convention, applied to new Irish plays and players, produced an exquisite effect that was neither purely Senecan nor naturalistic, but an extraordinary blend of simplicity and polish – 'beauty like a tightened bow'. With the new plays the result was an entirely new style and an entirely new type of actor – represented by Cyril Cusack – that seemed to suit perfectly the sort of theatre we wanted. I doubt if even Hunt knew the secret of what he was doing, for its presence could be detected only because by Friday –

unless the players were closely watched – it began to rub off, the opposite of what usually happens in repertory, where the players gradually begin to settle into their parts.

There was an interval of peace when some of the players left to tour America with Higgins as manager. The tour got off to a disastrous start. Hunt was keeping the theatre open with a second company, and we wanted a fair split, reserving a stiffening of the older players, while letting American critics have a glimpse of the new talent being produced by the Abbey. However, the older players, thinking of Hollywood contracts, resented this and got at our American manager, who cabled his own list of players, which we had to accept.

In America Higgins dropped the company altogether, and all the news we could get of them was from American newspapers, which described furious scenes between rival lawyers. Higgins simply ignored our cables, though after a month or so I got one report from him which was a masterpiece of wild humour, but told me nothing we really wanted to know. Blythe wanted to dismiss Higgins by cable and appoint Arthur Shields in his place, but Yeats simply mocked at the idea. 'What you and Blythe want is a three-pound-a-week clerk,' he snorted. 'You can't buy a genius for three pounds a week.' But we didn't want a genius; we merely wanted someone to keep that wretched touring company out of our hair while Hunt went on with the real business of the theatre, which was producing new plays.

And that was no easy task. For years I had been haunted by the subject of the Invincibles, a little group of Dublin terrorists who assassinated the British Chief Secretary in Ireland, Lord Frederick Cavendish, in 1882. I drafted a play about them. It was a bad subject for me because it is a peculiarly Dublin tragedy and would have needed an O'Casey to handle it. When Hunt agreed to join me as collaborator, putting real theatrical bones into my dramatized history, it became still more unsuitable, because, though in real life he was a brave and patriotic Englishman, as a man of the theatre he felt bound to identify himself with his subject, and no amount of lecturing would keep him from writing lines like 'Christ, we'll cut the throats of all the dirty English bastards!' It is, as Arnold said, the tragedy of the artist – 'we become what we sing' – and I was watching Hugh Hunt turn into a terrorist under my eyes.

During the production two things happened that I shall never forget. One was Cyril Cusack's performance. Hunt had asked me not to embarrass him by attending rehearsals, for fear I should compromise the cause of terrorism any further, and I had loyally agreed. He suddenly asked me to attend the last rehearsal but one, and speak to Cusack, who was behaving very badly. So far as I was concerned he was Hunt's discovery – a great actor, and, as Hunt explained to me, 'Not Irish at all, you know; straight Cockney'. Cusack played the part of young Tim Kelly, the choirboy who followed his older friend, Joe Brady, the stonemason, to the gallows. I went to the rehearsal and listened in dismay. I knew Cusack's part was vilely written, but he was deliberately ignoring the most commonplace theatrical effects as though they bored him. Maybe they did. At the same time I realized that it was far too late to interfere because anything I suggested would only throw off the other players, particularly Willie O'Gorman, who, as Joe Brady, was carrying the whole play magnificently on his shoulders.

Next day I went to the dress rehearsal and listened to Cusack again. He hadn't changed an iota of his interpretation; he still seemed to throw away every speech, but after a few minutes I began to feel a physical chill in the theatre. I looked round and saw two of the actresses weeping openly. When actors weep at someone else's performance in dress rehearsal it has to be pretty good. Of that unspeakable part Cusack had created something that wasn't in any line of it, a loneliness so terrifying that it made you wonder how the human mind could sustain it. I had always known what a great writer could do. That day showed me what a great actor could do.

The other thing I remember is Robinson's extraordinary behaviour. As a member of the Board he had read and approved the play. He had done more than that. He had taken me aside and pointed out to me the simple but important mistake I was making. I had written the play almost entirely in brief speeches, as a storyteller writes, and ignored the fact that in the theatre brief speeches – the equivalent of the Greek stichomythia – must be interrupted by long, expository ones, to give the actor and audience breathing space. I was grateful and pleased because I felt that Robinson was treating me like a friend, but there was small hope of that. By the time the play was ready for production, word had reached us through the Dublin underground that the Left Wing groups disapproved because they thought the play exploited and caricatured terrorism, and they proposed to wreck the theatre. On the first night this looked more than likely because Yeats' old girlfriend Maud Gonne came in for the first time and took her place in the stalls. There was no riot that night because Maud apparently decided it might not be understood, and the only protest came from a Nazi visitor who thought the play was directed against Hitler and wrote to the papers to say how shocked he was at this defence of tyrannicide. But while the players were still wondering whether or not they would have to fight, Robinson went to a debate at the rival theatre across the road and denounced Hunt and me bitterly for having dramatized a subject that was bound to cause pain to the relatives of the men who had been hanged by the British fifty years before. On the whole, the relatives of the men who had been hanged didn't seem to be too upset, and when Joe Brady's sister arrived at the theatre – to lend us the suit that her brother died in, for our production – Hunt felt it his duty to receive her as if she was royalty.

But everybody in the theatre realized that Robinson's remarks were a stab in the back and that he was trying to provoke a riot of his own. Hayes immediately tabled a resolution demanding his dismissal from the Board. It would have been plain common sense on my part to support Hayes, but before the meeting Yeats invited me to meet him for tea so that he could explain why he must oppose the resolution 'for personal reasons'. He knew he didn't have to tell me what the personal reasons were. Robinson was his friend whom he had already defended against Lady Gregory, and he had been a good friend to Mrs Yeats when she needed friends, and he was adored by Yeats' children. Yeats knew Robinson was in the wrong and was obviously distressed – a different Yeats altogether from the one who knew he was in the right and was determined on proving it to you. I merely told him that in any matter that concerned his peace of mind he could rely on me, which was perhaps disloyal to Hayes, though I don't think Hayes would have regarded it so.

It was a queer, agonizing evening. It began on the theatre backstairs. Yeats was obviously very ill and could only climb a step or two before pausing for breath. It seemed rude to stand behind him for minutes on end, waiting to see him take the next step. If it had been Russell, I should have taken his arm and lifted him up, but I knew Yeats wouldn't tolerate that from me. I could have run ahead and chattered from the top of the stairs, but I had been trying, without much success, to get the other members of the Board to stand up when he came into the room, and that didn't seem right either. He was doing this on Robinson's account, not mine.

At last we got up and he fell into a chair with Robinson on his left-hand side and Hayes at the foot of the table on my right. Hayes moved his resolution quietly – normally he was the quietest of men. Mr MacNamara had been asked to resign from the Board because he had given in to a hot-headed impulse that everyone understood and sympathized with. Could any member of the Board sympathize with Mr Robinson in an act of calculated treachery, and if so how could they justify their behaviour to a loyal colleague like Mr MacNamara? Hayes had the grand manner, and he could be stinging on an occasion like this. He looked directly at Robinson and asked why – since Mr Robinson was so sympathetic with the relatives of the executed men – he had waited until the previous Sunday to express his sympathy. Robinson sat with downcast eyes and did not reply.

Then Yeats made his speech and I have not forgotten the opening words. It began: 'Every member of this Board realizes that Lennix Robinson is no longer responsible for his actions' and went on to say, 'Robinson will apologize for his behaviour and his apology will be published in the Dublin newspapers.' Robinson sat that out too; his very despondency was his greatest strength. It was a technique I was now beginning to recognize. At times it was almost as though he enjoyed his own humiliation, as, with that strong masochistic element in his character, he may have done. And yet I knew he worshipped Yeats and that it must have been agony for him to endure that humiliating apologia, as it was for Yeats to offer it. We were all glad when it ended. After the meeting Yeats left without speaking to him. He was angry at finding himself in the wrong camp and angrier still at having been forced to humiliate a friend in front of strangers.

There was some truth in what he said about Robinson not being responsible. Robinson wrote an apology which was merely a repetition of everything he had said about Hunt and myself. When Hayes saw it he grew really angry. 'Send that to Yeats!' he said. 'If he's prepared to stand over that, he and Robinson are in this thing together.' I did what he suggested, and by return came a handsome apology, which may or may not have been published. But even that Yeats had to write for him, as I later learned.

There were other signs of mental deterioration in Robinson. He could no longer afford to keep up his home on Dublin Bay. He embarrassed me and delighted Higgins by producing a completely dotty scheme according to which Bernard Shaw ('He has lots of money') would buy the house, set him up as custodian, and he would provide a residence ('at a trifling cost') for younger writers like ourselves with books to finish, which needed to be finished in the beauty and repose of Killiney. He was drifting into the part of the literary panhandler, the famous figure whom every mediocrity in Dublin could afford to patronize. Yet those who knew him in those years still remember little touches of consideration and sweetness which showed that the old Robinson was still there.

FOUR

The death of Yeats

20

The row between Yeats and Higgins and Hunt and me had now got completely out of hand. It isn't, as I have said, that most of the time I was not entirely on Yeats' side and didn't try again and again to explain to Hunt the sort of acting that the older type of play required. There was, for instance, the little matter of *Dervorgilla*, Lady Gregory's beautiful one-act play, which I had insisted on restoring to the repertory. Hunt mistakenly gave the part of Dervorgilla to a young and inexperienced actress, and – again I think mistakenly – allowed the tremendous final speech of the old queen to be broken by the young actress's sobbing (as though Dervorgilla, realizing that, because of her love affair with the King of Leinster, Ireland had become a subject province and herself a woman whose memory would be execrated, would regard it merely as another example of the old saying that 'the woman always pays'). This was a clear example of the way English naturalistic production inevitably turns Deirdre into 'The Second Mrs Conchobhar'. I squabbled with Hunt about it at the dress rehearsal, and later, visiting Yeats on other business, told him what I had done. 'Is it ever permissible for an actor to sob before the final curtain?' I asked, and Yeats snapped, 'Never.'

During that visit Yeats was in a state of delight over a Chinese carving in lapis lazuli which some friend had given him, and he was writing his acknowledgment in verse. It was characteristic of him that when he was in a mood of excitement every casual conversation got swept into the poetry, sometimes with alarming results to the logic. That night my Advice to the Players somehow got itself embodied into Yeats thank-you poem as:

> Yet they, should the last scene be there,
> The great stage curtain about to drop,

If worthy their prominent part in the play,
Do not break up their lines to weep.

Once, when O'Faolain and I were at the house together, Yeats read us the Meru poem on the Trinity and asked if we understood it. O'Faolain, being both clever and well-brought-up, replied, 'Oh, yes', but I said, 'I don't understand a word of it, W.B.' Higgins reported that Yeats had said to him later that night, 'O'Faolain and O'Connor were here, and I read them the Meru poem, and O'Faolain said he understood it and he didn't, and O'Connor said he didn't understand a word of it, and he understood it perfectly.' (Nothing would ever persuade Yeats but that I was cleverer than I was.) And sure enough his next poem in the series begins, 'Although you said you understood no word'.

Still, I don't think he ever understood that I was on his side, or maybe he felt I was but was too arrogant to admit it. Next time he came back to Dublin from the Riviera, he and I had one of our biggest set-tos. By this time I was convinced that it was impossible to keep Hunt on over the opposition of Yeats and Higgins, which was usually unreasonable and often ungenerous.

If I couldn't have Hunt I wanted Denis Johnston, but the very name of Johnston made Higgins cringe. Like most of the other members of the Board, he wanted to keep the theatre under his own personal supervision, and if he couldn't do this with Hunt, what chance had he with Johnston? Like members of the Opposition everywhere, he wanted a weak government, and I finally agreed that we should look round for some young man of the theatre whom Hunt could train. Hunt, who was completely selfless in his devotion to the theatre and in Roman times would probably have trained the lion to devour him piecemeal in order not to spoil the show, chose two young men he thought he could train and gave them plays to produce. I went to the rehearsal of one of them and said I was not interested. I didn't go to the other's rehearsals because he had cast himself for the principal part and would have so much trouble producing himself that he would have no time for the other members of the cast.

What sank me completely was Hunt's production of *The Playboy of the Western World*, and Cyril Cusack as Christy Mahon. This was as misconceived as it was magnificent. Cusack – the greatest Irish actor I have seen – interpreted the part brilliantly, but there is nothing in it that the words do not interpret better; as with *Deirdre* and *Dervorgilla* it was the English inability to get out of the way of poetry. The long surging lines, which must be spoken in the manner of Racine's alexandrines, either in one breath or with the trained singer's tricks of imperceptible breathing, were broken up by the elaboration of points that were only a distraction, and were of the same order as picking up matches.

Higgins and I had an angry scene about it. Yeats was abroad; Higgins was in the position of unofficial widow, and I could not get him to admit how sensitive the production was, how lovingly every detail of background and lighting had been re-created, or how beautiful Ann Alery was as Pegeen Mike. All he could see was that Cusack had chopped up the 'porthery', and in Hunt's absence he went to Cusack's dressing-room to make a scene about it. I only learned this when Hunt told me he intended to complain, and I felt he was justified in doing so. There are better ways of indicating to a great actor that you disapprove of his performance than by going to his dressing-room when he is overwrought and starting a fight.

So I supported Hunt and Cusack, while Higgins complained to Yeats, who, after his return, arrived at the next Board meeting looking like the terrible judge of Michelangelo's *Last Judgment*. He ignored me and delivered a long speech on the sanctity of the Abbey tradition and a violent attack on Hunt's *Playboy*. That made me furious to begin with. For a man of the theatre to criticize a performance he hasn't even seen is unforgivable, and I had no intention of letting Yeats get away with it. When my time came I replied at length and said that, while I agreed with him about the speaking of poetry, I could find no evidence for the existence of a tradition in the theatre except a lot of bad acting. This was trailing my coat with a vengeance, and the reader is fully entitled to blame me. The very memory of this hurts me now, and I often blame myself for this deliberate trampling on Yeats' toes, but at the time I felt that Yeats had trailed his coat a bit, and if he was going to gang up with Higgins and his infernal 'porthery' I was going to gang up with Hunt.

Then Yeats made a serious tactical mistake, which left him wide open. He lost his temper and turned the attack on me. 'And you—' he stammered, 'you said you'd try to find some man to take Hunt's place, and when two young men produced their plays you weren't even there.' This was true enough so far as it went, and I had an answer to it (one of the young men was Cusack, whom I was defending), but at this stage our difference had gone beyond discussion of the Abbey and it was Higgins who had come between us. I had Yeats where I wanted him. 'If you're dissatisfied with my work as a member of this Board, you can have my resignation right now.' I said, 'but while I am a director of this theatre there is one thing I will not do, and that is reply to green-room gossip.'

There was no doubt about who had won that round, because Yeats was the most loyal of colleagues, and he *had* repeated green-room gossip, only the green-room gossip had not originated with the theatre company, but with Higgins, and I hadn't the sense to see it. Yeats went white. It was the sort of imputation he could not bear, and at our last meeting, just before he went to France to die, the charge still rankled, for when he wanted to tell me that he trusted me he had to begin with the complaint that I did not trust him. '*You* think I listen to green-room gossip . . .'

But if I had won that round, he won the match, because no one but myself would stand up to him in one of his bullying moods. Hunt was debarred from all further productions of Synge, Lady Gregory and Yeats; and, in atonement to Synge's memory, Higgins was invited to produce a 'classical' performance of the *Playboy* directed by one of the old players.

Higgins was a good poet, but he couldn't produce a child's recitation. He went into a dither of excitement, begging the players to remember their 'Peasant Quality' and pronounce every 'st' as 'sht' and say 'Cashelbar' instead of 'Castlebar'. This seemed to me exactly the same fault of excessive naturalism that Hunt had been blamed for. The performance was a nightmare. Such an evening of uncontrolled caterwauling and wailing was never heard in any theatre, while the players tried to demonstrate their 'Peasant Quality' and did their best to imitate Higgins' imitation of a County Mayo accent. Hunt's splendid lighting was entirely dispensed with, and instead every stage light was turned on full, masked by yellow screens, which, of course, reduced the apparent depth of a stage that was impracticably shallow anyhow to about six feet. Sitting in the stalls with Yeats, I kept expecting that every time a player rushed on stage he or she was going to land in my lap. There are at least six imperative changes of lighting, all of which were blandly ignored. People came on with a lantern, and the light didn't change; they went off with it and the light didn't change, and finally Pegeen Mike quenched the only conceivable source of illumination, and still the stage remained looking like Times Square on Christmas Eve.

'What do you think of that?' I asked Yeats as the curtain fell.
'Oh, very fine, very fine,' he replied with an abstracted air.
'I think it's absurd,' I said and walked out of the theatre.

But no reasonable human being could fight for long with Yeats. As well as a successor for Hunt I had to find a successor for Tanya Moiseiwitsch, who insisted on leaving with him, and I arranged to send Yeats' daughter, Anne, who had been assisting Tanya, to study stage design with Baty and Jouvet in Paris. I had warned Anne Yeats that Baty was a magnificent director of players with no notion of stage design. God alone knows what complicated intrigue Yeats saw in this, for it would simply never have occurred to him that I had been watching his daughter's work with interest, but as no one was allowed to excel Yeats in courtesy he arranged to publish a superb edition of my translation of 'The Lament for Art O'Leary', with coloured drawings by his brother, Jack.

A short time later I invited myself out to Rathfarnham to present a friend of mine to Mrs Yeats. At once Yeats started explaining to me that as a father he could not possibly allow his daughter to go to Paris unprotected, and that she must go to the Old Vic instead, where she could be looked after by some aunt, cousin or friend. I replied that nothing I had seen in the Old Vic had given me the idea that we had anything to learn from it and that I wouldn't consent to spend a penny of the theatre's money on sending Anne there. Yeats grew sulkier and sulkier, but George, seeing us to the door later in the evening, lifted my spirits by doing a dance step in the hall. 'That old bully!' she said. 'It's about time someone stood up to him. He's always trying to push people around.'

It was not the first time she had saved an evening for me, but it may perhaps explain why I shut Higgins up when he talked of the Yeats' domestic affairs. I knew the apparent childish selfishness of Yeats, because once when I was seeing him home, he went to his club, and told me that George was ill with some infectious disease and that he couldn't go home. I, thinking of George by herself in the house, said 'Oh, that's awful!' and Yeats replied mournfully, 'Yes. You see, I can't even get at my books.' But I also saw the other side, which apparently Higgins didn't see. Once, when we went in a taxi to some Board meeting, I paid the taxi driver and Yeats grabbed the money frantically from his hand and created a scene while he tried to find money of his own – always a difficult task for him as he never could make out where his pockets were. I said, 'Oh, stop it, W.B.,' and he turned on me. 'You don't understand, O'Connor,' he gasped. 'I wouldn't mind, but my wife would never forgive me.' Maybe only a storyteller can understand that, but I knew that a man who worried about what he was going to tell his wife about who paid the taxi fare was a man in love, whatever anybody else might think.

By this time I was in a bad state of unrest myself. I was unwell, and now, to the difficulty of holding down a job as librarian, running a runaway theatre and trying to write, was added an annulment action in the ecclesiastical courts that might go on for years. My publisher, Harold Macmillan, had said to me in his wise way, 'You've reached the stage where you must decide whether you're going to be a good writer or a good public servant. You can't be both.' I knew he was right, but it wasn't an easy choice. The only security I had ever known was the position I had made for myself, and I knew that once I gave it up I should never find another. I had got myself too much of the reputation of a firebrand. While I hung on to my job I could be ejected only with difficulty, but once out of it there would be plenty to see that I never got another chance. At last I gathered up what little courage I possessed, threw up my job, and went to live in County Wicklow.

And that, in some ways, was even worse. A writer is as conditioned to his methods of work as any old horse, and I found that the long day's leisure away from the activities that interested me was simply something I was not trained to take advantage of, so that when I did sit down to work at my usual hour after supper the day's idleness had already drained and dispirited me so that I wrote without aim or conviction.

Another source of anxiety was that I knew that until the annulment went through I should be a source of danger to the theatre. This was precisely the sort of weapon that its enemies would use, and not long before, when Hayes and other members of the Board had sat joking about a love affair between two of the players which had caused some scenes, I had said, 'This is no joking matter, and if I hear of it officially I shall ask for the resignation of both. The theatre is more important than anyone's feelings.' I decided to see Yeats and ask him to let me resign quietly. Hayes knew what I intended doing and, in his wise way, he tried to dissuade me. I liked being dissuaded, because there was nothing I wanted to do less than resign, but I had the puritanical sense I had inherited from Mother and Corkery and felt that though what I chose might be wrong I still had to choose. Yeats and I went out to dinner, and I explained how I felt about it. I even explained what I had already said about the players, and he was amused. 'That is quite different, O'Connor. If it had been a question of a Protestant director and a Catholic actress, I should have asked for his resignation immediately. But a Catholic director and a Protestant actress – we are unassailable.' Besides, in his romantic way he was thrilled by the more ceremonial usage of the ecclesiastical courts and said wistfully, 'I suppose the case will go to Rome', obviously thinking of the fine figure he would have cut himself in an atmosphere of Renaissance diplomacy.

And then, growing serious and becoming the Yeats I loved, he said, 'I can't accept your resignation, O'Connor. I know you think I listen to green-room gossip' – the old rebuke that he brooded over for months – 'but when I die I want to leave my theatre to you and Higgins.' There, again, was the essential Yeats – the man who never ignored a rebuke or an obligation.

This opened the way for a general discussion, and I begged him again to bring Denis Johnston in as producer. Of course I was attacking the obsession with Higgins, and the stubborn Yeats was aroused by his loyalty. Because he was feeling fond of me, he let me down lightly. Whenever he wanted to compliment me he quoted his wife as his authority and he said: 'You and George have exactly the same admiration for Denis Johnston. George made me listen to a radio programme of his on the Siege of Derry, and it was a masterpiece. But I can't help thinking he is a young man who would want his own way.' I knew perfectly well that Johnston would want his own way – was there ever a gifted man who didn't? – but I wondered what he thought Higgins and Blythe wanted.

The discussion swayed to and fro as such discussions must between a young man and an old one. Then he said sternly: 'At the next meeting of the Board I attend I want you to propose the dismissal of Robinson. When you quarrelled with him before, I knew you were right, but I had to oppose you; I had certain personal commitments. They no longer exist. I know Robinson is a danger to the theatre, and he must go.'

Well Yeats might talk of commitments. For years I had been watching what George Yeats was doing for him – and long after his death she told me that I was the first person who recognized that she was doing a job for him. But she wasn't being fair, any more than Yeats or Robinson or I was being fair. How could any of us be fair? I worshipped George Yeats, and I admired Robinson because it seemed to me that he too understood what she was doing. So I said to Yeats, 'Having accepted a public apology from Robinson I can't very well ask for his dismissal.' 'That was because you didn't know who wrote the public apology,' said Yeats. 'I wrote it, and I said to him, "Sign that." And he signed it,' Yeats added bitterly, and I knew that this was what upset him, and that if Robinson had pulled himself together and told Yeats to go to hell, Yeats would have been so proud of him that no one on earth could have attacked him.

While we ate, he went on, reminiscing about their relationship and the dozens of minor treacheries it had involved. And yet more revealing of Yeats' real nature were his last words on Robinson. After he had told me everything he had against him, he raised his finger and said sternly, 'But remember, O'Connor, that was Lennix Robinson the drunken intriguer, not Lennix Robinson who was your friend and mine.' Even today I can hear Yeats' voice as he uttered that magnificent line. I never did think him worth a damn as a love poet, but as a poet of friendship I felt he had no equal. How else could he have written:

> For friendship never ends
> And what if mind seemed changed
> And it seem changed with mind;
> When thoughts rise up unbid
> On generous things that he did,
> And I grow half-contented to be blind?

At times like this Yeats fascinated me. I had seen it once or twice before, most clearly on the night when Miss Horniman's death was announced, and he suddenly poured forth stories of her and her friends which are not in the official histories. It was not so much that the stories were particularly interesting in themselves, but that they threw such an extraordinary light on his own character. Anyone who had listened to him talk of Lennox Robinson in earlier days might have been forgiven for regarding him as a foolish, fond old man; listening to him when he suddenly decided to talk freely one realized that the foolish, fond old man was only half the personality, the personality that made the poetry, but that beneath it was another sort of personality altogether, sensitive and compassionate, but watchful, cool and without illusion, the mind of a novelist rather than that of a poet. This, of course, was what gave him his extraordinary capacity for development, and even in the few years I had known him I had seen his poetry getting nearer and nearer to my own ideal of poetry. He warmed my heart so much that night that I picked up enough courage to pay him a compliment. I said that if God gave him another ten years he would be the greatest lyric poet who had ever lived. He took this modestly, as Mother took praise of her good looks, and said, 'All the things I wanted to do when I was eighteen I am doing now that I'm an old man.' He was, and with the craziest of equipment. He was writing popular songs with no one but Higgins to give him a hand with the tunes, and poetry that has much of the quality of Old Irish verse on the basis of some translations of mine.

But if he thought that Higgins and I were going to perpetuate the sort of theatre he had dreamed of when he was young, he was very wide of the mark. All the same, things looked promising. Suddenly the Government offered a vast sum of money for the rebuilding of the Abbey as a national theatre. Yeats was enthusiastic. It looked as though after his death the theatre would be continued as an institution like the Comédie Française; he had heard me say at Russell's graveside that we had grown up in a country without institutions, and he would have wished the theatre to be one of them. Everybody was enthusiastic but myself. When Blythe produced his draft agreement with the Government I had to point out that all we were doing was handing over everything we possessed to the Government with no guarantee that we should have the least voice in the eventual policy of the theatre. I was then asked to draft an agreement of my own, and I did, and took it to Yeats for his approval. We went through it clause by clause. He was in an emotional state and talked of what it meant to him that, after all the hostility and violence, he, Synge and Lady Gregory should at last be accepted by their own people. I felt just the same; and I think the proposal of mine that pleased him best was that the main theatre must be called the Gregory Theatre. But the money made me unhappy and in the middle of our conversation I dropped my usual brick.

'Hasn't it occurred to you that we have created vested interests?' I asked, and Yeats gave me an angry look and said bitterly, 'Did you think I wasn't aware of it?'

Nowadays I wonder if he wasn't, and if that cool, watchful intelligence had not already warned him of what was going to happen after his death. Nothing had warned me except an old fear of money in the arts, and yet God knows that I should have been made suspicious by the peculiar things that were happening about me. I had just been involved in a most peculiar row about Yeats' play *The Herne's Egg*. I should have had more sense, but at the time the incident completely befuddled me. Yeats had read it to me while he was writing it and, apart from one of our usual wrangles about a music-hall joke in the first scene, I had admired it greatly. But when it was submitted to the Board at a meeting not attended by Yeats, the members rejected it because it was obscene. Only Ernest Blythe supported me, and he did so on the grounds that the play was so obscure that no one would notice that it was obscene. This was not what I felt at all, and it seemed to me intolerable that the Board which Yeats had selected himself should coolly reject one of the finest plays of its founder. Hayes became really violent and threatened to resign if it was produced. When I argued with Hayes afterwards, he told me that Higgins had assured him that Yeats' intention was that the seven men who rape the priestess should represent the seven sacraments. This interpretation appeared to me to be the utmost nonsense, but I saw no reason to disbelieve Higgins' story – did I say I was simple-minded? – for I knew that when Yeats was bored or depressed he was capable of saying the most outrageous things. (Indeed, I had heard him not long before tell a young woman who had drunk up his entire ration of whiskey for the night that 'the Blessed Trinity was an invention of a homosexual monk'.) But I did know Catholic doctrine as Higgins – and Hayes apparently – didn't, and I could not see how anybody of reasonable intelligence could accept such a stupid interpretation. Now, the play isn't very difficult. Any reader of Yeats can test that argument for himself. Clearly, the seven men represent the sciences and the priestess revealed religion, while the rape is merely a stylization of the nineteenth-century assault on religion. From the point of view of Christian orthodoxy you could comfortably produce *The Herne's Egg* in any ecclesiastical seminary. Indeed, an ecclesiastical seminary might be about the only place you could produce it where it would be fully understood. But I could not persuade Hayes, a really pious man – and by pious I don't mean prissy – that Yeats had no intention of being blasphemous.

Finally, in a fit of exasperation, I said I would produce the play myself at my own expense. When I told Yeats, he turned on me with real anger, and I saw that under all the good-humoured detachment he was bitterly hurt at the rejection of his beautiful play by a group of nonentities. 'And why did you not insist on its being produced when you had a majority of the Board behind you?' he shouted. I didn't know what to say, because the meeting had taken place some time before, and I could not immediately recall the details. I fobbed him off with Hayes' threat of resignation and said we'd had too many resignations. It wasn't until later that I remembered that nobody but Blythe had supported me, and that Higgins, Yeats' friend, was not only one of the play's bitterest opponents at the meeting, but was the person who had influenced Hayes by relating what Yeats was supposed to have said. All Yeats' information came from Higgins, and I was the one who had been presented as having got cold feet. But I still thought the whole thing was a misunderstanding and wondered only if Yeats' supposed blasphemies had not been a misunderstanding as well. I knew it was no use attacking his hero, Higgins, but I did ask him if he had interpreted the play in this way to anyone at any time. He looked at me in bewilderment and grew furious. 'How could I have said anything so silly?' he asked, which was exactly what I had wondered myself. I should have had sense enough to appeal directly to him at the beginning. He was quite right in his joke about me that I didn't think the vast majority of people meant much harm to each other for the greater part of the time, but, all the same, he wasn't too bright himself. Here were we, two grown men being put at cross purposes by schoolboy gossip and intrigue, and neither of us could see through it.

If I had the talent of a comic novelist I should love to describe how that brilliant and delightful man put us all by the ears. Higgins didn't even make a secret of it. He lived in what seemed to be an almost enchanted world of extemporization, imagination and intrigue. After his death, his old friends were approached for the manuscript of his last masterpiece, a play in which the characters were the picture cards in a pack. I knew that play better than I knew most of my own work. We had listened to it scene by scene and only waited to vote for its production; but, as each of us passed the buck, it became plain that that brilliant play never existed except in Higgins' head.

Yet Higgins was the man he had appointed director of his publishing firm and Managing Director of the Theatre. I had been Managing Director during the absence of the touring company and had asked Yeats how I should conduct myself. 'I asked Lady Gregory exactly the same thing when I became Managing Director,' he said, 'and she told me, "Give very few orders but see that they are obeyed." ' (Knowing her Yeats, the old lady knew that he wouldn't recognize her advice as a quotation from *Don Quixote*.) Nominally Higgins' appointment was for six months, to give us time to find a successor to Hunt. I knew perfectly well that there was no work for a full-time Managing Director, but Higgins entertained himself by doing Hunt's job as well. 'Giving very few orders' was not much in the line of that excitable man. 'My heavens,' he wrote to me, 'things are terrible here – all in a state of chassis. The BBC treated [threatened] to cancel broadcast because we could [couldn't] give the cast Hunt offered – of which we knew nothing. However, had a visit from a BBC official and together we hammered out a suitable cast. Also Hunt never consulted Belfast Opera House *re* our plays for Belfast etc.' (It is only fair to say that Higgins was ill. He had had an attack of Bell's Palsy, which had blasted his handsome face and interfered with his speech, but left him as excitable and enthusiastic as ever.) I admit that the six months' appointment never took me in, for I knew that an Irishman approaches a job in the spirit of the marriage service – 'till death do us part'. But even I never guessed that not only had Higgins dug himself in for life, but that his successor would do the same, and that twenty years later the non-existent job would still be flourishing. 'Vested interests' indeed!

I saw the theatre only at Board meetings, and I did not like the way things were going, with Hunt on the point of departure, and a new man, an Irish-speaking protégé of Blythe, taking over. But everything seemed to move with extraordinary rapidity towards one point – the death of Yeats. A day or two before he left for the South of France for the last time, he had a furious quarrel with Higgins. 'W.B. has left in a difficult temper owing to a personal awkwardness,' Higgins wrote to me. 'Personal awkwardness' was a mild description of Yeats' discovery that Higgins had been playing fast and loose with him all over the shop. After this, Higgins refused to reply to his letters at all, and Yeats, knowing he had only a short time to live, dictated a letter to me. He asked that, if I agreed with him, I should telegraph him and he would take a plane home, dismiss the whole Board of directors, and start again with one chosen by ourselves. But I had no way of knowing how ill he really was, or whether his letter meant anything more than a fit of pique with Higgins, so I wrote him a soothing reply to tell him not to worry. I was in Chester at the time, and as I took my letter to the post I bought a *Daily Telegraph* and read of his death. (Years later, when two young writers had staged a public protest in the Abbey Theatre against its commercialism, I took a book from my shelves and out dropped my last letter to Yeats, unposted, stamped and sealed. I read it between tears, because it brought him back to me so vividly, and shame, to think I should have been such a fool.)

That night I walked for a long time about the old walls of the city, saying over and over the lines from *The Herne's Egg* that seem to me so much a better epitaph than the one he composed for himself. 'Cast a cold eye/On life, on death' is a caricature of Yeats, who was never cold; often angry, often stupid beyond belief, but always young in heart, passionate, involved:

> Strong sinew and soft flesh
> Are foliage round the shaft
> Before the arrowsmith
> Has stripped it, and I pray
> That I, all foliage gone,
> May shoot into my joy.

21

I had no idea that night what the death of Yeats would mean to me. In the long run it meant that I took a major decision, one which I have never regretted since, but my blindness at the time, both towards myself and the happenings at the Abbey, guaranteed that I would take the most painful road in changing the course of my life.

I thought that night that I knew what I had lost in Yeats. Not a friend, but somebody who might have been a friend. During his last stay in Ireland his sister, Elizabeth, had asked me straight out, 'Why don't you go and see W.B.?' She was a woman of great beauty, who had what in America would be recognized as the gift of calculated indiscretion – the sort of thing one associates with old American families. And as always when one has to deal with calculated indiscretion I dropped into uncalculated indiscretion and said, 'Oh, I'd be afraid of boring him.' 'I don't think so, you know,' she said innocently, 'because when you do call, he always talks about it. He's very lonely, you know.'

God help us, I did know it. I had known it from the moment George Yeats had sat down beside me at Gogarty's party years before. I went to see Yeats and found him very depressed. He needed a holiday, he said, and I, greatly daring, asked, 'Why don't you come and stay with us? We could look after you very well.' For a moment he didn't know what to say, and then he gave me a boyish grin. 'Old people stay with old friends,' he replied. 'They can be very trying to anybody else.'

When a great man dies, not only does a legend spring up, but a phase of reality ends. Yeats himself realized it when he called one of his own autobiographical books *Ireland after Parnell*. Some day someone will write a book called 'Ireland after Yeats'. The things that happen after the death of a man like that have already been happening before he dies, but because he is alive they seem of no great importance. Death suddenly reveals their importance by isolating them.

For a year before his death little things had been happening which had depressed and irritated me. One evening I attended a Board meeting at which the three other directors explained to me with chuckles that I need not read a play by a Minister's wife because it would have to be accepted if we were to keep the Government grant. I didn't know which angered me most, the insult to me, the insult to the Minister and his wife, or the insult to our audience, who relied on us to be incorruptible. On another occasion the theatre was running a competition for plays in Gaelic which Blythe was supervising and Mícheál MacLiammóir adjudicating. I learned by the merest accident that Sean O'Faolain had submitted a play. When I inquired what it was like, Blythe said, 'Well, really, it wasn't good enough to submit to the adjudicator,' and this surprised me, because I did not think there was that much talent among writers in Irish. In the play which was shown to the judge and did win the prize, the principal characters were the Devil and the Blessed Virgin.

Living in the country at Woodenbridge and involved in my own difficulties, it was impossible to be watchful enough. Higgins asked me not to bother reading Cecil Salkeld's play about Germany, *A Gay Goodnight*. 'A ridiculous play; the usual Anglo-Irish rubbish' was how he described it. At the time I didn't know that Higgins and Salkeld had quarrelled and that Salkeld was supposed to have hit Higgins in the theatre bar (somebody was always hitting Higgins). It wasn't until years later, when I saw 'the usual Anglo-Irish rubbish' produced in a stable by a group of amateurs, that I realized Salkeld's play was a little masterpiece.

With Yeats permanently gone, I began now to realize that mediocrity was in control, and against mediocrity there is no challenge or appeal. Talent, like any other form of creative activity, has its own dialectic, and from its noisy and bitter conflicts some synthesis emerges, but mediocrity, having neither thesis nor antithesis, leads only a sort of biological life.

But there was worse to come. One evening, after a Board meeting, Higgins asked me in a whisper to remain behind when the others had gone. He was in his usual state of conspiratorial exaltation, and I assumed he had unearthed another plot. He had. When we were by ourselves he opened the minute book and pointed to a resolution that had been proposed by Hayes and passed. At this time I was editing a re-issue of Yeats' old theatre magazine, the *Arrow*; the resolution required me to submit everything I wrote in it to Lennox Robinson for his approval. A short time before, Hayes himself had moved the resolution demanding the dismissal of Robinson from the Board, and Yeats had replied, 'Everybody on this Board realizes that Lennix Robinson is no longer responsible for his actions.' He was now being made responsible for mine, and, being Robinson, probably saw nothing in the least inappropriate about it. Suddenly the door of the boardroom opened and Hayes was standing there. 'I'm waiting to walk home with you, Michael,' he said plaintively. I could barely speak and said without looking at him that I had some work to do. By this time he realized what Higgins had shown me. 'Oh, very well,' he said in a hurt voice and left. 'And now let me tell you something else,' Higgins said triumphantly. 'You asked why the Board did not give Tanya Moiseiwitsch a dinner before she left. We did, but Blythe insisted that you should not be asked. Here's the report of the dinner, if you don't believe me.'

I left the theatre in a frenzy. I felt that as a result of the death of Yeats I was left alone with a group of men not one of whom I should trust. Hayes' treachery was the thing that mattered most to me because for years he had been my closest friend. A critic of the theatre has described him as an arch-intriguer, though I did not find him so, and his machinations struck me as those of a very innocent and disinterested man. I think that, like many of his generation, he had adopted an idealistic pose too lofty for his own simple character, and that something – something perhaps in me that he couldn't understand – had caused it to break down. Years later, when Higgins was already dead, I was standing at the desk in the National Library when I suddenly felt an arm about my shoulders and heard Hayes say, 'My dear Michael, won't you shake hands with me?' It was one of the few occasions in my life when I shrank away from a man. Remembering the years of good fellowship and kindness, it is something I try to regret, but with little success, for it was more than Hayes I was turning my back on.

What I did regret in 1939 was leaving the theatre of Yeats, and Synge and Lady Gregory, and the end of their dream of a national theatre that would perpetuate their work. The alternative for me was to remain on and fight the Board, not on the terms of the founders, but on the terms of the current members. But there would be no Yeats to whom the members would ultimately have to defend themselves. Genius is often a light by which we occasionally see ourselves and so refrain from some commonness of thought or action that the time allows. I knew then, as I know now, that this kind of infighting and intrigue was something I could not carry on alone. Their terms were those of the Nationalist-Catholic establishment – Christmas pantomimes in Gaelic guying the ancient sagas that Yeats had restored, and enlivened with Blythe's Gaelic versions of popular songs and vulgar farces. One by one they lost their great actors and replaced them with Irish speakers; one by one, as the members of the Board died or resigned, they replaced these with civil servants and lesser Party politicians.

A great man is one who acts and speaks from a vision of himself. It is not that he is always right and everyone else wrong – often it is the other way round – but that even when he is wrong he is speaking from 'the foul rag-and-bone shop of the heart', the central volcano from which all creation comes. In so far as he interprets his country, as Yeats interpreted Ireland, he has no other source of authority. Once when we were arguing about politics, Yeats quoted a remark of de Valera's of which his enemies were making great capital – 'When I want to know what Ireland thinks, I look into my own heart.' 'Where else could he look?' growled Yeats.

But it takes a large heart to hold even a small country, and since Yeats' death there has been no other that could hold us, with all our follies and heroism.

Years before, he had asked me suddenly one night, 'O'Connor, do you believe you can transmit genius?' I was taken by surprise and did not realize until later that it was his own children he had been worrying about, so I replied, 'Genius? Hardly genius! Talent one can certainly transmit. The Bachs are a good example.' Then I realized that in my usual manner I had said something to make him cross, and he sulked at me for a few minutes. Finally he snorted, 'An old aunt of mine used to say' – the standard beginning for a crushing retort – 'you can transmit anything you like provided you take care not to marry the girl next door.'

It was in war-time England some time later that I came to realize the full significance for me of Yeats' death and my resignation from the Abbey. I was staying with Leonard and Sylvia Strong and had a dream one night which a psychiatrist friend of theirs sought to interpret for me. Suddenly I knew perfectly well what the dream meant and that it was a warning never again to allow the man of action in me to get on top. There was more wisdom in Harold Macmillan's advice than I had thought. Before Yeats died he told me that the time had come to decide whether I wanted to be a good public official, and I had resigned my job as librarian. Now I saw that the man of action was still on top; with nothing like Yeats' talent I had been playing Yeats' game. At once I resigned from every organization I belonged to and sat down, at last, to write.

Sean O'Casey
Autobiographies 1 £2.50

Sean O'Casey wrote his autobiography in six books over more than two decades. In this first volume, containing *I knock at the door*, *Pictures in the hallway* and *Drums under the windows*, O'Casey recreates his Dublin childhood of poverty and physical hardship, tells of his growth to manhood, and finally presents a portrait of Ireland and his countrymen from 1906 to that 'rare time of death in Ireland' – Easter 1916.

Autobiographies 2 £3.95

This second volume of Sean O'Casey's autobiography contains *Inishfallen, fare thee well*, *Rose and crown* and *Sunset and evening star*, the final three books of the autobiography he wrote over more than two decades. Independence and the Civil War heralded O'Casey's early triumphs at the Abbey Theatre, Dublin, and he vividly recreates the events and personalities of the period. He writes of his departure for London in 1926, the crowded years of his life in England, his marriage, America, the war and his friendship with Shaw. But underlining it all remains his concern for the people of Ireland.

Ralph Glasser
Growing Up in the Gorbals £2.95

' . . . a classic . . . He reveals a hidden face of Glasgow and gives a unique and fascinating insight into his early life . . . All the "No Mean City" ingredients – the filth and the squalor, the gang fights, the religious bigotry, the violence of the "tallymen", the mating rites of the midden, the pleasure of the "steamie" – are present' GLASGOW EVENING TIMES

'*Growing up in the Gorbals*, and its promised sequel, may well take their place beside the *Wesker Trilogy* as prime evidence of what culture has been for the most conscious working people in these last two generations' LISTENER

'Glasser has performed a service in recreating that ambivalent world of iciness and warmth, material poverty and spiritual richness, the hopes of dreamers and the dour resignation of "Expect nothing and you will never be disappointed" ' JEWISH CHRONICLE

Karen Armstrong
Through the Narrow Gate £3.50

At the age of only seventeen Karen Armstrong entered a holy order of nuns. Turning her back on the world, her family and friends, on any possibility of becoming a wife and mother, she embraced vows of poverty, chastity and obedience. While her generation enjoyed the swinging sixties, Karen suffered indignity, squalor and emotional anguish in a nightmare that could have come out of the Middle Ages. This is a nun's own story of a life that most of us could never imagine.

George Clare
Last Waltz in Vienna £3.50
the destruction of a family 1842–1942

On Saturday 26 February 1938 seventeen-year-old George Klaar took his girl Lisl to his first ball at the Konzerthaus. His family were proudly Austrian. They were also Jewish. Just two weeks later came the *Anschluss*. A family had been condemned to death by holocaust.

'They are like actors in a Lehar operetta suddenly cast in the roles of a Greek tragedy' ARTHUR KOESTLER, SUNDAY TIMES

'Mr Clare leads us gently, but inexorably, to the edge of the pit and then leaves us to look down into it' EDWARD CRANKSHAW, OBSERVER

Leslie Thomas
This Time Next Week £2.50

The autobiography of a happy orphan

'It's a school. Down in Devon. The masters play soldiers in the woods and the fields with the boys. I've heard they have a very good time. But you will write, won't you?'

Leslie's vivid reminiscences of life in Dr Barnardo's homes in Kingsbridge in Devon and later in the house at the corner of Galsworthy Road and Kingston Hill in London are often hilarious and sometimes unbearably touching. It was all a strange and wonderful misadventure which also provided the seed-bed for the talent that was later to flower so spectacularly.

'Mr Thomas's book is all humanity, to which is added a Welshman's mastery of words' OBSERVER

'One of the funniest and also one of the most moving accounts of childhood that I have ever read' DAILY EXPRESS

Glyn Hughes
Millstone Grit £3.95
A Pennine Journey

'I am writing about, I am living in, that block of the Pennine hills made of millstone grit and ringed by textile towns: Yorkshire wool to the east and Lancashire cotton to the west. Majestic places, they once were . . .'

Combining the poetic and the humorous, Glyn Hughes threads together personal experience, local lore, history, myth, and legendary names from a bygone age, to bring vividly to life the beauty of this remarkable region and the unique qualities of its people, past and present.

'The work of a subtle poet with the ear of a stand-up comic and the eye of the most delicate of watercolourists. It is a work of sadness and savagery . . . of gentle compassion . . . a grand book. Grand' THE TIMES

'Enjoyable both verbally and visually . . . You can hear the brass bands, you can smell the gas and coke and you can hear the winds moaning over the moors by just looking at the magnificently gloomy and absolutely appropriate photographs' DERBYSHIRE LIFE AND COUNTRYSIDE

Fred Archer
Fred Archer, Farmer's Son £3.50
A Cotswold childhood in the 1920s

'In the many country books he has written, Fred Archer demonstrates again and again just how deeply he can sink his memory into the past. This book must be one of his most personal to date: an honest, down-to-earth account of a Cotswold childhood which no passage of time is allowed to sentimentalize or blur' COTSWOLD LIFE

'Vividly recalls day-to-day life in the Worcestershire countryside . . . he describes aspects of rural life which by today's standards seem almost incredible – bathing in a tub by the fire; the privy in the garden; young boys being sent beneath hayricks with scissors to cut straws used as "ladders" by mice; the arrival of the miracles of telephone, radio and motor car' WARWICKSHIRE & WORCESTERSHIRE LIFE

'An evocative tale of a life that has gone for ever . . . the round of the seasons, the round of the farm, the hardships and simple pleasures, ploughing with a team of four, village life, grammar school and market place, a hayfield seduction. In short, the sun, the moon, and the stars . . . this book rings every bell in my recollection' EASTERN DAILY PRESS

All Pan books are available at your local bookshop or newsagent, or can be ordered direct from the publisher. Indicate the number of copies required and fill in the form below.

Send to: **CS Department, Pan Books Ltd., P.O. Box 40, Basingstoke, Hants. RG21 2YT.**

or phone: 0256 469551 (Ansaphone), quoting title, author and Credit Card number.

Please enclose a remittance* to the value of the cover price plus: 60p for the first book plus 30p per copy for each additional book ordered to a maximum charge of £2.40 to cover postage and packing.

*Payment may be made in sterling by UK personal cheque, postal order, sterling draft or international money order, made payable to Pan Books Ltd.

Alternatively by Barclaycard/Access:

Card No.

Signature:

Applicable only in the UK and Republic of Ireland.

While every effort is made to keep prices low, it is sometimes necessary to increase prices at short notice. Pan Books reserve the right to show on covers and charge new retail prices which may differ from those advertised in the text or elsewhere.

NAME AND ADDRESS IN BLOCK LETTERS PLEASE:

....

Name————————————————————————

Address————————————————————————

————————————————————————

————————————————————————

————————————————————————

3/87